MW00387334

SHOWSTOPPERS

F
I
L
M

A
N
D

C
U
L
T
U
R
E

John Belton, General Editor

FILM AND CULTURE
A Series of Columbia University Press
Edited by John Belton

What Made Pistachio Nuts?
Henry Jenkins

SHOWSTOPPERS

BUSBY BERKELEY AND THE TRADITION OF SPECTACLE

COLUMBIA UNIVERSITY PRESS NEW YORK

MARTIN RUBIN

Columbia University Press
New York Chichester, West Sussex

Library of Congress Cataloging-in-Publication Data
Rubin, Martin
Showstoppers : Busby Berkeley and the tradition of spectacle / Martin Rubin.
p. cm. — (Film and culture)
Stageography: p.
Filmography: p.
Includes bibliographical references and index.
ISBN 978-0-231-08054-5
1. Berkeley, Busby,—1895- —Criticism and interpretation.
2. Musical films—United States—History and criticism. 3. Musical theater—United States—History. I. Title. II. Series.
PN1998.3.B475R8 1993
791.43'0233'092—dc20 92-37956

 CIP

Casebound editions of Columbia University Press books are Smyth-sewn and printed on permanent and durable acid-free paper.

Printed in the United States of America
c 10 9 8 7

To Penney

I only have eyes for you . . .

CONTENTS

Please note: The photographs used in this book are production stills, not frame enlargements. Although they provide a record of the general appearance of the scenes depicted, they are not identical with those scenes as they appear on the screen. Framing, camera angle, and the arrangement of actors and props are often significantly different.

Photos from Broadway shows are reproduced with the permission of The Billy Rose Theatre Collection, The New York Library for the Performing Arts, Astor, Lenox and Tilden Foundations.

ACKNOWLEDGMENTS

Without John Belton, in his capacities as teacher, editor, and friend, this book would have been inconceivable on several levels. I could never adequately express my thanks to him.

Jennifer Crewe, Senior Executive Editor; Anne McCoy, Managing Editor; and Roy Thomas, Copy Editor, provided an exceptionally friendly and professional working relationship with Columbia University Press.

Professors Richard Koszarski and Philip Rosen nurtured this project in its early stages.

Greg Ford, Barrv Gillam, Bob Kalish, Ed Maguire, and Rick Scheckman went out of their way to help me view Berkeley's films. I am grateful for their friendship as well as their assistance.

Terry Geesken of the Film Stills Archive of the Museum of Modern Art, Howard Mandelbaum of Photofest, Charles Silver of the Film Study Center of the Museum of Modern Art, and Stephen M. Vallillo of TheatResearch were especially helpful in providing research materials.

My wife Penney and my parents David and Doris Rubin have blessed me with support, patience, and love over the many years that this project has consumed.

SHOWSTOPPERS

INTRODUCTION: BERKELEY AND THE BERKELEYESQUE

Introduction: Berkeley and the Berkeleyesque

The American Thesaurus of Slang contains, as a lower-case noun, the entry *busby berkeley*. The term is defined as "any elaborate dance number."[1]

When people think of dancing in a musical, they might think first of Fred Astaire and Ginger Rogers, Gene Kelly, or perhaps Bill Robinson. When they think of singing in a musical, they might think of Judy Garland or Barbra Streisand or Maurice Chevalier. But when they think of the production number—that is, the number that depends on sheer spectacle, on the deployment of hordes of chorus dancers in a grandiose setting—one name probably springs to mind before all others: Busby Berkeley.

A filmmaker with one of the most familiar "signatures" of any Hollywood director, Berkeley is identified with a form that still enjoys great recognition. Films, television commercials, and music videos continue to employ "Berkeleyesque" configurations as part of a vital cultural vocabulary, long after Berkeley himself and the genre that nourished him have largely faded from the scene. Yet despite his high profile and his involvement with popular culture, Berkeley was something of a peripheral figure within the Hollywood system—a flamboyant anomaly who operated an eye-catching sideshow under the big top of mainstream cinema. In fact, Berkeley was an anomaly within an anomaly. His trademark genre, the musical, is the most anomalous of all major genres sanctioned under the impure orthodoxy of Hollywood classicism. The musical makes mischief with dominant values of realism, consistency, and narrativity, dancing giddily close to their counterparts—contradiction, inconsistency, and showstopping spectacle. But as the musical film became more attached to a gospel of integration between story and music, Berkeley's brand of "gratuitous" spectacle (i.e., not narratively functional) began to appear increasingly anachronistic, excessive, and even outré.

However, one should not overstate the extent of Berkeley's marginality within the Hollywood system. He was not an idiosyncratic fringe figure like such little-known "cult" directors as Rowland Brown, Edgar G. Ulmer, Gerd Oswald, or Monte Hellman; indeed, Berkeley was one of the most celebrated filmmakers of the thirties, a "superstar" director long before the concept became commonplace.[2] Although his career suffered an eventual decline, Berkeley's perceived indulgences did not cast him outside the Hollywood pale, in the manner of Erich von Stroheim or Orson Welles. On the one hand, Berkeley's style became somewhat diluted in his later films; on the other hand, his excesses continued to create friction within increasingly restrictive production contexts. Nevertheless, he remained active in Hollywood for twenty-five years and was still accomplishing major work in a distinctive vein well into the 1950s.[3]

Those distinctive qualities of Berkeley's numbers are usually thought of as essentially cinematic, representing a form that has its roots in the evolution of the early sound musical (beginning around 1929) and the concurrent evolution of Berkeley as a film choreographer (beginning in 1930 with *Whoopee!*). The standard historical interpretation of the evolution of the early movie musical presents the following scenario: In the first rush of talking pictures (1929–30), a huge number of Broadway musicals were transposed to the screen with little attempt to make them cinematic; they were essentially canned theater. Then, beginning with either *Whoopee!* (Berkeley's first film) or *42nd Street* (1933; his first film for Warner Brothers), Berkeley appeared on the scene and almost singlehandedly lifted the movie musical out of its static, primitive, and stagebound state.[4] Berkeley's contribution was that he "made the camera dance." Rather than passively recording numbers that were presented much as they would be on a theatrical stage, Berkeley created numbers *for* the camera, chiefly through the use of elaborate crane shots, striking camera angles, and various editing tricks.[5]

Berkeley's significance in the history of the musical

film has been interpreted primarily in terms of a substantial break with theatrical tradition. He is seen (with nods to Ernst Lubitsch and Rouben Mamoulian) as the filmmaker who pioneered a truly cinematic musical genre conceived in filmic rather than theatrical terms. This scenario indicates a limited interpretation not only of Berkeley's film musicals but of the film musical in general. Stage elements have always been an overt and central element of the classical movie musical, which throughout its history has clung tenaciously to its theatrical roots. "Staginess" is an integral part of this movie genre, more so than of any other.[6]

Berkeley himself did much to contribute to the neglect of stage influences on his movie musical style. In several interviews, he recounted the same story about his genesis as a filmmaker: After being hired by Samuel Goldwyn to direct the dances in the film version of *Whoopee!*, Berkeley went out to Hollywood to observe how movie musicals were made. On the soundstage, he immediately saw that musical numbers were being staged essentially as they were in the theater. Four cameras passively recorded the action, and the various angles were sorted out later in the cutting room. "I realized, of course, that the technique [of filmmaking] was entirely different from the stage," Berkeley related. "At the end of a few moments I understood that the camera can have only *one* eye, and I said to myself: 'Buzz, you can do an infinite number of things with the camera, it's your first film, you might as well begin at once!'" On his first day of shooting, Berkeley, confronted with four camera crews, dismissed three of them, asserting, "It's not my technique. I use only one camera, so let the others go."[7] Film choreography was seemingly born on the spot, like a tap-dancing goddess from the forehead of her one-eyed Zeus.

Until recently, historians of the film musical have generally been content to follow Berkeley's lead. John Kobal, in *Gotta Sing Gotta Dance*, states, "The outrageous extravaganzas he whipped up could never have originated on a theatre stage." Robert C. Roman, in an article on Berkeley in *Dance Magazine*, writes, "It was Berkeley who *first* recognized the great differences between screen dance and stage dance." According to John Springer in *All Talking! All Singing! All Dancing!* "[*42nd Street*] introduced a new element—song and dance numbers created by Busby Berkeley especially for movies, bursting far beyond the bounds of what could be done on a stage." Berkeley himself said, "I have staged many shows on Broadway as well and so I know very thoroughly that they require an entirely different technique. The staging of a music hall spectacle is one thing, that of a cinematographic spectacle is another."[8]

What tends to get blurred together in statements like these is, on the one hand, the manifest fact that many of Berkeley's numbers create effects beyond the scope of a realistically presented theatrical stage and, on the other hand, the more questionable implication that Berkeley's film numbers are fundamentally "another thing" from the Broadway stage tradition that preceded them. In their emphasis on Berkeley's undeniable achievements with cinematic effects, historians have tended to overlook or minimize the considerable influence of theatrical elements on the form of his movie musical numbers. Although Berkeley's previous theatrical experience is occasionally noted, it is rarely seen as a major element of his film work. Instead, historians frequently relate Berkeley's film style not to any stage tradition but to the avant-garde, abstract, and surreal traditions of nonnarrative cinema.[9]

As mentioned above, Berkeley, despite his anomalous position in relation to the Hollywood mainstream, was a resoundingly popular artist in all senses of the term. Although they certainly contributed to the aesthetic background of the Berkeleyesque, surrealism and avant-gardism seem unlikely candidates to be the major traditions behind such popular art. Was Berkeley then a diluter of avant-garde devices into tamer and more acceptable forms? This is a more likely possibility, but notions of dilution and tameness still seem inadequate in the face of the qualities of intensity and excess that mark Berkeley's work. It seems more plausible that his accessibly eccentric film style can be accounted for as the apogee of a *popular* tradition—one that contributed to but did not dominate classical Hollywood cinema.

Historians and Berkeley alike have stressed the *break* that his film work represents from theatrical forms. It is the purpose of this study to restore an equally important sense of the *continuity* between Berkeley's film style and preceding theatrical forms—particularly those forms deriving from a particular stage tradition, designated here the "Tradition of Spectacle." This is a primarily nineteenth-century tradition of popular entertainment: the tradition of P. T. Barnum, the minstrel show, vaudeville, the three-ring circus, Buffalo Bill Cody's Wild West Show, burlesque, and the *Ziegfeld Follies*. It is a tradition based on creating feelings of abundance, variety, and wonder. It offers a fundamentally different approach to entertainment from those more modern forms that are oriented predominantly toward unity, continuity, and integration.

Although a major concern of this book is the Tradition of Spectacle, I would like to point out that the reference here is to a *particular* (albeit extensive) form of popular/spectacular entertainment. The book is not intended to be a general theoretical investigation of the role of spectacle in the cinema, with Berkeley's work serving primarily as a typical test case to illustrate such issues. It would be difficult to posit Berkeley's work as "typical," and I do not intend to try. The proposal of any major artist as typical or a test case seems a dubious enterprise anyway. Berkeley is less of interest here for what he represents or typifies in himself than for the manner in which his work mediates between a number of different, often contradictory cultural/aesthetic/historical systems and inflects them into especially resonant configurations: between stage and screen; between nineteenth- and twentieth-century entertainment forms; between the conflicting demands of narrative and spectacle; between classical Hollywood and its most "renegade" genre, the musical film; between mainstream cinema and the powerful alternative impulses it manages to incorporate.

The centering of a film studies book upon the work of a single director inevitably raises the specter of auteurism. This school of film criticism, which arose in France in the 1950s and migrated to England, America, and points beyond in the 1960s, analyzes films primarily in terms of personal "authorship." In a film, the director is commonly seen as the most significant author, and auteurist criticism concentrates on consistencies and developments of theme and style over a number of works by the same director.

In its heyday, auteurism was widely attacked both for slighting the contributions of other filmmaking collaborators and for overrating the work of several then-disreputable Hollywood directors. However, it has since become apparent that the general concept of auteurism can easily be expanded to include other film "authors" (screenwriters, cinematographers, actors, etc.), and most of auteurism's embattled favorites (such as Alfred Hitchcock, Nicholas Ray, and Howard Hawks) have passed into the ranks of widely accepted, *New York Times*–approved Old Masters.

Later attacks on auteurism, borrowing from French theorists such as Michel Foucault and Roland Barthes, shifted their criticism to the basic notion of authorship itself, which was seen as a historicized concept tied to a certain time (post-Enlightenment), place (Euro-America), and political ideology (bourgeois capitalism). Auteurism was faulted for failing to discern that meanings are culturally rather than personally determined, and for promoting an overly idealistic and consistent image of works of art. Rather than unified expressions of the artist's "vision," works of art were increasingly seen as battlegrounds upon which various discourses, hidden contradictions, and cultural/political interests struggled. Auteurism is currently considered an unfashionable approach in the field of film studies, although its influence continues to be wide and is not always fully acknowledged. It is not uncommon for scholarly writings to begin with an obligatory attack on auteurism and then proceed to incorporate many of its assumptions. Many recent film scholars could be described as "closet" auteurists to a greater or lesser degree.

This book seeks not to reject auteurism but rather to problematize it—and to use that issue as the pivot of its investigation. It is important to emphasize that the focus of this study is not so much Busby Berkeley the author but a quality (or series of associated qualities) that can be termed the *Berkeleyesque*. The subject here is less an individual artist or a personal style than a general descriptive category (as noted above, the words *busby berkeley* have come to mean "any elaborate dance number"). Qualities of the Berkeleyesque—that is, qualities which, by custom and usage, have come to be loosely associated with the name Busby Berkeley—include: (1) large numbers of chorus girls in regimented and geometrical formations, (2) overhead shots that form kaleidoscopic patterns, (3) an impression of extravagance and excess in setting and camerawork, (4) extended and spectacular crane shots, (5) stylized uses of the female body in abstract and object-like ways, (6) elements of fetishistic eroticism, and (7) the use of giant, multiple, and bizarre props.

However, Berkeley often (especially in the 1940s and 1950s) did effective work outside the Berkeleyesque qualities described above. Also, as this study will demonstrate, most of those elements commonly identified with the Berkeleyesque both surpass and precede the career of Berkeley himself. Just as Busby Berkeley is more than the Berkeleyesque, the Berkeleyesque is more than Busby Berkeley. The term "Berkeleyesque" is intended to refer precisely to that combination of the personal and the cultural, to the somewhat volatile and problematic transactions between the individual Busby Berkeley and the tradition he came to represent.

Film historians tend to characterize many movie musical numbers of the 1930s (those involving kaleidoscopic overhead shots, giant props, surreal fancies, platoons of chorines, etc.) as being derivative of Berkeley. For instance, Ethan Mordden in *The Hollywood Musical* cites two numbers as prime examples of "the Berkeley imitation": "Too Marvelous for Words," from the film *Ready, Willing and Able* (1937), in which the upraised legs of concealed chorines form the keys of a gigantic typewriter (see photo 1); and "You Gotta Pull Strings," from *The Great Ziegfeld* (1936), in which about twenty suspended chorus girls are arranged on a giant doily.[10] In actuality, "Too Marvelous for Words" is a close replica of a number ("The Typing Place") that appeared in *The Perfect Fool*, an Ed Wynn revue that opened in 1921 (that is, four years before Berkeley began staging numbers on Broadway, and nine years before his first film). Similarly, giant doily/plate/fan/bouquet arrangements in the vein of the *Great Ziegfeld* number were standard fare on the musical stage long before Berkeley arrived on the scene.

Although Berkeley's influence on the development of the early film musical was undoubtedly great, one should be cautious in drawing conclusions about his influence on numbers staged by his contemporaries. Such caution is especially appropriate when one considers that many of the top Hollywood dance directors during the 1930s (Bobby Connolly, Seymour Felix, Sammy Lee, etc.) were veterans of the same Broadway tradition that nurtured Berkeley. Rather than being classified as an isolated and eccentric innovator, Berkeley can be more accurately understood as the transmitter—in some ways, the apotheosis—of a very rich, long-standing tradition in theater and popular entertainment.

Berkeley absorbed this declining theatrical tradition

during his career as a Broadway dance director (1925–30) and then helped to revitalize it by transferring it to the new context of the early movie musical. Although he was not the only purveyor of this tradition, Berkeley became its purest and most celebrated representative—too pure, in fact, for the primarily realistic and narrative-oriented institution of classical Hollywood cinema. As a result, Berkeley's film career became increasingly marked by tension and constraint after his heyday in the early thirties. However, the type of entertainment tradition represented by Berkeley continued to operate in a more adulterated form as an important component of the movie musical—a genre that to a certain extent escapes the domination of narrativity and realistic consistency. It is my contention that a greater acknowledgment of this tradition would lead to a more accurate assessment of the tensions and contradictions that lie at the heart of the movie musical genre and give it a distinct identity within the Hollywood system.

Another central contention of this study is that the *context* of a musical number—its relationship to the show as a whole—is a crucial factor in determining the style and characteristics of that number. Those qualities identified with the Berkeleyesque flourished in certain contexts and not in others. Accordingly, the descriptions below of Berkeley's stage and film work often devote considerable attention not only to descriptions of the numbers themselves but also to their contextualization: the type of show in which they appeared, their placement within the whole show, and their relationship to the other elements of the show.

The field of film studies has recently been undergoing a shift of emphasis from theory to history. This book seeks to historicize such topics as authorship and genre in order to ground Busby Berkeley's work as a cultural phenomenon. It deals with the work of an individual artist in terms of the artist's placement *within* a particular tradition and within particular conditions of production. Previously dominant approaches in film studies have tended to concentrate on one context at a time in a way that maintains methodological purity but tends to impoverish the overall model. *Showstoppers* seeks an integrated approach that springs from a synthesis of genre study, history, and aesthetic analysis. It attempts to conceive of both Berkeley and the Berkeleyesque in a manner that is not static but contextualized and historicized, as they are viewed through a series of multiple and shifting contexts—including genre history, institutional history, studio history, film history, and theatrical history.

This book hopes to contribute toward a developing direction in film studies that is more flexible, wide-ranging, and interactive. By looking at films in this way, categories such as "authorship" and "genre" can be realigned and decompartmentalized. Such an approach can also provide a historically specific means for engaging *films* again in ways that are less romanticized than the traditional auteurism of the 1960s and less abstract than the poststructural theoretical approaches of the 1970s and 1980s.

The first part of this study investigates the Berkeleyesque mode in terms of its relationship to the larger context of the musical genre. The general emphasis here is on the central tensions that lie at the heart of the genre, its evolution out of various nineteenth-century entertainment forms, and the development of forms especially receptive to large-scale musical spectacle. More specific issues involve the rise of "aggregate" entertainment forms, the spectacular qualities of mainstream nineteenth-century theater, and the evolution of the revue (which eventually evolved into the backstage musical—the optimum context for Berkeley's production numbers).

The second section deals with Berkeley's stage career, centering on the ways in which it both anticipates his subsequent film work and reflects the influence of a previous tradition of popular stage entertainment. Included here are a discussion of the major stage productions on which Berkeley worked, a descriptive catalogue of spectacular effects employed on the Broadway stage (and later assimilated by Berkeley in his stage and screen numbers), and a brief history of the chorus line and other stylized ways in which female bodies were incorporated into the architecture of the spectacular production number.

The third section presents an overview of Berkeley's films in relation to these issues. His film career is divided into six phases. Each of these can be conceptualized in terms of its receptiveness to Berkeleyesque spectacle, which flourished in the special context of the early thirties Warner Bros. backstage musical but then became increasingly restrained and readjusted in response to changing trends in the musical genre. Representative major works are examined to demonstrate the operation of the spectacular mode, which frequently involves both the retention of relevant stage techniques and the extension of those techniques to specifically cinematic forms.

This study does not pretend to be a comprehensive or definitive examination of Berkeley's work. Although he was a filmmaker of limited and specialized range, Berkeley's career provides an extraordinarily rich point of convergence for a wide range of cultural and artistic contexts. Only a small portion of that range is dealt with here, but it is a portion that calls for a fuller appreciation of both an exuberant artist and an expansive entertainment tradition whose prodigious attractions are often patronized and oversimplified.

PART ONE

BERKELEYESQUE TRADITIONS

1 ROOTS: FROM BARNUM TO ZIEGFELD

Integration and the Musical

In analyzing the production numbers of Busby Berkeley (or those of any other musical/dance director), it is important to consider those numbers not only in terms of themselves but in terms of their relationship to the musical work as a whole. Those qualities now commonly identified with the Berkeleyesque flourished in the context of a particular type of musical show and were greatly curtailed in the context of other types. These different types (different in terms of the ways in which individual numbers relate to the entire show) are allied with distinct trends in the evolution of the musical and with certain operations that serve to define the genre.

Musical numbers seldom exist in and of themselves as independent, self-enclosed units in the manner of short subjects but are almost always part of an enclosing larger work, usually a narrative of some kind. On the other hand, a musical number does not have the same relationship to the surrounding narrative that a scene does in a conventional nonmusical narrative. The shift in discourse from spoken dialogue to performance that is sung and/or danced (including the typical popular-song format wherein—unlike in an opera—each song functions as a somewhat discrete entity) insures that there will always be a certain amount of structural autonomy for a musical number in relation to the narrative or surrounding show.[1] This leads to the issue of "integration," around which most historical and theoretical accounts of the musical genre have been centered.

Traditional chroniclers of the stage musical—Gerald Bordman, David Ewen, Stanley Green, Richard Kislan, Cecil Smith, etc.—commonly interpret its history in idealistic terms as a progressive development toward an ever greater and more seamless integration of plot and music, with shows such as *Show Boat* (1927), *Oklahoma!* (1943), and *My Fair Lady* (1956) frequently cited as milestones in this evolution.[2] Kislan's *The Musical: A Look at the American Musical Theater* contains a representative statement of the traditional pro-integration position:

> What emerged was a more fluid and compact union of song and story. Many called it the new musical comedy; in reality, it was a new form, the musical play. . . . Within the book, no elements were intended to function without the others. . . . Character, situation, mood, and theme were placed ahead of hit song, star, gags, and formula. To weave music deeper into the fabric of the musical drama, [*Show Boat* composer Jerome] Kern drew on the example of the "leitmotif" theory from opera composition. The songs that were once adjacent to or companions of the drama now became an essential part of the drama. Music began to personify character, foreshadow mood, echo emotion, underscore dialogue, and parallel the libretto's emerging patterns of action and rest.[3]

Analysts of the film musical have generally followed this lead, stating the matter in terms of the mastering of disruptive spectacle elements by other, integrative elements. These can be narrativization (Patricia Mellancamp), "internal narrative logic" (Thomas Schatz), thematic unity (Stanley J. Solomon), the body and voice of the singer/star (Jacque Schultz), "transformative energy" (J. P. Telotte), connections of musical performance to ordinary life (Michael Wood), a utopian dissolving of oppositions (Rick Altman), or an overall fusion of all the elements of the musical (Timothy E. Scheurer).[4] In each case, the primary value is placed upon a unifying principle that serves to transcend the inherently divided structure of the musical.

However, it could be argued that nonintegration—a built-in and formalized resistance to the ultimate homogeneity or hierarchy of discourse—is essential to the musical genre, which is based precisely on a shifting and volatile dialectic between integrative and nonintegrative elements.[5] Viewed in this way, the history of the musical becomes not so much a relentless, unidirectional drive toward effacing the last stubborn remnants of nonintegration, but a succession of different ways of articulating the tension and interplay between integrative (chiefly narrative) and nonintegrative (chiefly spectacle) elements.

This interpretation of the musical corresponds to a vision of genres as being based on the maintenance of certain central, unresolved tensions (which may be formal, structural, ideological, or thematic). Genres that resolve their central "problems" too definitively often eliminate their raison d'être at the same time, as the recent decline and near-extinction of the movie western has demonstrated. In a similar way, any such complete and universally applied "solution" of the problem of integration would probably spell the end of the musical genre. Musicals would then be supplanted by mere films-with-music, which are quite a different thing.

If integration were indeed the goal of the musical genre, then a question might be raised regarding the examples provided by eighteenth-and nineteenth-century prototypical forms such as ballad opera, comic opera, and operetta.[6] These early forms of the musical were all relatively cohesive and integration-oriented in form, and they pointed a clear path for the developing genre to follow.

However, the musical genre declined to rush toward the promised land of integration. As has happened so often in its history, for every step taken forward along the road to integration, another was taken backward. One possible reason for this recalcitrance might be that forms such as ballad opera, comic opera, and operetta are *too* well-integrated to be considered true musicals. They diminish that element of problematic, semiautonomous spectacle which, in tandem and constant struggle with the impulse toward integration, supplies the central dynamic that propels the musical genre.

The history of the evolution of the musical is not only the history of relatively integrated forms but also of those elements that pull in the opposite direction, that work to deintegrate and problematize the unity of the discourse of the narrative. These deintegrative elements should not necessarily be seen negatively, as crude and embarrassing drawbacks that need to be effaced. They can also be seen as essential elements in the musical genre's continuing and enriching struggle between integration and nonintegration, between the contradictory demands of narrative and spectacle.

The intention here is not to go to the opposite extreme and aggrandize certain types of musical simply for their hardy primitivism and their lack of bourgeoisified integrative elements. The idea, rather, is to point out that most histories of the musical, in their zeal to elevate its integration-oriented side, often overlook or underestimate the importance of nonintegration in the dynamic of the genre. These nonintegrative elements are a significant factor in the systems of virtually all individual musicals, including the predominantly integration-oriented ones, such as *Show Boat* and *Oklahoma!* In addition, those musicals in which nonintegrative elements are dominant need not be simply dismissed as stumbling blocks on the road to integration. Collectively, they form an important and lively tradition demonstrating that musicals can have much to offer outside the achievement of consistency.

It is to this spectacle-oriented, nonintegrative tradition that the Berkeleyesque is essentially linked. Indeed, in the cinema Busby Berkeley was that tradition's most prominent perpetrator. Accordingly, at this point it is appropriate to trace the development of that somewhat disreputable tradition, which Berkeley did so much to transfer to the screen.

Aggregate Forms

> Do I contradict myself?
> Very well then. . . . I contradict myself;
> I am large. . . . I contain multitudes.
> —Walt Whitman,
> "Song of Myself"[7]

The spectacle-oriented mode of the musical (and, on a broader level, the entire musical genre) owes its genesis not only to the evolution of early musical forms such as ballad opera and comic opera but also to more general trends in nineteenth-century American popular culture. These trends spawned a whole series of related entertainment forms in a mode that might be termed (per *Webster's Ninth New Collegiate Dictionary*) a *conglomeration* ("a mixed coherent mass") or, perhaps better, the *aggregate* ("a mass or body of units or parts somewhat loosely associated with one another").

One of the pioneers in the evolution of nineteenth-century aggregate forms was the showman P. T. Barnum, a key figure in the history of American popular culture. Although today Barnum's name is mainly associated with the circus, his most important contribution to the world of entertainment concerned another type of institution: the so-called dime museum (Barnum actually charged a quarter). In 1841, Barnum acquired Scudder's American Museum in downtown Manhattan, a typical collection of natural history exhibits, scientific displays, and assorted curiosities. Renaming the place Barnum's American Museum, he converted it into a sensationally popular attraction by adding to the existing stock of educational exhibits diverse elements of the "freak" show, the circus, and the variety show.[8]

Barnum's American Museum was an early example of an aggregate entertainment form. It was a place where heterogeneity ruled, where as much diversity as possible was included under one roof. Rather than attempting to figure out what his customers wanted, then selecting and organizing the exhibits accordingly, Barnum operated on the principle of simply overwhelming his customers by including everything. In addition to the exhibits themselves, the museum also included a theater, which presented continuous performances of variety acts (singers, acrobats, animal acts, etc.), popular plays, and melodramas. All told, a patron of Barnum's American Museum could expect to receive an extraordinarily plentiful and diverse range of entertainment for the single admission price. In his autobiography, Barnum included this Whitmanesque catalogue of some of the bounty offered his customers:

> The transient attractions of the Museum were constantly diversified, and educated dogs, industrious fleas, automatons, jugglers, ventriloquists, living statuary, tableaux, gipsies, albinos, fat boys, giants, dwarfs, rope-dancers, live "Yankees," pantomime, instrumental music, singing and dancing in great variety, dioramas, panoramas, models of Niagara, Dublin, Paris, and Jerusalem; Hannington's dioramas of the Creation, the Deluge, Fairy Grotto, Storm at Sea; the first English Punch and Judy in this country, Italian fantoccini, mechanical figures, fancy glass-blowing, knitting machines and other triumphs of the mechanical arts; dissolving views, American Indians, who enacted their warlike and religious ceremonies on the stage—these, among others, were all exceedingly successful.[9]

After Barnum's American Museum was destroyed by fires in 1865 and 1868, he became primarily associated with the institution for which he is most famous today: the circus. Operating concurrently and sometimes in partnership with other leading showmen such as George A. Bailey, W. C. Coup, Dan Castello, and Adam Forepaugh, Barnum was involved in a major transformation of the circus form in the latter part of the nineteenth century. Previously, the circus had been based primarily on skilled performers displaying their acts one at a time, much like in a variety show. Beginning in the 1870s, the American circus turned in a direction where spectacle, extravagance, and opulence were stressed as much as were individual skills. Hundreds of performers were paraded, first in two rings, then in three, with the idea of presenting the audience with a *superabundance*, with more than could possibly be absorbed at a single sitting by any single spectator.[10]

It is this concept of superabundance that links the three-ring circus to Barnum's American Museum and to other aggregate entertainment forms. As Barnum wrote of his Museum:

> No one could go through the halls, as they were when they came under my proprietorship, and see one-half there was worth seeing in a single day; and then, as I always justly boasted afterwards, no one could visit my Museum and go away without feeling that he had received the full worth of his money. . . .
>
> From the first, it was my study to give my patrons a superfluity of novelties, and for this I make no special claim to generosity, for it was strictly a business transaction. To send away my visitors more than doubly satisfied, was to induce them to come again and to bring their friends. I meant to make people talk about my Museum; to exclaim over its wonders; to have men and women

all over the country say: "There is not another place in the United States where so much can be seen for twenty-five cents as in Barnum's American Museum."[11]

Another important example of the aggregate tradition is the minstrel show, which reigned as the most popular American entertainment form in the period 1840–80. The minstrel show was a collection of comic and musical elements organized very loosely around a fixed format that consisted of three main parts. In the first part (which is the part corresponding to the subsequent popular image of the minstrel show), a group of performers in blackface seated themselves in a semicircular arrangement. Dominated by the central emcee (known as the Interlocutor) and the two disruptive end men (known as Tambo and Bones), this group presented a program of song, dance, and comedy tied to a heavily mythicized vision of the antebellum South. This first part was then followed by the olio (a series of variety acts) and the afterpiece (a one-act skit, usually a type of parody or burlesque common to the theatrical practice of the period).[12]

The minstrel show was very much in the aggregate vein: a conglomeration of diverse parts in which each act was presented as a self-contained unit designed to stop the show.[13] As Gerald Bordman writes of the minstrel show: "The show was held together by an external framework—what today's jargon would call a format—rather than by any internal cohesion or organically dictated form. Its devil-may-care indifference to even the vaguest dramatic unities helped establish a not altogether healthy slapdash tradition in the American Musical Theatre."[14] Centering on the two main elements of music and comedy, the minstrel show in some ways prefigured the nascent form of musical comedy, although two key elements were still lacking: narrative and spectacle.[15] These were supplied by the seminal 1866 show *The Black Crook*, which will be discussed below.

The next dominant form of American entertainment, vaudeville, was basically an extension of the minstrel show's olio: a series of separate acts in the music, comedy, and novelty modes.[16] American vaudeville differed from its French and British equivalents (known as music hall) in that music hall shows were less diversified, tailored more for specific class strata, and directed more toward establishing a sense of intimacy and rapport with the audience (often reinforced by having an emcee or host figure to tie the show together). American vaudeville did not feature an emcee; its variegated acts, pitched at a heterogeneous mass audience, succeeded each other without introductions or bridging elements; and it was generally a more objective and compartmentalized form than were its European equivalents.[17]

However, this does not mean that American vaudeville was merely an undifferentiated hodgepodge. The several acts (usually between seven and nine) of the standard vaudeville show were structured according to certain principles of logic and design, based on pacing, orchestration, and a consciousness of audience response, with the aim of creating an optimum overall impression of diversity and abundance.[18]

Other nineteenth-century-derived aggregate forms include the medicine show (something of a small-scale vaudeville show), the Wild West show (combining elements of the western, the circus, and vaudeville, and most famously represented by Buffalo Bill Cody's Wild West Show), the Tom Show (in which touring companies used the familiar story of *Uncle Tom's Cabin* as an elastic format allowing for the casual inclusion of novelty, specialty, and song-and-dance acts), and burlesque (which aggregated music, dance, comedy, and display of the female body).

Also of relevance to the aggregate tradition is the amusement park, particularly the type of self-enclosed, spectacular, all-inclusive bazaar pioneered by the opening of Coney Island's Steeplechase Park in 1897. It is worth noting some direct connections between the amusement park and the turn-of-the-century musical/spectacular stage. Frederic Thompson and Skip Dundy, founders of the legendary Hippodrome in New York, had previously made their mark by building Luna Park, the most beautiful and spectacular of Coney Island's great parks, in 1903. Florenz Ziegfeld, the most important figure in the creation of the American spectacular revue, got his show business start in the fairground/amusement-park field, first as a talent scout for the 1893 World's Columbian Exposition in Chicago and then as the promoter of strongman Eugene Sandow.[19]

Even the mainstream dramatic theater of the eighteenth and nineteenth centuries partook heavily of this aggregate impulse. Music, songs, and dances were freely interpolated into virtually every form of play. Between acts of plays, audiences were usually regaled with variety acts (singing, dancing, juggling, satire, pantomime, etc.), no matter whether the play was a Shakespeare tragedy or a potboiler melodrama.[20]

The texts of the plays themselves were often treated in a similar manner. Nineteenth-century performance style was based on treating each scene, each big speech, as a self-enclosed high point, almost in the manner of a vaudeville show.[21] Accordingly, a nineteenth-century production of a Shakespeare play might become something on the order of selected big moments from the play, with a few new songs and other interpolations thrown in for good measure.

One of the most striking examples of this casual approach to the unities of dramatic structure occurred during the 1888 Broadway revival of Johann Strauss's *Prince Methusalem*, a period Ruritanian operetta set in the requisite mythical European principality. During the show's run, the lead actor, De Wolf Hopper, bought performance rights to a new poem by Ernest L. Thayer entitled "Casey at the Bat," a recitation of which Hopper inserted forthwith into the middle of the second act.[22] It is perhaps difficult to imagine today how audiences of the time accommodated this sudden transition from Ruritania to Mudville, but they did accommodate it—indeed, it became the popular highlight of the show. Notions of unity and narrative consistency were not as paramount in the nineteenth-century theater as they have been in other times. Audiences of the day were more receptive to the concept of a theatrical show as a collection of powerful, autonomous moments and spectacular effects.

Although these aggregate forms are by no means completely random and disorganized in their structure, they generally lack the overriding sense of centrality and homogeneity that characterizes more strongly narrativized forms. A useful analogy (frequently called upon in recent art theory and criticism) concerns the idea of Renaissance perspective as the dominant system in Western representational painting (and photography), based on the use of a single dominant center (the vanishing point) to direct the viewer's gaze. This system can be contrasted with other systems of representation, such as Cubism or Oriental art, which are based more on the balance and arrangement of elements, and on a series of multiple "centers" dispersed throughout the frame. Narrative can be seen as a centering device analogous to Renaissance perspective, with a similar function of directing attention and containing the potential disruptiveness of heterogeneous elements.[23]

The types of arrangements used in alternative representational systems (such as pre-Renaissance, "primitive," Oriental, and Cubist art) bear a certain analogy to the nineteenth-century aggregate forms discussed above, which are based on a concept of multiple centers and which strive to make each unit, each act, each number, a self-contained highlight—a "showstopper." The very phrase "stopping the show" (frequently used to describe the effect of musical numbers) is itself of great interest in relation to these issues, especially when compared to the concept of narrativity, which is based on principles of sustained continuity and temporal flow.

To a certain extent, all musicals bear the mark of their ancestry in nineteenth-century aggregate forms, with the musical numbers functioning as a series of self-contained highlights that work to weaken the dominance of a homogeneous, hierarchical narrative continuity. In a similar sense, all musical numbers are spectacles, by virtue of the way in which they function as semiautonomous exhibitions somewhat distinct from the discourse of the narrative.

It is important to emphasize that here the concept of "spectacle" need not be limited to the large-scale but may include anything that sets itself apart from the dominant narrative flow and calls attention to itself as an object of display. In these broad terms, something as simple as a provocatively garbed (or ungarbed) female body or a musical performer turning to address a song directly to the audience can function as an element of spectacle.

While all musicals bear the mark of their aggregate heritage, and all musical numbers are to a certain extent spectacles, certain musicals work to efface as much as possible the marks of spectacle and aggregation. These musicals belong to the tradition of the "integrated" musical, generally esteemed by critics and historians as the more modern, sophisticated, and artful tradition: ballad opera, opéra bouffe, comic opera, operetta, the Princess Theatre shows, *Show Boat*, *Oklahoma!*, etc.[24] The other major tradition in the evolution of the musical (and one generally viewed as the more primitive, unsophisticated, and artless) works to maximize heterogeneity, excess, and spectacle in the manner of nineteenth- and early twentieth-century aggregate entertainment forms.

The pleasure offered by these aggregate forms is largely directed toward creating feelings of copiousness, superabundance, variety, heterogeneity, inclusiveness, and blatant spectacle, based around a loosely organized series of self-enclosed units or climactic moments. In aggregate forms these qualities are stressed more than in integrated forms where the spectator's pleasure is more directly based on a unified, hierarchical, centered, closure-oriented experience, leading the spectator along a continuous path that organizes, arranges, and absorbs the various elements of the show/film/narrative.

Although recent film and narrative theory has placed major emphasis on the primacy of these latter, integrative elements in mainstream modes of art and entertainment, the example of divergent aggregate forms suggests that the narrative/integrative impulse ("integrated" being essentially just another term for narrative-dominated) has not always or necessarily been such a dominant force in a work of entertainment. The musical genre itself—something of a holdover from these more archaic entertainment forms—remains more or less in a state of unresolved suspension between aggregative and conventional narrative impulses. A major stylistic and structural choice in a musical therefore concerns the type of interrelationship it establishes between these two aspects of the genre. In the Berkeleyesque musical, it is definitely the aggregative side of the genre that is emphasized (in particular ways that will be discussed throughout this book).

The Black Crook

As noted above, several key elements of the musical—music, comedy, song-and-dance, and vernacular music and performance styles—were already inherent in such aggregate forms as the minstrel show and vaudeville. Of the remaining elements contributing to the evolution of the musical, the most crucial were *narrative* and *spectacle*. Both of these elements were supplied abundantly—even overabundantly—by the celebrated 1866 production of *The Black Crook*.

The origins of the show have passed into theatrical legend. A stroke of circumstance (the burning of the Academy of Music in New York City) caused a visiting French ballet troupe to be hastily incorporated into a fantastic melodrama written by a little-known author named Charles M. Barras. The resulting hybrid was a tremendous success, and *The Black Crook* continued to be revived profitably for over twenty-five years.[25] Few commentators have ever attributed the show's popularity to Barras's long-winded drama; rather, the crucial ingredient was the presence of seventy ballet girls, wearing then-scandalous tights and performing interpolated numbers such as "The Grand Ballet of the Gems" and "The March of the Amazons."[26]

The Black Crook is frequently cited in histories as the first American musical. In much the same way that film scholars treat claims for *The Birth of a Nation* (1915) as the first feature film or for *The Jazz Singer* (1927) as the first talkie, *The Black Crook*'s claims to primacy are usually heavily qualified and even discredited by scholars of the musical theater. One of the foremost of *The Black Crook*'s detractors is Julian Mates, a leading historian of the early American musical. In an article entitled "The Black Crook Myth," Mates asserts that there is nothing to justify the preeminence accorded to *The Black Crook* by theatrical historians. In the first place, Mates maintains, none of the individual forms and conventions employed by *The Black Crook* was novel. Its plot, its music, its spectacle, its display of female anatomy—all of these derived from stage traditions established long before 1866. In the second place, *The Black Crook*, according to Mates, offered no new ways of combining these unoriginal elements. He notes that combinations of ballet and drama were common in the pantomime, and that narrative dances (i.e., dances telling a self-enclosed story) were often used as entr'actes during stage productions. Furthermore, *The Black Crook* cannot be counted as a "genuine musical comedy," because its music was the work of several composers, because there was a disunity of conception between the libretto and the score, and because the music failed to illuminate the characters and actions of the narrative.[27]

Although *The Black Crook* was certainly no *Oklahoma!*, and its status as a full-fledged musical can be challenged on other grounds (notably, its divorcement from vernacular music and dance styles), it is possible to question Mates's underlying assumptions on several points. Granting that *The Black Crook* employed no entirely new elements, one can nevertheless claim that its method of combining these elements was, if not utterly unprecedented, still highly and influentially distinctive in a pioneering sense. Although it may be true that, as Mates states, ballet and drama were previously combined in pantomimes, and narrative dances were commonly used as entr'actes, these forms do not completely cover the possibilities for combining narrative and dance that were explored in *The Black Crook*.

Mates's argument is based on a conception of the musical that is too one-sidedly weighted toward integration as the sole rationale of the genre. If one views the musical (as suggested above) as a more or less unwieldy interaction between integrative and nonintegrative elements, then the significance of *The Black Crook* to the evolution of the genre becomes less tenuous. *The Black Crook* offered a method of combining musical performance and dramatic narrative that was neither as self-inclusively separate-unto-itself as an entr'acte piece (or an olio/vaudeville act) nor as homogeneously aligned with the rest of the show as a pantomime ballet. The ballet numbers, through their scale and provocativeness, were given a semiautonomous (but not completely autonomous) weight that enabled them to become a competing center of gravity vis-à-vis Barras's already quite weighty plot.

As noted above, the musical genre is based on two main impulses—the integrative and the aggregative. These two impulses in the musical are neither completely contradictory nor completely resolvable but coexist in a constant state of unreconciled tension. If the musical is conceptualized in these asymptotic terms (rather than as a relentless march to stamp out the aggregative and enshrine the integrative), then *The Black Crook* can be seen not as an irrelevant and overrated antique but as a major step in articulating a tension that lies at the core of the genre.[28]

A final objection to Mates's argument concerns his implicit identification of the "true" musical with music that illuminates character and action. Mates here is reducing the established range of the musical genre to a single one of its possible modes. What could be called the Berkeleyesque musical is based precisely on music (and musical numbers) that "fails to illuminate particular kinds of action or particular characters."[29] One might arguably consider this to be a primitive or inferior strain of the musical, but it has nevertheless been a significant and long-lived one in the history of the genre, far more significant and enduring than "integrationist" historians have generally acknowledged.

Spectacle Forms

The Black Crook also exemplifies the evolving musical's intersection with a general trend affecting nineteenth-century stagecraft: the prominence of pictorial spectacle in theatrical performance. Whereas the stage of previous eras had been based primarily on the spoken word, the physical/vocal presence of the actor, and a predominantly abstract setting, the period running roughly from the late eighteenth century to the early twentieth century witnessed an increasing emphasis on visual realism, spectacle, and sensationalism.[30]

The traditional apron stage, which thrusts the actor

out onto an abstract platform for declamation, was superseded by the proscenium arch, which places a literal frame around the stage "picture" and throws the action back into a more self-enclosed and concretized space. Settings, which previously had been perfunctory and abstract, became increasingly elaborate and detailed, often drawing considerable attention away from the written/spoken text and in some cases even eliminating actors completely (as in the cases of dioramas and panoramas—"performances" that were all setting, with no actors). Two-dimensional flats became more lavish and were augmented by the use of wings, traps, bridges, cuts, and lighting effects. These devices produced a more fully visualized environment, a wide variety of special effects, and an illusion of three-dimensional depth. This last quality was enhanced by the widespread introduction of box sets in the early 1900s.[31]

Boosted by the shift in power from actor-managers to producer-directors (such as Augustin Daly, Steele Mackaye, David Belasco, André Antoine, and Dion Boucicault), this drive toward pictorial theater reached its peak in the late nineteenth century.[32] During this period, the stage was the frequent site of large-scale battle scenes, floods, fires, storms, and chariot races (with real horses), as well as the gargantuan ballets and "Amazon marches" in musicals and protomusicals such as *The Black Crook* (1866), *The White Fawn* (1867), *Humpty Dumpty* (1868), and *The Twelve Temptations* (1869). Casts and supernumeraries became more numerous. To accommodate these colossal displays, theaters became necessarily larger, culminating in Steele Mackaye's legendary (and never realized) Spectatorium and the equally celebrated New York Hippodrome (described in chapter 4).

Existing repertory was retailored to conform to the prevailing fashion (as in Henry Irving's renderings of Shakespeare plays as elaborately detailed period pieces), and new forms were developed to meet it. Melodrama, perhaps the most popular new theatrical form of the nineteenth century, was a highly visualized form of drama, heavily dependent on spectacular stage effects and "the pictorial value of settings and their physical aspects."[33] Producers chose plays on the basis of their spectacular elements and expended most of the budgets on these elements because of their great box-office appeal. As a result, "hundreds of plays were written solely as vehicles for magic, special effects, or elaborately trapped settings."[34]

Entire stage forms evolved that were largely or wholly oriented toward visual spectacle. These included hippodramas (which incorporated circuslike equestrian maneuvers into staged drama), aquadramas (which existed mainly as opportunities to reenact sea battles), dioramas (wherein the audience sat on a revolving platform that gradually disclosed large-scale scenic paintings enhanced with lighting effects), panoramas (similar to dioramas, but involving a stationary platform surrounded by a 360-degree painting), and biblical spectacles such as *Quo Vadis?*, *Ben Hur*, and *Judith of Bethulia*, which emphasized three-dimensional spectacular realism even more than did melodramas.[35]

Two of these spectacle-oriented forms that developed during the nineteenth century merit special mention in relation to the musical and to the Berkeleyesque style of the musical. The first is the pantomime. Derived from the commedia dell'arte (a highly conventionalized comic form that originated in Italy in the sixteenth century) and the harlequinade (a later British importation of the form), pantomime presented a fairy-tale or nursery-rhyme subject that was enlivened by comedy, music, and ballet. The performance built toward a climactic and magical transformation effect that transported the main drama into the realm of fairyland.[36]

As far back as the 1690s, pantomimes and related stage forms in Italy (then the leading area in the development of scenic and mechanical stage effects) were giving special prominence to spectacular visual displays, especially in regard to transformation effects. In one late seventeenth-century production, stage soldiers grouped together to form the figure of an elephant with their shields—a predecessor of the placard and flag effects of later musicals (described in chapter 4). In a 1698 production at the Theatre Capranio in Rome, an actress representing the ghost of a woman suddenly transformed herself into a palace, complete with wings and courtyard, while the guards attempting to capture her turned into fountains, cascades, and trees, forming "a charming garden before the palace." Another production at the same venue included a spectacular descent into Hell, featuring an enormous dragonlike monster that, at the climax, transformed itself into a multitude of white butterflies.[37]

In the nineteenth century, the pantomime reached a peak of popularity in Britain, where it incorporated ballet and music-hall elements and eventually evolved into the traditional Christmas pantomime. By 1850 the pantomime had become almost completely dominated by visual spectacle, with most of the energy and expense of the production being sunk into the scenery and transformation effects.[38] R. J. Broadbent, in *A History of Pantomime*, notes, "All this love of spectacular display soon began to supersede the good old-fashioned Christmas Pantomime."[39] Brooks McNamara, in an article on popular entertainment stagecraft, concurs, "Many of the traditional English Christmas pantomimes were little more than frameworks for elaborate transformation scenes."[40]

In the eighteenth century, the pantomime was imported to the United States, where, in a somewhat impure form, it eventually intersected with the evolving form of the musical. G. L. Fox's immensely successful *Humpty Dumpty* (1868, and often revived thereafter), which is cited in nearly all histories as a landmark in the development of the American musical, combined topical humor and *Black Crook*-like ballets with a pantomime story involving such characters as Humpty Dumpty, Goody Two Shoes, Harlequin, Columbine, and Pantaloon.[41]

Other notable pantomime/musicals followed *Humpty Dumpty*, including *Hiccory Diccory Dock* (1869), *Wee Willie Winkie* (1870), *Azreal, or The Magic Charm* (1873), and *Babes in the Wood, or Who Killed Cock Robin?* (1877). By the 1920s, the pantomime was largely defunct as an integral entity in the American theater, but its spirit survived in musical/revue formats (especially at the Hippodrome) in the form of individual numbers in the pantomime vein. Examples include "The Toy Shop" in *A World of Pleasure* (1915), featuring toy soldiers coming to life in an oversized toy-shop setting; the similarly themed "A Toy Store" in *Good Times* (1920); "Snowflake" in the 1921 edition of the *Greenwich Village Follies*, with allegorical figures representing Jack Frost, the Winter Night, the North Star, the Aurora, and Moonbeams; and "The Land of Mystery" in *Better Times* (1922), in which a sleeper's bed transformed into a motor car and drove off, giving way to a nightmarish fairyland filled with flying witches, harlequins, marionettes, and row upon row of dancing skeletons.[42]

The pantomime tradition feeds into the Berkeleyesque in several ways. One is the frequent use of giant props and animated objects. Another is the way in which an initially established narrative situation is arbitrarily dissolved into pure spectacle (several Berkeley film numbers employ a similar structure—e.g., "Shanghai Lil," "I Only Have Eyes for You," "Spin a Little Web of Dreams"). Most importantly, there is the central use of transformation effects to create a sense of wonder and surprise. In addition to the climactic transformation (typically from a gloomy cavern to a resplendent palace), nineteenth-century pantomime usually also featured a major earlier transformation, which turned the principals of the nursery-rhyme/fairy-tale opening into the traditional harlequinade figures (Harlequin, Columbine, Pantaloon, Clown), followed by any number of localized transformations effected by Harlequin's magic bat.[43] As will be discussed elsewhere in this study, transformation is a key element of Berkeley's numbers, by virtue of its power to create a magical world of fluid, constantly shifting spatial and temporal boundaries.

The second of these pre-1900 spectacle "genres" to be singled out here is the extravaganza. In the late eighteenth century, as elements of spectacle became increasingly important in existing forms such as the pantomime and the masque, these elements began to coalesce into a separate, more self-enclosed form. This could be appended as an afterpiece or entr'acte to a dramatic play or, more commonly, presented by itself as a full-length performance.[44]

In these productions, known as extravaganzas, plot elements were downplayed and often completely eliminated, while scenic effects became the production's raison d'être. "Scenery was so elaborate . . . that the actor sometimes found himself crowded entirely off the stage, the manager relying chiefly on the magic of paint and canvas to pack the house."[45]

This form of extravaganza reached a peak of popularity in America in the 1790s, but the term continued to be used more loosely throughout the nineteenth century to designate several types of theatrical performance. These included early forms of the burlesque and revue, and also musical entertainments with a heavy emphasis on semiautonomous spectacle, such as the aforementioned *The Black Crook*.[46] The major idea underlying these various applications of the term "extravaganza" seems to be that a weakening of narrative dominance leads to correspondingly increased opportunities for *extravagance*—whether that extravagance be in the form of scenic/spectacular effects or in the form of outrageous foolishness and wit. Indeed, it is precisely these two "extravagant" ingredients—spectacle and comedy—that form the basis of the last in this line of major aggregative/spectacular/musical forms, the revue (discussed below).

The movement toward increased visual spectacle on the nineteenth-century stage is commonly seen as reaching toward the cinema, which would be able to present spectacle much more grandiosely, efficiently, and economically than could even the most elaborate theatrical production.[47] The advent of the cinema superseded the spectacle-oriented mode of theater, which gradually declined (without, however, completely disappearing) in the early 1900s. But one area in particular carried on and even augmented the tradition of the nineteenth-century spectacle stage well into the 1920s. That area was the musical theater. The spectacular musical was not quickly superseded by the cinema, one self-evident reason being that the screen musical did not establish itself until approximately 1929, after the entrenchment of talking pictures.

Another reason for the survival of spectacle on the musical stage in the period from 1905 to 1930 can be inferred from certain leads in A. Nicholas Vardac's study *Stage to Screen*. Vardac maintains that the drive toward spectacle on the nineteenth-century stage was mixed with a simultaneous drive toward ever-greater realism. These two drives, although not unrelated, were fundamentally in conflict with each other. The elements of spectacle tended toward glamorous and romanticized sensationalism, while the realistic elements (such as the use of authentic settings and props) tended toward naturalism and verisimilitude.[48]

As a result, according to Vardac, most nineteenth-century productions in the oxymoronic "spectacular realism" vein were unsatisfactory mélanges of constrained romantic sensationalism and half-achieved realism. Naturalistic details pointed up all the more the inherent artificiality of stage space and plot contrivances; the use of three-dimensional perspective in two-dimensional painted flats only emphasized their inescapable two-dimensionality; the use of more realistic electric lighting (vs. the soft, shadowy haze of gas lighting) made more apparent the unreality of the settings; and so on. The nineteenth-century stage was littered with these incongruous mixtures of the realistic and unrealistic. This irreconcilable tension between realism and spectacle was eventually relieved by the cinema, which was better suited to accommodating both values, whether singly or in combination. The theater was then liberated to move freely into more coherent and consistent experimental, intimate, expressionistic, and exclusively realistic forms.[49]

The musical theater, however, was less immediately affected by these developments, not only because there were no musical films at the time but also because the musical is a form that is not as closely bound as others are by notions of realism and consistency. The phrase "realistic musical" can only be a relative term. Traditional musicals are a priori unrealistic in the sense that nobody realistically breaks into sudden outbursts of spontaneously composed, choreographed, and orchestrated song-and-dance.

The consistency of discourse central to classical realism is continually undermined in musicals.[50] All musicals are mélanges, to a lesser or greater extent; they are all more or less incongruous mixtures of the realistic and the antirealistic. The quality of spectacle is less easily shed by the musical than by dramatic (and even melodramatic) forms, because spectacle (in the broad sense) is an intrinsic element of the musical genre, not an optional adornment. For these and other reasons, the nineteenth-century Tradition of Spectacle continued to flourish in the musical theater well after 1900; it was still flourishing there when Busby Berkeley entered the scene as a dance director in the 1920s; and, after its decline in the theater after 1929, it enjoyed a new lease on life in the Berkeleyesque film musicals of the early 1930s.

Revue Forms

The form of musical theater in which the Tradition of Spectacle continued to flourish most of all during the early twentieth century was the revue. The revue is a highly flexible and amorphous form (British producer Charles B. Cochran called it "the most plastic of all theatrical forms"), and it is difficult to find a precise definition of it in any of the major texts on the subject.[51] However, a few basic parameters can be set forth.

Like vaudeville, music hall, burlesque, and minstrel show (especially the olio section), the revue is a mixture of self-contained acts, with a general emphasis on music and comedy. However, the format of the revue is more solid and "anchored" than that of its predecessor, vaudeville. Unlike in vaudeville, the acts of a revue may be (but do not have to be) loosely linked by some sort of continuity. This may be a tenuous plot (as in the three Shubert revues on which Berkeley worked in the late 1920s), a general theme (the Orient, the Four Seasons, Unionism, etc.), the music score (an innovation in some revues of the 1920s was to have all the music written by the same composer), the decor (e.g., the *Ziegfeld Follies of 1915* was designed throughout in varying shades of blue by Joseph Urban), or the overriding concept of an individual producer (e.g., Ziegfeld's imposition of lavish tastefulness as the keynote of the *Follies*).

Unlike in vaudeville, the same performers may appear several times in the course of the show, and a strong star/host figure can dominate the proceedings to a certain extent (e.g., W. C. Fields in the *Earl Carroll Vanities of 1928*; Josephine Baker or Maurice Chevalier in several big Parisian revues of the 1920s). The material for the revue is largely unique and conceived specifically for that particular production, rather than being, as in vaudeville, a "bill" of preexisting acts.[52]

Unlike vaudeville shows, which moved itinerantly from venue to venue, a revue was usually grounded in a single theater (excepting tryouts and touring companies). Many of the most famous big revue series were strongly identified with the theaters in which they were habitually performed: the *Follies* with the New Amsterdam, the *Passing Show* series with the Winter Garden, the "*Folie*" series of Parisian revues with the Folies-Bergère, etc. Vaudeville acts usually took place in a generalized, neutral performance space, which could then be altered by the personality of the artist and the few props he or she provided. Revues, on the other hand, could utilize all the resources of theatrical production to create a full and elaborate scenic environment.[53]

In terms of the evolution of the Berkeleyesque, the most significant aspect of the revue form is that, of all musically oriented forms of popular theater, it offered the greatest opportunity for spectacle. On the one hand, the revue was not bound by the constraints of narrative consistency. The most elaborate production concepts could be fully indulged with a minimal regard for integration, plot sequence, or simple logic. A revue could mount a Parisian number and then follow it with an Arabian number, without bothering to connect the two to any external framework.

On the other hand, a revue had available to it all the scenic and production resources of the mainstream dramatic stage. A vaudeville show might have as flexible a format as a revue, but, thrown together with little advance preparation and constantly on the move, it could not afford to be encumbered with ambitious, large-scale production elements. However, a revue, conceived as a unique, long-running production and rooted in a single (and often quite sizable) locale, could take full advantage of extensive preplanning, stable performance space, and elaborate physical resources to produce the dimensions and excess of full-scale spectacle. The development of the Berkeleyesque depended heavily on the revue and closely related forms, such as the tour-of-the-town and the backstage show-within-a-show.

The revue form—as the French spelling indicates—is generally acknowledged to have originated in Paris, where revues first attained popularity in the 1840s. The earliest phase of the revue, closely related to the burlesque, was based on topical humor: a series of satirical sketches and songs aimed at contemporary events. One of the most popular targets of early revues was the past theatrical season, whose various productions would be lampooned or simply excerpted. The term "revue" thus derives from the idea of "end-of-the-year review" or "review of the past season," as indicated by the following full title of an early British revue: *A Revue of Eighteen Hundred and Sixty-three; or the Sensations of the Past Season, with a Shameful Revelation of Lady Somebody's Secret.*[54]

Although this quality of topicality was not as dominant in the subsequent history of the revue, in which music and spectacle received increasing emphasis, it nevertheless continued to hold an important place. For instance, an impression of topicality was maintained by the common practice (especially in the United States) of bringing out yearly editions and/or affixing the current year to the title of the production (e.g., *The Passing Show of 1912, . . . 1913, . . . 1914,* etc.; *Topics of 1923*; *Nic Nax of 1926*).[55] A revue was usually not expected or intended to last more than a single season, and the form was strongly identified with ideas of novelty, currency, ephemerality, le dernier cri.

The revue form was quickly imported from France to England, where the review-of-the-current-season format also proved popular, with increasing doses of "pictorial and scenic accessories" added to the satiric brew.[56] Although there are the requisite precedents and prototypes, the first American revue is considered to have been *The Passing Show*, which opened on May 12, 1894, at New York's Casino Theatre, a venue well-known for its lavish production values and its beauteous chorus line. The show was billed not as a revue but as a "topical extravaganza," indicating its connection to the traditions of both topical satire/burlesque and *Black Crook*-like spectacle. Tied together by a thin and largely irrelevant plot involving a father's attempt to stop his son's marriage, *The Passing Show*'s main focus was on satirical songs and sketches spoofing such topics as contemporary theater, "living pictures" of the type then popularized by Edward Kilyani, and current-affairs items like Coxey's Army.[57]

The *New York Times* critic expressed confusion over the use of the term "topical extravaganza" to describe the show.[58] Surfacing in the *Times* critic's confusion is a basic tension between two impulses that lie at the heart of the revue form: one toward comedy, lightness, intimacy, and topicality, and the other toward spectacle, lavishness, impersonality, and female display. This tension eventually led to the splitting of the revue form into two different modes—the intimate revue and the spectacular revue.

It should be noted that both modes rarely exist in the pure form. Predominantly intimate revues—such as the *Music Box Revue*, *Greenwich Village Follies*, *Garrick Gaieties*, and *Chauve Souris*—often strove for such spectacle effects as were possible within their limitations of budget and space, while the spectacular revues (with the possible exception of the gargantuan Hippodrome shows) always contained a significant share of intimate elements.

In a similar fashion, although the Berkeleyesque is predominantly associated with the spectacular tradition, it is easy to overlook the importance of intimate elements in Berkeley's movie numbers. Indeed, one of the most distinctive and admirable elements of Berkeley's style is the ability to shift fluidly and even breathtakingly from the spectacular to the intimate, from the large-scale to the small-scale. The latter quality is often located in the bathetic codas of Berkeley's spectacular numbers (e.g., the ersatz bird's nest at the end of "By a Waterfall," the neglected kitten near the end of "Lullaby of Broadway").

After the moderate success of *The Passing Show* (which spawned a handful of minor revues in the topical mode), the American revue went into a general eclipse for the next decade. The next significant dates were 1905, which marked the year of the first of the mammoth Hippodrome shows, and 1907, which saw the inauguration of Ziegfeld's famous *Follies*. Although the situation would soon change, this first edition of the *Follies* laid more stress on topical satire than on showgirls and spectacle. The title of the show reputedly derived from a newspaper column, "Follies of the Day," which had been written by the show's prolific librettist/lyricist Harry B. Smith.[59]

The 1909 edition of the *Follies* is generally considered to have been the first to achieve Ziegfeld's distinctive blend of comedy, spectacle, pretty girls, and melodies, all served up with a garnish of high-class production values. Among the features of the 1909 *Follies* were a jungle number satirizing Teddy Roosevelt's hunting expeditions, showgirl Lillian Lorraine circling over the audience in a miniature airplane, forty-eight showgirls wearing battleship-model headgear with twinkling electric lights, and a finale ("Come On, Play Ball with Me") in which the cast tossed 500 balls into the audience.[60]

The period of the First World War and the early 1920s was the heyday of the spectacular revue on Broadway (as well as in Paris and London). This era saw the flourishing of the great annual series, led by the *Ziegfeld Follies* and also including *The Passing Show* (the Shuberts' answer to the *Follies*), *George White's Scandals* (a fast-paced, Jazz-Age revue produced by dancer George White and featuring heavy doses of dancing and comedy), the *Earl Carroll Vanities* (reputed to be the raunchiest of the lot), the *Greenwich*

Village Follies (known for its combination of sophistication and beauty, with a strong emphasis on music), and the *Music Box Revue* (a small-scale, gemlike series, composed and coproduced by Irving Berlin).

By the late 1920s, these spectacular revues, although still active, were being viewed as bloated dinosaurs by many critics and sophisticates. A typical example was e. e. cummings's characterization of the big American revue as "a mammoth collection of boudoir-paintings-come-to-life."[61] Critical attention was being monopolized by an influx of witty, intimate revues, many of them foreign-imported or foreign-influenced: *Elsie Janis and Her Gang* (1922), *Chauve Souris* (1922), *Charlot's Revue* (1924), *Grand Street Follies* (1924–29), the *Garrick Gaities* (1925–26, 1930), *This Year of Grace* (1928).

The big revues lumbered through the end of the 1920s, until talking pictures and the Crash sent them on the road to extinction. A few attempts were made to revive the spectacular formula, but the 1930s saw a marked decline in the number of revues produced and a predominance of satire over spectacle in the few that succeeded: *The Little Show* (1929), *Three's a Crowd* (1930), *The Band Wagon* (1931), *As Thousands Cheer* (1934), *Life Begins at 8:40* (1934), *The Show Is On* (1936), *Pins and Needles* (1937). It can be observed that Busby Berkeley came on the scene of the big Broadway revue during the period of its overripe maturity and imminent decline.

The decline of the spectacular stage revue can be attributed to three main causes. The first is the Crash of 1929, which cut deeply into the available funds of producers and investors, making even less feasible the maintenance of an opulent and highly budgeted form that was already teetering on the brink of dubious solvency. Second, even before the Crash, the spectacular revue was beginning to go out of fashion. As noted above, critics had for some time been viewing the Ziegfeld-style revue as ponderous and old-hat.[62] In his history of the form, Gerald Bordman (*American Musical Revue*) suggests that the Ziegfeld-style revue—plush, overstuffed, and leisurely—was a relic of the Victorian Age and thus belonged to the same era as the sentimental operettas of Victor Herbert and Franz Lehar.[63] By the 1920s, public and critical taste was turning toward brasher, snappier, more streamlined musical forms on the stage, and the big revue's heyday had passed.

The third factor in the decline of the spectacular Broadway revue was the ascendancy of the sound film in 1929. What had befallen the stage spectacle in the early 1900s now came to pass for the musical spectacle after its quarter-century period of grace. Movies provided a more economical, expansive, and innovative means of rendering a form that was approaching exhaustion on the stage. As it had done for the melodrama earlier, the cinema gave a new lease on life to the spectacular production number and to the revue form that nurtured it. The most important and inventive figure in carrying over this tradition of spectacle from the musical stage to the musical film was Busby Berkeley.

The first major wave of talking pictures in 1929–30 saw the screen inundated with musical films—more, in fact, than in any other period of American film history. The majority of these early movie musicals were more or less direct transcriptions of Broadway properties and/or Broadway stage techniques. Some of the most important early movie musicals were pure plotless revues: *The Hollywood Revue of 1929*, *The Show of Shows* (1929), *King of Jazz* (1930), *Paramount on Parade* (1930). (See photo 2.) Others, such as *The Broadway Melody* (1929; winner of the Academy Award for Best Picture), and *Glorifying the American Girl* (1929; produced under the supervision of Florenz Ziegfeld), employed backstage plots concerning the production of a spectacular stage revue.

Both forms—the plotless revue film and the plot with a revue within it—were used as frameworks to include production numbers in the manner of the spectacular Broadway stage revue of the 1920s. Examples include: "The Tableau of Jewels" in *The Hollywood Revue of 1929* (ornately costumed showgirls posed on revolving platforms inside a giant crown); "Chinese Fantasy" in *The Show of Shows* (parade of showgirls in an Oriental setting featuring a giant genie and oversized umbrella); "Rhapsody in Blue" in *King of Jazz* (Paul Whiteman's entire orchestra rising from the innards of a giant piano with no less than five pianists at its elongated keyboard) (see photo 3); "The Wedding of the Painted Doll" in *The Broadway Melody* (scenic effects achieved exclusively through theatrical devices such as traps, cutouts, banked steps, etc., filmed from camera angles that never penetrate the proscenium). All of these numbers were staged much as they would have been on the Broadway stage of the period, with very little adjustment or expansion in terms of film technique.

Since approximately 1907, the mainstream commercial cinema has been almost completely dominated by narrative forms. The place of the plotless musical revue is an extremely minor one in American film history, limited mainly to the anything-goes, music-crazy period of the conversion to sound. The temporary decline in popularity of the movie musical in 1931–32 brought with it the general demise of the pure plotless revue on the screen, with the exception of a few isolated, novelty-oriented revivals of the form, such as *Ziegfeld Follies* (1945) and *New Faces* (1954). However, the backstage plot with a revue-like setting (or, in subsequent variations, a radio station, shipboard, or country-house benefit setting) proved more durable, especially in the mid- and late 1930s.[64]

After 1940 the leading preserves of the revue tradition in Hollywood were the composer/performer biography and, during the war, a series of variations on the guest-stars-for-victory formula.[65] *Million Dollar Mermaid* (1952), to which Berkeley contributed two numbers, is an example of the performer-biography mode, and *The Gang's All Here* (1943), his greatest achievement of the 1940s, contains elements of the wartime-rally mode. However, both of these forms are much more oriented toward personality/performance than they are toward spectacle. The 1940s in general witnessed a decline of the Berkeleyesque in the movie musical—and also (although not necessarily in a direct cause-and-effect relationship) a decline of Busby Berkeley himself, whose career reached rock bottom in 1945–46

THE BACKSTAGE FORMAT

2

Evolution of the Backstage Musical

During his film career, Berkeley never worked in the revue form per se. However, this fact does not diminish the importance of the revue tradition in the development of Berkeleyesque spectacle on the screen. The revue impulse also extends to a range of adulterated forms that incorporate narrative while at the same time maintaining a pronounced autonomy of the musical passages. There are several precedents for this in the history of the musical theater. As previously noted, early revues, especially in the pre-1915 era, commonly incorporated flimsy plots to string together their specialty acts. This structure, although less popular during the era of the big annual revues, was still practicable enough to be employed when Berkeley worked on such late twenties Broadway revues as *A Night in Venice*, *Pleasure Bound*, and *Broadway Nights*.

Other relevant antecedents of these loosely narrativized musical forms preceded the advent of the revue proper. One such form was the "tour-of-the-town" show, introduced to New York by the successful 1823 importation of Pierce Egan's London hit, *Tom and Jerry; or, Life in London. Tom and Jerry* centered loosely on a country cousin's adventures and misadventures during a whirlwind tour of the big city. The show's peripatetic structure allowed for "rapidly shifting scenes, great diversity of city types and of character, and a large amount of consequent spectacle, song and dance."[1]

The success of the first *Tom and Jerry* show led to a number of variations on the tour-of-the-town format over the next half-century, including *A Glance at New York in 1848* (1848), *The World's Fair; or, London in 1851* (1851), *Apollo in New York* (1854), *Life in New York; or, Tom and Jerry on a Visit* (1856), *Round the Clock, or New York by Dark* (1872), and Harrigan and Hart's *The Donovans* (1875). The celebrated 1875 spectacle *Around the World in 80 Days* extended the tour-of-the-town format on a global scale. It should be noted that *Good Boy* (1928), one of the most important shows that Berkeley worked on during his Broadway period, was substantially in the tour-of-the-town tradition, utilizing the basic Tom-and-Jerry format of a country bumpkin's visit to the city as the pretext for a series of rapidly shifting scenes filled with song and dance.

A later form closely related to the tour-of-the-town was the "farce-comedy." This employed a rudimentary plot, usually just enough to bring the characters into a setting, such as a theater or cabaret or ocean-liner salon, where they could watch and/or perform a program of specialty and musical acts, much like the olio of a minstrel show. Farce-comedies appeared regularly on the New York stage from 1879 until well into the 1890s. Charles Hoyt's *A Trip to Chinatown* (1891), one of the most successful and important nineteenth-century musicals, was largely derived from the farce-comedy mode.[2]

The final example of these narrative forms with revue tendencies is the backstage musical. The previous two forms (tour-of-the-town and farce-comedy) mainly work externally, bringing the narrative from someplace outside to a place or places where a show can be performed. The backstage musical, on the other hand, works primarily from the inside, originating from the venue where the show is made and centering on the relationships between the performers who make it.

The backstage musical has always been far more popular and important on the screen than it has been on the stage.[3] The predominance of the form in the film musical was established virtually from the beginning. *The Jazz Singer* (1927), the first movie musical, has strong backstage elements. Several of the most important musical films of 1929—including *The Broadway Melody*, *Syncopation*, *Close Harmony*, *William Fox Movietone Follies of 1929*, *Glorifying the American Girl*, *Broadway*, *Broadway Babies*, *Dance of Life*, *Broadway Scandals*, *Gold Diggers of Broadway*, *On with the Show*, and *Footlights and Fools*—are full-blown examples of the backstage form.

It is remarkable how quickly the backstage form achieved maturity in the movie musical. *The Broadway Melody* (released in February 1929) still holds up as a classic of its form. *On with the Show* (May 1929), a lesser-known early musical sometimes overstatedly cited as the first version of *42nd Street*, demonstrates a remarkably assured use of the show-within-a-show form.[4] One effect of this is the enhanced dynamism of the film's style. Even though it employs only a few camera movements, *On with the Show* rarely seems static in the manner of some early talkies, mainly because of the fluid interplay it sets up between onstage action and backstage action through crosscutting and foreground/background relationships. Although not as accomplished as *On with the Show*, *Broadway* (May 1929) uses its backstage framework (here applied to a nightclub setting) as an excuse to send the cinema's reputed first bonafide camera-crane soaring self-indulgently skyward for every song-and-dance number. In these pioneer musical films, the backstage/show-within-a-show format has a liberating effect on film technique and on opportunities for spectacle, setting a pattern that would be continued in the subsequent history of the movie musical.

The major Warner Bros./Berkeley musicals of the early 1930s—*42nd Street*, *Gold Diggers of 1933*, *Footlight Parade*, *Dames*, *Gold Diggers of 1935*—are widely acknowledged (especially the first three) to be pinnacles of the backstage format, which flourished throughout the 1930s at all studios. The backstage format continued to thrive in the 1940s, often overlapping with the musical-biography and let's-put-on-a-show-for-the-USO modes. In the 1950s, it provided a refuge for the spectacular, semiautonomous production number (even in the face of the growing trend toward integrated, plot-oriented musicals): "Broadway Rhythm" in *Singin' in the Rain* (1952), "Girl Hunt" in *The Band Wagon* (1953), "Born in a Trunk" in *A Star Is Born* (1954). After 1960 the backstage format was used occasionally for spectacle-oriented purposes, often with a nostalgic or parodic inflection, as in *Funny Girl* (1968—especially the "His Love Makes Me Beautiful" number), *The Producers* (1968), *The Boy Friend* (1971), and *Funny Lady* (1975).

The backstage format's relationship to spectacle-oriented and integration-oriented modes of the musical is shifting and analogical; it may lean toward one mode or the other, or be open to both within a single film. For example, backstage musicals like *Glorifying the American Girl*, *Footlight Parade*, and *The Boy Friend* are mainly spectacle-oriented (i.e., based on a marked distinction—both qualitative and quantitative—between the discourse of the narrative and the discourse of the production numbers). On the other hand, *Babes in Arms* (1939), *The Barkleys of Broadway* (1949), and *Cabaret* (1972) are more integration-oriented (i.e., based on a tighter and more consistent relationship between numbers and narrative), while backstagers such as *Gold Diggers of 1935*, *Folies Bergère* (1935), and *The Band Wagon* are more open to both modes.

By the same token, modes such as tour-of-the-town, farce-comedy, and backstage musical are by no means mutually exclusive; they easily combine and blend into one another. It could be argued, for instance, that the Warners/Berkeley classic *Footlight Parade* contains elements of all three modes in its whirling progress from venue to venue (tour-of-the-town), in the progression of the narrative toward the place of serial, olio-like performances (farce-comedy), and in the narrative's concentration on behind-the-scenes preparations and the relationships between show people (backstage musical).

The common denominator that seems to be essential to the establishment of spectacle in the backstage musical is primarily a *spatial* one rather than a musical or narrative one. The film must work to establish a space (or a series of homologous spaces) that are, to a certain extent, self-enclosed and independent of the surrounding narrative. This renders the space accessible to spectacular expansions and distortions that can be clearly in excess of the narrative without necessarily disrupting it. The main requirement is that this space be a special or bracketed space, adjoining the primary space of the narrative but not completely subordinated to it. The strong demarcation of the space of the numbers as distinct from that of the offstage narrative is an essential ingredient of Berkeleyesque cinema.

An "Impossible" Genre

In the classic Warners/Berkeley musicals of the early 1930s, this spatial demarcation of the musical numbers takes on a special intensity and a special inflection. It is overdetermined in a very particular way.

In his valuable article, "Realism and the Cinema: Notes on Some Brechtian Theses," Colin MacCabe defines the "classic realist text" (a category that includes classical narrative cinema—the dominant mode of Hollywood filmmaking) as one in which the various discourses in the text form a hierarchy. This hierarchy is surmounted by a dominant discourse that resolves or rationalizes all the other discourses and provides a frame of reference off which they can be read. In classical narrative cinema, this dominant discourse is the main narrative line.[5]

A simple example of the operation of the dominant discourse is the inclusion within the narrative of dream and fantasy sequences (comprising different "discourses" or modes of address), which are ultimately referred back to the dominant "reality" of the surrounding narrative framework. On the other hand, this type of discursive divagation might be kept more deliberately ambiguous or outright contradictory in other forms of cinema, such as European art cinema, radical cinema, avant-garde cinema, etc. MacCabe writes, "The classic realist text cannot deal with the real as contradictory."[6]

The musical genre constitutes something of a special case within the institution of classical narrative cinema, because musicals are based on a central contradiction between the discourse of the narrative and the discourse of at least a significant portion of the musical numbers. The narrative and the musical numbers appear to be based on different laws or ground rules. This contradiction is never (or, at best, only weakly) resolved in the musical, so that the narrative's status as the dominant discourse remains excessively problematic.

One way of stating this concept is to say that many of the numbers in a musical are "impossible"—that is, impossible from the standpoint of the realistic discourse of the narrative. Typical examples of this impossibility include:

1. Gaylord Ravenal (Allan Jones) and Magnolia Hawks (Irene Dunne), meeting for the first time, spontaneously perform the beautiful duet, "Only Make Believe" (*Show Boat*, 1936).
2. Pete Peters (Fred Astaire) and Linda Keene (Ginger Rogers), previously established as having had no experience with roller skates, flawlessly execute the great roller-skate number, "Let's Call the Whole Thing Off" (*Shall We Dance*, 1937).
3. Unknown singer Lily Mars (Judy Garland) stumbles accidentally onto a bandstand and immediately launches into a perfect vocal arrangement of "Tom, Tom, the Piper's Song" with the orchestra (*Presenting Lily Mars*, 1943).
4. Ninotchka (Cyd Charisse), a Russian envoy with no apparent composing talents or familiarity with popular music, bursts into the song, "Love's a Chemical Reaction, That's All" (*Silk Stockings*, 1957).

A possible working definition of the musical (at least in its traditional form) might therefore be: a musical is a film containing a significant proportion of musical numbers that are "impossible"—that is, persistently contradictory in relation to the realistic discourse of the narrative. This definition is useful for distinguishing bonafide generic musicals from movies that are merely films with musical performances in them—films like *She Done Him Wrong* (1933), *Young Man with a Horn* (1950), *The Glenn Miller Story* (1954), *River of No Return* (1954), *Nashville* (1975), *Coal Miner's Daughter* (1980), *Dirty Dancing* (1987). These films all feature many musical numbers, but the numbers do not create sustained problems in terms of a dominant realistic discourse. There are no (or hardly any) "impossible" numbers; the numbers can all be rationalized on the level of the narrative as professional stage performances, prerehearsed routines, etc.[7]

Space and Discourse

In most traditional musicals, this requisite impossibility is concentrated along the transitional points between narrative and performance—that is, at those points where the character "feels a song (or dance) coming on" and bursts into spontaneous, purportedly unrehearsed, but perfectly executed performance. However, the classic Warners/Berkeley musicals of the early 1930s, which comprise the most celebrated monuments of the Berkeleyesque, are based on a significantly different configuration.

With a few exceptions (all of which occur in *Dames* and *Gold Diggers of 1935*, transitional films between the declining Warners/Berkeley and ascendant RKO/Astaire formulas), the numbers in the major Warners/Berkeley musicals do not create discursive difficulties in terms of the numbers' placement within the narrative. In other words, there is no "impossibility" at the points of transition from narrative to performance—no leaps into magically spontaneous, unrehearsed, perfectly and elaborately executed song-and-dance. In almost every case, the numbers in these films are realistically established performances taking place on a theatrical stage, their previous origination painstakingly developed in the backstage plot, which shows (or, at least, frequently refers to) the preparation, rehearsal, and execution of those numbers. Even when Brad (Dick Powell) spontaneously sings "I've Got to Sing a Torch Song" to express his romantic feelings toward Polly (Ruby Keeler) in *Gold Diggers of 1933*, there is no rupture of discourse. It has already been clearly established in the narrative that Brad is a songwriter engaged to write tunes for the show and that he has been working on this and other songs. He performs the number seated at his piano, with a music sheet in front of him and a pencil, presumably still warm with inspiration, lodged behind his ear.

However, this does not mean that the numbers in the Warners/Berkeley musicals are realistically aligned in relation to the discourse of the narrative, with no problematical consequences of impossibility, and that these films therefore fall into the category of films with music rather than that of full-scale generic musicals. The major shift in discourse in these films occurs not in the transition from narrative to performance but within the performance itself.

Although the introduction of the numbers into the narrative in the Warners/Berkeley musicals creates no impossibility, the numbers *themselves* (as many commentators have noted) are blatantly and audaciously impossible in terms of the theatrical space in which they are supposedly taking place. There is no problem of realistic consistency in terms of getting to the performance space of the musical numbers, but, once within that performance space, things begin to happen that could never possibly happen on any realistically presented theatrical stage.

These impossibilities occur on two main levels: the level of scale and the level of effects. On the level of scale, the numbers create a constant and rapid progress into new and enormous spaces that could not possibly accommodate them all (or, often, even individually) within the confines of any theatrical stage, not even that of the mammoth Hippodrome.

Examples of scale include: the huge stucco pool in "By a Waterfall," and the enormously long bar set (complete with backroom opium den) and even more enormous street set in "Shanghai Lil" (*Footlight Parade*, 1933); the movement from street set to subway to abstract dreamspace in "I Only Have Eyes for You," and the infinitely expanding abstract spaces in "Dames" (*Dames*, 1934); the fifty-two pianos that appear out of nowhere in "The Words Are in My Heart," and the Grand Central–sized nightclub (plus apartment house plus street sets) in "Lullaby of Broadway" (*Gold Diggers of 1935*, 1935).

In terms of effects, the numbers create configurations that are feasible only with a movie camera, on an editing table, or in a special effects lab, and that would be either impossible or incomprehensible on a theatrical stage. These include: the kaleidoscopic overhead shots and location-shifting concealed cuts in many Berkeley numbers, the underwater shots in "By a Waterfall," the crowds that "all disappear from view" in "I Only Have Eyes For You," the reverse-motion effects in "Dames" and "Lullaby of Broadway," the face of Wini Shaw looming up to fill the screen and then dissolving into the skyline of New York in "Lullaby of Broadway," etc.

As with the stage revue and its related forms, a spatial concept is essential to determining the effect of the Warners/Berkeley narrativized film musicals. Spatial elements are exactly aligned with discursive elements in these films. Unlike in the typical film musical, the "impossible" discourse of the numbers does not encroach on the "realistic" discourse of the narrative. This distinction is then doubled and reinforced in spatial terms: performance space is kept separate from narrative space, with each having its own qualities, laws, and modes of address. The "musical-ness" (a quality commonly associated with artificiality, impossibility, antirealism) of the Warners/Berkeley musicals is exclusively concentrated in the space of the musical numbers: a designated, demarcated, "official" space (e.g., a theatrical stage) in which the impossible can occur.

This rigid alignment of performance space and performance discourse is crucial to the development of the Berkeleyesque in the classic Warners musicals of the early 1930s. The clear and absolute separation of performance space/discourse from narrative space/discourse (the partitioning off of the films' "musicalness") imparts to the musical numbers a revue-like autonomy, freed from the demands of even the most tenuous narrative-to-numbers consistency. This allows full, unrestrained indulgence and extension of the impulse toward spectacle, of the Berkeleyesque.

In effect, Berkeley is allowed to operate his own musical sideshow within the context of a narrative film. As stated (perhaps with some exaggeration) in a 1970 interview/article by William Murray in the *New York Times*, "Berkeley himself never cared much about the story line and regarded it merely as a convenient skeleton on which to flesh out his fantasies, much in the manner of Rossini draping his gorgeous solos, duets and ensembles all over the framework of whatever hack libretto an impresario handed him. 'I did my numbers and the director did the story,' Berkeley recalls. 'Sometimes I'd even forget who was directing.'"[8]

Berkeley vs. Sandrich

This central strategy of the Warners/Berkeley musicals can be contrasted with that of the next dominant mode of the movie musical: the Astaire-Rogers musicals produced at RKO Radio Pictures, Inc., especially those directed by Mark Sandrich. In the Warners/Berkeley musicals of the early 1930s, the world of the numbers is compartmentalized and set apart from the world of the narrative. This separation occurs not only spatially and discursively but also economically, presenting a world of opulence and excess in contrast to the world of struggling chorus girls and Depression hard times in the narrative. On the other hand, in the RKO/Astaire musicals of the mid- and late 1930s, the world of the musical numbers and the world of the narrative are made more homogeneous and more continuous with each other.

This is accomplished by two complementary strategies: (1) by making the world of the musical numbers more natural and restrained (rather than a radically excessive world with its own laws of time and space à la Berkeley), and (2) by making the world of the narrative more artificial and stylized. The former effect is accomplished by a reduction of scale and a naturalizing of musical performance style. The latter effect is enhanced by the use of extremely artificial dialogue that seems almost as blatantly stylized as song lyrics. In addition, everyday activities and environments are denaturalized by being set to choreographed rhythms (e.g., the "Walking the Dog" scenes in 1937's *Shall We Dance*, or the rhythmic engine-room pistons mimicked by Astaire's dance steps in the stunning "Slap That Bass" number from the same film). As a result, the gap between the performance world and the narrative world, though not eliminated, is narrowed and smoothed over.

Performance space in the RKO/Astaire musicals is not confined to a separate, compartmentalized domain like a theatrical stage. Instead, any place becomes a potential performance space: a roller-skating rink, a bedroom, a nightclub, a park, a ship's deck, a city street, a foggy woods, a ferryboat. Transitions from narrative to performance are stylized and "impossible" in the I-feel-a-song-coming-on mode, leading to an encroachment of performance discourse into narrative discourse. However, this discursive rupture is then smoothed over by the consistencies of tone, style, and scale between the narrative and musical performance passages. Mark Sandrich, the crucial director involved in the series (Thornton Freeland, William A. Seiter, George Stevens, and H. C. Potter were never able to match Sandrich's impeccably superficial touch), disliked numbers that were cut off from the narrative in the Warners/Berkeley manner. For instance, "The Continental" in *The Gay Divorcee* (1934) was originally conceived as a totally self-enclosed Berkeley-like spectacle, but Sandrich insisted on breaking up the number and interweaving it with narrative passages.[9]

In the key Warners/Berkeley musicals, the production numbers are transcendent episodes in an otherwise realistic, gritty, wisecracking, hardbitten Depression context. In the RKO/Astaire musicals, the nonmusical passages are basically as stylized and artificial as the musical numbers, and the two blend together into a smoothly syncopated surface—an unbroken, swanky, bon ton world of luxury hotels, ocean liners, art deco nightclubs, and country estates.

The Importance of Excess

The segregation and independence of the production numbers from the body of the film occurs on three interlocking and mutually reinforcing levels in the Warners/Berkeley musicals of the early 1930s: narrative (they bear little relation to the surrounding plot); spatial (the space of the musical numbers is a separate domain from that of the narrative); and discursive (the "impossible" discourse of the musical numbers does not impinge on the "realistic" discourse of the narrative). This imparts to the production numbers an unusual degree of autonomy, allying them with the revue/aggregate tradition that nurtured the Berkeleyesque and giving them greater access to the full indulgence of spectacle. Largely liberated from the necessities of serving plot, characterization, and cause-and-effect logic, with little or no obligation to maintaining the consistency of a fictional world, spectacle in Berkeley's numbers becomes an end in itself.

Of crucial importance to the creation of Berkeleyesque spectacle is a sense of gratuitousness, of uselessness, of extravagance, of rampant excess, of over-indulgence, of flaunting, of conspicuous consumption, of display for the sake of display, of elements calling attention to themselves rather than serving a higher, all-encompassing concept such as the narrative. (Narrativity, on the other hand, is a more economical process, working to "use up" its elements—to contain them, absorb them, and invest them into their function within the plot.)[10]

The DeMillesque

In these respects, Berkeleyesque musical spectacle intersects with another, more narrativized form of generic spectacle: the type of epic/historical/biblical spectacle that became popularly identified with director Cecil B. DeMille in such films as *The Ten Commandments* (1923, 1956), *The Sign of the Cross* (1932), and *Samson and Delilah* (1949). DeMille himself directed a semi-Berkeleyesque musical, *Madame Satan* (1930). The scene of Antony's seduction on a magnificent barge in DeMille's nonmusical *Cleopatra* (1934)—with voluptuous water nymphs bearing jewel-filled clam shells, giant platters groaning with steaming delicacies, leopard-skinned slave girls driven by a whip-wielding keeper and tumbling through flaming hoops, etc.—is virtually a full-scale Berkeley production number. (See photo 4.) For his part, Berkeley crossed paths with the "DeMillesque" in such mixtures of the monumental, the exotic, and the erotic as "No More Love" (*Roman Scandals*, 1933) and "Totem Tom Tom" (*Rose Marie*, 1954).

This relationship between DeMillesque spectacle and Berkeleyesque spectacle was noted by critics even before Berkeley came to Hollywood. For example, Wilella Waldorf wrote in her *New York Post* review of the *Earl Carroll Vanities of 1928* (for which Berkeley staged the musical numbers), "The display set forth last night in Mr. Carroll's theatre indicates a complete tie-up of spangled goods and plumed headdress industries for some time to come. It is doubtful, in fact, if Cecil B. DeMille will be able to scrape together enough material for a new epic for at least a year, so completely has Mr. Carroll cornered the market."[11] Similarly, a *New York Times* news item on the Philadelphia tryout of the *International Revue* (1930; special dance arrangements by Berkeley) reported, "The Philadelphia Public Ledger was moved to say tersely, 'More DeMilleish than DeMille'—an erudite synonym for splendor."[12]

The major difference between DeMillesque spectacle and Berkeleyesque spectacle is that the former, no matter how extravagant and self-aggrandizing, is still fully integrated with the narrative in spatial and discursive terms, whereas Berkeleyesque spectacle, even in a relatively modest instance, is held apart from the narrative in those terms. The seduction-scene spectacle of DeMille's *Cleopatra* inflates the world of the narrative but does not rupture it in any way; the slave-market spectacle of Berkeley's "No More Love" takes the film substantially out of that world and into another. Berkeleyesque spectacle not only calls attention to itself *within* the narrative but also asserts its autonomy *from* the narrative.

Spectacularization of the Camera

This notion of segregated, autonomous spectacle extends, in Berkeley's case, not only to mise-en-scène elements such as props, sets, chorus girls, etc., but also to the camera itself. In effect, Berkeley *spectacularizes the camera*. Just as the structure of the Berkeleyesque musical severs the domain of the production numbers from that of the narrative, the camera itself is liberated from the demands of narrativity (and, to a degree, from the demands of any form of subordinate expressivity) in order to assert its own presence as an element of autonomous display—that is, of spectacle. As Jean-Louis Comolli has written, Berkeley's cinema is a "cinema that resolves itself totally into spectacle, these images, these shots, these scenes . . . have no other function, no other meaning and no other existence but visual beauty."[13]

The concept of "spectacularization of the camera" here refers not only to the camera apparatus itself. It also encompasses more generally all those situations where realistic consistency is violated for the sake of producing a cinematic effect. These include the intrusion into onstage numbers of purely cinematic configurations, such as trick cuts, reverse motion, patterns visible only from certain camera angles, etc. Also involved are those situations where the camera ostentatiously asserts its presence (for instance, through an especially elaborate and massive camera movement) in a manner that seems totally arbitrary or, at least, greatly in excess of any possible function of displaying the performance, expressing the number's "inner feeling," and so on.

Technique in classic cinema is subordinated to and largely absorbed into the narrative.[14] This accounts for the exceptional nature of the moment in *Gold Diggers of 1933*'s opening "We're in the Money" number when the camera dollies in on Ginger Rogers's face without following focus; the shot remains blurred for a moment before coming back into focus. Although out-of-focus effects are not infrequently used in classical cinema, the device is almost always motivated by a narrative rationale, such as the subjective state of one of the characters (the character is drunk, losing consciousness, going blind, etc.). However, this direct and blatant invocation of the camera in "We're in the Money" is without any narrative or subjective referent; the effect is purely arbitrary and gratuitous.[15] As such, it constitutes something of a declaration of independence for the Berkeleyesque camera, an affirmation of its power to inscribe itself directly into the film as an element of spectacular design.

Berkeley's contribution to the evolution of the movie musical can be seen not so much as the replacement of a theatrical mode by a cinematic one, but as the *extension* and *expansion* of a theatrical tradition—the Tradition of Spectacle—to include specifically cinematic elements. Editing, camera angle, camera movement, optical effects, and other cinematic devices are freed from the constraints of realistic, narrativized, cause-and-effect discourse and become liberated elements of play and display. Cut loose from the space and discourse of the narrative, they are free to soar into the realms of pure design and abstraction. This helps to account for the frequently drawn parallels between Berkeley's numbers and largely nonnarrative modes of cinema such as abstract, surrealist, and avant-garde film.

But even this description ultimately seems too limiting to encompass the full scope of Berkeleyesque cinema. More accurately, one could say that Berkeleyesque cinema is free not merely to operate in the realm of pure, nonnarrative, antirealistic, spectacular abstraction but to roam a broad spectrum of modes and discourses, ranging from the mundanely realistic to the spectacularly abstract. A great deal of the effect of Berkeley's best production numbers derives not only from their indulgence of grandiose spectacle but also from their ability to shift rapidly, fluidly, and even dizzyingly from the particular to the immense, from the narrativized to the abstract, from the realistic to the fantastic, from the bathetic to the elevated, from the mundane to the extravagant. It is, of course, in the best aggregate tradition for Berkeleyesque cinema to strive in this way to include everything and anything.

PART TWO

BERKELEYESQUE THEATER

3 BERKELEY ON BROADWAY

Apprenticeship: Operettas and Obscurity (1925–1927)

Before coming to Hollywood, Berkeley spent six years in the Broadway musical theater, staging numbers for at least twenty shows and gaining a reputation as one of the era's most innovative dance directors (the term "choreographer" was reserved for non-vernacular dance in those days). His Broadway career falls chronologically into three main phases, each identified primarily with a certain type of musical show: (1) operettas (1925–27), (2) musical comedies (1927–28), and (3) revues (1928–30).[1] The order of this progression is extremely important in terms of Berkeley's alignment with those Berkeleyesque elements on which his reputation would subsequently be based—an alignment that did not occur until relatively late in his stage career.

Berkeley's first assignment on Broadway was as dance director of *Holka Polka* (opened October 14, 1925). This dance-heavy *mit-tel*-European romance rode in on the coattails of a general resurgence of operetta on Broadway in the mid-1920s, led by 1924's smash hit, *Rose-Marie*.[2] *Holka Polka* was followed by Berkeley's collaboration on two operettas composed by *Rose-Marie*'s Rudolf Friml: *The Wild Rose* (October 20, 1926) and *The White Eagle* (December 26, 1927). In addition, Berkeley handled the ensembles for the pre-Broadway Chicago production of *Castles in the Air* (November 22, 1925), a hybrid operetta and musical comedy with some strong resemblances to the hit 1924 operetta, *The Student Prince*. He also staged the musical numbers for *Rainbow* (November 21, 1928), an Americanized operetta following (and faltering) in the footsteps of the 1927 landmark *Show Boat*.

Represented by the work of such composers as Johann Strauss, Franz Lehar, Victor Herbert, Rudolf Friml, and Sigmund Romberg, operetta is characterized by its European origins, its elegance and sophistication of tone, its use of melodic, waltz-time music, its picturesque and exotic settings, and its strongly integrative organization around a melodramatic, romance-oriented book.[3] The opulence of the settings and costumes link the operetta with the spectacular revue. However, unlike in the revue, such elements are more integrated than blatant; they stem from the exoticism and elevation of the narrative settings (typically a palace in a foreign land). These settings, distanced in time and place (often in mythical Ruritanian/Graustarkian principalities), impart a timeless quality to the operetta world, which distinguishes it from the vernacularized topicality typical of both the musical comedy and the revue. In an operetta, the male chorus (often in the form of a military unit) is frequently given more prominence than the female chorus, and singing performance is usually more important than dancing performance.

Berkeley's dance direction was well-received but largely buried in the general lavishness of the operetta productions to which he contributed. The spectacular qualities of operetta are invested into naturalism and narrative rather than into the autonomous fantasy of Berkeleyesque spectacle. As noted above, the spectacle of operetta numbers is primarily a function of the settings, which are themselves a function of the narrative. This contrasts with the more "segregated," unanchored spectacle space available in the stage revue and its Berkeleyesque film equivalent, the backstage musical. In addition, the tempos of operetta music generally preclude the types of rhythmic inventiveness that gained Berkeley distinction when he worked in musical comedy.

Breakthrough: *A Connecticut Yankee* (1927)

Although Berkeley had scored personal successes with his dance direction for the first Broadway shows with which he was associated, the shows themselves were all flops, and he was still an obscure figure in the theatrical world. *A Connecticut Yankee* (November 3, 1927) provided Berkeley with his first big break, when he was selected as dance director for the show. With a major score by Richard Rodgers and Lorenz

Hart (including the standards "Thou Swell" and "My Heart Stood Still"), a solid book (especially in the first act) derived by Herbert Fields from Mark Twain's novel, and gaudy, controversial sets by John F. Hawkins, Jr., the show was a substantial hit.

Musical comedy has been described as a fusion of operetta and traditional (i.e., pre-striptease) burlesque, taking from the former a sense of classical continuity in plot and musical score, and from the latter a lightness of tone, a certain looseness of structure, and a penchant for topicality and satire.[4] This genealogy is especially apparent in *A Connecticut Yankee*, where it is inscribed overtly into the text itself. After a prologue set in the modern day, the play moves (via a dream structure) to Olde Camelot, an operetta-like domain of castles, royalty, and military regalia. (See photo 5.) The twist is that the mythical remoteness of operetta is suddenly thrust into a present-day context through the use of modern gadgetry and up-to-the-minute twenties slang ("Methinks yon damsel is a lovely broad," "Away, varlet, thou art full of the juice of the prune," "Thou hast said a snootful," etc.).[5] *A Connecticut Yankee* embodies in its book the conquest of operetta by musical comedy, of the traditional form by the modern one.[6]

Working with a stronger book and a smaller ensemble than ever before (twenty-eight members, including only twelve girls—less than half of what he had worked with in any previous show), Berkeley seems to have successfully tailored his style to the unified and intimate standards of this production.[7] (See photo 6.) His dance direction shared in the general glory of the show, and, combined with his involvement in the next Rodgers and Hart hit, *Present Arms* (April 26, 1928), caused Berkeley to be reckoned among the leading dance directors on Broadway. He was often grouped with Seymour Felix, Sammy Lee, and Bobby Connolly as one of the new breed who were revolutionizing vernacular theatrical dancing.[8] However, it is important to note that at this time Berkeley's style was seen to be developing in directions quite different from the ones with which he would later be associated.

On July 22, 1928, the *New York Times* published a lengthy feature article on Busby Berkeley, written by the paper's dance critic, John Martin. Rather than the usual gossip/interview piece, the *Times* article was a serious attempt to evaluate and analyze Berkeley's contribution to the evolution of dance in musical comedy. Although the article mistakenly assumed that Berkeley had only two Broadway credits to his name (*A Connecticut Yankee* and *Present Arms*), he was proclaimed to be one of the most important innovators in the popular musical theater—"a man of the hour who has appeared at a time when he is needed."[9]

According to Martin, dance in musical comedy had only very recently begun to be considered an object worthy of serious critical attention. However, the rapid strides being made in the field were in danger of coming to a dead end. Broadway dance directors had built their numbers on two basic ingredients: speed and novelty. The first had already reached its limit; it was impossible to conceive of the human body being pushed any further in this direction. For novelty, Dave Bennett's "Totem Tom Tom" number in *Rose-Marie* (1924) and the "Parade of the Wooden Soldiers" in the imported revue *Chauve Souris* (1922) were cited as paradigms, but this vein, too, was becoming rapidly exhausted, confined more and more to repetitions and reshufflings of previous efforts. Acrobatic chorus maneuvers were likewise wearing thin, with cartwheels, splits, and leaps becoming increasingly routine to their jaded audiences. A new direction was needed, a new outlet for novelty, if Broadway dance was to continue to develop. And it was here, the article declared, that "Busby Berkeley assumes the mantle of a kind of minor prophet."[10]

What Berkeley had done, according to Martin, was to discover a new and more productive basis on which to build novelty: the rhythmic structure of the number. Berkeley was expanding this dimension in a jazz-like manner, introducing complicated and offbeat syncopations, executing broken rhythms, and employing two or three different rhythms simultaneously. The advantage of this type of novelty, in contrast to the more superficial forms previously used, was that it grew directly out of the internal structure of the number rather than being a tacked-on external device. In this way, it became intrinsically linked with the book and the musical score. In other words, it became a contributor to that perennial ideal of musical theater: the unified show (or, as it would later be called, the integrated musical).

> The results he has achieved in this direction are not only novel but unwontedly artistic in their manner of utilizing to the fullest extent the actual material which author and composer have provided for him.
>
> Here is a substantial type of novelty which depends not upon the inventiveness of one man but grows as well out of the creative work of his collaborators, as the direction of a dramatic work grows out of the work itself rather than out of the imagination of the director.[11]

Martin noted that Berkeley still had not completely shaken off some of the old bad habits; his rhythmic innovations were often diluted by "stunts," "acrobatic tricks," and "bits of external cleverness." But, the article ventured optimistically, "Obviously [Berkeley's] heart is in the mazes of syncopation and not in the superficial tricks which are actually 'playing down.'"[12]

One week before the *Times* piece, the magazine *New York Amusements* (a handout self-described as "Broadway's Official Guide") ran an article on Berkeley that made some of the same observations in a sketchier and less sophisticated manner: "[He] is known to the chorus girls as 'Off-Beat' Berkeley, they say that his heart beats on the off-beat, girls who work for him are afraid they'll never be able to dance in rhythm."[13]

By mid-1928, then, Berkeley had built a reputation

as an innovator of intricate and offbeat rhythms, an apostle of new integrated musical comedy forms, and a leader in the break away from the more primitive traditions of external novelty, visual spectacle, and regimented "precision dancing." It is remarkable how different these qualities are from those for which Berkeley later became celebrated.[14]

Spectacle: *Earl Carroll Vanities of 1928*

The *Earl Carroll Vanities of 1928* (August 6, 1928) represents the second major turning point in Berkeley's Broadway career (the first being *A Connecticut Yankee*). Whereas *A Connecticut Yankee* and *Present Arms* established Berkeley as a major innovator working in the rapidly evolving musical comedy form, the *Earl Carroll Vanities* marked his first direct involvement with an older, more stagnant, and even moribund stage tradition. This is the tradition of the big Broadway revue, in which numbers function more as autonomous spectacles than as organic extensions of narrative, score, and characterization.

Berkeley's initial reputation as a rhythmic innovator in musical comedy did not indicate the direction his career would later take nor the elements on which his fame would be based. On the other hand, it is precisely at that point where Berkeley begins to work regularly in the revue format that one begins to find, recognizably and consistently, a predominance of those elements commonly identified with the Berkeleyesque. In other words, it is at this point that the individual Busby Berkeley begins to merge with the Berkeleyesque—that larger, transpersonal set of interrelated qualities that provide the essential link between his most celebrated film numbers and a longstanding popular entertainment tradition.

Presented in more or less yearly editions beginning in 1923, the *Earl Carroll Vanities* was in the top rank of the big annual Broadway revue series (including *George White's Scandals*, John Murray Anderson's *Greenwich Village Follies*, and the Shuberts' *The Passing Show/Artists and Models* series) that attempted to rival the acknowledged leader in the field—the *Ziegfeld Follies*. Whereas the *Follies* was known as a "class act," striving for an impression of elegance and tasteful lavishness, the *Earl Carroll Vanities* (its motto: "Through These Portals Pass the Most Beautiful Girls in the World") was more prone to garishness and sensationalism. It had a reputation (at times strongly challenged by the Shubert shows) as the raunchiest of the big revues and the one most heavily oriented toward the blatant display of female bodies.[15] One review of the 1928 edition noted, "From the drop of the hat it is skin, skin, skin. Bare backs to the right of one, uncovered knees to the left, undraped thighs in unserried rank in front of one, and naked scapulae, patenae, and various odds and ends of anatomy in every nook and corner of the stage."[16]

The *Earl Carroll Vanities of 1928*, fronted by W. C. Fields and stocked with beauty contest winners, was widely considered to be the most elaborately produced of all the *Vanities* shows.[17] The production numbers were rich in elements that can be related—both generally and specifically—to the characteristic features of Berkeley's subsequent film work. Photographs of the *Earl Carroll Vanities of 1928* show ornate production numbers with scantily clad showgirls forming parts of columns, "human fountains," and layer-cake-like platforms (see photo 7). Such arrangements are recognizably similar to those later found in Berkeley's film production numbers such as "By a Waterfall" (with its six-tiered revolving platform) and "Spin a Little Web of Dreams" (with its display of "human harps").[18]

The opening number, "Say It with Girls," introduced the main theme of the show and included an optical device (called "Vanities Votaphonevitotone Movies") that projected onto a screen enlarged close-up images of various showgirls.[19] The opening was followed by "Pretty Girl," featuring thirteen showgirls dressed in yellow *robes du style* with huge pink roses painted on the skirts.[20] This segued into "Garden of Beautiful Girls," which continued the rose theme. The setting featured a long flight of stairs topped by a curtained, silver-canopied alcove. Out of the alcove, two at a time, stepped showgirls representing roses. Attended by two short-tuniced pages, each pair wore low-slung satin bodices and hugely flared tulle skirts of progressively deeper shades, beginning with light pink and working up to American Beauty.[21] "Raquel," the most elaborate of several curtain numbers in the show, featured a jeweled red-and-silver curtain, adorned with showgirls in the form of living tassels (see photo 8).[22]

"The Machinery Ballet," which opened the second act, excited more comment than any other number in the show. Inspired, the programme asserted, by a visit to a Ford automobile plant, the number began at the gates of a factory, then moved to an expressionistic assembly line. There, amid lurid flashes of fire and smoke, the chorus, in metallic robot-style costumes emblazoned with dials and switches, shuttled and whirled mechanically in an endless circle. Their route took them across a series of platforms surmounted by a female dancer turning continuous slow cartwheels, which transformed her into a living cogwheel. Critics, for the most part greatly impressed, compared the number to Russian Constructivist Art, Fritz Lang's film *Metropolis* (1926), and Karel Capek's play *R.U.R.* (1923), while the *Journal of Electrical Workers and Operators* found in it a healthy sign that Broadway was finally taking note of the processes of mass production upon which modern civilization is built.[23] Berkeley later used an assembly-line setting in the tongue-in-cheek bakery number that opens the film *Palmy Days* (1931), but the assembly-line image seems more relevant as a generalized association underlying the synchronized chorus movements, conveyor-like treadmills, and elaborate revolving machine-structures that figure prominently in such major Berkeley numbers as "Remember My Forgotten Man" (*Gold Diggers of 1933*), "Don't Say Goodnight" (*Wonder Bar*, 1934), "I Only Have Eyes for You" (*Dames*, 1934), and "Fascinatin' Rhythm" (*Lady Be Good*, 1941).

"I'm Flying High," sung by Lillian Roth, featured a novelty formation in which the chorus arranged themselves collectively into the shape of an airplane, with cartwheeling Dorothy Lull forming the propeller; a virtually identical effect was later used by Berkeley for the "Flying High" number in the 1931 film *Flying High*.[24] In "The Collegiate Vaniteaser," filmed scenes of various colleges were flashed onto a white curtain, through which sixteen girls poked their heads in turn, singing the school song appropriate to each campus; a somewhat similar structure was employed by Berkeley for the collegiate grand finale of the film *Varsity Show* (1937).[25] The *Earl Carroll Vanities of 1928* concluded with the chorus waving goodbye to the audience through a curtain of plumes—an intimation of Berkeley's plume-laden "Spin a Little Web of Dreams" number in the film *Fashions of 1934* (1934).[26]

Fluidity: *Good Boy* (1928)

Berkeley's next show, *Good Boy* (September 5, 1928), gave further indication of the direction in which his dance direction style was heading. Self-described as a "musical play," its ambience and plot (country boy journeys to Broadway in search of fame and romance) placed it squarely in the domain of musical comedy. However, several critics still designated the show a revue because of the manner in which its thin plot was overwhelmed by its spectacularly ingenious staging and its succession of rapidly shifting scenes.[27] The *Boston Transcript* critic suggested that the most appropriate label for the show might be "musical play panoramic"—a reference to the panorama, a popular nineteenth-century entertainment form in which scenic views of foreign locales, famous battles, etc., were displayed to the audience.[28] Indeed, *Good Boy*, with its extensive use of cutouts, flats, treadmills, and scenic transformations, owed much to the pictorial-spectacular tradition of late nineteenth-century/early twentieth-century stagecraft.[29]

The outstanding qualities of the production were its speed and fluidity. The principle vehicle for achieving these qualities was a set of treadmills that carried the cast and the settings (at various speeds and in various directions) through a nearly continuous series of brief, whirlwind scenes tracing the hero's frenetic progress around Manhattan. The seventeen scenes of the first act and the sixteen scenes of the second act were presented in a seamless, uninterrupted flow, without a single pause (save for the customary between-acts intermission) to change scenery. The *New York World* critic wrote that this constant movement "has much the same effect as the motion picture camera has when mounted on wheels."[30]

To keep up the pace, the treadmills were supplemented with revolving sets and a screen on which were projected animated and live-action films. An excerpt from the *New York American* review conveys some of the excitement of the physical production:

> The country boy arrived in New York, the maelstrom of America, the syncopated, nerve-tearing epitome of the machine age, gone drunk with speed and din. Sidewalks became animated and whirled a dizzy kaleidoscope of reeling skyscrapers across the stage, nondescript beings rushed and ran but never got anywhere.
>
> The lights failed, and on screen an astonished audience saw the tall spires of America's Babylon sway and swirl into a chaos of gyrating atoms. All this to the tune of thundering traffic, raucous trumpeting of automobile horns and the ominous wailing of ambulance sirens.[31]

The first act was especially dazzling in this respect. It opened with the hero Wally (Eddie Buzzell) bidding farewell to his family in an Arkansas farmyard. A drop curtain shifted the scene to a sleeping car aboard the "Arkansas Flyer," whose progress northward was depicted on an animated map. Wally appeared on the deck of a ferryboat from Jersey City, with the silhouetted skyline of Manhattan looming up from the background. This gave way to moving-picture images of the bustling metropolis. Then the treadmills took over, moving the hero uptown from the 23rd Street Ferry to the Great White Way in a rapid series of eleven brief scenes. Throngs of pedestrians and impressionistic, black-backdropped fragments of Manhattan (soft-drink stands, fire hydrants, skyscrapers, ashcans) glided on and off the stage, capped by the facade of the Paramount Theatre with a glittering silver doorman out front. Wally met the ingenue Betty (Barbara Newberry) in front of a boarding house, whose exterior slipped away as the couple walked through the front door and into the kitchen.

The action moved briefly back to Arkansas, then to a Broadway rehearsal attended by Wally and Betty. Afterward they sped away in a taxi, which, facing the audience, bounced up and down while the couple necked in the backseat. The entrance to a hotel slid onto the stage to meet them. As they entered an elevator, the lobby set rolled off to disclose a full-stage set depicting a hotel suite where a party was in progress. To climax the first act, the interior swung away, instantaneously transforming itself into an exterior, with Wally and Betty looking down from a balcony while dancing couples filled the terrace below and the lights of upper Manhattan stretched across the background.[32]

Good Boy's kaleidoscopic collage of an overheated metropolis anticipated the frenetic urban visions of two of Berkeley's most famous film numbers: "42nd Street" from the 1933 film of the same name and "Lullaby of Broadway" from *Gold Diggers of 1935*. Berkeley later incorporated the device of opposing treadmills into *Gold Diggers of 1933*'s "Remember My Forgotten Man" (the military parade) and the title number of *Dames* (the dames trooping off to work); and movable cutouts were used extensively in "42nd Street" and "Dames," among others. More important than any of these specific associations, however, is *Good Boy's* special relevance to the general principle of hyperfluidity, of whirlwind transitions and transformations, which is extremely central to nearly all of Berkeley's major film work.

Broadway and "42nd Street": *International Revue* (1930)

In early 1929, Berkeley solidified his association with the revue format by working on three consecutive lavish shows produced by the Shubert Brothers: *Pleasure Bound* (February 18, 1929), *A Night in Venice* (May 21, 1929), and *Broadway Nights* (July 15, 1929). The era's most powerful producers and theater owners, the Shuberts were important if somewhat derivative figures in the development of the American musical revue. They answered the first (1907) edition of the *Ziegfeld Follies* with their own *The Mimic World* in 1908; their major revue series, *The Passing Show*, was inaugurated in 1912. The most prolific of revue producers, the Shuberts were responsible for over a hundred revues in the period from 1906 to 1943.[33]

The Shubert shows frequently aped the *Follies*, although they tended to be less meticulously produced and to place a greater emphasis on satire and female nudity. One notable innovation of the Shuberts was the runway (introduced in *The Passing Show of 1913*), which, by bringing showgirl and spectator closer together, spurred a general reduction in the size of showgirls from their previously imposing dimensions. The Shuberts are also often credited with introducing full-figure female nudity to the legitimate Broadway stage—reputedly when the ill-tempered J. J. Shubert took a dislike to some showgirls' costumes, ripped them off, and then decided he liked the effect.[34]

The last phase of Berkeley's Broadway career is dominated by revues. In addition to the three Shubert shows mentioned above, he also contributed production numbers to Ruth Selwyn's ambitious but unwieldy *Nine Fifteen Revue* (February 11, 1930), Lew Leslie's global-themed *International Revue* (February 25, 1930), and Billy Rose's raunchy confection *Sweet and Low* (November 17, 1930).

In terms of Berkeley's later career, the most interesting of this batch is the *International Revue*. It was a sumptuous production, staged in the old Ziegfeld style, with a greater emphasis on opulence than wit—in contrast to the intimate style of revue that was then becoming more popular.[35] Berkeley shared the dance direction duties with Chester Hale, a ballet-trained choreographer whose twenty "Chester Hale's International Girls," supplemented by eleven showgirls, comprised the chorus. The elaborate Indian extravaganza, "Big Papoose on the Loose," featured the chorus in huge feathered headdresses—an effect soon to appear again in the climactic number of Berkeley's first film, *Whoopee!* (1930). An especially Berkeleyesque effect was achieved in "Keys to My Heart," in which the chorus, dressed in half-black, half-white outfits, were human piano keys dancing up and down a giant keyboard.[36]

The show's most interesting number in relation to Berkeley's later film career is "The Rout," a pantomime dance featuring Anton Dolin (billed as the "Irish Star of the Diaghilieff Russian Ballet"). Set in Montmartre in 1880, the number began with an impressionistic panorama of the motley life of the quarter: drunks, a dope addict, an organ grinder, a knife grinder, beggars, strollers, society swells, a live donkey, goat, and dog. Denizens playing cards and reading newspapers were glimpsed through windows. A flower girl was knocked down by a drunk. A young *apache* (Dolin) lounged in a doorway. Suddenly a gunshot was heard. A young woman, apparently the victim of a sexual assault, jumped out of a second-story window, was caught by the *apache* below, and launched into a dance with him. A dispute with a rival *apache* followed, and the young woman was stabbed fatally in the back. Everyone fled from the scene, and the number ended with a lone old man hobbling slowly across the stage.[37]

"The Rout" is remarkable for its close parallels to the basic structure of one of Berkeley's most famous film numbers, "42nd Street," which transposes many of its predecessor's elements to a Manhattan context. It subtracts the livestock and the French ambience and adds taxicabs, skyscrapers, and a chorus in big-buttoned slit skirts. Like "The Rout," "42nd Street" begins with impressionistic vignettes of life on the "naughty, bawdy" street. Then a scream is heard; the camera cranes up to a second-story window where a man grabs a young woman and flings her onto a bed. She jumps out of the window and is caught by the crowd below. She dances on the pavement with an *apache*-style Manhattanite until she is finally stabbed by her attacker from upstairs.

There are also strong resemblances between "The Rout" and another Berkeley street-scene number, "Night over Shanghai" from the film *The Singing Marine* (1937). Both develop a similar structure of milieu-establishing vignettes, sordid urban atmosphere, a sudden outbreak of violence climaxing in a woman's death, and a mournful coda with a lone figure on the deserted stage. In "Night over Shanghai," sailor Dick Powell, strolling through the bustling streets of Shanghai, encounters Caucasian chanteuse Doris Weston singing in a shady cafe. He attempts to rescue her from her Oriental captors; she is shot in the scuffle; and the stage is cleared except for a lone harmonica player.

There are two major generalizations to be drawn from this brief overview of Berkeley's stage career. The first is that his progression from operetta to musical comedy to revue is a movement toward the increased importance of key elements closely identified with the

Berkeleyesque. These include the use of jazz/tap-dance rhythms, an emphasis on spectacle, and the weakening of an "integrated" format that strongly links the musical numbers to the narrative. In short, this chronology demonstrates the eventual confluence of Berkeley and the Berkeleyesque—his increasing engagement with the aggregative principles and popular entertainment traditions described in the preceding chapters.

The second generalization is that this progression ran against the grain of the prevailing developments in Broadway musical theater at that time. In the late 1920s, Broadway was moving toward more intimate, satirical revues and, especially, toward a merger of operetta and musical comedy into the form of the classical (then considered "modern") integrated musical. Berkeley's progression toward the obsolescent large-scale, spectacular revue is something of a retrogression in terms of the history of the musical theater. The Berkeleyesque mode itself was becoming increasingly anachronistic on the stage, just as it would in film a few years later.

1. *Ready, Willing and Able* (1937). "Too Marvelous for Words": Busby Berkeley became identified with a certain type of musical number. Other dance directors working in that vein have been accused of imitating him, when in fact they were drawing upon a common tradition of stage spectacle. Using a concept derived from a pre-Berkeley stage show, this Warner Bros. number (staged by Bobby Connolly) sends Ruby Keeler and Lee Dixon hunting and pecking across the keyboard of a giant typewriter.

2. *The Hollywood Revue of 1929* (1929). The big Broadway revue was the theatrical form most conducive to Berkeleyesque spectacle. Although the spectacular revue declined on Broadway in the late 1920s, it enjoyed a revival in Hollywood during the music-crazy period of early talking pictures. Jack Benny emcees one of the several plotless revues filmed in 1929–30, with steps employed to enhance the vertical patterning of the chorus behind him.

3. *King of Jazz* (1930). "Rhapsody in Blue": The use of giant-sized props was one of several Berkeleyesque devices that were commonly used in stage spectacles and early film musicals before Berkeley himself used them. This early sound musical revue employed a piano large enough to accommodate five pianists at its keyboard and to contain the entire Paul Whiteman orchestra inside it.

4. *Cleopatra* (1934). Cecil B. DeMille's elaborate visualization of Cleopatra's seduction of Antony is not far removed from a Berkeleyesque production number. The essential difference lies in the spectacle's relation to the narrative.

5. *A Connecticut Yankee* (1927). Berkeley's breakthrough on Broadway was this Rodgers and Hart hit. The medieval setting recalled the sumptuous operettas Berkeley had previously worked on, but this invocation of the operetta tradition served mainly to indicate its usurpation by newer musical comedy forms. (*Courtesy of The New York Public Library*)

6. *A Connecticut Yankee* (1927).The chorus is pictured in a peppy musical comedy arrangement. Working with a smaller ensemble than ever before, Berkeley concentrated on rhythmic variety and inventiveness rather than spectacle. His initial reputation as an innovative Broadway dance director was based on qualities quite different from those of his famous movie numbers. (*Courtesy of The New York Public Library*)

7. *Earl Carroll Vanities of 1928* (1928). When Berkeley began working regularly in spectacular Broadway revues, he connected with the forms that would later be identified with his name. This "human fountain" arrangement anticipates such Berkeley film numbers as "By a Waterfall" and "Spin a Little Web of Dreams." (*Courtesy of The New York Public Library*)

8. *Earl Carroll Vanities of 1928* (1928). Numbers such as this Living Curtain provided the first recognizably Berkeleyesque elements in Berkeley's stage career. The use of chorus girls as part of the decor or architecture was a device practiced widely in his film numbers. (*Courtesy of The New York Public Library*)

GD-92

10. *Follies of 1909* (1909). Chorus girls could represent virtually anything in a spectacular production number: cigarettes, flapjacks, icicles, mosquitoes, raindrops, taxicabs, watermelons, zeppelins, or (as depicted here) battleships, cruising into New York Harbor. (*Courtesy of The New York Public Library*)

11. *Buds of 1927* (1927). In this clever arrangement, a showgirl becomes a clock. It should be noted that Berkeley himself rarely used such directly metaphorical images, although he made extensive use of more generalized methods of objectifying the female body. (*Courtesy of The New York Public Library*)

9. *Gold Diggers of 1933* (1933). "The Shadow Waltz": Numbers in which musical instruments figure prominently as props were one of the stage traditions Berkeley drew upon in his movie musical numbers. Blonde-wigged Ruby Keeler leads the violin-playing chorus.

12. *The Passing Show of 1923* (1923). "The Living Chandelier": One method of objectifying the female body was to treat it as a form of inanimate decor or building material. The concept is illustrated by this number from a typically lavish Shubert revue of the 1920s. (*Courtesy of The New York Public Library*)

13. *Rain or Shine* (1928). The semicircular pinwheel patterns formed by the chorus in this Broadway show (featuring comedian Joe Cook) can be seen as an antecedent of the kaleidoscopic overhead shots identified with Berkeley's film numbers (*see* photos 20, 39, and 49). (*Courtesy of The New York Public Library*)

14. *The Passing Show of 1914* (1914). "The Sloping Path": Although lacking the benefits of the high-angle shots and camera cranes favored by Berkeley in his film numbers, early stage musicals could simulate height in other ways. This Shubert revue created verticality with tiers. Berkeley employed a similar arrangement in the title number of the Warner Bros. musical *Dames* (1934). (*Courtesy of The New York Public Library*)

15. *The Show of Shows* (1929). The use of steps and tiers to create group patterns carried over from the stage to several stagelike early film musicals, such as this Warner Bros. revue.

16. *King of Jazz* (1930). One of the last entries from the brief heyday of the musical film revue, this opulent Universal production provided another example of the use of steps to create a group pattern. Although Berkeley never worked in the pure revue form during his film career, he used the backstage musical format to create a revue-like autonomy of the musical numbers from the plot.

17. *Glorifying the American Girl* (1929). This *Follies*-set backstage film musical was coproduced (nominally) by Florenz Ziegfeld himself. It imported a repertory of spectacular stage devices, such as the incorporation of female bodies into living curtains and columns.

18. *Ziegfeld Follies of 1923* (1923). The Gertrude Hoffman Girls, a showgirl troupe with a fondness for acrobatics, graced several revues of the 1920s. Their aerial maneuvers provided another possibility for creating vertically oriented patterns without the benefit of cinematic techniques. (*Courtesy of The New York Public Library*)

19. *Whoopee!* (1930) was the first film Berkeley worked on, and he quickly began using the camera in a more aggressive way than other early film musicals had done. Here he is seen setting up the type of provocative camera angle that would become identified with his name.

20. *Whoopee!* (1930). "The Song of the Setting Sun": The war-bonneted chorus provides an early example of a Berkeley overhead pattern. Although he later became popularly identified with this device, it had previously been used in movies by other dance directors who came out of the same stage tradition of musical spectacle.

21. *Whoopee!* (1930). "The Song of the Setting Sun": Based on Ziegfeld's 1928 stage production, *Whoopee!* enabled Berkeley to continue the association with musical spectacle that had developed late in his Broadway career. The film's climactic number derives from the "beauty parade" employed in many Ziegfeldian revues.

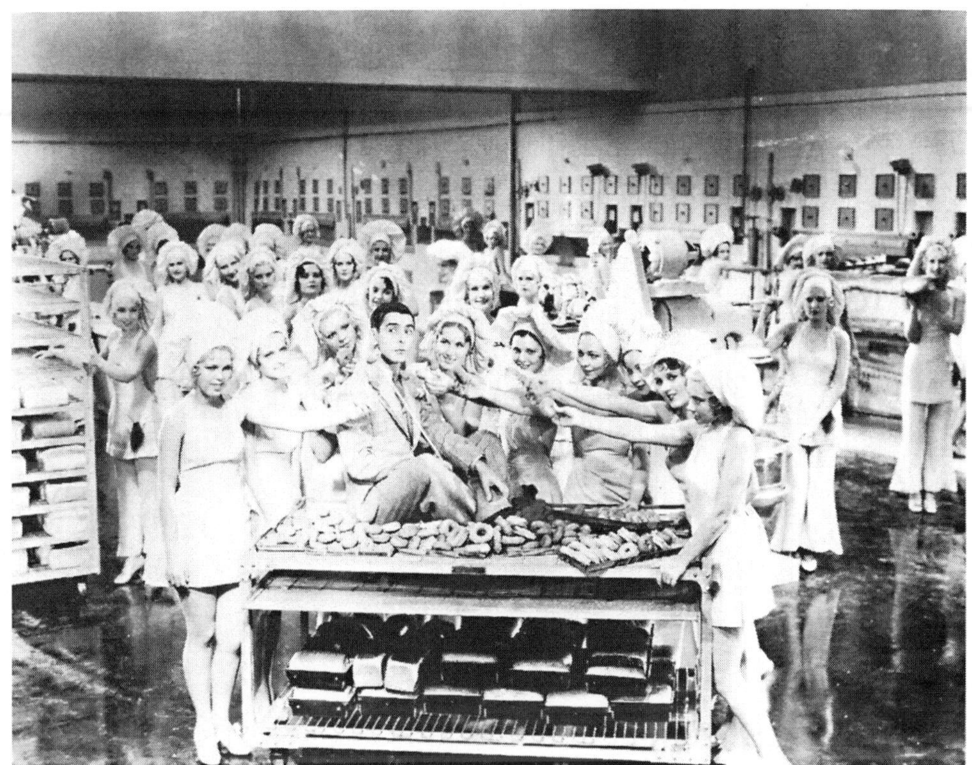

22. *Palmy Days* (1931) was the second of four films Berkeley worked on with comedian Eddie Cantor and producer Samuel Goldwyn. The Goldwyn Girls (seen with Cantor, who does not actually appear in this number) glorify the American donut in the film's bakery prologue, which satirizes the mechanistic precision and cookie-cutter interchangeability of the traditional chorus line.

23. *Palmy Days* (1931). "Bend Down Sister": Keeping in shape for their cooking chores, the Goldwyn Girls repair to the bakery's in-house gymnasium for synchronized calisthenics. This type of all-female "seraglio" environment was used by Berkeley in several of his 1930s numbers.

24. *The Kid from Spain* (1932). "The College Song": The third Berkeley/Cantor/Goldwyn collaboration opens with another number in the "seraglio" mode, this time depicting the rising, bathing, and dressing rituals of the inhabitants of a girls' college dormitory.

25. *The Kid from Spain* (1932). "What a Perfect Combination": Berkeley occasionally resorted to the time-honored theatrical device of having the chorines form a picture or representational pattern. In this Latinized number, the circular patterns of chorus and platform evoke the forms of the wide-brimmed hats they wear.

26. *Roman Scandals* (1933). "No More Love" is the most famous of Berkeley's Goldwyn numbers, thanks to its kinky subject matter and its chorus girls reputedly clad only in their long blonde wigs. Its emphasis on narrative and sadism is atypical for Berkeley, whose numbers usually gravitate toward abstraction and voyeuristic reverie.

27. Ruby Keeler and Dick Powell were the most durable stars of Warner Bros. musicals in the 1930s. Their charming innocuousness suited the Berkeleyesque style better than did the high-powered charisma of Mickey Rooney and Judy Garland at MGM.

28. *42nd Street* (1933). "Shuffle Off to Buffalo": Berkeley's move to Warner Bros. in 1933 provided him with the optimum conditions for creating musical spectacle on the screen, but he did not immediately exploit the situation to the fullest. His continued reliance on stagecraft rather than sleight-of-camera to produce spectacular effects is demonstrated here.

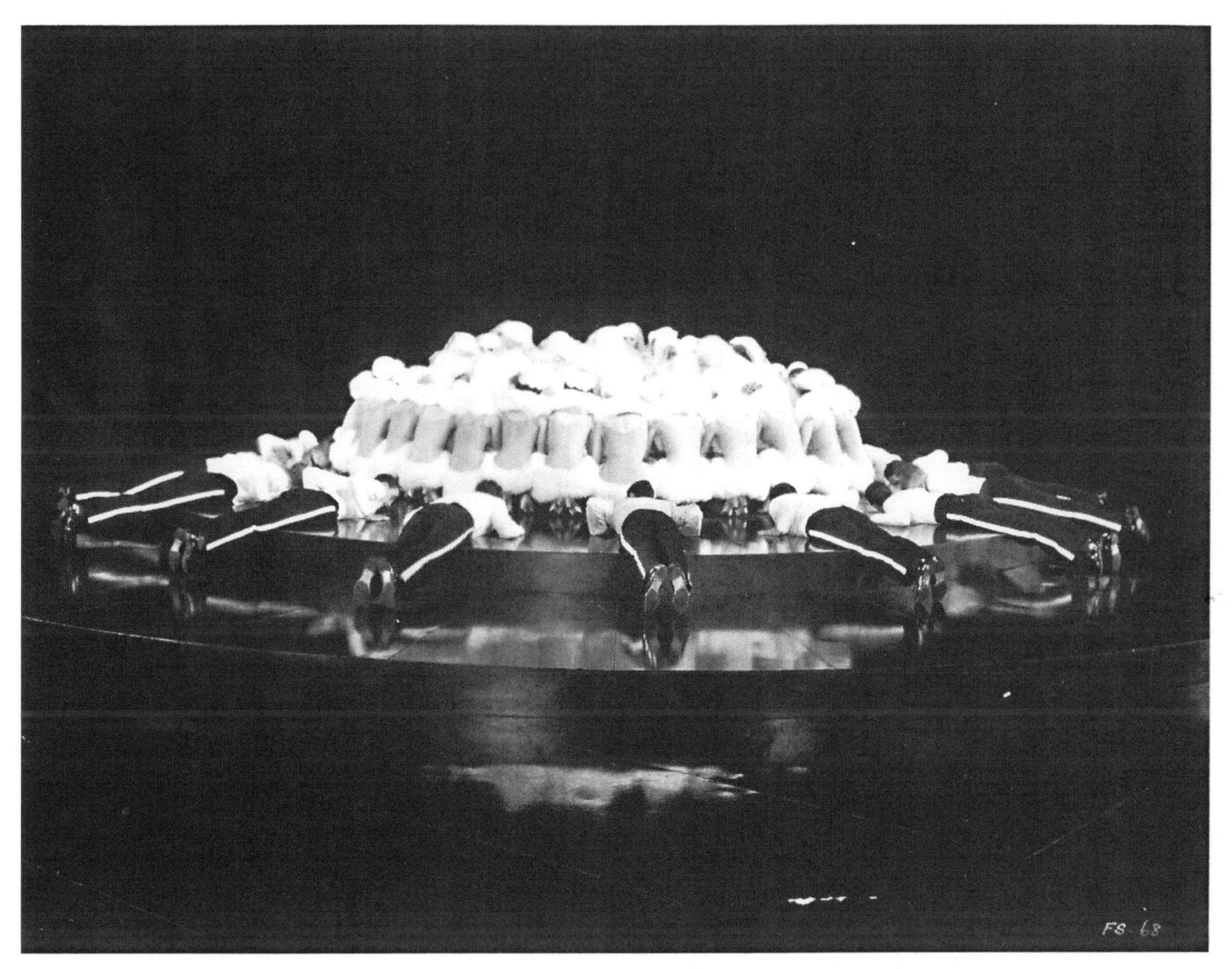

29. *42nd Street* (1933). "Young and Healthy": The first of Berkeley's elegant black-polished-floor numbers, it demonstrates the subordination of anatomy to geometry but remains confined to possible stage dimensions. Berkeley's later and more adventurous numbers would audaciously soar beyond the confines of a realistic stage space.

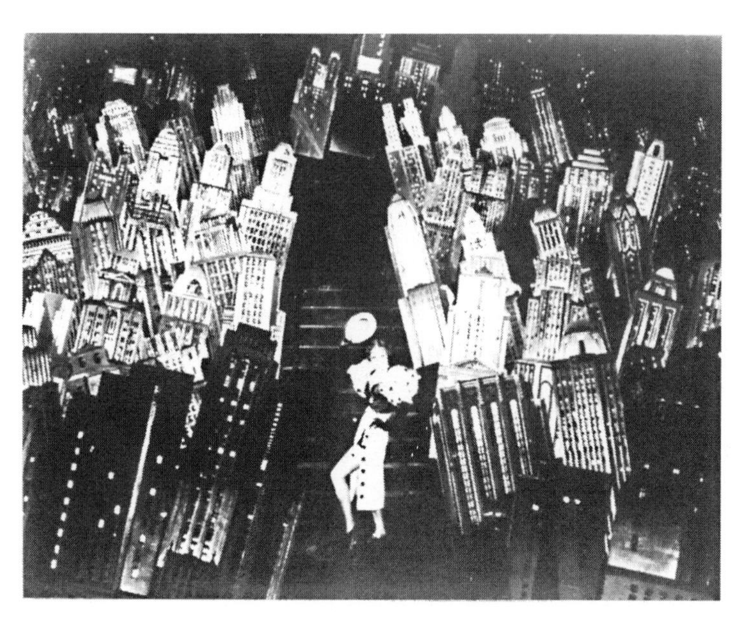

30. *42nd Street* (1933). "42nd Street": Rather than replace theatrical effects with cinematic effects, Berkeley often employs them both in excessive combination. The skyscraper placards displayed at the number's climax offer another example of a recycled effect from the theatrical past.

31. *Gold Diggers of 1933* (1933). "Pettin' in the Park": Autumn strollers receive a police escort on roller skates. The decorative showgirls in the background carry on the "living architecture" tradition of theatrical spectacle.

32. *Gold Diggers of 1933* (1933). "We're in the Money": The film's opening number immediately establishes a central link between sexuality and money. This production still employs an angle not used in the film itself; camera tracks can be seen in the lower left corner.

33. *Gold Diggers of 1933* (1933). "Pettin' in the Park": The seasons pass; spring brings neckers out and skirts up. Berkeley's big Warner Bros. numbers are usually stacked together at the end of the film. This risqué spectacle is atypically placed midway through the film, helping to set a naughty, flippant tone for the second half of the story.

34. *Gold Diggers of 1933* (1933). "The Shadow Waltz": Berkeley (right), art director Anton Grot (left), and assorted chorines flank director Mervyn LeRoy as they contemplate a model of the number's main set.

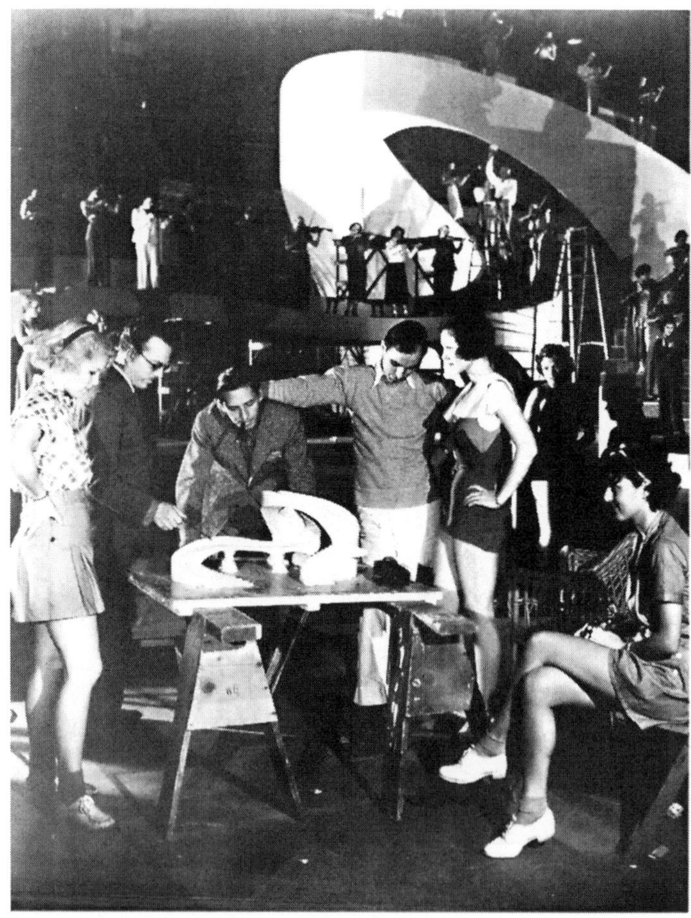

35. *Gold Diggers of 1933* (1933). "The Shadow Waltz": The set itself is seen here. Its curvilinear form and the hooped skirts of the chorus evoke a floral motif without literally representing flowers.

36. *Gold Diggers of 1933* (1933). "Remember My Forgotten Man": The film's powerful finale extends the link between sexual power and economic power established in the "We're in the Money" opener. In the final tableau, the forgotten men of the Depression kneel before images of their former military (and employed) glory.

37. *Footlight Parade* (1933) is the greatest of the Warner Bros. backstage musicals, combining spectacular Berkeley numbers with a snappy narrative and a dynamic James Cagney performance. In this publicity photo, Berkeley and chorus girls intermingle with two-dimensional images of the film's stars.

38. *Footlight Parade* (1933). "By a Waterfall": Berkeley's definitive water spectacle features some of his boldest effects yet in manipulating realistic space and transforming it into spectacle space. Camera magic transforms a woodsy waterfall into an ornate swimming pool and transports the chorus from the water to a five-tiered revolving fountain.

39. *Footlight Parade* (1933). "By a Waterfall": The fountain near the number's end provides another variation on the Berkeleyesque kaleidoscope and the architectural use of chorus girls.

40. *Footlight Parade* (1933). "Shanghai Lil": The film's finale is a dynamic blend of spectacular and intimate elements. This publicity photo shows Berkeley and Dick Powell watching Ruby Keeler and James Cagney rehearse the number.

41. *Footlight Parade* (1933). "Shanghai Lil": The AWOL sailor Bill (James Cagney) defends his lost love Lil's notorious name in the chaotic central section of the number.

42. *Footlight Parade* (1933). "Shanghai Lil": Order begins to emerge out of chaos as Bill and Lil (Ruby Keeler) tap dance together—one of the few examples of individualized "personality" dancing in a major Warners/Berkeley spectacle.

43. *Footlight Parade* (1933). "Shanghai Lil": A bugle sounds, ending the tap dance and summoning Bill to rejoin his ship. Order is firmly reestablished in the climactic parade, but there's room for Lil, too, in Berkeley's navy.

4

BROADWAY BEFORE BERKELEY

Specific Antecedents

The previous chapter pointed out a number of instances in which characteristic elements of Berkeley's film numbers were clearly anticipated in the stage shows on which he collaborated. It is apparent that there was a significant carryover from Berkeley's Broadway experience to his Hollywood oeuvre, sometimes occurring on a very specific level (e.g., from "I'm Flying High" in *Earl Carroll Vanities of 1928* to "Flying High" in the film *Flying High*; from "The Rout" in *International Revue* to "42nd Street" in the film *42nd Street*).

Elements now commonly associated with Busby Berkeley can also be found in the following stage production numbers:

1. "The Typing Place"—The legs of six concealed chorines formed the key-bars of a gigantic typewriter, striking the keys and writing an enormous letter as the lights of Broadway sparkled through the window.[1]

2. "Dining Out"—In a restaurant setting, diners at a table rose slowly into midair. Beneath them appeared showgirls rigged up as various culinary delights: for example, an appropriately costumed girl seated atop a giant pastry dish to represent "French Pastry," or girls seated inside bathtub-sized vegetable dishes to portray "Mushroom" and "Cauliflower."[2]
3. "The Rotisserie"—On a giant, three-level rotisserie, eighteen chorus girls were trussed to huge spits and turned like broiling fowl until they were "done."[3]
4. "The Story of a Fan"—While Nanette Flack, Virginia Futrelle, and Frank Johnson sang "Just a Fan," chorus girls trooped down golden stairways on either side of the stage. The backs of their costumes formed, peacock-like, fans of all colors and styles and nations: Dresden, Watteau, Louis XIV, Egyptian, and so on. The fan-girls, 144 in all, divided into groups of six, congregated on stage, and danced in ensemble, creating constantly shifting patterns of color. At the climax of the number, thirty-nine large, vividly colored fans, each with a spread of forty feet, sprouted up from the floor. From the ceiling descended an even more enormous fan, its span nearly the entire width of the 200-foot proscenium, suspended by cables and illuminated with hundreds of colored electric lights. Attached to this giant fan and forming its ribs were twenty nearly nude showgirls.[4]

The catch is that Busby Berkeley had nothing to do with any of the four numbers described above. "The Typing Place" was from *The Perfect Fool*, a successful Ed Wynn revue that opened in 1921 and was staged by the veteran director of musicals, Julian Mitchell. "Dining Out" was featured in the first (1921) edition of Irving Berlin's *Music Box Revue*, staged by Hassard Short. "The Rotisserie" created a splash in the third edition of the Shubert revue *Artists and Models*, which opened on June 24, 1925, and was staged by J. J. Shubert himself.[5] "The Story of a Fan" was one of the sensations of the 1922 Hippodrome extravaganza *Better Times*; the number was designed by Mark Lawson under the direction of Hippodrome perennial R. H. Burnside.

In other words, all four of these "Berkeleyesque" numbers were produced before Berkeley made his Broadway debut as a dance director in November 1925. The point here is that, when discussing the influence of Berkeley's stage work on his films, it is less accurate to see him as an isolated theatrical innovator than as the inheritor of already flourishing stage and popular entertainment traditions—those of the musical, the extravaganza, the big production number, the chorus line, the spectacular revue, and various "aggregate" forms of entertainment. Elements that are now popularly identified with Busby Berkeley in many cases predated his advent as a dance director by years and even decades. The "Berkeleyesque" existed as a full-fledged tradition long before Berkeley ever arrived on the scene.[6]

This rendezvous with the Berkeleyesque appears to have been less a matter of innovation than of confluence. As noted above, Berkeley's reputation as an innovative Broadway dance director was initially and primarily based on qualities quite different from those that characterize his most famous movie numbers. In the last part of his stage career, Berkeley "found himself" by connecting with an existing set of forms and traditions that, even as they tapered off on the stage, were about to flare up in the nascent film musical and become identified with his name. During this period, Berkeley was at least as much an apprentice, an observer, and an assimilator as he was an innovator. The following sections deal with correspondences between motifs and devices found in Berkeley's film numbers and their previous use in the musical theater. The intention here is not to prove that Berkeley was influenced by any particular stage number but to indicate some relevant general trends and methods in the stage tradition from which he evolved.

Radium Numbers

One of Berkeley's most celebrated effects occurs in "The Shadow Waltz" number in *Gold Diggers of 1933* when the lights go down and the screen is filled with neon-outlined violins. The spectacular "Polka Dot Polka" climax of *The Gang's All Here* features myriad neonized hoops hovering in a darkened void.

There are many precedents for this type of effect in the "radium numbers" and other glow-in-the-dark effects used on the American musical stage. One of the earliest examples occurred in the bizarre 1902 science-fiction musical *King Highball*; in one number, the stage was illuminated only by tiny light bulbs twinkling on the dresses of the chorus girls. The 1904 Eddie Foy musical *Piff! Paff! Pouf!* featured a "Radium Dance" in which chorus girls in luminescent costumes jumped luminescent ropes.[7]

The 1915 *Follies* included a number, "My Radium Girl," which set the shimmering white dresses of the chorus against a solid black background. These types of effects became popular in subsequent editions of the *Follies*. In the 1917 edition, sixty chorines in Chinese costumes climbed up ladders that glowed in the dark. The most spectacular number of the 1922 *Follies* was called "Lace-Land," in which showgirls appeared in exquisite lace gowns; then the lights went out, leaving the gowns shimmering in multicolored luminous paints. One enthusiastic reviewer reported, "The audience fairly shouted in its joy. The effect was astonishing. There have been other beautiful 'radium' stage pictures, but nothing like 'Lace-Land.'"[8]

Instruments

Numbers in which musical instruments figure prominently as props are a likely self-referential phenomenon in the musical. In Berkeley's numbers of this type, the emphasis given to instruments as props is often elaborated to the point where they seem to take on a life of their own. The most famous of these numbers are "The Shadow Waltz" (*Gold Diggers of 1933*), in which sixty girls perform with neonized white violins (see photo 9), and "The Words Are in My Heart" (*Gold Diggers of 1935*), with fifty-six girls seated at dancing white pianos. Also relevant here are "Spin a Little Web of Dreams" (*Fashions of 1934*), with its bent-back showgirls forming the frames of harps; the finale of *Broadway Serenade* (1939), with its platoons of grotesquely masked instrumentalists; and "Fascinatin' Rhythm" (*Lady Be Good*, 1941), with its giant silhouettes of instrumentalists and its succession of grand pianos. A fitting climax to this development is the surrealistic "I've Gotta Hear That Beat" (*Small Town Girl*, 1953), in which Ann Miller tap dances her way through an orchestra composed entirely of disembodied hands and the instruments they are playing.

A precedent for the instrument-oriented number can be found at least as far back as 1873, when, in *Humpty Dumpty Abroad*, "the cast paraded dressed as brasses, wood winds, cellos, and drums."[9] Violins were highlighted in a number in *The Passing Show of 1918* (Chicago edition), which the *Variety* critic described with uncommon awareness of the number's Freudian overtones: "The dancing violin girls . . . background [Herman] Timberg in a beautiful setting appropriately designated 'Viol-Inn.' Timberg and the girls carry their sweethearts along. Their sweethearts are violins. They make love to them on the stage, and the result brings sighs of adoration and contentment from the other side of the footlights."[10]

In *Gay Paree* (1925) there was an anticipation of "The Words Are in My Heart" in a number called "A Baby's Baby Grand," where the chorus performed with miniature pianos slung over them like drums.[11] In the Berkeley-choreographed *International Revue* (1930), human piano keys danced along a giant keyboard.

One of the most elaborate instrument-oriented numbers of the era occurred in the 1927 edition of the *Ziegfeld Follies*:

> The big ensemble comes at the end of the first act and completely kills the second act. Building up and piling up until it seems as though [set designer Joseph] Urban and [costume designer John] Harkrider and [dance director] Sammy Lee have outdone any Ziegfeld ensemble to date. Twenty girls form a jazz band and around them the scene piles up. Color scheme is yellow and white, with high plumed military headgears and on the staircases on either side are a dozen gold pianos (practical) with the girls actually playing. Full company then amplifies this group of thirty girl musicians by the use of kazoos and with a wind-up melody based on Sousa's 'Stars and Stripes Forever.' It brings the audience right up on its feet and nearly takes the roof off the theatre.[12]

Ziegfeld biographer Charles Higham uses this number to surmise that "Ziegfeld was the natural father of Busby Berkeley." Berkeley himself attributed the inspirations for both "The Shadow Waltz" and "The Words Are in My Heart" to vaudeville acts he had seen at the Palace Theatre.[13]

Gigantism

Gigantism—the use of giant-sized props—has long been a staple effect of musical numbers on both stage and screen. Examples of gigantism are cited elsewhere in this chapter: the typewriter in *The Perfect Fool*, the fans in *Better Times*, the paint boxes in *Greenwich Village Follies of 1923* and *Artists and Models of 1925*, the powder-box in *Delmar's Revels* (1927), the keyboard in the *International Revue*, etc.

Examples of gigantism abound in other Broadway shows. Earl Carroll's *Vanities of 1923* featured an enormous revolving wedding cake with star Peggy Hopkins Joyce perched atop it. In the short-lived *Topics of 1923*, showgirls wore huge floral headdresses and stalklike skirts which, when combined with the stalklike columns on which the showgirls stood, gave the illusion of rafters-reaching flowers. In the 1923 *Follies*, apparently doll-sized actors disported around a Brobdingnagian tabletop. The 1924 black revue *Dixie to Broadway* grouped showgirls around an immense piano.[14]

For an 1898 Anna Held show, Florenz Ziegfeld had a massive music-sheet fill the background, with the protruding heads of black singers forming the notes; an oversized music-sheet is used in Berkeley's finale of the 1937 film *Varsity Show*.[15] The "Grand Opera Ball" number in the 1922 Hippodrome spectacle *Better Times* centered on a king-size cabinet-style phonograph, through whose door emerged actors representing various recording stars; in a Berkeley number for the film *Two Tickets to Broadway* (1951), Tony Martin sings an operatic selection while standing on a gigantic phonograph turntable.[16] In the famous all-black revue *Blackbirds of 1928*, a huge watermelon was suspended above the stage; Berkeley's racial-stereotype extravaganza "Goin' to Heaven on a Mule" in the film *Wonder Bar* (1934) includes a watermelon large enough to contain a tap-dancer inside.[17]

Other instances of gigantism in Berkeley's films include the colossal coins in "We're in the Money" (*Gold Diggers of 1933*), the giant-sized naval cap that descends in the finale of *Gold Diggers in Paris* (1938), the mammoth bananas and strawberries in "The Lady in the Tutti-Frutti Hat" (*The Gang's All Here*), and the titanic tom-toms (beaten by giant mechanical hands) that frame the stage for "I've Gotta Hear That Beat" (*Small Town Girl*). Of course, Berkeley was far from the only movie choreographer employing giant props—two well-known examples are the table-sized straw hats in Dave Gould's Oscar-winning "Straw Hat" number for *Folies Bergère* (1935), and the gargantuan outspread legs and feet between which Fred Astaire dances in the Astaire/Hermes Pan "Bojangles of Harlem" number in *Swing Time* (1936).

It is possible to find in this tradition of gigantism

the root of one of Berkeley's most characteristic and dazzling film devices: the juggling of different perceptions of scale. One of the many astounding effects in *Dames*'s "I Only Have Eyes For You" occurs when Ruby Keeler, standing inside a circular frame, becomes a frozen picture on the back of a hand-mirror held by a now giant-sized Keeler. Similarly, in the "Dames" number later in the same film, a long shot of an arrangement of chorus girls turns into a still photograph through which bursts the gigantic grinning face of Dick Powell.

A particularly rich example of this device is found in "The Words Are in My Heart" (*Gold Diggers of 1935*) when the entire number—fifty-six pianos and all—is revealed to have apparently taken place inside another piano, beside which are standing a relatively oversized female singing trio. On top of this piano is a miniature toy garden, into which the camera dips to disclose the life-sized costars Dick Powell and Gloria Stuart.

Berkeley had a Swiftian fascination with the gigantic and the miniature. This can be traced in part to the widespread use of giant props on the musical stage, but the resources of film editing gave him an enhanced flexibility to manipulate the viewer's sense of large and small.

Transformations

Shifts in scale are just one of several forms of metamorphosis that occur in Berkeley's work. The world of his numbers is a fluid and deceptive one, in which appearances are constantly being transformed. One type of transformation involves space or location. For example, at the beginning of "42nd Street" Ruby Keeler is seen dancing in front of a backdrop of the street. A detail shot shows her feet; then a cut to medium shot reveals her to be dancing now on the roof of a taxicab in a full-scale set of 42nd Street. In "By a Waterfall," a trick cut instantly changes the location from a leafy glade to an ornate stucco pool.

In "42nd Street," a two-dimensional backdrop becomes a three-dimensional set; a row of chorus girls becomes a skyline of skyscrapers; and down becomes up, as a shot looking down the floor becomes a shot looking "up" at Powell and Keeler apparently atop a skyscraper. In "Dames," a girl seated at her vanity sprays perfume at the camera lens, which becomes a window being wiped clean by a black cleaning woman inside an office. In "Lullaby of Broadway," Wini Shaw's face becomes an aerial view of Manhattan, and a vertiginous shot of the street to which she falls becomes the spinning dial of a clock tower. In "Minnie from Trinidad" (*Ziegfeld Girl*, 1941), the camera tracks into a piece of coral in a fishtank; the coral is then revealed to be part of an elaborate headdress worn by a Ziegfeld girl. This last example shows how different types of transformations—size, location, object—can be intertwined: the concealed cut here changes the object and scale from a tiny piece of coral to a large headdress, and the location from a fishtank to a theatrical stage.

Transformations of this sort are obviously more difficult to achieve on the stage than on the screen, where one has such resources as dissolves and concealed cuts at one's disposal. Nevertheless, rapid transformations of setting and object—accomplished with the aid of drops, revolving platforms, special lighting effects, etc.—were a staple of nineteenth-century stagecraft and continued to be practiced on the Broadway musical stage of the 1920s.[18]

In the 1921 edition of *Greenwich Village Follies*, for a number entitled "When Dreams Come True," the interior of a house was suddenly transformed into a garden exterior by means of a magnified stereopticon and a lighting change. In *Lady Butterfly* (1923), a corner of a reception hall in an English home revolved to disclose an old-fashioned saloon in full operation. *Happy Days* (1919) opened in a nursery school dormitory where children's beds suddenly arranged themselves into a railroad train. In the dream sequence of "The Land of Mystery" in *Better Times* (1922), a man's bed turned into a motor car and drove off. In the 1924 editions of both the *Music Box Revue* and *Artists and Models*, a change in lighting suddenly turned an all-white chorus into "shiny-skinned darkies."[19]

In the 1907 Hippodrome show *The Auto Race*, a summertime ballet of butterfly-costumed girls was suddenly transformed into a winter scene complete with onstage blizzard; in Berkeley's "Pettin' in the Park" (*Gold Diggers of 1933*), a ball flung at the camera instantly changes a winter scene into springtime. In the 1910 *Follies*, Anna Held was seen on film as a hurtling comet in the heavens; then Held herself, seated atop a silver rocket, burst through the screen—an effect somewhat similar to that of the above-mentioned climax of "Dames," where Dick Powell's head bursts through the photographic surface.[20]

Placards

One particular form of transformation involves the use of placards or like objects which, when reversed, form a picture or a pattern. A well-known example of this occurs at the end of "42nd Street" when the chorus, their backs to the camera, turn around to reveal skyscraper placards that combine to form a Manhattan skyline. The 1929 edition of the stage revue *George White's Scandals* ended in a very similar way: "At the finish the coryphées turn their backs to the audience to exhibit elaborate trappings imitative of skyscrapers, which in combination form an approximation of the skyline of New York."[21]

In "I Only Have Eyes for You," a chorus of Ruby Keeler lookalikes bend over, and placards on their backs form, jigsaw-fashion, a giant image of Keeler's face. In the 1927 Shubert revue *A Night in Spain*, for a number called "Promenade the Esplanade," girls with shawls arranged themselves on stairways and then, by reversing their shawls, formed a single giant image of a Spanish shawl.[22]

Near the end of "Shanghai Lil" (*Footlight Parade*,

1933), marching chorus girls and sailor boys use placards to form a gigantic American flag with FDR's face superimposed on it. A similarly patriotic transformation occurred in "The Land I Love," the first-act finale of the 1920 Hippodrome show *Good Times*. At the climax of this all-American extravaganza, a seventy-foot map of the United States, outlined in electric lights, was suddenly illuminated at the back of the stage. In front of this a chain of high ladders dropped from the ceiling. The chorus marched to the footlights, where each took hold of a wide streamer of ribbon. Then they rushed backstage and clambered sixty feet up the ladders. When they reached the top, the ribbons were reversed, forming a composite American flag that stretched across the entire width of the Hippodrome's huge proscenium.[23]

Scale

The vast scale of Berkeley's movie numbers such as "Dames," "I Only Have Eyes for You," "By a Waterfall," and "Lullaby of Broadway" seems far beyond the reach of a theatrical stage. But, in the above-mentioned Hippodrome Theatre, one can find at least an approximate theatrical precedent for the magnitude of Berkeley's most ambitious movie numbers. The Hippodrome—popularly known as "The Hip"—opened on April 12, 1905. It was the brainchild of two men, Frederic Thompson (the creative half) and Skip Dundy (the business half). Their previous experience had been in expositions (participating in the turn-of-the-century "world's fair" craze) and amusement parks (opening Coney Island's legendary Luna Park in 1903). The Hippodrome covered an entire city block between 43rd and 44th Streets at Sixth Avenue. The seating capacity was 5,200. The stage was 200 feet wide and 110 feet deep. (By comparison, the stage of Radio City Music Hall measures 144 feet by 80 feet.) It could easily accommodate 600 performers, not to mention elephants, waterfalls, a water tank fourteen feet deep, and various mammoth scenic effects, such as a thirty-foot high airship, a hurricane, and a nearly full-scale baseball game. Among the Hippodrome's idiosyncrasies were a curtain that descended (rather than rose) to reveal the stage, and the changing of the scenery by precision-drilled stagehands working in full view of the audience.[24]

Losing money due to excess overhead, Thompson and Dundy "retired," and the theater was taken over by the Shuberts in 1906. In 1915 the Shuberts sold out to impresario Charles B. Dillingham. An unusually courtly and well-liked producer, Dillingham had a reputation for leaving his creative people alone. It was during his ownership, lasting until 1922, that the Hippodrome enjoyed its most fertile and spectacular period, with veteran writer-director R. H. Burnside the key collaborator.[25]

Two of the Hippodrome's characteristically grandiose numbers—"The Story of a Fan" and "The Land I Love"—have already been described above. For good measure, here is another example, "The Harbor of Prosperity," which was the climactic number of the last of Dillingham's Hippodrome shows, *Better Times* (1922). This spectacle began with large mountains rising from the edges of a pool. Through waterfalls at the rear of the stage marched a phalanx of ten rows of female Water Guards, eight abreast, dressed in gold armor and helmets. Without breaking step, the Water Guards continued marching straight down the steps of the pool and disappeared beneath the water. This was followed by a ballet of water nymphs amid spouting fountains, while Nanette Flack sang "My Golden Dream Ship." Then, its masts slowly emerging like periscopes, there rose from the depths of the pool an enormous golden ship, its outline ablaze with electric lights, its decks and rigging filled with the gleaming figures of the previously submerged Water Guards.[26]

The 1918 Hippodrome show was simply called *Everything*, and no one seemed to find the title presumptuous. The last show staged at the Hippodrome was, appropriately enough, the Billy Rose circus musical *Jumbo*. No other theater was considered large enough for this spectacular production, and the shuttered Hippodrome was reopened to accommodate it in 1935. The mammoth structure was torn down in 1939. Busby Berkeley worked on the 1962 film version of *Jumbo*; it marked the end of his film career.

Water Spectacles

Water, as an image of dissolution and romantic sublimation, is an important element in Berkeley's oeuvre, not only in such celebrated water spectacles as "By a Waterfall" and the aquatic numbers of the Esther Williams vehicles *Million Dollar Mermaid* (1952) and *Easy to Love* (1953) but also, more subtly, as a leitmotif or coda in several of his numbers. For example, both "The Shadow Waltz" and "The Words Are in My Heart" end with images of their two principals' rippling reflections in a pool; "I Only Have Eyes For You" ends with Keeler and Powell walking off in the rain; curtains of colored spray frame the final numbers of *The Gang's All Here*; "The Closer You Are" (*Two Tickets to Broadway*) is played against a rainy background; a fountain erupts at the end of "Love Is Back in Business" (*Call Me Mister*, 1951).

Water spectacles were a thriving genre in the nineteenth-century theater, primarily for the purpose of recreating naval battles.[27] With the turn of the century, the primary focus of water spectacles shifted from battleships to bathing beauties. This development was closely linked to liberalized stage standards that were extending the display of the female figure in various ways, bathing costumes among them.

For all types of water spectacle, the Hippodrome, with its huge permanent tank, was unsurpassed. The 1906 underwater fantasy *Neptune's Daughter* included an onstage hurricane and, for the first time, the celebrated Hippodrome effect in which the chorus marched resolutely into the water tank, disappeared beneath the surface, and, to the perpetual amazement of the spectators, never emerged again (or, alternatively, emerged many minutes later—without a drop of water on them). *The Big Show* (1916) included a mammoth aquatic number called "The Enchanted Waterfall," which was peopled with hordes of mermaids, sprites, and naiads, and climaxed with a sensational Annette Kellerman high dive.[28] The aquatic spectacle in *Good Times* (1920) featured "a whole school of divers, headed by Miss Dorothy Gates, who does a 122-ft. plunge from the Hippodrome ceiling. . . . Electric lights and gushing geysers are used in the stupendous spectacle at the final curtain."[29]

Although not as immense as those at the Hippodrome, water spectacles were a regular feature of the *Ziegfeld Follies* in the 1910s. To celebrate the opening of the Panama Canal that year, the 1913 *Follies* presented a spectacle that immersed girls in the waters released when the locks of a simulated canal were opened.[30] The 1914 *Follies* included the number "Neptune's Daughter," featuring Annette Kellerman in her famous skintight bathing suit.[31] It was presumably this sort of thing to which Berkeley was referring when he described the conception of "By a Waterfall": "I can see a big waterfall coming down through the rocks, with girls sliding down the rapids into a huge Ziegfeldian pool."[32]

"My Luve Is Like a Zeppelin"

A rose is a rose is a rose, but a chorus girl could be virtually anything, including a rose. Indeed, she frequently was a rose, or some other form of blossom. The floral incarnation was one of the most venerable production number devices, and chorus girls adorned gardens, bouquets, and trellises in countless productions.[33] Berkeley himself pitched in with a rose number for the *Earl Carroll Vanities of 1928*.

Woman-as-flower has been a common enough image throughout the ages: "O, my Luve is like a red, red rose." But what about "My Luve is like a cigarette" or "My Luve is like a Zeppelin"? Here one enters a broader area—that of woman as object—which is again part of a venerable tradition on the musical stage. For example, in *Music Hall Parade*, an anecdotal history of the British music hall tradition, there is the following entry on London's rival Alhambra and Empire theaters during the 1880s:

> Both houses became temples of that type of ballet in which almost anything was translated in terms of pretty girls. One night the *corps de ballet* would personify the Armies of All Nations. Another night they would be All the Ingredients of a Salad, not forgetting the mustard-pot and slices of hard-boiled egg.[34]

A similar phenomenon was noted by the reviewer of an American revue produced some thirty years later:

The Passing Show of 1917 is seriously affected by the new custom of dressing chorus girls, if at all, in things that are not so much gowns as structures. Just now at the Winter Garden they came out as fans and as drinks and as restaurant tables.[35]

Here is a list of just a few of the things that chorus girls represented in musical shows of the era:

1. Battleships, cruising into New York Harbor (Ziegfeld's *Follies of 1909*: see photo 10)[36]
2. Bubbles (*Better Times*, 1922)[37]
3. Candelabra (*The Passing Show of 1924*)[38]
4. Candles in a birthday cake (*Greenwich Village Follies of 1920*)[39]
5. Cigarettes, tucked away in boxes (*A Night in Paris*, 1925)[40]
6. A clock, with the underside of the chorine's flared skirt forming the face, and her black-stockinged legs forming the minute- and hour-hands (*Buds of 1927*: see photo 11)[41]
7. Coins, from pennies through dollars (*I'll Say She Is!*, 1924) or plated in silver and gold (*Up in the Clouds*, 1922)[42]
8. Flapjacks (*The Comic Supplement*, 1925)[43]
9. Fruits of various kinds, arranged in a large fruit basket (*The Passing Show of 1923*)[44]
10. Good-luck omens—horseshoe, four-leaf clover, etc. (*George White's Scandals of 1926*)[45]
11. Handbags, emerging from the lining of a giant beaded bag (*The Passing Show of 1924*)[46]
12. Icicles (*In Gay New York*, 1896)[47]
13. Machine cogs and electrical wiring in a factory (*Steel Blues*, 1930)[48]
14. Mosquitoes, hovering over the New Jersey marshes (Ziegfeld's *Follies of 1908*)[49]
15. Paints of various hues, emerging from a paint box (*Greenwich Village Follies of 1923*)[50]
16. Peaches, adorning an orchard of peach trees (*Better Times*, 1922)[51]
17. The pendulum of a clock (*Earl Carroll Vanities of 1925*; *Strand Roof Revue*, c. 1926)[52]
18. Perfumes, enclosed within illuminated crystal jars (*Gay Paree*, 1925)[53]
19. Porcelain plates of every style—Wedgwood, Sevres, Delft, Dresden, etc. (*The Passing Show of 1924*)[54]
20. Powder puffs (*A Night in Paris*, 1926)[55]
21. Precious stones (*The Merry World*, 1926; *Broadway Nights*, 1929)[56]
22. A railroad train (*Broadway Nights*, 1929)[57]
23. Raindrops (*Little Nemo*, 1908)[58]
24. Skyscrapers, combining to form the skyline of Manhattan (*George White's Scandals of 1929*)[59]
25. Snowballs (*Earl Carroll Vanities of 1923*; *Greenwich Village Follies of 1925*)[60]
26. Switchboards, to which patrons could connect their telephones (Ziegfeld's roof revue, *Frolics*, 1915)[61]
27. Taxicabs, complete with headlights and meters in front, and spare tires and red lights aft (Ziegfeld's *Follies of 1908*)[62]
28. Totem-poles (*The Yankee Tourist*, 1907; *Rose-Marie*, 1924)[63]

29. Tree-trunks (*Music Box Revue*, 1924)[64]
30. Watermelons (*The Rogers Brothers in Washington*, 1901)[65]
31. Wine bottles (*Up in the Clouds*, 1922)[66]
32. Zeppelins, with searchlights sweeping over them (*Frolics*, 1915)[67]

Objectification of the Feminine

This concept of the objectification of the feminine is deeply ingrained in the evolution of the production number. It is also a central ingredient of some of Berkeley's best-known production numbers—for example, the opening "We're in the Money" number of *Gold Diggers of 1933*, where the chorus girls represent coins, or the "Spin a Little Web of Dreams" number in *Fashions of 1934*, where they are turned into "Human Harps."

One does not find these types of girls-equal-objects images in Berkeley's movies as often as one might expect, and it would be difficult to cite more than the two examples above. However, this does not mean that the concept is not still an important one in Berkeley's numbers. There are at least three forms that the objectification of the feminine can take:

1. The female *represents* a particular object, as discussed above.
2. The female is *associated* with an object, generally in the form of a prop.
3. The female is *treated* like an object, generally as a decorative or deindividualized part of a larger arrangement.

In contrast to many stage musicals of the early twentieth century, Berkeley in his movies resorts to the second alternative more frequently and more memorably than to the first. To cite a couple of his most celebrated numbers: In *Gold Diggers of 1933*'s "The Shadow Waltz," the chorines do not become "Human Violins"; instead, they all *play* violins. And in *The Gang's All Here*'s legendary "The Lady in the Tutti-Frutti Hat," the chorus does not turn into giant bananas and strawberries; more provocatively, they carry and manipulate giant bananas and strawberries. The metonymical relationship of the chorine to the object is emphasized more than her metaphorical identification with it.

The device of having women directly represent objects on the screen seems mainly limited in its effect to the grotesque or the tongue-in-cheek—for example, Debbie Reynolds as a human football in the charming MGM minimusical *I Love Melvin* (1953), or the "Dancing Dildoes" number in the parodic *The First Nudie Musical* (1976). This type of anthropomorphism seems better suited to the more fluid and stylized world of the animated cartoon. In live-action cinema, as opposed to the early musical stage, dance directors have usually preferred to present such imagery one step removed.

The third form of objectifying the feminine—treating the female like an object—is also widely practiced by Berkeley (indeed, it is the most pervasive form of the three), and it, too, derives from an extensive stage tradition. The most obvious illustration of this occurs when the chorus girl, while retaining human form, is presented as inanimate decoration or living architecture, as if she were made of stone or marble or wood or stucco. One of the best examples of this in a Berkeley movie number is the aforementioned "Human Harps" effect from "Spin a Little Web of Dreams," where the girls' arched bodies form the normally wooden frames of the harps. Other examples include the girls who appear as statuary in the park setting of *Gold Diggers of 1933*'s "Pettin' in the Park," and the Indian maidens who seem like extensions of the rock face of the cliff in *Rose Marie*'s "Totem Tom Tom." In an interview, Berkeley once described how, while stopping at a red light, he became fascinated by the diamond-shaped patterns formed by hod-carriers as they piled their bricks into the hod: "I said, 'Someday I'll do that with girls'—and I did."[68]

Such reductions of the female body to a form of attractive building material were widely practiced on the musical stage of the 1910s and 1920s. For example, a typical revue like *The Passing Show of 1923* featured seminude girls as the ribs of chandeliers, the stems of candelabra, and the stuff of living statues and curtains (see photo 12). In the *Earl Carroll Vanities of 1925*, they formed a colonnade of "living pillars." In the *Earl Carroll Vanities of 1928* (a show with which Berkeley was associated), they appeared as columns and as the buttresses of an ornate fountain. A White Studio photograph of *The Circus Princess* (an Emmerich Kalman operetta imported by the Shuberts in 1927) shows a large, striking setting with seven small archways at the bottom. Inside each archway, a pair of chorines bend forward facing each other, their posture echoing the shape of the arch so that they themselves become a part of the architecture.[69]

Part of a Pattern

The next step in the treatment of the female as an object involves not her conversion into architecture but her transformation into a deindividualized unit, a subsidiary part of a larger representational pattern. One of the most famous examples from Berkeley's film work occurs in "The Shadow Waltz" when the chorines with their neon-illuminated violins combine to form the outline of a single, giant violin. Other examples include the title number in *Flying High*, where the chorus arranges itself into the outline of an airplane, or the finale of *Varsity Show* (1937), where the chorus boys and girls form the initials and insignias of leading universities.

Once again, antecedents abound in theatrical history. In Julian Mitchell's staging of *An Arabian Girl and Forty Thieves* (1899), the corps de ballet formed a giant dragon. For "The Song of the Flowers" in the 1905 Hippodrome show *A Society Circus*, 144 ballerinas in flowery dresses bunched together into a gigantic dancing bouquet. As noted above, the Shubert revue *A Night in Spain* (1927) had shawl-wearing girls forming the pattern of a single mammoth shawl. Another Shubert revue, *The Merry World* (1926), featured a number, "The Enchanted Forest," in which an ensemble of forty Tiller Girls used synchronized undulating arm gestures to form a snake that wriggled on and off the stage.[70]

Of course, the patterns in a production number need not be pictorial in order to produce objectification, and more abstract and complex arrangements are found in nearly every one of Berkeley's major movie numbers. The important factor is the chorus's incorporation into a transcendent pattern that subordinates individuality to totality, anatomy to geometry.

In Berkeley's films the human body can reach a point of abstraction that is startling and even disturbing. Perhaps the most remarkable instance of this occurs in "By a Waterfall" when the chorus transform themselves into triangular, cell-like units. Nearly as striking examples can be found in most of Berkeley's amazingly varied overhead patterns, in which recognizably human forms seem to dissolve into a fluid sequence of pulsating circles, angles, and lines.

The Kaleidoscope

The most celebrated of Berkeley's abstract patterns are his bird's-eye shots of chorus girls arranged in concentric circles, their limbs and torsos intersecting to form kaleidoscope-like patterns. Although he did not originate this device on the screen, it has certainly become his trademark, so closely identified with him that the use of it in such latter-day parodies as Mel Brooks's *The Producers* (1968) and Ken Russell's *The Boy Friend* (1971) instantly evokes Berkeley without any need of mentioning his name.

These kaleidoscopic effects are evidently unique to the cinema. They require a camera mounted in the ceiling or atop a high crane. If a theatrical chorus were to lie on the floor and arrange themselves in a similar manner, anyone seated in the orchestra would be able to see little except the shoe-soles of half the participants. Yet it is still possible to find some theatrical equivalents for the overhead shots in Berkeley's movie numbers.

The trick is that, even if stage directors could not suddenly place their audiences sixty feet directly above the stage, they could still work in a vertical direction on the stage itself, building patterns on the axis perpendicular to that of the floor. In *Princess April* (1924), scantily dressed chorines formed vertical-plane geometric patterns by means of outstretched arms, bent backs, aligned legs, etc. In the 1928 Joe Cook vehicle *Rain or Shine*, three groups of five chorines each linked hands, placed their feet together, and leaned outward to form semicircular pinwheel patterns. If the other half of the circle were completed, one would have a simplified ancestor of a Busby Berkeley kaleidoscope (see photo 13).[71]

The examples above are limited in scope by the constraints of gravity. Other, more ambitious numbers went further by building straight up. The most spectacular number in *The Passing Show of 1914* was "The Sloping Path." It featured four connected rows sloping straight upward in zigzag fashion; each row contained around a dozen seated and barelegged chorines against a black background (see photo 14). A similar effect, also called "The Sloping Path," was used in the 1914 British revue *Not Likely!*[72] This type of stage effect can be seen as an antecedent of Berkeley's elaborate "Dames" number, which also features vertically planed rows of seated girls.

Another solution to the problem of giving stage audiences an overview of choral patterns can be found in the early sound musicals *The Hollywood Revue of 1929*, *The Show of Shows* (1929), and *King of Jazz* (1930).[73] These films employ a steep, wide bank of steps (around thirty steps high in *The Show of Shows*) on which the chorus can march up and down, forming various patterns that would be visible to a stage audience as if from a high-angle shot (see photos 15 and 16). A review of the Chicago edition of *A Night in Venice* (1929), for which Berkeley served as dance director of the original Broadway version, notes the use of "a high, stage-wide flight of steps" to display novelty tableaux and drill effects.[74] Berkeley later used large-scale banked-step arrangements in his film numbers "Dames" and the *Varsity Show* finale.

Also of relevance here are the various "Living Curtain" numbers that adorned numerous stage revues of the period (including the Berkeley-choreographed *Earl Carroll Vanities of 1928*), with showgirls suspended in vertical patterns reaching nearly to the flies (see photo 17). In several respects, these numbers are like Berkeley kaleidoscopes turned up on their sides. The same point could be made about the many human-fan and giant-plate arrangements, some of which have been cited earlier.

Another example of gravity-defying decorativeness was the Gertrude Hoffman Girls, an acrobatically inclined troupe that graced several revues of the 1920s. Among their many talents, the Hoffman Girls could clamber up ropes and trellises and arrange themselves in a variety of pleasing patterns (see photo 18). Here is a description of some of their antics from a review of *Artists and Models of 1925*:

> They are happiest when they can match agility with daring; when they can clamber gaily up a green-gold lattice that fills half the stage; when they can lunge and feint in the quick barter of a fencing drill; or when, depending in geometric disarray from long strands of webbing, they can weave sinuous figures far above the footlights or, with hands linked to ankles behind supple torsos, swing provocative arcs over a gaping populace.[75]

The widespread use of such devices as vertically planed patterns, "sloping paths," banked steps, living curtains, and aerial ensembles might explain why

Broadway dance directors, when engaged to work on the first musical films, were able to begin using overhead patterns almost immediately. These effects appear in such pioneer musical films as *The Hollywood Revue of 1929*, *Byron of Broadway* (1929), *The Cocoanuts* (1929), and *King of Jazz* (1930), all made before Berkeley arrived on the movie scene to create his first kaleidoscopes for *Whoopee!*

Faces on Parade

Next to the overhead kaleidoscope shot, the most familiar Berkeley screen figure is probably the "parade of faces"—a continuous series of faces of smiling chorines. This effect is created either by cutting together a succession of close-ups or by having a line of chorines march directly up to the camera (alternatively, the camera moves toward them) and then turn off to the side, one by one, to reveal the next girl in line. The origination of this figure is generally credited to Berkeley; as he said, "In *Whoopee* what I did, for the first time in the history of films, was close-ups of pretty girls. That had never been done in musical comedies."[76]

Like the kaleidoscope shot, the close-up is essentially a cinematic device. Yet it is again possible to find theatrical precedents for the Berkeley "parade of faces." A trademark of the *Ziegfeld Follies*, beginning with the 1912 edition, was the beauty parade, in which each showgirl came forward into the spotlight. As Allen Churchill writes in *The Theatrical Twenties*, "Each girl had at least one precious individual moment in a *Follies*, usually when she swayed center stage to pause for a moment, the focus of all eyes."[77] The roll call of beauty soon became a feature of other revues; for example, the *Earl Carroll Vanities of 1925* contained a number in which a platoon of showgirls, named for the principal cities of the United States, were called forth one by one.[78]

Especially relevant in this respect was the *Earl Carroll Vanities of 1928*, where, during the ensemble number "Say It with Girls," a device called "Vanities Votaphonevitotone Movies" presented enlarged close-ups of several of the showgirls.[79] It should be recalled that Berkeley was dance director for the 1928 *Vanities*, and, although he may not have had anything to do with creating this effect (the programme credits it to Max Teuber), he was certainly in a position to notice it.

Evolution of the Chorus Line

Even when the results are not as dramatic as a giant picture or a kaleidoscopic pattern, virtually any precision chorus number involves a certain degree of objectification of the feminine—a loss of individuality as a result of being made part of a mass, synchronized unit. From its beginnings, the development of the musical has been closely bound up with the display of massed female bodies, as evidenced by the previously discussed pioneer musical *The Black Crook* (1866).[80]

The use of the massed chorus continued to grow. The 1875 spectacle *Azurine* featured a chorus of "300 young ladies." The vast stage of the Hippodrome Theatre, as described above, was capable of holding over 600 people at once, and the house maintained a company of 200 ballet dancers, 400 chorus girls, and 100 chorus boys.[81] Berkeley's fondness for filling the frame with dancers harks back to a somewhat primitive stage tradition of massive ensembles.

The practice of "precision dancing" on the American musical stage can be traced back at least as far as *A Glance at New York in 1848* (1848), in which Gerald Bordman finds evidence of a "primitive chorus line."[82] The form was greatly popularized in 1868 by the arrival in New York of Lydia Thompson and her British Blondes, a troupe of amazingly hefty (by today's standards) showgirls, who wore tights and executed synchronized high kicks and other figures. The elementary configurations of the Thompson troupe were succeeded in 1888 by another British importation, "skirt dancing," in which, instead of the once-requisite tights, the chorus girls wore long, flowing skirts, imparting a more graceful and flowing line to their movements.[83]

This trend toward greater grace and sophistication was continued in 1894 by the arrival in America of British impresario George Edwardes's Gaiety Girls, whose aspect was classier and more individualized (as well as considerably slimmer) than that of the now-defunct Lydia Thompson troupe.[84] In 1907 a sensation was created by the American premiere of Franz Lehar's operetta *The Merry Widow*, with its celebrated "Merry Widow Waltz." According to historian Cecil Smith, what made the show such a great hit was neither its book nor even its music:

> It was the dancing, the animation of the waltz presented in the intimate, gallant terms of the ballroom rather than the formal figurations prescribed by established conventions. In *The Merry Widow* the ballroom dance was glorified as a symbol of romantic love, and placed in the focus of attention. The "Merry Widow Waltz" did in fact start a new era. . . . It dealt a death blow to the marches, drills, and empty convolutions that had punctuated musical-comedy performances until then. It opened the way for Vernon and Irene Castle, the tango, the turkey-trot, and the fox-trot. It humanized dancing, and made it warm, immediate, and personal.[85]

Smith overstates the case by speaking of a "death blow" to the tradition of "formal figurations" and "empty convolutions." It would be more accurate to speak merely of the establishment of a countertradition, one based on grace, personality, and intimacy rather than on spectacle and mass movement. This intimate tradition was carried on by such personality dancers as Vernon and Irene Castle, Tony and Sally DeMarco, and Fred and Adele Astaire, and by Broadway dance directors such as Jack Haskell, George Hale, and Boots McKenna.

In the 1910s and 1920s, the "spectacle" number and its corollary, deindividualized precision dancing, continued to flourish on the stage. In the realm of precision dancing, the rudimentary maneuvers of Lydia Thompson were succeeded by the more elaborate unison-configurations of the John Tiller Dancers. Tiller, a British businessman and producer of church pageants, began training precision dancers in the 1880s. Different troupes of Tiller Girls (ranging in number from eight to forty, with sixteen the most common) were then sent out all over Britain and Europe. A troupe first arrived in the United States in 1912, and various groups of Tiller Girls continued to populate American musicals for many years afterward.[86] Their rivals in the field included such groups as the Gertrude Hoffman Girls, Russell Markert's Roxyettes (from whom Radio City Music Hall's famed Rockettes evolved), the Albertina Rasch Troupe, the Allen K. Foster Girls, and the Chester Hale Girls (the last two groups appearing in Berkeley-choreographed stage musicals). All these ensembles stressed the virtues of precision, synchronization, and regimentation.[87]

The coexistence of these two stage dance traditions (spectacle/precision and intimacy/individuality) carried over into the early history of the movie musical. The tradition of mass spectacle, with Busby Berkeley as its leading exponent, dominated dance numbers in the movie musicals of the early 1930s. In the mid-1930s, it began to be overtaken by the tradition of intimacy and individual grace epitomized (and imported directly from the stage) by Fred Astaire. As the movie musical gravitated toward more narrativized and integration-oriented structures, the individualized dance style became increasingly predominant. However, the more "primitive" spectacle style is rarely completely absent from movie musicals, although its position is usually more subordinate and its effects less blatant than in the tradition represented by Berkeley and the stage spectacles that preceded him.[88]

PART THREE

BERKELEYESQUE CINEMA

5

AN INTRODUCTORY OUTLINE OF BERKELEY'S FILM CAREER

Phases and Variables

Busby Berkeley's film career can be divided into six main phases, with occasional overlaps and anomalies:

1. Early Period (1930–33), centering on the Eddie Cantor vehicles produced by Samuel Goldwyn
2. Classic Warner Bros. Period (1933–34), including those films with which both Berkeley and the Berkeleyesque are most strongly identified (i.e., *42nd Street*, *Gold Diggers of 1933*, *Footlight Parade*, and *Dames*)
3. Later Warner Bros. Period (1935–39), a transitional period shaped by changing trends in the movie musical
4. MGM Period (1939–43), typified by the Mickey Rooney/Judy Garland vehicles and marked by strong tensions between studio style and Berkeley's impulse toward spectacle
5. Fox Period (1943), consisting of only one film, *The Gang's All Here*, but one that represents Berkeley's most ambitious attempt to spectacularize an entire film

6. Late Period (1949–54, 1962), in which Berkeley's spectacle style enjoyed a modest revival achieved through simplification and modulation.

The following chapters do not attempt a comprehensive overview of Berkeley's film career but rather propose a limited interpretation of it in terms of the main issues raised in the first part of this study. Those issues concern the relationship of the Berkeleyesque to Berkeley's stage work and to a longstanding theatrical tradition that he inherited. Berkeley's alliance with the Tradition of Spectacle, forged relatively late in his stage career, carried over into his first films. His early successes in that vein and the almost immediate linking of his reputation with it consummated Berkeley's marriage, for better or worse, to a spectacle style and defined a set of parameters that remained in effect throughout his career. These parameters can be read in terms of the relationship between aggregative and integrative tendencies in the musical. As noted previously, both sides are always at work in the genre, but the film musical gravitated in a direction leaning more (although never exclusively) toward the integrative side. The result was a widening gap between those qualities that made Berkeley's work distinctive and the main currents of the American movie musical. This necessitated a series of solutions, conflicts, compromises, and adjustments in order to sustain Berkeley's career and to create a place for the Berkeleyesque within the Hollywood system—two goals that were interdependent but not always in perfect agreement.

Major dimensions of Berkeley's oeuvre—including the social-historical dimension, the dimension of psychological and sexual imagery, and the dimension of auteur thematics—are barely touched upon here. The emphasis is on the Berkeleyesque, that mode which links Berkeley to the Tradition of Spectacle in American popular entertainment. These chapters concentrate on the extent to which the Berkeleyesque flourished (or was constrained) in different production contexts, and the various ways in which Berkeleyesque spectacle was achieved (or not achieved or only partially achieved) in the different stages of his career.

Berkeley's filmography is approached here not as a self-enclosed model but as an open system—a dynamic matrix within which a number of variables intersect and interact. One especially pertinent area concerns the genre in which Berkeley specialized—the musical film. The historical development of the movie musical and its different modes and their relevance to the Berkeleyesque are referred to at some length in the following chapters. In general, these developments describe an increasing regularization and narrativization in the musical that made it more difficult for the Berkeleyesque to sustain itself or else obligated it to seek out receptive pockets (such as the Fox wartime musical or certain retrograde forms available in the 1950s) where it could operate effectively. Some other variables relevant to the central concerns of this study are treated briefly in the remainder of the chapter.

Studio

The 1930s represented a period of maturity and solidification for the Hollywood studio system. After the concurrent shake-ups of the 1929 Crash and the conversion to sound, the studios settled into the basic financial/management structures that would dominate Hollywood until this particular phase of the studio system began to erode in the late 1940s. Although the basic principles of distribution and exhibition were similar for all the studios (especially the so-called Big Five: Fox, MGM, Paramount, RKO, and Warner Bros.), a greater degree of variation and individuation from studio to studio occurred at the production level.[1] There are numerous examples of the work of major directors undergoing profound alteration as they moved from studio to studio—for example, Raoul Walsh, whose directorial "identity" shifted from rowdy populist to studio hack to ace action director as he moved from Fox to Paramount to Warner Bros. in the thirties, or Alfred Hitchcock, whose films for the independent Selznick company were generally more romance-oriented than was his output for other studios during the 1940s.

Berkeley was no exception to this pattern. In fact, his somewhat limited range and his position as a peripheral specialist made his work in the Berkeleyesque mode especially sensitive to shifts in studio and in studio policy. This involved not only "artistic differences" regarding stylistic orientation but also the more mundane matters of budget, priorities, and access to production facilities. The full exercise of the spectacle style required a substantial commitment of resources, and the tendency of Berkeley's production numbers to strain a film's budget often led to conflicts with the studio hierarchy and feelings of constriction on Berkeley's part.

In addition to the studio as a whole, there were subunits within the studio structure that could exert a special input of their own. This is especially true of the Arthur Freed production unit at MGM, which implemented an unusually strong and influential concept of the musical film. The Freed approach had a pronounced effect on Berkeley's style and ultimately provoked several outright clashes, including his firing from *Girl Crazy* in 1943 and his apparent exile from the Freed unit in the 1950s. On the other hand, Berkeley and especially the Berkeleyesque seem to have found a more hospitable context in several non-Freed MGM musicals of the early 1950s.

Collaborators

Although the following chapters do not deal in great detail with specific collaborators, the issue is still important, in relation both to individual contributions and to broader issues concerning the general context of the Berkeleyesque. In terms of directors, it is noted briefly below how a Warner Bros. musical directed by, say, Lloyd Bacon differed from one directed by Mervyn LeRoy. Even more crucial is the fact (not always sufficiently acknowledged by critics and historians) that Berkeley was usually not the director of the films containing his numbers. This raises questions of multiple authorship with particular vividness and creates a built-in, pronounced heterogeneity that harks back to the aggregative tradition of the nineteenth century, when shows were a series of acts by individual specialists, with little or no attempt to impose upon them an impression of central, transcendent authorship.

In a similar way, the question of star performers in Berkeley's numbers concerns not only the differing individual styles of the actors involved (e.g., the comparatively low-key Dick Powell and Ruby Keeler vs. the more aggressive and charismatic Mickey Rooney and Judy Garland) but also general issues concerning the dominance of individual performers, the extent to which the films are "star vehicles," and studio attitudes toward large-scale spectacular digressions that might distract from the luminescence of their featured contract players. Warner Bros. was probably the least star-driven of the major Hollywood studios, just as MGM was the most.[2] The Warners musicals often featured ensemble configurations in which several players were given prominence; this differed from the typical setup of Berkeley's MGM films, which concentrated more heavily on the central star or, at most, the star couple.

In general, the Berkeleyesque mode fared best in those situations where a certain diminishment of the star performers was possible, and Berkeley's spectacularized camera was permitted, in effect, to become a "star." Advantages of this type of configuration to the Berkeleyesque mode include: the elevation of the chorus to a status greater than that of a backdrop to the featured stars; the ability both to drop the star performers for extended periods and also to weave them more freely in and out of the chorus (an important element of several of Berkeley's greatest numbers, such as "By a Waterfall," "Shanghai Lil," and "I Only Have Eyes for You"); and greater access to flights of spectacular fancy and large-scale, abstract patterning.[3]

Stylistic and Structural Contexts

Although these categories overlap with those cited above, it is important to note that the Berkeleyesque mode, especially as developed most fully by Berkeley himself in the cinema, was more than simply a catalog of spectacular motifs (e.g., large choruses, kaleidoscopic overhead shots, enormous sets, extended crane shots, etc.). It also involved a series of basic structural and stylistic relationships allowing for the greater or lesser expansion of the Berkeleyesque.

The relationship of the surrounding narrative structure to the production numbers—and the advantages of the backstage structure in particular—are discussed at length elsewhere in this study. Also crucial is the placement of the numbers in relation to the narrative. As discussed below, the "stacking" together of several big numbers near the end of the film enhances the autonomy of Berkeleyesque spectacle from the surrounding narrative. On the other hand, the "spotting" of numbers at more or less even intervals throughout the film works to increase their subordination to the gravitational pull of the story line. A strong sense of self-enclosure (often augmented by such devices as symmetry and spatial barriers) is essential to Berkeleyesque spectacle, inhibiting the narrative's ability to break into the numbers through inserted dialogue passages, crosscutting, etc.

The issue of integration in the musical is usually conceptualized in terms of narrative causality and characterization. In the first case, the songs directly further (rather the interrupt) the progress of the narrative. The second case attains its ideal form in the "personality number," whose performance is strongly tied to a specific character. Early musicals, however, employed songs that could be passed from one character to another (and even one plot to another) with little loss of significance. The maturity of the genre was measured by its increasing reliance upon musical passages that would make little sense unless performed by a particular character in a particular situation.

For achieving such effects, the Berkeleyesque mode is greatly limited. Its operations work to elevate pattern over personality, and they depend upon a pronounced separation from the narrative on several levels. In terms of the evolutionary rhetoric of the integrated musical, the Berkeleyesque can be seen as something of a throwback to earlier, more aggregative stages in the genre's development.

However, in seeking to differentiate the Berkeleyesque mode from the integrated musical tradition, one should avoid overstating the case. The films still have access to a number of generalized strategies for relating the individual numbers to the larger context of the narrative. The musical numbers can highlight a general theme of special relevance to the story (e.g., the announcement in "We're in the Money" of the underlying link between money and sexual power that informs *Gold Diggers of 1933*). They can develop a powerful set of thematic and formal parallels with the other production numbers in the film, as is detailed in the discussion below of *Footlight Parade*. They can establish a tone that carries over to and colors the subsequent narrative scenes, as exemplified by the risqué "Pettin' in the Park" in *Gold Diggers of 1933*. They can provide a one-step-removed expression of a relationship in the narrative, achieved either through fictional surrogates played by the parties involved themselves (as when the resolution of the Dick Powell—Ruby Keeler romance is capped by the romantic maneuvers of their onstage personae for "The Words Are in My Heart" in *Gold Diggers of 1935*) or through entirely different parties (as when stars Howard Keel and Ann Blyth witness but do not participate in the erotic spectacle of "Totem Tom Tom" in *Rose Marie*). However, situations in which musical numbers provide a direct unmediated expression of the characters' feelings and actions in the narrative are confined to rare and minor occurrences in the most characteristic Berkeleyesque musicals (e.g., when Dick Powell sings "I've Got to Sing a Torch Song" to express his affection for Ruby Keeler in *Gold Diggers of 1933*). This relative poverty of plot function combined with the lavishness of the production numbers creates an imbalance in the narrative-based economy of classical cinema and thus contributes to the sense of ostentation and excess so central to Berkeleyesque spectacle.

A very simple instance is the length of the numbers—they go on too long in relation to whatever narrative function they might serve. "Lullaby of Broadway" consumes fourteen minutes of *Gold Diggers of 1935*'s total 95-minute running time, and its relationship to the main storyline is peripheral at best. Many of Berkeley's major numbers of the 1930s run in excess of ten minutes apiece. The extended length of these spectacle passages adds to their autonomous weight, and it also makes more feasible a certain type of structural complexity. Berkeley's major numbers of the thirties feature a series of bracketings—the creation of frames within frames within frames. This contributes to a sense of strongly demarcated microcosm, as the spectator is lead away from the narrative world into a realm of spectacle with its own laws and properties. Even Berkeley's most ambitious numbers of the 1950s generally run around half as long as their early thirties counterparts, and, as a result, their structures are much simpler and more monolithic. Although their physical properties are often as spectacular as those of the thirties numbers, they lack the room to develop the intricate structures of Berkeley's classic period and thus demonstrate the progressive attenuation of the Berkeleyesque in the course of Hollywood history.

In other respects, however, the Berkeleyesque is not attached to the type of self-contained complexity exemplified by the structures of his major numbers of the 1930s. Although Berkeley is popularly associated with lavishness and excess, it is important to note that the settings for his major numbers are often relatively simple and even minimalistic. In this respect, Berkeley's work departs from the plushness and clutter that characterize the otherwise influential Ziegfeldian stage tradition (and also many of the "Berkeleyesque" numbers staged by film choreographers other than Berkeley). Overly elaborate, concrete, and detailed settings tend to "ground" the numbers too much, inhibiting their flexibility, their suitability for rapid transformation, and their access to abstraction. A strongly defined proscenium is important at the outset of Berkeley's numbers in order to establish a sense of self-enclosure and separation from the outer world of the narrative. However, after this initial establishment, Berkeley's numbers tend to break down a sense of clearly defined dimensions, dissolving the boundaries and creating increasingly ambiguous and even void-like spaces (as found in the central sections of "I Only Have Eyes for You," "All's Fair in Love and War," the *Broadway Serenade* finale, etc.). Such nebulous locales drift easily into realms of abstraction, hyperfluid mutability, and detached formalism, which facilitate the spectacularization essential to the Berkeleyesque.

These and other related stylistic/structural issues are dealt with more specifically and extensively in the remainder of the book. In general, the Berkeleyesque was a somewhat specialized, inflexible, and even cumbersome mode. Its increasing archaism and its problematic relationship to the Hollywood mainstream made it especially dependent on the types of special contexts and conditions indicated above. The following treatment of Berkeley's film career traces what is, in varying degrees, a volatile interplay of tensions, gaps, and resistant factors, not all of which can be recuperated into an impression of artistic coherence.

6 EARLY PERIOD (1930–1933)

The Early Film Musical and the Berkeleyesque

While financial straits and changing tastes were causing the Tradition of Spectacle to decline on the Broadway stage, it was enjoying a vogue on the Hollywood screen. As a new and somewhat renegade genre in the American cinema, the musical developed vigorously and diversely. The years 1929–30 witnessed a rash of musical production unsurpassed in movie history. The nearly indiscriminate appropriation of musical material during these years included a number of pure, plotless revues (*The Show of Shows*, *The Hollywood Revue of 1929*, *King of Jazz*, etc.). There were also pioneer backstage movie musicals (such as *Glorifying the American Girl* and *The Broadway Melody*) that employed a revue as the show-within-the-show. As previously discussed, the revue is the stage form most receptive to Berkeleyesque spectacle, and several early musical films presented numbers closely approximating the stage spectacles that had characterized the Ziegfeldian/Hippodromean/Shubertian revue.

In addition, the conversion to sound in general created a

partial breach in Hollywood conventions that allowed for a greater degree of innovation and hybridization. Early sound films were apt to mix silent and talking passages, color and black-and-white images, raw documentary and flagrant theatricality, and other diverse elements in a manner more explicitly heterogeneous than normal in American movies. It is fitting that the musical film, the most inherently hybridized and heterogeneous of all Hollywood genres, entered the cinema at this point. The novelty value of sound produced a foregrounding—in some senses, a spectacularization—of film technique that deviated from the somewhat overstated ideal of "invisibility" (i.e., the subordination of film technique to narrative function) usually identified with American classical cinema. Also attached to the coming of sound was an increased influx of theatrical influences into American movies, involving personnel, subject matter, and entertainment forms. As noted above, these theatrical influences often drew upon the aggregate/spectacle tradition that formed the primary heritage of the Berkeleyesque. All these factors enabled an element of autonomous, weakly narrativized, and archaic theatrical spectacle to establish an unusually prominent if tenuous foothold in the American cinema.

The Cantor Comedies

When Berkeley entered the movies, the first flush of musical film production was already starting to come to an end. In 1931–32 there was a "crash" in the genre, with many productions being abandoned, truncated, or hastily converted into nonmusicals. The brief movie heyday of the plotless revue came to an end, never really to rise again. However, a haven for musical spectacle was provided by the continuing commercial viability of a certain subgenre of comedy—"comedian comedy" (as it was later called), featuring a comedian or comedy team with strong roots in the vaudeville/revue tradition (e.g., the Marx Brothers, Wheeler and Woolsey, Eddie Cantor) and employing a loose, semiabsurdist structure that easily allowed for the incursion of individual production numbers.

Berkeley's early work in Hollywood centered on his work as dance director in four musical comedies starring Eddie Cantor and produced by independent producer Samuel Goldwyn for United Artists. Also included in this early period were brief side trips to MGM (*Flying High*, 1931), Universal (*Night World*, 1932), Howard Hughes (*Sky Devils*, 1932), and RKO (*Bird of Paradise*, 1932).

The Cantor films are musical comedies with a decided emphasis on comedy over music. They are prime examples of the aforementioned subgenre that Steve Seidman has termed "comedian comedy." Seidman describes comedian comedies as films in which the personality of the star comedian–often strongly preestablished in another medium such as the stage, radio, or (later) television—supersedes the consistency of the fictional world. This produces frequent ruptures of that consistency in the form of asides and direct addresses to the camera, steppings in and out of character, references to the comedian's extra-fictional persona, flagrant violations of cause-and-effect logic, self-reflexive tropes, and absurdist, cartoonlike antirealism.[1]

This loosening of fictional and structural consistency creates a certain amount of overlap between the concerns of comedian comedy and those of the musical genre, Berkeleyesque spectacle, and the aggregate/revue tradition (like many preradio comics, Cantor established his reputation largely in vaudeville and revues). As a result, the Cantor films provided enough of a nonintegrative framework to allow Berkeley the discursive latitude to inject "extraneous" and abstract visual effects (such as overhead kaleidoscopic shots, beauty-parade closeups, white-and-black patterning, and through-the-legs tracking shots: see photo 19), to begin opening up realistic narrative space into antirealistic spectacle space, to develop erotic motifs, and to establish structures of segregation (sexual, narrative, spatial) congenial to the enlargement of Berkeleyesque spectacle.

However, the numbers in the Goldwyn/Cantor films are still on a scale commensurate to a theatrical stage, and they are still consistent in terms of themselves. There are no confounding shifts of scale, no trick cuts and magical transitions, no surreal visual effects, and only a few, limited spectacularizations of the camera. In short, there is none of the free indulgence of "impossibility" that marks the full expression of the Berkeleyesque.

Whoopee! (1930)

Whoopee! (directed by Thornton Freeland), Berkeley's first film as a dance director, is a retailored version of Florenz Ziegfeld's successful 1928 stage production.[2] Conceived as an Eddie Cantor vehicle, this loosely plotted musical comedy takes place in a not-so-wild West of dude ranchers and tourist-shop Indians. The entire film, except for a few inserted scenic long shots, is confined to studio sets. The overall effect is extremely and homogeneously stagebound, diminishing the potential separation of narrative discourse and performance discourse that enhances the Berkeleyesque mode.

Several of the song numbers ("Making Whoopee," "My Baby Just Cares for Me," "A Girlfriend of a Boyfriend of Mine") are solo comic specialties by Cantor. Three chorus numbers qualify as rudimentary Berkeleyesque spectacles, and these are spaced throughout the film: "Cowboy Number" at the beginning, "Stetson" around the middle, and "The Song of the Setting Sun" near the end. For the most part, the spectacle aspects of these numbers are circumscribed in terms of both scale and concept. There is nothing in them that could not be comfortably accommodated on a normal theatrical stage (even though the story has no backstage elements that would anchor it to a theatrical setting), and none of them is partitioned off into a formal stage environment.

Whoopee! marks Berkeley's first uses of some of the specifically cinematic effects with which he would later be strongly identified, even though he did not necessarily originate them. "Cowboy Number" marks Berkeley's first use of an overhead pattern, with ten-gallon hats contributing strongly to the geometry—an effect augmented with war bonnets in the even more vividly kaleidoscopic patterns of "The Song of the Setting Sun" (see photo 20). "Stetson" contains Berkeley's first "parade of faces" effect, with the chorus girls advancing in sequence toward the camera, each one raising a hat to reveal her face as she passes by. The beauty-parade roots of this device are made explicit in the finale's literal parade of "Indian maidens" on horseback, each in turn parting her robe to reveal a skimpy but ornate outfit underneath. "Stetson" also contains Berkeley's first use of a priapic tracking shot through the spread legs of the chorus—an effect he would use more emphatically in "Young and Healthy" (*42nd Street*) and "Dames." The choreography of *Whoopee!*'s dance numbers is fairly rudimentary; in a manner already characteristic of this avowedly visually oriented choreographer, there is as much emphasis on headgear (cowboy hats, war bonnets) and hand/arm maneuvers as there is on footwork in the chorus effects (see photo 21).

Whoopee! immediately and explicitly established the connection between Berkeley's film work and the Ziegfeldian stage tradition. The nature of this connection and the ways in which it could be extended in a cinematic direction are laid out in a lucid, even schematic fashion. This gives *Whoopee!* considerable charm as a museum-piece; however, the subsequent Goldwyn/Cantor/Berkeley vehicles, though not as well known or as influential in their impact, actually develop these Berkeleyesque concepts more thoroughly and extensively.

Palmy Days (1931)

Palmy Days (directed by Edward Sutherland), another Eddie Cantor comedy produced by Samuel Goldwyn, is slightly more ambitious in its creation of musical spectacle than *Whoopee!* had been. The three Berkeleyesque production numbers bookend the narrative, with the bakery prologue and the gymnasium number ("Bend Down Sister") coming back-to-back at the beginning of the film, and "My Honey Said Yes, Yes" located right before the final plot resolution.[3]

The main locale of the action is a bakery, entirely staffed by comely bakerettes who also constitute the film's chorus line. The mechanistic precision and cookie-cutter interchangeability of the traditional chorus line are satirized here in the explicit parallel drawn between the girls and the product they manufacture on the assembly line. (See photo 22.) Their bakery's motto is "Glorifying the American Donut"—a play on the "Glorifying the American Girl" motto of the

Ziegfeld Follies. In order to keep in shape for their baking chores, the chorus repair frequently to the in-house gymnasium, which provides the theme for "Bend Down Sister." This athletic spectacle features synchronized calisthenics and high-angle shots that utilize the chorus's exercise-sticks to form diaphragm-like patterns and, at the number's end, a loose representation of a galley being "rowed" across the floor (see photo 23).

The final "My Honey Said Yes, Yes" number—the only one in the film with a formal audience and designated stage-space—is set at the bakery boss's mansion. It involves Cantor and the chorus, the latter manipulating hatbox-sized discs, black on one side and white on the other, to form extremely abstract overhead patterns. At the end of the number, the chorus combines two-dimensional cutout sections to form a Niagara-bound Pullman car (intimations of "Shuffle off to Buffalo" and "Honeymoon Hotel"). This marks Berkeley's first use in a film of the "jigsaw-puzzle" effect in which the chorus becomes pieces in the formation of a transcendent representational image, as in "Shanghai Lil" (the American flag and FDR's face) and "I Only Have Eyes for You" (Ruby Keeler's inescapable face). Stars Cantor and Charlotte Greenwood bring up the rear of the train, their heads poking through holes in bride-and-groom drawings of the type used in novelty photographs. Seen here is Berkeley's first play on shifting the image back and forth between two-and three-dimensionality, an effect that will be developed much more elaborately in "Shanghai Lil," "I Only Have Eyes for You," and "Dames."

Although *Palmy Days* (like the other Cantor musicals) contains virtually nothing of a backstage structure, it does begin to articulate some of the principles of "segregation" that are at the heart of the Berkeleyesque musical. The production numbers in *Palmy Days*, although not segregated from the body of the film on a stage/offstage axis, are nevertheless segregated on three other mutually reinforcing levels: (1) sexual, (2) spatial, and (3) narrative.[4]

1. *Sexual:* With a single exception (noted below), the production numbers involve only women and/or take place in all-female environments. The bakery, quite fancifully, is staffed only by female employees. The gymnasium is off-limits to men. The final number involves the all-female chorus, comedienne Charlotte Greenwood, and (the lone male exception) Eddie Cantor.

2. *Spatial:* The feminized environment of each of the production numbers is given a self-enclosed, detached spatial locus: the bakery, the gymnasium, the stagelike area of the final number. In each case, an actual physical barrier underscores the idea of spatial separation: the vestibule separating the kitchen in the back of the bakery from the tea shop in front; the glass doors enclosing the gymnasium; the moatlike pool in front of the space of the final number.

3. *Narrative:* The Berkeleyesque production numbers do not involve the main functionaries of the plot

(again, with the exception of Cantor in "My Honey Said Yes, Yes"): ingenue Joan Clark, male romantic lead Paul Page, villains Charles Middleton and George Raft, father Spencer Charters, etc. The production numbers have no bearing whatsoever on the development of the narrative. From the standpoint of the narrative, the Berkeleyesque production numbers are almost completely gratuitous. They have only the most tenuous relationship—spatially, stylistically, and narratively—to the rest of the film. Collectively, they nudge the whole production closer to the revue side of the musical spectrum.

The Kid from Spain (1932)

The use of feminized environments that characterizes the bakery shop production numbers of *Palmy Days* is carried over into the next Goldwyn/Cantor/Berkeley musical, *The Kid from Spain* (directed by Leo McCarey). Its opening number, "The College Song," lovingly describes the rising, bathing, and dressing rituals of the inhabitants of a girls' college dormitory (played by the Goldwyn Girls chorus: see photo 24). This type of demarcation of an all-female space could be called the "seraglio effect." It recurs in later Berkeley numbers that create, in whole or in part, voyeuristic, "no-men-allowed" areas that can be penetrated only by the viewer's gaze or, occasionally, by the lecherous "baby" played by Billy Barty: "Pettin' in the Park," "The Shadow Waltz," "Honeymoon Hotel," "By a Waterfall," "I Only Have Eyes for You," "Dames," "The Words Are in My Heart," "All's Fair in Love and War."

On a broader level, the "seraglio effect" extends the strongly segregative configuration of the Berkeleyesque musical to a sexual dimension. In other words, just as the backstage world is separated from the non-showbiz "civilian" world in the classic Warner Bros./Berkeley musicals, and just as the spectacle is separated from the narrative on both a spatial and discursive level, so is a unisexual female world often separated from both a male world and a male-female world. This separation, it should be noted, heightens rather than diminishes the eroticism of the numbers, by virtue both of its relationship to the barrier essential to voyeuristic spectacle, and of the playfully titillating manner with which this separation is usually treated. This occurs most overtly in "Dames" (where dames in dishabille coyly thrust powder puffs and perfume spray at the nosy camera) and "All's Fair in Love and War" (where males and females are divided into entrenched but hardly hostile "armies").

"The College Song" is the pre-*42nd Street* Berkeley number that is richest in nascent Berkeleyesque film effects: girls undressing in silhouette behind screens, long lists of beautiful faces, recitative delivery of lyrics, space expanding fluidly and antirealistically. The coeds' morning dip into the swimming pool, complete with overhead patterns, represents the first of Berkeley's filmed water spectacles, later to be expanded in

"By a Waterfall" and the Esther Williams aquacades of *Million Dollar Mermaid* (1952) and *Easy to Love* (1953).

The Kid from Spain's only other excursion into the Berkeleyesque, "What a Perfect Combination," is a less ambitious number, set in an elegant Mexican cafe, with Cantor in blackface performing amid the Goldwyn Girls chorus. The chorus girls are fitted out in lacy black-or-white Latin-style outfits (including some of the tightest trousers in movie history) and flat, wide-brimmed hats. Among the patterns formed by the chorus are circular arrangements that implicitly evoke, on a giganticized scale, the hats they are wearing (see photo 25). As usual, Berkeley manages to come up with inventive variations on his basic overhead-shot device, this time by having the girls remove their hats to reveal blackfaces painted on the tops of their heads and mirroring the blackfaced Cantor standing in their center. The number ends with a "jigsaw puzzle" effect, the girls coming together to form a giant mock-up of a bull's head, which segues into the film's climactic slapstick bullfight.

Roman Scandals (1933)

Roman Scandals (directed by Frank Tuttle), the last of the Goldwyn/Cantor/Berkeley collaborations, was actually made after Berkeley's transfer to Warner Bros., in settlement of his remaining contractual obligations to Goldwyn. As such, it represents something of a throwback in the development of his style. The three spectacle-oriented numbers are spaced throughout the film, without any backstage connections. Despite the provocativeness of their initial concepts, these numbers seem restrained in comparison to the peak Warners work being done by Berkeley at this time. This momentary attenuation of Berkeley's style in the midst of its heyday at Warner Bros. indicates (much as his move from MGM to Fox would do in the early 1940s) that the flourishing of the Berkeleyesque was far more dependent on objective production conditions than on subjective factors such as inspiration, personal decline, etc.

"No More Love" is the most famous of Berkeley's Goldwyn numbers, thanks mainly to the kinky nature of the subject matter and the now-legendary tale (spread by Berkeley in numerous interviews) of how several of the chorus girls were clad only in their long blonde wigs.[5] The three-tiered, wedding-cake-like circular structure on and around which the number takes place is strongly in the *Ziegfeld Follies/Earl Carroll Vanities* theatrical mode. The number remains rooted to this setting throughout, without any of the startling expansions and elaborations of space that characterize Berkeley's big Warner Bros. numbers of this period.

With its chained girls, forced striptease, whip-wielding slave-dealer, and fat, leering bidder, the voyeuristic spectacle here is more explicitly aggressive-sadistic than is usual for Berkeley (see photo 26), who normally leans more toward what Laura Mulvey terms "fetishistic scopophilia." In keeping with the sadistic scenario, the number is marked by an increased degree of narrativization.[6] Unlike other Berkeley spectacles in the Goldwyn films, it is strongly related to the dilemma of a character in the main body of the narrative: Olga (Ruth Etting), the emperor's former favorite, has been deposed and sent to the slave market, moving her to sing "the woman's cry of despair." "No More Love" also has a more sustained *dramatic* (as opposed to spectacular) impact than any other Berkeley number before "Lullaby of Broadway," whose death-plunge-and-final-lament ending it anticipates. However, "Lullaby of Broadway" has a much more adventurous spectacular dimension to accompany its dramatic dimension, which is partly why it is one of Berkeley's greatest numbers, and "No More Love" a relatively minor one.

The last spectacle in *Roman Scandals*, "Keep Young and Beautiful," is a prime example of the "seraglio effect." The number features a blackfaced Cantor at loose in the women's bathhouse, where Roman beauties are glimpsed receiving massages, applying make-up, fixing their hair, etc. Berkeley's penchant for rendering the chorus into white-and-black patterns was demonstrated previously in the black- and white-sided disks wielded by the chorus in *Palmy Days*'s "My Honey Said Yes, Yes," in the black-or-white outfitted señoritas in *The Kid From Spain*'s "What a Perfect Combination," and in the alternating blonde and brunette groups of slave girls in "No More Love." The effect is intensified in "Keep Young and Beautiful," whose visual design is centered on the contrast between the white-skinned bathers and their black-skinned female attendants. These white-and-black patternings are related to a drive toward abstraction that is a central element of the Berkeleyesque and receives its most extreme payoffs in the climactic sections of "By a Waterfall," "Dames," and "The Polka Dot Polka/A Journey to a Star" (*The Gang's All Here*).

In general, Berkeley's Goldwyn period is characterized by tentative experiments in the assertion of Berkeleyesque devices and their adaptation to cinematic contexts. These early efforts contain lively but still rudimentary flashes of the audacious, paradoxical tropes that mark Berkeley's great Warner Bros. numbers. The Goldwyn/Cantor films provided an amenable though not optimal framework for the development of the Berkeleyesque in Berkeley's early films—far more amenable than the operettas and musical comedies that formed the bulk of his early stage career, but not as amenable as the classic Warner Bros. musicals of the mid-1930s. Unlike the latter, the Cantor films do not use the backstage format to a significant degree. They employ the more familiar structure of interspersing numbers throughout narrative situations, rather than grouping them together in a self-enclosed show at the end. These films can be seen as experimental precursors to the full flowering of the Berkeleyesque that would take place in the classic Warner Bros. musicals.

It is important to note that Berkeley was not responsible for introducing the "Berkeleyesque" mode to the screen; instead, his early film work resumed his alliance with a strongly established stage tradition, an alliance that had been initiated in the latter part of his Broadway career. This tradition was being assimilated into Hollywood movies well before Berkeley's arrival. Its assimilation involved not just the transposition of stage elements but also the evolution of cinematic equivalents for them—a development popularly credited to Berkeley but one that was already well on its way before his flamboyant appropriation of it caused it to be popularly linked with his name. For example, the overhead kaleidoscopic pattern, perhaps the most familiar of all Berkeleyesque film devices, appears in movie musicals almost immediately, in such 1929 productions as *The Cocoanuts*, *The Hollywood Revue of 1929*, and *Happy Days*. Just as he had on the Broadway stage, Berkeley extended rather than initiated a tradition of musical spectacle. However, on stage this tradition was long established, even approaching exhaustion, while in film it was still nascent and inchoate. Much as Ziegfeld had become identified with the already developing American spectacular (henceforth Ziegfeldian) revue in the early 1900s, Berkeley was positioned to become identified with the Hollywood spectacular (henceforth Berkeleyesque) production number in the early 1930s. The particular format of the Warner Bros. backstage musical would enable him to seize that opportunity.

7

Classic Warner Bros. Period (1933–1934)

Advantages of the Warner Bros. Musical

The classic Warner Bros. period represents the pinnacle of the Berkeleyesque in cinema. Although other factors (Depression sociology, early New Deal ideology, pre-Code screen morality, etc.) were undoubtedly important, the key determining factor was the prevailing form of the Warner Bros. musical at this time. Warners musicals of the early thirties featured the following aspects of special congeniality to the Berkeleyesque mode:

1. *The Backstage Format:* This format (described in chapter 2) allows for maximum isolation of musical spectacle within a narrative framework. It constitutes a distinct alternative to more integration-oriented formats also popular in the period, such as the screen operetta identified with Ernst Lubitsch, Rouben Mamoulian, Maurice Chevalier, Jeanette MacDonald, etc., or the homogeneously glitzy Astaire/Sandrich mode that was just coming into its own in films such as *Melody Cruise* (1933), *Flying Down to Rio* (1933), and *The Gay Divorcee* (1934).

2. *Urban Realism:* In the early 1930s Warner Bros. was producing a number of films noted for their relatively gritty urban realism (*Little Caesar*, *The Public Enemy*, *I Am a Fugitive from a Chain Gang*, *Employees Entrance*, *Blessed Event*, etc.). In the studio's musicals of the period, this aspect served to enhance the self-enclosed separation and heterogeneity of Berkeleyesque spectacle, as the opulent production numbers seemed to exist in another realm from the proletarian, wolf-at-the-door world of the narrative, especially in *42nd Street*, *Gold Diggers of 1933*, and *Footlight Parade*.

3. *Less Dominant Stars:* Except for the rapidly fading Al Jolson (who starred in *Wonder Bar*, a minor Berkeley-choreographed musical of the period), Warners in the mid-1930s did not have any high-powered musical superstars on the order of Fred Astaire, Maurice Chevalier, Eddie Cantor, Mae West, Shirley Temple, Bing Crosby, etc. As a result, the Warners/Berkeley musicals were relieved of some of the necessity of being star vehicles. Rather than being delimited by the egos and preexisting personae of celebrated performers, Berkeley's numbers were given increased latitude to elevate spectacle over personality. In contrast to Berkeley's later work at MGM, his musical numbers of this period were largely built around pleasant but low-key (and presumably more malleable) performers like Dick Powell, Ruby Keeler, Joan Blondell, Wini Shaw, and a pre-Astaire Ginger Rogers. (See photo 27.) The one major exception is James Cagney's memorably dynamic performance in *Footlight Parade* (including the Berkeley number "Shanghai Lil"). However, because Cagney had never appeared in a screen musical before, he brought no strong pre-established *musical* persona to the film (his spirited Oscar-winning performance in *Yankee Doodle Dandy* was some nine years in the future); thus, Cagney here blended quite well into the Berkeleyesque universe.

4. *Stacking: 42nd Street* inaugurated the Warners/Berkeley practice of stacking all or most of the big musical numbers at the end of the film, rather than spacing them out more proportionately throughout the narrative (as had been done in the Goldwyn/Cantor films). In *42nd Street*, one full number ("You're Getting To Be a Habit with Me") is performed in rehearsal about midway through the film. The three major numbers—"Shuffle Off to Buffalo," "Young and Healthy," and "42nd Street"—come one after another at the climax of the film, leaving room only for a brief but punchy plot coda.

Gold Diggers of 1933 opens with an in-rehearsal number, "We're in the Money," and places "Pettin' in the Park" halfway through the film. It unloads its two most spectacular numbers, "The Shadow Waltz" and "Remember My Forgotten Man," back-to-back at the end, dispensing altogether with any postshow plot wrap-up.

Footlight Parade presents the purest of these stacking arrangements. A truncated rehearsal number

("Sitting on a Backyard Fence") occurs midway through. Then three large-scale production numbers ("Honeymoon Hotel," "By a Waterfall," "Shanghai Lil") are presented consecutively at the end, leaving just enough room for a breathless afterthought of a reconciliation between Cagney and Blondell as the curtain is coming down and the film is fading out.

Dames, a transitional film that is starting to slip out of the classic backstage format, spreads out its numbers more evenly. However, its two biggest ("I Only Have Eyes for You" and "Dames") are saved for a double-wallop in the late stages of the film.

The general effect of these stacking arrangements is to inhibit the interpenetration of narrative and spectacle. The big musical numbers, stacked together at the end of the film, coalesce into a semiautonomous bloc that overbalances the narrative and separates out from it to a significant extent.[1]

For the sake of contrast, consider the typical structure of the RKO/Astaire films, particularly those directed by Mark Sandrich. Before shooting these films, Sandrich would plot them out on flow charts that meticulously broke down the continuity in terms of locale, night/day, music/dialogue, and singing/dancing, resulting in a kind of macro-rhythmic alternating pattern.[2] The RKO/Astaire musical takes the shape of a vast checkerboard design, the numbers interlaced with the narrative. In the classic Warner Bros./Berkeley musical, the form taken is more like a wave, in which the climactic spectacle breaks away from and virtually engulfs the narrative resolution.

42nd Street (1933)

42nd Street (directed by Lloyd Bacon) is the first of Berkeley's films to employ a full backstage structure; however, in terms of the Berkeleyesque, it does not take maximum advantage of the situation. Snatches of upcoming musical numbers (especially "42nd Street") are heard in rehearsal in the early stages of the film, and one entire number ("You're Getting to Be a Habit with Me") is performed on a bare rehearsal stage. But these serve only as appetizers for the three big numbers stacked together at the end of the film.

The scale and spectacle of these final numbers are relatively restrained and stagebound. With the exceptions of the overhead patterns in "Young and Healthy" and the trick cut that moves tap-dancing Ruby Keeler from the apron of the stage to the roof of a taxicab in "42nd Street," there is little in the film's numbers that could not be presented within the confines of a realistic theatrical stage (although the dimensions of the set in "42nd Street" might stretch credibility to the utmost).

The clever effects of "Shuffle Off to Buffalo" are conceived in terms of the limitations of the stage, with the Pullman car splitting open to reveal its cross-sectioned interior (see photo 28). By 1934–35, Berkeley would probably have used a camera movement or a cut (as he did in the subway scenes of "I Only Have Eyes for You" and "Lullaby of Broadway") in order to move the camera to a viewpoint inside the train (and presumably inaccessible to the stage audience).

"Young and Healthy" is built primarily on cinematic effects (overhead shots, a through-the-legs tracking shot, the use of the frameline to conceal the chorus behind Dick Powell and his costar after they kiss), but the staging of the number itself is clearly within possible stage dimensions. (See photo 29.) As in "Shuffle Off to Buffalo," a scene shift is handled via a theatrical rather than a cinematic device: a prop bench sinks below the floor and becomes part of a revolving platform.

"42nd Street"

It is the climactic "42nd Street" number that begins most notably to strain against the confines of realistic stage address, as in the trick cut to the taxicab roof and in the exploration of a detailed and continually expanding stage space established initially via a simple backdrop. The most important developments for Berkeley in his numbers for *42nd Street* are in the areas of pacing and compression. The tightness and fluidity of the camerawork are far in advance of anything he had attempted before. This is especially true of the "42nd Street" number, in which fast, sweeping crane shots pick out a rapid-fire series of brief vignettes depicting life on the "naughty, bawdy" street. This enhancement of speed and fluidity sets up some dazzling, dizzying transitions of the type that would become a hallmark of Berkeley's film style, notably:

1. The breathtaking shift in tone when the woman is stabbed and the camera immediately swoops up to a second-story window from which debonair playboy Dick Powell looks down, singing nonchalantly while his valet mixes a cocktail in the background (a detail unlikely to be visible to a stage audience);
2. The shift from three-dimensional to two-dimensional space when the chorus holds up cutouts to form the skyline of Manhattan (see photo 30);
3. The shift in perspective when the camera, moving horizontally across the stage floor, appears to be looking up at Keeler and Powell as they kiss on "top" of an elongated skyscraper;
4. The shift in scale when Powell pulls down a miniature asbestos curtain that fills the frame and ends the number.

It should be noted that the skyscraper effect is essentially a theatrical one. In fact, virtually the same effect was employed in the stage show *George White's Scandals of 1929*.[3] In the same vein, the series of dizzying shifts of perspective and scale that climax the number are based mainly on the clever manipulation of space within a confined area, rather than on the type of hyperbolically expansive space that characterizes the later Berkeley manner.

Lloyd Bacon

Mervyn LeRoy was originally assigned to direct the narrative portions of *42nd Street*, but illness forced him to withdraw in favor of Lloyd Bacon.[4] This circumstance was probably a beneficial one for the overall shape of the film. It is noteworthy that, of the classic Warners/Berkeley musicals, the two directed by Bacon (*42nd Street* and *Footlight Parade*) are clearly those with the least insipid narratives. Although a less ambitious director than LeRoy, Bacon had a superior sense of pacing. The narrative scenes maintain a drive and overall punchiness that prevent them from being overwhelmed by the big Berkeley numbers at the end (the same cannot be said for the LeRoy-directed *Gold Diggers of 1933*). While the sketchy plot resolutions of the other Warner Bros. musicals are almost totally eclipsed by Berkeley's spectacular musical finales, *42nd Street* has enough dramatic thunder left at the end to counter the Berkeleyesque fireworks of "42nd Street" with the powerful epilogue of manic-depressive director Julian Marsh (Warner Baxter) sitting alone, exhausted, and unappreciated in the alley outside the theater where his show has just succeeded so gloriously.

In general, *42nd Street* has the strongest, most serious plot and performances of any of the early thirties Warner Bros. musicals. The relative strength of the narrative passages and the relative restraint of the musical numbers (relative, that is, to the types of spectaculars Berkeley would be pulling off in his next few films) make this the most "integrated" of the Warners/Berkeley musicals. However, the concept of integration here applies not in the sense of the musical numbers expressing plot and character, but in the sense of the musical numbers being similar in tone and scale to the narrative and therefore not standing out from it so obtrusively. This is a good part of the reason *42nd Street* stands high in the integration-inclined canon of classic musicals, but not as high in the ranks of full-fledged, hyperspectacularized Berkeleyesque cinema.

Gold Diggers of 1933 (1933)

Gold Diggers of 1933 (directed by Mervyn LeRoy), the second entry in the series of classic Warners/Berkeley backstage musicals, represents a further development from the relatively restrained explorations of the Goldwyn/Cantor films and *42nd Street* toward the fully developed spectacular style of "By a Waterfall," "I Only Have Eyes for You," "Dames," and "Lullaby of Broadway." All of the numbers in *Gold Diggers of 1933* are in the realistically motivated performance mode. Two, occurring back-to-back early in the film, are at-home demonstrations of tunes fresh from the pen of budding songwriter Dick Powell. The first of these ("The Shadow Waltz") is directed at the pretty showgirl (Ruby Keeler) who lives across the way. The second ("I've Got to Sing a Torch Song") is performed for the benefit of Broadway producer Ned Sparks, with Keeler lovingly looking on from the sidelines. The other four numbers (that is, the ones staged by Berkeley) all take place on the stage, according to the classic backstage formula.

However, *Gold Diggers of 1933* also represents a tentative first attempt in the Warners/Berkeley musicals to relate the world of performance and spectacle more meaningfully to the surrounding world of the narrative. Although it would be going much too far to imply that the Berkeley-directed onstage numbers here are intertwined with the narrative in the manner of an integration-oriented musical, there is still a certain degree of correspondence between numbers and narrative on a generalized, thematic level.

Unlike any of the other classic Warners/Berkeley musicals, *Gold Diggers of 1933* begins directly with a production number, "We're in the Money" (aka "The Gold Diggers' Song"). With its giant coins and dollar signs, and its chorines dressed in little but a few strategically placed coins, "We're in the Money" serves to announce the central themes of the ensuing narrative: the overriding importance of money in the Depression milieu and the strong links between money and sexuality. (See photo 32.) At the end of the number, the lawmen strip the coins off the cowering, seminude chorus girls, effecting an equation between loss of economic power and loss of sexual power. This is a theme that will be expanded in the "Remember My Forgotten Man" finale.

"We're in the Money" moves in the direction of continuously increasing contextualization. It begins with a close shot of singer Ginger Rogers, then gradually expands to include the other chorines, the set, the entire stage, and the interior of the theater. The number climaxes with the irruption of the sheriff's deputies from the alley outside to close down the show for nonpayment of debts. The effect is of the Depression literally forcing its way into the opulent insularity of the Berkeleyesque production number. In a final twist, the brash confidence of the song ("And when we see the landlord, we can look that guy right in the eye!") segues into the Depression realities of the next scene, which opens with a Rent Overdue notice being slipped under the chorus girls' apartment door.

As in *42nd Street*, *Footlight Parade*, and *Dames*, the last three (and biggest) numbers of *Gold Diggers of 1933* are part of the pivotal show-within-the-show. But *Gold Diggers of 1933* works a major variation on the standard "stacking" arrangement by pushing up the first of these big numbers ("Pettin' in the Park") to a position about midway through the film. As a result of this maneuver, "Pettin' in the Park"—one of Berkeley's most risqué numbers—serves to set a naughty, flippant tone for the ensuing portion of the narrative, which concerns the cynical efforts of showgirls Joan Blondell and Aline MacMahon to seduce, extort, and generally lead around by their noses the two wealthy stuffed-shirts played by Warren William and Guy Kibbee.

As the first half of the climactic show, the elegant, romantic "The Shadow Waltz," serves to underscore the narrative-side romance of Keeler and Powell, who play the lovers in the number also. This association is strengthened by the fact that "The Shadow Waltz" was previously used in the narrative as part of Powell's romantic artillery for wooing Keeler.

After a brief backstage plot wrap-up, the final number, "Remember My Forgotten Man," sums up the film as a whole. It encapsulates the story's Depression milieu (as previously described by producer Sparks, "Yes, that's what this show's about—the Depression . . . . Men marching, marching . . . The Big Parade of tears. . . . Jobs, jobs . . ."). It also climaxes the film's thematic equation of sexual and economic power, which is established in the opening "We're in the Money" number, permeates the whole of the narrative, and then is applied in this finale to the male side of the ledger, where joblessness is linked with a loss of sexual potency.

Deprived Women, Forgotten Men

The production numbers in *Gold Diggers of 1933* contain some of Berkeley's boldest ventures in creating purely cinematic effects, but at the same time they remain very strongly attached to motifs and devices steeped in the tradition of the spectacle stage. In fact, these numbers exemplify a general characteristic of Berkeleyesque cinema that corresponds to the *additive* principle of the aggregate/spectacle tradition. Spectacularization of the camera does not supplant or diminish theatricalized spectacle (as is often implied by film historians and by Berkeley himself in interviews) but is simply (or complexly) *superadded* to it. It is wholly in the nature of the aggregate/spectacle tradition to leave nothing out, no matter how apparently contradictory or superfluous. Paraphrasing Freud's famous statement on dreams, one could say that there is no "no" in full-scale Berkeleyesque spectacle.

"We're in the Money"

The opening "We're in the Money" number is the one with the most direct relation to theatrical traditions and techniques. Indeed, the number is marked by an archly old-fashioned staginess in many of its devices. Gigantic coins dominate the background. A twin-doored entranceway is emblazoned with an oversized dollar-sign, beneath which enter a double row of chorus girls. Coin-draped outfits and oversized coins are sported by the chorines themselves (as noted previously, Berkeley's film numbers are rarely so blatantly and directly metaphorical in their imagery). In terms of scale, the number is entirely stage-possible. The purely cinematic effects are largely confined to the margins: the blurry focus-change as Ginger Rogers renders the song in pig-Latin, and the restricted framings that make possible the gradual expansion of the number as well as the trick effect in which Rogers appears at both the front and rear of a line of chorines.

"Pettin' in the Park"

"Pettin' in the Park"—a lively, racy number in the vein of "Shuffle Off to Buffalo" (*42nd Street*) and "Honeymoon Hotel" (*Footlight Parade*)—is relatively restrained in scale. Its largest-scaled effects involve the ranks of roller-skating girls and policemen near the beginning (see photo 31), the overhead patterns (embellished by the manipulation of beachball-sized globes) in the wintertime section, and the climactic display of rain-soaked chorus girls disrobing in silhouette inside a double-tiered bank of dressing cubicles.

Like several other Berkeley numbers from this period, "Pettin' in the Park" opens in a deliberately restricted, shallow setting—in this case, Powell and Keeler singing by a prop bench in front of a curtain. It then expands into a space that becomes increasingly difficult to comprehend (although not yet blatantly confounding) in terms of realistic stage dimensions.

The number's most striking cine-spectacular effects are reserved for transitions in time and space. The main section of the number is opened up by a dissolve from the monkeys pictured on Keeler's Animal Crackers box to live monkeys in the park zoo. Another dissolve transforms the autumnal park setting into a wintry landscape filled with snowball-flinging chorus girls. A ball rolls into the foreground of the wintertime scene, covering the camera lens, then bounces back to reveal a grassy springscape filled with necking couples. (See photo 33.)

"The Shadow Waltz"

"The Shadow Waltz" is a number in the elegant, abstract, black-polished-floor mode also represented by "Young and Healthy," "Don't Say Goodnight" (*Wonder Bar*), and "The Words Are in My Heart." The main ingredients of "The Shadow Waltz" relate clearly to established spectacle-stage traditions involving musical instruments (sixty chorus girls playing violins), radium/luminescent numbers (the lights go down, and the violins are outlined in neon), and gigantism/representational patterns (the neonized violins form into the pattern of a giant violin, "played" by a giant neon bow).[5]

The number is built—although not overinsistently—around a floral motif. The prologue ends with a tracking shot into a close-up of a white flower held by Ruby Keeler. This blossom is echoed in the wide, hooped skirts of the chorus, which evoke a floral form without literally representing a flower. The motif is extended in the petal-like shapes of the overhead kaleidoscope patterns and is more loosely associated with the large, curvilinear staircase structure on which the central section of the number is set. (See photos 34 and 35.)

Spectacularized camera effects include the magically dissolved-in appearance of four violin-girls at the beginning of the number. An extremely confounding, disorienting effect occurs when the image is turned on its side and the chorus, symmetrically paired with their reflections, swirl "down" the frame. In a final, lyrical effect, Powell and Keeler are seen reflected in a pool. As they kiss, the flower held by Keeler drops into the water, dissolving the image into a pattern of liquid ripples.

"Remember My Forgotten Man"

Even more than "We're in the Money," the climactic "Remember My Forgotten Man" number (with its explicit tie-in to the recent Bonus March of Summer, 1932) evokes the tradition of topicality that was closely associated with the stage revue form from its earliest days. In fact, "Remember My Forgotten Man" stands as one of Hollywood's most hard-hitting political statements of the 1930s, surpassed only by *I Am a Fugitive from a Chain Gang* (Warner Bros., 1932). Berkeley modulates his style effectively to suit the occasion. Distinguished by its economy as much as by its spectacle, "Remember My Forgotten Man" is the most straightforward of the big numbers in the classic Warners/Berkeley musicals. Its directness is a consequence of its political commitment.

The number begins on a stark street-corner set. Lead singer Joan Blondell walks over to a bum, lights her cigarette from his butt, and gives him the fresh cigarette. Wistfully caressing a lamp post, she sings in recitative, "You sent him far away./You shouted hip-hooray./But look at him today . . ." Blondell's lament, soon seconded by women of various races and ages, is twofold. She wants two things: a job *for* her man and love *from* her man. The latter is dependent on the former: "And once he used to love me,/I was happy then. /Won't you bring him back again?/For ever since the world began,/A woman needs a man./Forgetting him, you see,/Means you're forgetting me."

Picking up the thread established in "We're in the Money," the number is based on an equation between economics and sex, a confluence of the social and psychological levels. For working men in the Depression, the loss of their jobs or the decrease in their earning power represented a loss of masculine pride—a form of impotence.[6] What Blondell and the other women in the number are saying is: Because my man can't get a job, he has lost his virility—he can't love me the way he used to.

After this downbeat introduction, the number suddenly opens up to a flashback of men marching off to war, erect, proud, *employed*—images of virility. Blackout: the screen parts to show the soldiers trudging back from battle, wounded, bleeding, sagging—images of castration. Blackout: the screen parts again, this time to reveal a line of unemployed men in a soup kitchen. A series of sliding associations has been made: War/Castration/Depression.

The number's only large-scale spectacular effect is the grand tableau at the end, which depicts men of the Depression kneeling before images of their past glory, in the form of a three-tiered, semicircular display of marching soldiers (see photo 36). Most of the hyperbolic effect of "Remember My Forgotten Man" is invested in its intensified pacing, which vigorously moves the central section of the number from setting to setting via the series of brilliantly judged blackouts that drive home the number's thematic connections. Although it employs elements of spectacle, "Remember My Forgotten Man" also demonstrates Berkeley's ability to modify his spectacle style in order to intensify the impact of one of his simplest and most powerful numbers.

Footlight Parade (1933)

After working on *Roman Scandals* to fulfill his Goldwyn obligation, Berkeley returned to Warner Bros. for *Footlight Parade* (directed by Lloyd Bacon), the greatest of the Warners/Berkeley backstage musicals. (See photo 37.) There may be better individual numbers in other films ("I Only Have Eyes for You" in *Dames*, "Lullaby of Broadway" in *Gold Diggers of 1935*), and *42nd Street* may have a stronger narrative, but *Footlight Parade* attains the highest simultaneous quality of both numbers and narrative. It features three top Berkeley numbers (two of them—"By a Waterfall" and "Shanghai Lil"—ranking among his greatest spectacles) and a fast-moving, entertaining plot graced with a dynamic James Cagney performance.

Under Lloyd Bacon's direction, the pacing of the narrative is admirably sustained over a panoramic series of brief, snappy scenes keyed on rapid dialogue delivery and bustling activity. Scene transitions are frequently accomplished through wipes and direct cuts (rather than the then more common fades and dissolves), adding to the sense of urgent forward propulsion. Romantic passages are caught on the run, in breathless snatches on the periphery of the action, so that the inevitable Dick-and-Ruby interludes do not bog down the film too much. Cagney's performance as musical-prologue producer Chester Kent (a lighter version of Warner Baxter's obsessive Julian Marsh in *42nd Street*) is the finest in any Warner Bros. musical, but *Footlight Parade*'s mosaic-like structure (jumping rapidly from subplot to subplot) prevents the film from congealing into a straight star vehicle.

The placement of the musical numbers in *Footlight Parade* has the three big extravaganzas presented in a familiar stacking arrangement at the end. One earlier number, "Sitting on a Backyard Fence," involving a feline chorus, is placed about midway through the film. However, it is so brief (less than three minutes—the other three numbers average over ten minutes apiece) and so disjointed (suggesting that a longer version was truncated in the editing room) that it does not register nearly strongly enough to counterbalance the three stacked numbers at the end. The separation of the onstage world from the offstage world, so conducive to Berkeleyesque spectacle, is underscored within the narrative when the musical company barricade themselves from the rest of the world for three days of secret rehearsals in order to prevent a rival producer from stealing their routines.

Footlight Parade also demonstrates Berkeley's increased confidence in detaching the numbers from their realistic narrative context. The staging of the numbers in *42nd Street* is, with the exception of a few camera angles, realistically conceivable on a theatrical stage. *Gold Diggers of 1933* becomes more adventurous in its handling of transitions (e.g., the hidden cuts that shift the seasons in "Pettin' in the Park," the blackouts in "Remember My Forgotten Man"), but the scale of the numbers and most of the effects still remain primarily within the range of possible stage address. Only "The Shadow Waltz," with its dissolves and overhead patterns, seriously strains the illusion that everything is taking place on a stage. In both *42nd Street* and *Gold Diggers of 1933*, the numbers generally begin with a very modestly scaled prologue set on the apron of the stage, which acts as a buffer zone between the outer realm of the realistic narrative and the inner realm of Berkeleyesque spectacle.

Footlight Parade takes this progression a step further in two main ways: (1) the transitions into the realm of Berkeleyesque spectacle are accomplished more quickly and boldly, and (2) the scale of the numbers (especially the last two) is more consistently extravagant than ever before in Berkeley's film work. However, *Footlight Parade* does not go as far in these directions as do later numbers like "I Only Have Eyes for You" and "Lullaby of Broadway," which plunge more directly into expansive, cine-spectacular address, with little regard at all for realistic stage limitations.

The three big numbers are structured on a principle of the sustained expansion of theatrical space into spectacle space. This expansion is established first in a lateral direction, across the surface of the screen, and then in a perpendicular direction, extending the space in depth. The numbers move generally in the direction of greater contextualization and increasing spectacle, with a final movement that symmetrically repeats or inverts the movement that initiated the number.

"Honeymoon Hotel"

"Honeymoon Hotel" is one of Berkeley's most successful comic numbers. It begins on the legs of a couple walking in a rightward direction. As the camera tracks laterally with them, bits of context are filled in: a sidewalk, a fire hydrant, a baggage cart.[7] The shot pans up to a pile of stacked baggage filling the entire foreground with a solid, impenetrable wall that pushes the visual field of the shot forward and invokes the surface of the screen. Porters' hands reach in and dismantle the wall piece by piece, revealing Dick Powell and

Ruby Keeler standing behind it. After a duet filmed entirely in medium two-shots, Dick and Ruby look at a newspaper ad depicting the doorman of the Honeymoon Hotel. A close-up of the ad collapses the image into surface again, and a matching dissolve shifts the locale from the train station to the hotel itself, where the doorman, in the flesh, greets the couple as they enter screen left.

The lateral-right movement that began the number is picked up in a tracking shot that follows Dick and Ruby as they begin to walk across the lobby, and it is continued in a series of swish pans that introduce the various personnel of the hotel. Each swish pan is linked to the next by a concealed cut, and these two techniques work together to break down the integrity of realistic space, distorting it and eliding it. For instance, the first swish-pan-plus-concealed-cut, moving from the couple to the front desk clerk, telescopes the space of the lobby by bringing the desk much closer to the camera than it would be in a realistic configuration. The subsequent swish pans similarly elide large chunks of space, at one point drawing an apparent lateral link between the lobby and a maid who is actually standing in a corridor upstairs. Meanwhile, time as well as space is being distorted: at the conclusion of the series of swish pans, Dick and Ruby finally reach the front desk—it has apparently taken them over a minute to cross the short distance of the lobby.

After Dick and Ruby depart for the Justice of the Peace, the image collapses into surface again as animated postcards and envelopes jump out of their mail slots to form a silhouette-drawing of the marriage ceremony. The lateral-right pattern continues in a tracking shot that follows the just-married couple across the lobby to the elevator. The happy pair proceed to their honeymoon suite upstairs, where they are greeted by an unpleasant selection of the bride's relatives, including Berkeley's ubiquitous man-child, Billy Barty. At this point the orientation of the number rotates 90-degrees on its axis, shifting from the surface-oriented lateral-right configuration to a depth-oriented configuration defined by the receding hotel corridor in the center of the frame. The grooms all march off through the bathroom door in the center background, while the brides all pop their heads out the bedroom doors to exchange pleasantries.

Berkeley once again uses editing tricks to undermine one's sense of realistic space, in this case via the use of ambiguous eyeline-matches.[8] The brides are aligned on either side of the corridor. The first shot of the series is a close shot of Bride A looking screen right. The second shot shows Bride B looking screen left, apparently returning Bride A's gaze. But the third shot shows Bride C looking screen right and apparently returning Bride B's gaze. Is Bride B's gaze linked to Bride A's or Bride C's? This disorienting shift of spatial relationships continues through a series of six eyeline-matches.

After his trip to the bathroom and a scuffle with Billy Barty, Dick enters the bedroom in search of connubial bliss. As the light is turned out, the camera tracks left across the room, returning to the lateral configuration that began the number but reversing its direction from right to left. The movement to two-dimensionality is similarly reestablished when the camera movement ends on a table with a magazine, whose pages are riffled by the wind until they come to rest on a photograph of a beaming baby.

"By a Waterfall"

"By a Waterfall" is the most ambitiously spectacular number attempted by Berkeley up to this point in his career. The number opens with a proscenium shot of Dick Powell lounging on the grass of a rather cluttered and depthless pastoral glade setting. The second shot of the number shifts ninety degrees away from the proscenium axis (that is, away from the plane of normal stage address), facing Powell from the previously established screen-left. The number remains on this axis for the duration of the prologue—a device that serves to sever the number quickly from its narrative context. As Dick sings the refrain ("By a waterfall, I'm calling you-oo-oo-oo"), Ruby, in a gauzy white dress, appears on the rocks above, answering ("Oo-oo-oo-oo"), and skips down to join him. At the end of their duet, sleepy Dick's head sinks out of the frame, and Ruby's refrain is answered by a group of naiads who appear on a waterfall in the background. Doffing her dress, Ruby joins them in the water.

The reality-status of the events in the number becomes so ambiguous at this point that the entire question of reality-status tends to evaporate, anticipating the abstraction of the number's climactic section. Is Ruby to be interpreted as a flesh-and-blood person or as a fantasy-figure summoned up by Dick's rhapsodic imagination? And are Ruby's cavortings with the water nymphs, after Dick falls asleep, to be interpreted as originating from his dream or from her daydream? We appear to be witnessing a dream within a dream or, even more intricately, Ruby's dream within Dick's dream.

The initial series of water antics with Ruby and the naiads by the waterfall serves mainly as a preliminary to the more astounding maneuvers in the climactic section. The waterfall section is centered on a continual movement back and forth between above-water and underwater camera positions, a movement accentuated by matches-on-action that link the two viewpoints (e.g., an underwater shot shows nymphs swimming upward toward the surface of the water, followed by a match-on-action cut to an above-water viewpoint as they break the surface).[9] These cuts establish the surface of the water as the visual pivot of the section and also as an analogue for the surface of the film image. This association is reinforced by shots of a diving nymph's impact breaking her watery reflection and of nymph-splashed water blurring the surface of the camera lens. For one particularly astonishing shot, the camera moves not only under the water but *under* the underwater, as the surface of the screen is revealed to be also the water-tank's glass bottom, over which the water-nymphs blithely step. It is hardly necessary to point out that such effects, as well as the elaborate overhead patterns in the next section of the number, are totally inconceivable on a theatrical stage.

The section concludes with Ruby breaking the surface and smiling up at the camera, followed by a line of surfacing-and-smiling naiads in a familiar Berkeley parade-of-faces effect. A cut to high-angle shows the nymphs arranged in a circle; then the camera pulls back to reveal that the setting is no longer a "natural" woodsy waterfall but an enormous rectangular pool with elaborate stucco ornamentation and a fountain in the background.

The play on surface-of-the-water/surface-of-the-image, established in the previous waterfall section, is paid off here in a series of spectacular overhead formations in which the naiads, supported by hidden floats, lie back in the water and link intertwined arms and legs to form complex, rotating spokewheel patterns. As the lighting switches from above-water to underwater sources and then back again, the naiads appear to hover suspended in space, as if such distinctions as up/down, top/bottom, and air/water had been collapsed into the impalpable surface of the image.

The climactic series of overhead patterns in "By a Waterfall" achieve an intensity of abstraction that Berkeley equaled only in the title number of *Dames* and the finale of *The Gang's All Here*. The surface of the water, by eclipsing all of the nymphs' bodies except for their heads and arms, enables Berkeley to transform the female anatomy into a purer, less corporeal geometry than ever before. First, by arranging themselves in rows and resting a hand on each shoulder of the nymph directly in front of them, they become rectangular, vertebral sections in the snakelike pattern of the entire row. Then, detaching themselves from the mass, they duck their heads and clasp their extended arms at the wrists to form little triangular packets that cluster together and form circular patterns. The overall effect is as if the chorus had exchanged their human forms for simpler, more elemental ones, becoming cellular units in an overall body of abstraction.

A trick cut shifts the location once more: the nymphs are now out of the water, forming the architecture of a giant, revolving, five-tiered fountain (see photo 38). The scene is extended in depth by a high-angle long shot showing the fountain deep in the background and the pool occupying the foreground. Then the image collapses into surface again as the girls form overhead patterns and a watery curtain of spray covers the foreground (see photo 39). The camera cranes down to Ruby, who is now back in the water. She dips her head underneath the surface; a concealed cut shifts the setting back to the leafy glade in which the number opened. Ruby sloshes water onto Dick to wake him up; they embrace. In the homely coda, the camera cranes up a nearby tree to show a nest containing a momma bird and four baby birds (all ersatz), who open their hungry mouths one by one.

"Shanghai Lil"

The film's finale, "Shanghai Lil," is notable for its successful integration of spectacle elements with less typically Berkeleyesque elements. (See photo 40.) The frame of the number is unusually narrativized, especially in its first half (only "Lullaby of Broadway" is more plot-oriented among Berkeley's major numbers). Also, "Shanghai Lil" is dominated by a star personality—Cagney (again, especially in the first half). It contains an extended tap dance by Cagney and Keeler in the "personality" vein that emphasizes individual style rather than synchronized routines. In addition, the lead-in to the number has a much stronger connection to the outer narrative than is usual in the Warners/Berkeley backstage musicals. Producer Chester Kent (Cagney), during a pre-curtain scuffle with his drunken leading man, tumbles down a flight of stairs onto the stage. After a moment of suspense, he effortlessly takes the leading man's place in the number. This narrativized lead-in sets up the plot-heavy framework of the first part of "Shanghai Lil," which in turn sets up the dissolution of narrative into spectacle that marks the number's final section.

Even more emphatically than "Honeymoon Hotel," "Lil" opens with a series of sustained lateral-right camera movements that work to break down the viewer's sense of a theatrical proscenium frame. The number commences with an extended rightward tracking shot following the dissolute, tuxedoed Bill (Cagney) as he staggers across a decadent Oriental saloon in search of his lost love, Shanghai Lil. The movement ends as Bill reaches the bar (where we learn that he is a sailor who has jumped ship), but it is quickly followed by another extended lateral-right movement that leaves Bill in order to track down the long bar. There barflies of various sexes, races, and nationalities offer their comments on the notorious Lil. In this opening section, the spatial context of the number is only gradually and partially disclosed, with the backgrounds of shots confined to soft-focused glimpses.

The end of the camera movement picks up Bill again as he lurches through a doorway into a backroom opium den, which appears to be frequented exclusively by young Caucasian women; a series of close-ups captures their stupefied expressions. The monolithic left-to-right organization of the first section is now broken down through cutting (the series of close-ups) and through the splayed criss-cross patterns of latticework and shadows that frame the girls' faces. This visual fragmentation serves as a segue into the second, more chaotic section of the number.

A direct cut moves from a close-up of a comely opium-smoker to a profile close-up of a tough-looking bruiser hoisting a beer mug at the bar. As he drains the mug and leans back out of the frame, the shot rack-focuses to reveal the length of the bar receding in a deep diagonal—the first significant introduction of depth in the number. This shift to depth-orientation is sustained through the next series of shots. A high-angle long shot reveals the whole space of the saloon for the first time. A sailor jumps on a table and sullies Lil's name ("She's every sailor's pal,/She's anybody's gal"), inciting Bill to attack him. The ensuing large-scale brawl is shown in a series of deep, brief, chaotically organized shots. (See photo 41.)

After the Shore Patrol clears the saloon, Bill, now clad in a sailor suit, emerges from behind the bar, and Lil herself (an absurdly orientalized Ruby Keeler) pops out from under the lid of a trunk. A sense of order is restored by Cagney and Keeler's stylish tap dance along the top of the bar (see photo 42), which temporarily revives the lateral-right orientation of the first section of the number and serves as a transition to the purposeful organization of the final section. It is also at this point that the melodramatic narrative (much in the vein of the "Fallen Woman" melodramas popular in the early 1930s) begins to dissolve away in favor of the dreamlike logic of Berkeleyesque spectacle.[10]

A bugle sounds, abruptly ending the tap dance and sending Bill scurrying out into the streets to join the ranks of marching sailors (see photo 43). The drill patterns of the sailors maintain the strong sense of depth from the second section of the number, which is now transformed into an orderly, purposeful depth, with long rows of sailors extending into the background. The heterogeneous mixture of the first section is resolved into its component parts. The marching sailors are all male, Caucasian, and American; the cheering onlookers are all Oriental; and, at the climax of the maneuvers, a phalanx of Oriental women march through the ranks of the sailors in alternating rows.

As in "Honeymoon Hotel" and "By a Waterfall," the final movement of the number collapses depth into surface, here via placard formations depicting the American flag and FDR, and an overhead pattern in which the tops of the chorus's caps create an image of FDR's National Recovery Administration eagle. The sailors then march off to board their ship in a sustained leftward movement that reverses the direction of the number's opening. The coda of the number shows Bill and Lil (now sporting a sailor suit herself) marching off to sea together. In a final invocation of surface, Bill fans a deck of cards to produce a crudely animated image of the departing ship.

Paradigm Parade

The strongly foregrounded organization of *Footlight Parade*'s numbers around such visual motifs as depth/surface and lateral-right/lateral-left camera movements exemplifies the way in which Berkeleyesque spectacle makes use of these cinematic properties as elements of free formal play and display. They are not subordinated to the dictates of narrative logic, whether that narrative be a story told within the number or the story told around the number. These elements serve the qualities of gratuitousness and ostentatiousness that are so central to Berkeleyesque spectacle. In addition, the strong invocation of such elements as depth of field, surface of the screen, and camera movement emphasizes that these numbers are linked to a cinematic rather than a theatrical referent. This serves to underscore the separation of the world of the numbers (which flaunt many purely cinematic properties) from the world of the surrounding narrative (which insists that all this is nevertheless taking place on a theatrical stage)—another central principle of Berkeleyesque film spectacle.

Even though the numbers in *Footlight Parade* have little relationship to the surrounding narrative, they do have strong interrelationships to each other. This has already been indicated by the above-noted formal/structural resemblances between "Honeymoon Hotel" and "Shanghai Lil." Both open with extended lateral-right camera movements and a strong surface orientation. They then move to a central section with strong depth orientation and conclude with a return to surface orientation and lateral movement, the latter now reversed to the left. Both end with a collapsing of depth into a two-dimensional image: the baby photo in "Honeymoon Hotel" and the animated ship in "Shanghai Lil." Although the central number "By a Waterfall" is not as formally similar to the two others, it shares their concern with surface and, in the pool-and-fountain section, their temporary shift to depth orientation.

The interrelationships between the three numbers operate on other levels—theme, tone, imagery—as well. The light, risqué tone of "Honeymoon Hotel" and the grandiose, somewhat heavy spectacle of "By a Waterfall" come together in the finale "Shanghai Lil," with its successful blending of tones. The two heterosexual spectacles—"Honeymoon Hotel" and "Shanghai Lil"—bookend "By a Waterfall," which (with the exception of Powell's appearance in the prologue and epilogue) is set in an all-female fantasyland in the "seraglio" mode.

In "Honeymoon Hotel," the romantic couples turn into military-like ranks as the grooms march two abreast to the bathroom and the brides march three abreast to Ruby's door; in "Shanghai Lil," marching military ranks turn into a romantic couple—the sailor-suited Bill and Lil. The individual Bill is woven in and out of the mass of marching sailors in "Shanghai Lil" in much the same way that the individual Ruby is woven in and out of the mass of gamboling water nymphs in "By a Waterfall." The sailors in "Shanghai Lil" (seamen or "water/men") could be seen as male equivalents of the nymphs ("water/women") in "By a Waterfall." Both "Honeymoon Hotel" and "By a Waterfall" end with images of procreation: the baby photo in "Honeymoon Hotel," the baby birds in the nest in "By a Waterfall."

Many such equivalences, some more far-fetched than others, could be drawn among the numbers in *Footlight Parade*. Those above should be sufficient to support the ideas that the numbers in the film are not merely a serial arrangement of unrelated units in the manner of vaudeville acts, that there are strong thematic and formal links between the numbers, and that there are other ways of organizing material besides embedding it within a narrativized hierarchy. As Rick Altman has noted in his article, "The American Film Musical: Paradigmatic Structure and Mediatory Function," the numbers in a musical film usually form a strong network of paradigmatic relationships that is somewhat independent of the syntagmatic progression of the narrative.[11] But this characteristic property of the musical genre is highly overdetermined in a classic Warners/Berkeley musical like *Footlight Parade*, where the backstage format and the stacking arrangement cause the numbers to coalesce into a single, self-enclosed bloc at the end of the film.

Dames (1934)

Berkeley then worked on *Fashions of 1934* (1934, directed by William Dieterle), a programmer comedy-drama containing one musical number, "Spin a Little Web of Dreams." This plush (even overplush) Ziegfeldian extravaganza, fairly smothered in ostrich feathers, points out a certain divergence between Berkeley's film style and the Ziegfeld tradition. Berkeley's conception of spectacle does not usually depend as much on elaborate and ornate settings; the settings of his numbers tend to be more abstract and even streamlined.

This was followed by *Wonder Bar* (1934, directed by Lloyd Bacon), a *Grand Hotel*-like Al Jolson vehicle to which Berkeley contributed two large-scale production numbers. The first, "Don't Say Goodnight," is an impressive though somewhat diffuse entry in the elegant, black-polished-floor vein of *42nd Street*'s "Young and Healthy" and *Gold Diggers of 1933*'s "The Shadow Waltz." The second, "Goin' to Heaven on a Mule," is an embarrassing fiasco whose formal and structural deficiencies are ultimately more debilitating than the notorious racism of its imagery.

Berkeley's next major effort was *Dames* (directed by Ray Enright). In terms of plot elements, cast, and major numbers, *Dames* is much in the *Gold Diggers* mold (Jim Terry in *The Busby Berkeley Book* suggests that the film could easily have been called *Gold Diggers of 1934*), yet in some respects it marks the beginnings of a departure from the classic Warner Bros. backstage formula.[12]

Up to this point, the numbers in the Warners/Berkeley backstage musicals have all been realistically motivated, taking the form either of (1) small-scale rehearsals or song-demonstrations before the big show, or (2) large-scale production numbers from the climactic big show, stacked in a massive bloc that works to overwhelm narrative with spectacle. The film is thus effectively split into two parts: (1) the body of the film, which is intimate in tone and strongly focused on the narrative, with perhaps one or two minor song numbers, and (2) the climax of the film, which has a modicum of narrative elements and consists mainly of an onslaught of elaborate and fantastically expanded spectacle numbers. The types of numbers most commonly associated with the musical genre are those which have characters unrealistically bursting into spontaneous song and dance to express their emotions, and which work to intertwine the musical and narrative portions of the film more closely together. These types are conspicuously absent from the earlier Warners/Berkeley backstage musicals.

Dames represents an attempt to include a broader spectrum of musical numbers outside the onstage spectacle mode. It also attempts to utilize the numbers to give shape to the structure of the entire film, rather than dumping them all into a big, self-enclosed package at the end. There is a definite progression to the placement of the numbers in *Dames*, which works to ease the film more gradually into large-scale spectacle instead of just suddenly shifting gears at the climax, as was the case in the earlier Warners/Berkeley musicals. The numbers in *Dames* build toward Berkeleyesque spectacle in the following manner:

1. "When You Were a Smile on Your Mother's Lips and a Twinkle in Your Daddy's Eye": Shot outdoors (supposedly in Central Park). Spontaneous, unrealistically motivated love song sung by Dick Powell to Ruby Keeler as they sit by a pond. Dialogue leads into recitative, which leads into song. Filmed mainly in close two-shots. No other characters are present besides the two principals.

2. "I Only Have Eyes for You" (first rendition): Set on the Staten Island ferry (rear projection of New York harbor). Love song sung by Powell to Keeler. Realistically motivated (would-be producer Powell takes out a song sheet representing his latest composition and tells Keeler, "Just listen to this . . ."), but an unrealistic performance element intrudes when a cut to long shot reveals in the foreground a three-piece orchestra, which "impossibly" provides the accompaniment for Powell's crooning. The number begins intimately, with Powell and Keeler in two-shot, but subsequent cuts reveal the orchestra and other couples, who listen to the song and sigh.

3. "Try To See It My Way" (first rendition): Set in producer's office. Realistically motivated and performed. Powell, seated at a piano, demonstrates a song to prospective star Joan Blondell; also present are Keeler and the songwriters. Filmed mostly in two-shot.

4. "Dames" (instrumental only): Set on the stage. Realistically motivated and performed. While other chorines watch from the background and the rehearsal pianist plays the tune, Keeler, auditioning for a part, performs a brief but energetic tap dance. Shot mainly in close shots of Keeler's dancing feet and reaction shots of Powell and Blondell ("Hey! That kid can dance!").

5. "The Girl at the Ironing Board": The first of four onstage numbers occurring on the big show's opening night. A small-scale, comic number, centering on

Blondell and a small chorus of laundresses. However, the address of the number is unrealistic, being pointedly directed away from the theater audience and toward the movie camera.

6. "I Only Have Eyes for You" (second rendition): Onstage number. Realistically motivated but unrealistically performed—from the start, the number is largely inconceivable in theatrical terms. It begins fairly intimately, then expands into spectacle. Perhaps Berkeley's most fluid mixture of mass spectacle and personalized, intimate romance.

7. "Dames": Onstage number. It begins mostly realistically, then expands to an extremely grandiose scale. Many of its effects are comprehensible only in cinematic terms. Sheer spectacle and extreme abstraction, with little or no personal dimension.

8. "Try To See It My Way" (second rendition): Onstage number. Realistically motivated and performed by Joan Blondell and a relatively small (c. twenty-five-member) chorus on a modestly scaled staircase set. The number is addressed to the theater audience rather than to the movie camera, and there are no special cinematic effects. In a variation on *Gold Diggers of 1933*'s opening "We're in the Money," this closing number is discontinued by the intrusion of narrative elements (a gang of hired thugs charge the stage, and the police arrive to throw everybody in jail).

With the exception of the final number (which serves as something of a coda or wind-down, returning the film to plausible dimensions and leading into the final plot resolution), the progression of the numbers in *Dames* runs in the following interrelated directions:

From outdoors (the park, the ferryboat) to indoors (the office, the theater)
From small-scale (two characters) to grandiose (dozens of chorines)
From intimacy (two characters alone) to the presence of larger audiences
From informal situations to more formal, "official" performances
From situations with a strong relation to the narrative (e.g., Powell singing his love to Keeler, Powell trying to sell his production to potential backers) to production numbers that are self-enclosed and detached from the narrative
From (1) numbers that are unrealistic in terms of motivation and spontaneity but realistic in physical terms (scale, effects, setting), to (2) numbers that are realistic in terms of both motivation and scale, to (3) numbers that are realistically motivated but unrealistic in terms of scale, effects, and setting (the optimum Berkeleyesque mode).

This rudimentary gesture in *Dames* toward the domain of the integrated musical falls short. The earlier numbers are routine and forgettable; the film lapses into a familiar stacking arrangement at the end; and *Dames* is noteworthy almost entirely for its two big numbers, "I Only Have Eyes for You" and "Dames," which stand somewhat apart from the rest of the film.

"I Only Have Eyes for You"

"I Only Have Eyes for You" is one of Berkeley's greatest achievements, with complexities and thematic resonances beyond the scope of this analysis. The number plunges very quickly into straight cinematic address, bypassing the type of prologue that opens many of Berkeley's 1930s spectacles on a note of deceptive theatricality. Although the opening shot shows, in low angle, a street scene that could easily be encompassed on a stage set, an automobile then approaches the camera and drives directly over it. If this were a realistic stage set, the car would presumably topple off the apron and into the orchestra pit.

The opening section of the number is highly cinematized and narrativized. Camera movements follow Dick Powell and Ruby Keeler down a crowded street whose dimensions quickly eclipse those of a possible stage set, with the crowds magically dissolving away each time Powell sings, "But they all disappear from view,/And I only have eyes for you." In fact, the first part of "I Only Have Eyes for You" is in the mode of an integrated narrative number such as Gene Kelly's "Singin' in the Rain" (*Singin' in the Rain*, 1952) or Astaire and Rogers's "Let's Call the Whole Thing Off" (*Shall We Dance*, 1937). However, the importance of the backstage mode is demonstrated here. Because the number is initially established as a formal stage performance, it cannot be absorbed into the narrative. Instead, the fiction that this is all occurring on a stage serves as a bracketing device, holding the number always at one remove from the narrative and thus keeping it open to the free and arbitrary incursion of spectacle and abstraction.

Powell and Keeler move from the street to a subway car, where, as they fall asleep, the number opens out into the unrestrained spectacle of its central section. Once again, the onstage fiction is crucial here. Because the number always has to be taking place on a stage, its improbabilities cannot be rationalized away as the character's dream or subjective fantasy.[13] These remain impossible, astounding, and hence especially spectacular.

The central section of the number takes place in the type of endlessly dissolving, unbounded space that provides the most fertile ground for Berkeleyesque spectacle. Hovering in a black void, cutout blowups of Keeler's face proliferate and form various arrangements (see photo 44). The chorus—with each girl coiffed and dressed exactly like Keeler—is then revealed on an elaborate structure combining three staircases, a revolving platform, and a ferris-wheel-like contraption in the center (see photo 45). The chorus streams over this structure on different levels and in different directions, combining with Berkeley's moving camera to form complex arabesques of angle, motion, and shape.[14]

This section climaxes in a series of astonishing transitions that represent Berkeley's most sustained exercise in controlled disorientation—an orgy of paradox that juggles scales, perspectives, locations, and dimensions to a mind-boggling degree. This type of disorientation (although usually not carried to the extent that it is in "I Only Have Eyes for You") is a central strategy of Berkeleyesque spectacle, working to make the viewer lose all sense of the proscenium frame-of-reference and effectively severing spectacle space from the surrounding narrative space.

In extreme low angle, Keeler walks toward the camera and (via a glass floor) right over it. The hem of her long white skirt passes over the camera, revealing (via a concealed cut) that it is now in extreme high angle, with a sea of chorines seated in rows far below. The chorines stand up, bend over, and lift up the backs of their skirts, to which are attached placards that together form a giant puzzle of Keeler's face. The camera cranes down into the giant face's left eye, which opens like a lens to disgorge Ruby herself in the flesh. Standing in a black space, Ruby walks forward; the camera pulls back to reveal a circular gold frame around her and, below this frame, sixteen chorines seated in a row on an elongated couch. The couch splits in two and slides out of the frame. The chorines form a vertical row beneath the gold frame and are transformed into its handle. An apparently giant-sized Ruby steps into the shot, takes hold of the handle, and turns the frame (now bearing her frozen likeness) to reveal a mirror on its other side, in which Powell and Keeler are seen asleep in the subway car. This segues into the low-key, poignant finale: Powell and Keeler wake up, discover themselves at the end of the subway line (see photo 46), and walk off slowly across a rainy, deserted trainyard.

The extraordinary resonance of "I Only Have Eyes for You" serves as a reminder that, although the spectacular mode is Berkeley's forte and the quality for which he is most famous (as well as the featured subject of this study), this does not mean that his effectiveness is limited exclusively to the spectacular mode. Berkeley is a more fully rounded artist than that, and it is more accurate to see his style as being composed of a major key (spectacle, grandiosity, glitter) and a minor key (intimacy, banality, poignancy). This ability to play the minor key off the major key is at the heart of the resonance and depth of Berkeley's best numbers. It also generally distinguishes his work from that of colleagues and imitators who restrict themselves mainly to spectacular patterns in the Berkeleyesque manner.

No Berkeley number demonstrates this double-level principle more vividly than "I Only Have Eyes for You," where the rich interplay of the personal and the spectacular, the intimate and the grandiose, the individual and the mass is explicitly inscribed in the very subject and design of the number. "I Only Have Eyes for You" is built on a sustained back-and-forth between the couple and the crowd around them in the opening section, and on the continual reemergence of Ruby, in all her dubious glory, from the chorus of lookalikes. She is extraordinarily ordinary and infinitely replicable yet forever unique in the eyes of her beloved:

> You are here, so am I.
> Maybe millions of people go by,
> But they all disappear from view,
> And I only have eyes for you.

"Dames"

It is precisely the minor key that is missing in the film's biggest number, "Dames." This lack ranks "Dames" below Berkeley's major numbers despite its achievement of several of his most astounding and spectacular effects. The number opens modestly and somewhat stagily with a prologue set in a theatrical office. There producer Dick Powell presides over a debate concerning which is the ingredient most essential to a successful show: story, cast, publicity, music, etc. Powell, in song, supplies the correct answer: dames. The number then launches into the upper stratosphere of spectacular style, never to come down to earth again. There is no characteristic Berkeley coda or wind-down at the end of "Dames." Instead, it concludes on a high note of astonishment and tour de force, with an especially spectacular arrangement of chorus girls freezing into a still photograph, and Powell's head bursting through it to sing the final line.

"Dames" is the number, more than any other, where Berkeley throws in everything in the grand aggregate/spectacle tradition. If he leaves out the kitchen sink, he still manages to supply twenty-eight bathtubs, each containing a bubbly chorus girl while a companion primps herself before a neon-framed mirror attached to the tub. Also on hand are twenty-eight giant alarm clocks, twenty-eight double beds (each containing a brace of chorus girls: see photo 47), mass calisthenics, twenty-eight double vanity-sets, twenty-eight stage doors, and an enormous all-white structure containing over 100 embanked chorus girls. In addition, there are chorus girls parading, tap dancing, flying through the air, deploying themselves in kaleidoscopic patterns, and forming the walls of a gigantic revolving tunnel.

Berkeley attempts to counter the diffuseness of the number by organizing it around several simple but powerful motifs, most notably those of black/white and up/down. Everything in the main section of the number is realized in terms of white and black, contributing to an impression of intense abstraction. This reaches a peak in the patterns formed by the black-legged, white-topped chorus against a field of complete, dazzling whiteness, and in the proto–Op Art design of converging lines (alternating white and black) that resolves itself into a diamond-shaped vortex of chorus girls, all in white, spinning through a black void. (See photo 48.)

The up/down motif includes, besides Berkeley's customary shiftings between high angle and low angle, chorines flying straight up into the camera and black beach-balls dropping straight down to scatter the clustered chorus into an array of kaleidoscopic designs. (See photo 49.) The manipulation of up and down reaches a crescendo of disorientation when the chorines line up in single file and stand with their black-tighted legs spread apart, forming a triangle with its point on the top. The camera rotates 180 degrees, turning the triangle upside down, then tracks through the tunnel of parted legs, each girl bending down (or is it up?) to grin into the camera as it passes by. In a final twist that completely confounds all sense of direction, the camera, after tracking all the way through the parted legs, continues forward, revealing the chorines standing in a row in the white field far below. This effect represents an extreme example of the difference between narrative space, which (even when applied to fantasy situations) is constructed according to certain delimiting principles of causality and consistency, and spectacle space, which can be expanded and transformed to include anything and to go anywhere, with complete freedom and arbitrariness.

After the prologue, the number is addressed almost exclusively to the camera rather than to any conceivable stage audience. This idea is underlined by a couple of gaglike transitions in which chorines react with mock modesty to the presence of the camera, covering the lens with a powder puff or fogging it up with spray perfume. The number proceeds to employ a series of exclusively cinematic devices: trick cuts, jump cuts, overhead shots, freeze frames, animated graphics, etc.

However, at the same time that the number is being ostentatiously cinematic, it is also being just as ostentatiously theatrical. Alongside the cinematic devices, Berkeley employs a range of effects that strongly evoke the spectacle tradition of the stage. For instance, rather than using cuts or dissolves, several transitions are handled by the nineteenth-century stage device of having cutouts (the giant alarm clocks, the stage doors, a freeze-framed arrangement of girls) disappear through grooves in the floor. At another point, treadmills moving in different directions and at different speeds are used to convey an impression of the dames marching off to work—an effect much like those employed in the 1928 stage production *Good Boy*, with which Berkeley was associated. The first set of abstract chorus patterns in "Dames" is accomplished not through overhead shots but through vertically banked levels, a common practice of the spectacle stage.

Rather than abandon or diminish theatrical address in favor of cinematic address, "Dames" (like many other Berkeley numbers throughout his career) plays on a paradoxical simultaneity of stage and screen effects. This is, in fact, a common practice in many musical films—for instance, when performers dance and sing toward the camera rather than toward the fictional audience. However, the extravagance, ostentatiousness, and expansiveness with which this type of device is treated in numbers like "Dames" moves it out of the realm of ordinary musical practice and into the realm of the Berkeleyesque—a matter of degree here rather than of kind.

A third organizing motif employed in "Dames" is the key Berkeley motif of individual/group. However, it is here that the number's limitations become more clearly apparent. Although Berkeley dexterously juggles faces and patterns, close shots and group arrangements, the number lacks any "Ruby" or "Wini" ("Lullaby of Broadway") on which to focus its minor (i.e., intimate, personal) key. The dames of "Dames" are all completely anonymous. Nor is there any personal or romantic relationship established in the number's prologue as a springboard to the ensuing spectacle, as there is in numbers such as "Pettin' in the Park," "Remember My Forgotten Man," "By a Waterfall," "I Only Have Eyes for You," "Lullaby of Broadway," etc.

Because "Dames" lacks the concentrated emotional counterweight of those other numbers, it becomes primarily a display of detached and rambling pyrotechnics whose effect is more sequential than cumulative. Astounding but cold, lacking the richness of Berkeley's best numbers, "Dames" reveals some of the limitations of the spectacle style: even in the realm of the Berkeleyesque, it is possible to be *too* spectacular.

The Warner Bros. backstage musicals of the early thirties did not necessarily provide an ideal framework for Berkeleyesque spectacle. One could say that this format was better suited for expanding Berkeleyesque concepts than the Goldwyn/Cantor format had been, but not as much as a pure, unadulterated revue format might have been. However, purity is not always the most artistically productive course. While allowing for a great degree of autonomous spectacle, the Warners backstage format also enabled the Berkeleyesque mode to be enriched (rather than negated or adulterated) by other, contrapuntal tendencies. These included the more extensive development of a minor, intimate dimension to complement the major, spectacular dimension, and the limited employment of integrative strategies (e.g., general thematic correspondences to the narrative and paradigmatic parallels between the numbers). Such strategies added possibilities of significance to the production numbers (as noted above, the Berkeleyesque/aggregate tradition tends to be inclusionary rather than exclusionary) without drawing them too closely within the more constrictive orbit of the surrounding narrative. Given the constitutionally problematic nature of musical film, these "impurities" allowed Berkeley's work at Warner Bros. to remain more relevant (even if atypical) to the central dynamics and historical development of the genre.

The necessity of incorporating excessive spectacle into a relatively substantial narrative framework (as opposed to the rudimentary, vestigial narratives employed by some revues) also indicated ways in which the Berkeleyesque could make a place for itself within the confines of mainstream classical narrative cinema, through strategies of maximized if not total separation—such as the stacking of the musical numbers, the creation of distinct spaces to contain the numbers, and the use of discursive deviation (or "impossibility") within those spaces. In sum, the Warner Bros. backstage musical of the early 1930s provided the optimum context for the Berkeleyesque—if not the best possible, then the best that was to be feasible for Berkeley in the actuality of American film history. Hereafter, Berkeley's opportunities to implement the Berkeleyesque would be more limited at best and largely inimical at worst.

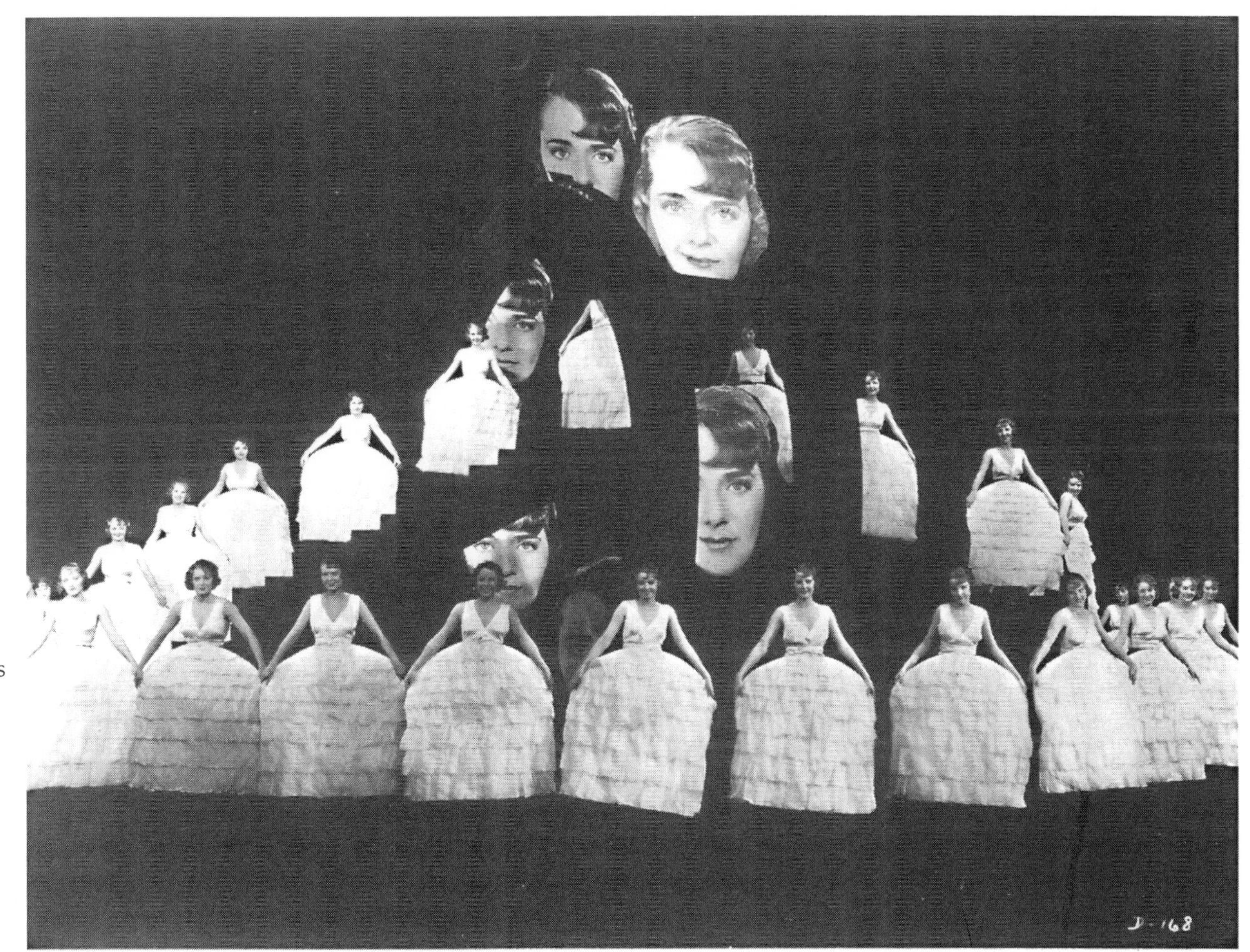

44. *Dames* (1934). "I Only Have Eyes for You" is one of Berkeley's most dazzling and moving numbers. After a prologue establishing young lovers Dick Powell and Ruby Keeler in the big city, it moves into an abstract dreamspace dominated by Ruby's inescapable face.

45. *Dames* (1934). "I Only Have Eyes for You": An elaborate structure of stairs and wheels surrounds Ruby with chorus girls dressed and coiffed exactly like her. A paradoxical relationship between the individual and the mass is at the heart of many Berkeley numbers. Extraordinarily ordinary and infinitely replicable, Ruby will always be unique in the eyes of her lover.

46. *Dames* (1934). "I Only Have Eyes for You": Returning from dreamland, Dick and Ruby wake up in an empty subway car. This poignant image from the end of the number illustrates Berkeley's often overlooked ability to shift fluidly from grandiosity to intimacy.

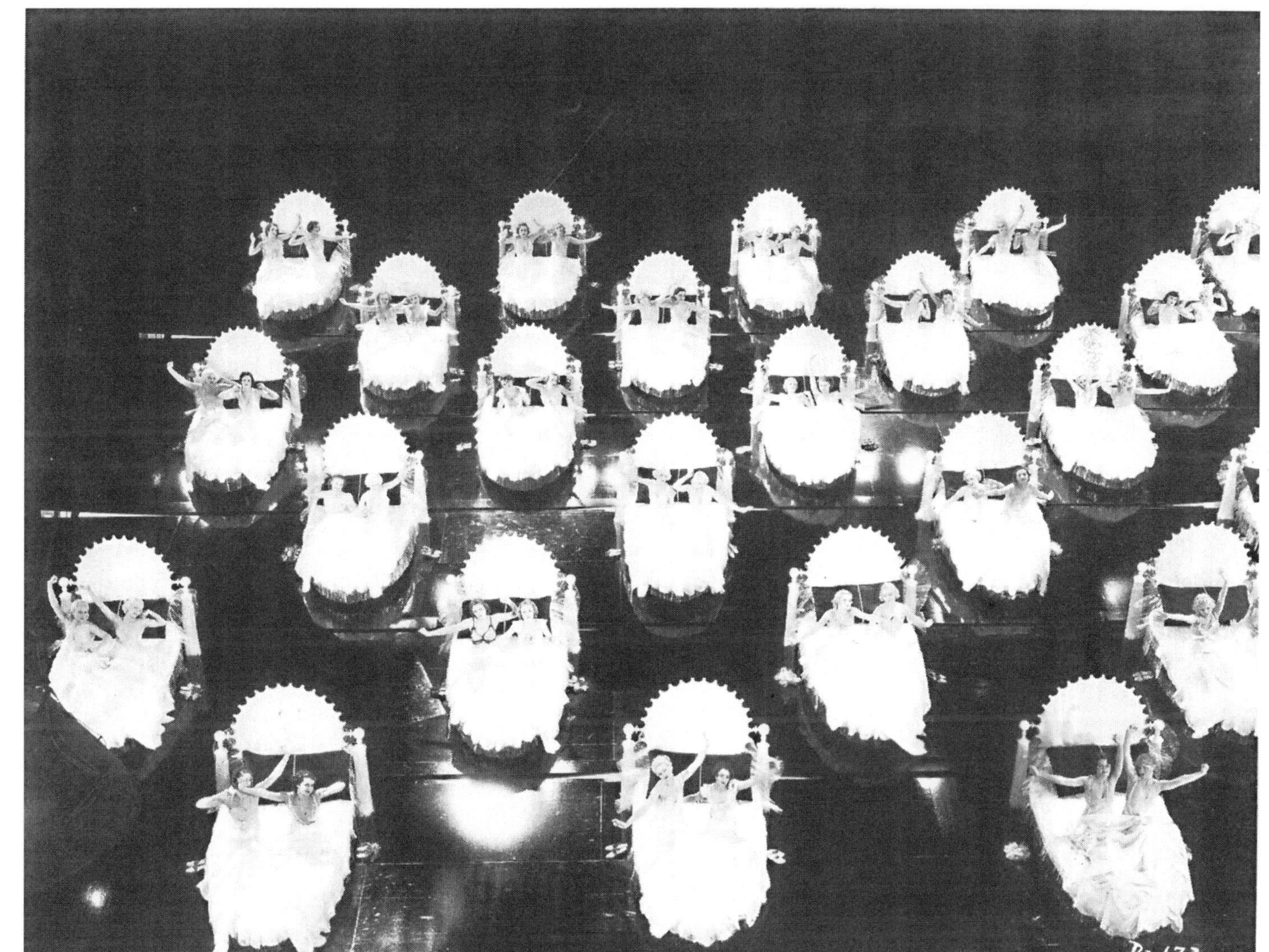

47. *Dames* (1934). "Dames": Chorus girls rise and shine in Berkeley's most purely spectacular number. However, "Dames" lacks the intimate dimension that enriches "I Only Have Eyes for You."

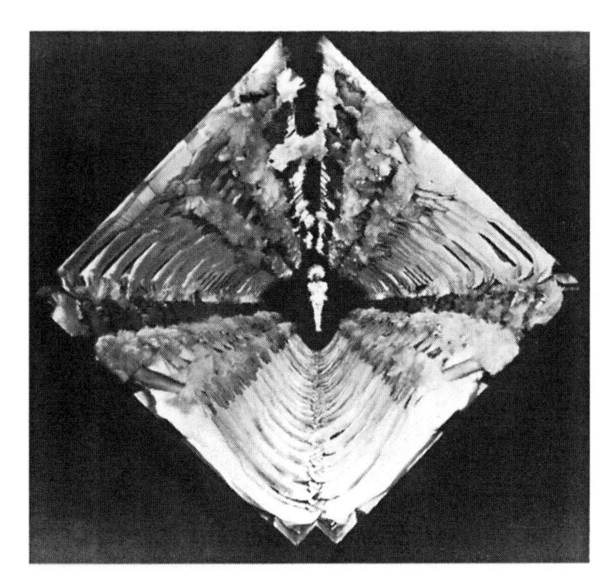

48. *Dames* (1934). "Dames": Abstraction and geometrizing of the female body reach a peak in this diamond-shaped vortex of chorus girls.

49. *Dames* (1934). "Dames": Black-and-white and up-and-down form the central organizing principles of the number's unmitigated abstraction. Black beach balls drop straight down to scatter the white-topped chorus into an array of kaleidoscopic designs.

50. *Gold Diggers of 1935* (1935) "The Words Are in My Heart": Fifty-six musical behemoths float like butterflies through this most accomplished of Berkeley's elegant numbers.

51. *Gold Diggers of 1935* (1935). Changing trends in the musical genre during the late 1930s caused alterations in Berkeley's style. The homogeneously swanky setting of the Wentworth Plaza Hotel (visited here by Gloria Stuart and Dick Powell) contrasts strongly with the gritty Depression milieu of the earlier Warners/Berkeley musicals.

52. *Gold Diggers of 1935* (1935). "Lullaby of Broadway" is the pinnacle of Berkeley's Warner Bros. numbers. After sleeping all day, playgirl Wini Shaw (seen upper right) goes nightclubbing with boyfriend Dick Powell (out of frame). They arrive at an extravagantly, even eerily vast establishment where they seem to be the only customers.

53. *Gold Diggers of 1935* (1935). "Lullaby of Broadway" can be seen as an epitaph for the unrestrained Berkeleyesque excess of the early thirties. The large chorus becomes oddly threatening, their stomping feet booming ominously through the cavernous nightclub, which takes on a haunted-house quality.

54. *Gold Diggers of 1935* (1935). "Lullaby of Broadway": Wini (center) is lured down to the dance floor, and the number reaches a frenzied peak, just before she takes her fatal plunge.

55. *The Singing Marine* (1937). "Night over Shanghai" is an orientalized variation on such urban mood pieces as "42nd Street" and "Lullaby of Broadway." Dick Powell contemplates harmonica player Larry Adler in the number's atmospheric conclusion, derived from a 1930 stage show that Berkeley had worked on.

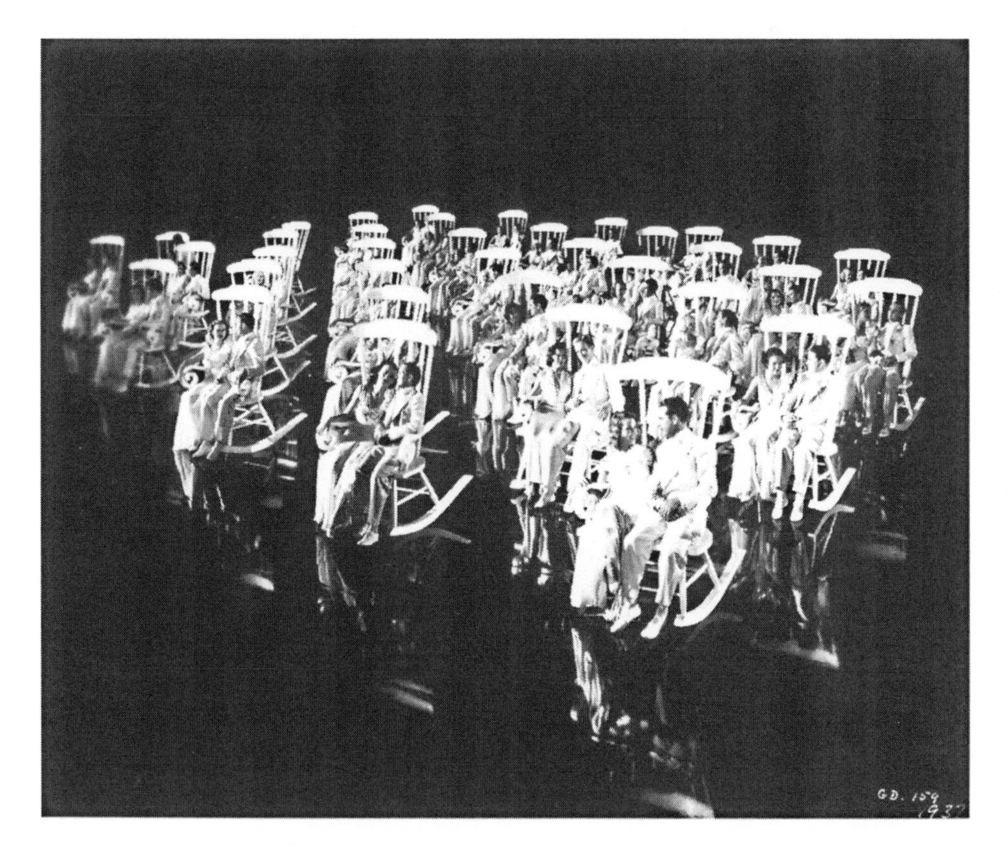

56. *Gold Diggers of 1937* (1936). "All's Fair in Love and War" was one of the last major spectacles of Berkeley's Warner Bros. period. In the opening section, gigantic rocking chairs provide commodious love-seats before the "hostilities" commence.

57. *Gold Diggers of 1937* (1936). "All's Fair in Love and War": The victorious women parade in triumph, their reflections setting up an especially ingenious Berkeleyesque effect in which the floor seems to melt away.

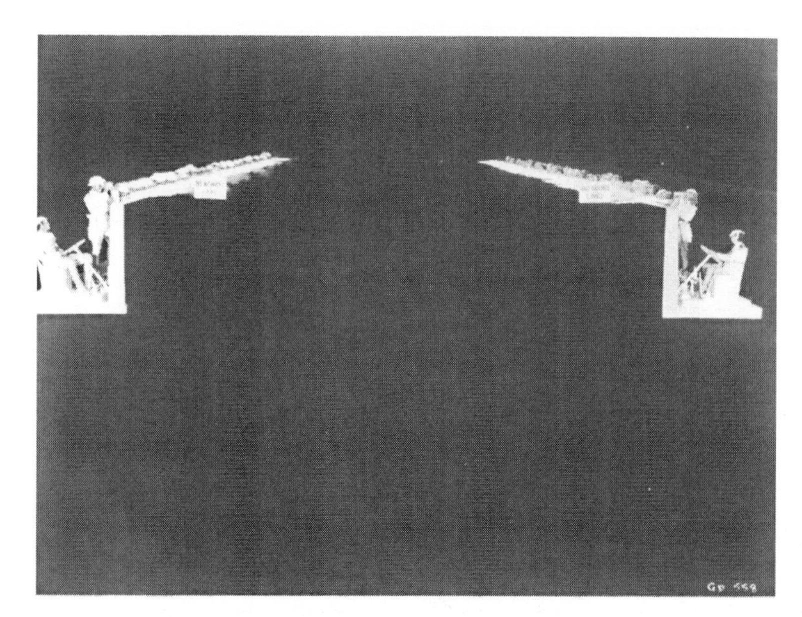

58. *Gold Diggers of 1937* (1936). "All's Fair in Love and War": The battle of the sexes is fancifully literalized in the form of these two motorized trenches, from which kisses and perfume attacks are launched.

59. *Hollywood Hotel* (1937). Edgar Kennedy chews the scenery in this Berkeley-directed musical comedy. Berkeley's comic touch was generally a heavy one, and this film in particular was overstuffed with manic character actors.

60. *Broadway Serenade* (1939). In 1939 Berkeley moved from Warner Bros. to MGM, whose integration-oriented musicals were less receptive to Berkeleyesque spectacle. The grotesque, funereal images of the *Broadway Serenade* finale provided a bizarre (and, as it turned out, uncharacteristic) beginning to Berkeley's MGM period.

61. *Strike Up the Band* (1940). The backbone of Berkeley's MGM tenure is the three musicals he directed with Mickey Rooney and Judy Garland. Seen here is a characteristic situation from the Rooney/Garland musicals: earnest Mickey seeks the approval of the adult world while Judy looks on with concern.

62. *Babes in Arms* (1939). Although Berkeley's MGM numbers often referred to Tradition of Spectacle forms (e.g., minstrel show, revue, vaudeville, melodrama, patriotic extravaganza), their own spectacularization was constrained. This Minstrel Show medley with Mickey Rooney, Douglas McPhail, and Judy Garland never expands beyond the limited stage dimensions depicted here.

63. *Strike Up the Band* (1940). "La Conga": The deployment of the ensemble here remains too loose and individualized to attain the intense abstraction of the Warner Bros. period. The inclusion of both spectators and performers within the same frame inhibits the ability of Berkeleyesque spectacle to break away from the narrative context.

64. *Strike Up the Band* (1940). "Strike Up the Band": Characteristic of Berkeley's MGM spectacles are the finale's patriotic fervor and its localized use of spectacular effects, here represented by the expansion of the stage apron. Judy Garland and Mickey Rooney salute Old Glory in the background as the band belts out the Gershwin anthem.

65. *Ziegfeld Girl* (1941). "You Stepped Out of a Dream": Leading ladies Lana Turner, Hedy Lamarr, and Judy Garland pose in the foreground. The ornate costumes and decor here are more Ziegfeldian than Berkeleyesque.

66. *Lady Be Good* (1941). "Fascinatin' Rhythm": The lone number Berkeley contributed to this otherwise modest musical is one of the major accomplishments of his MGM period. In the last part, Berkeley ventures into Astaire territory, as Eleanor Powell tap dances with a chorus of sophisticated gents.

68. *Girl Crazy* (1943). "I Got Rhythm": Tommy Dorsey joins Judy and Mickey in the foreground. Tightness is the keynote of this number, which works within the limited stage dimensions depicted here. However, it was still considered too self-indulgent by the MGM brass, and Berkeley was fired from the film.

67. *For Me and My Gal* (1942). Judy Garland inspects draft-dodger Gene Kelly's self-inflicted wound in a typically serious moment from one of Berkeley's most dramatic and least spectacularized films. Even though someone else handled the dance direction, Berkeley later picked this film as a personal favorite, indicating a possible desire to escape his identification with Berkeleyesque spectacle.

69. *Iceland* (1942). Berkeley moved on briefly to 20th Century-Fox, where he found a more receptive context for Berkeleyesque excess. Polynesia meets Iceland in this Sonja Henie vehicle (filmed before Berkeley's arrival at the studio) that illustrates the Fox musical's free and easy attitude toward plausibility.

70. *The Gang's All Here* (1943). "You Discover You're in New York": The expansive opening number is supposed to have taken place on this tiny nightclub stage, as Berkeley's spectacularized camera asserts its power to refashion space and to conjure up a fictional world.

72. *The Gang's All Here* (1943). "The Lady in the Tutti-Frutti Hat": These outrageous props became Camp icons in the 1960s.

73. *The Gang's All Here* (1943). "The Lady in the Tutti-Frutti Hat": The number's final tableau confounds two-dimensional and three-dimensional space, sustaining the pattern of astonishment and paradox that characterizes this remarkable musical.

71. *The Gang's All Here* (1943). "The Lady in the Tutti-Frutti Hat": Carmen Miranda, Fox's most flamboyant musical star, exemplified the studio's tolerance for freewheeling absurdity. As the centerpiece of Berkeley's legendary number, she perches on a cart laden with provocative fruit.

74. *The Gang's All Here* (1943). "The Polka Dot Polka/A Journey to a Star": The final number's central section moves from a realistic stage to a Berkeleyesque fantasyland. The disks wielded by the chorus sustain the polka dot motif, obscurely connected to the polka dance tune.

75. *Take Me Out to the Ball Game* (1949). "Yes, Indeedy": Vaudevillians-cum-ballplayers Frank Sinatra and Gene Kelly audition for their future teammates. Typically for the film (but not for Berkeley), the team members shift fluidly between the status of performers and spectators, and the area on top of and in front of the dugout functions as both narrative space and stage space.

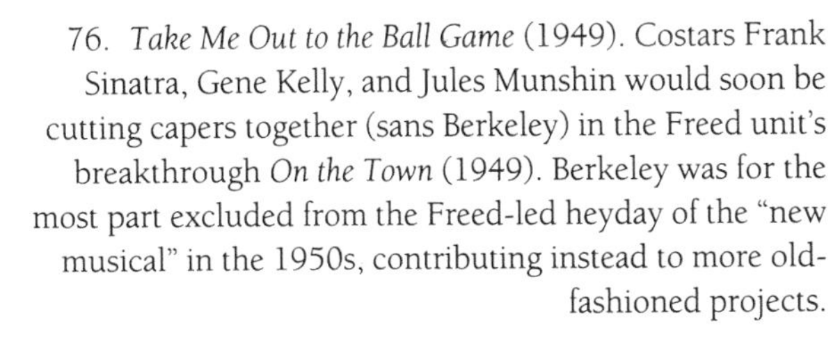

76. *Take Me Out to the Ball Game* (1949). Costars Frank Sinatra, Gene Kelly, and Jules Munshin would soon be cutting capers together (sans Berkeley) in the Freed unit's breakthrough *On the Town* (1949). Berkeley was for the most part excluded from the Freed-led heyday of the "new musical" in the 1950s, contributing instead to more old-fashioned projects.

77. *Call Me Mister* (1951). "Japanese Girl Love American Boy": One can easily imagine how this concept might have been spectacularized in Berkeleyesque terms. Instead, as in nearly all the film's numbers, spectacle is deferred in favor of star performance.

78. *Two Tickets to Broadway* (1951). "Manhattan": Tony Martin and Janet Leigh enact a vest-pocket equivalent of "Lullaby of Broadway." This little-known musical is one of the few Berkeley films to realize its limitations well.

79. *Two Tickets to Broadway* (1951). "Are You a Beautiful Dream?": In the film's final number, Janet Leigh inhabits the type of abstract dreamspace conducive to Berkeley-esque fantasy.

80. *Million Dollar Mermaid* (1952). "Smoke": This Esther Williams vehicle afforded Berkeley the opportunity to stage one of his most spectacular late numbers, with evident parallels to his earlier aquacade, "By a Waterfall." But, although Berkeley's 1950s numbers were often based on concepts as impressive as those of the 1930s, their development was less elaborate and complex.

81. *Million Dollar Mermaid* (1952). "Smoke": At the number's end, Williams is the centerpiece of a queen-and-court configuration, presiding over miracles of fire and water. The star-centered orientation of the number contrasts with Berkeley's earlier Warner Bros. spectacles, which were more "democratically" structured, with greater prominence given to the chorus.

82. *Small Town Girl* (1953). "I've Gotta Hear That Beat": Ann Miller's dance with the disembodied orchestra provided one of the most striking conceits of Berkeley's late period, as well as his final effort in the venerable Musical Instruments vein.

83. *The White Eagle* (1927). Twenty-seven years before he worked on the film version of *Rose Marie*, Broadway dance director Berkeley contributed an Indian spectacle to this ambitious but unsuccessful production of another Rudolf Friml operetta. (*Courtesy of The New York Public Library*)

84. *Rose Marie* (1954). "Totem Tom Tom": The final tableau of one of Berkeley's most erotic numbers shows chieftain's daughter Joan Taylor pinioned in a setting of priapic grandeur.

85. *Jumbo* (1962). "Over and Over Again": In Berkeley's final film assignment, the Berkeleyesque was reunited with its Barnumesque roots. In addition, this acrobatic display with Doris Day recalls the aerial configurations of the Gertrude Hoffman Girls that graced the spectacle stage of the 1920s.

8 LATER WARNER BROS. PERIOD (1935-1939)

A Genre in Transition

The mid-1930s saw a major shift in the course of the Hollywood musical. The Berkeleyesque spectacle style, far from being creatively exhausted, was actually reaching a peak of achievement—not only for Berkeley himself (especially in "The Words Are in My Heart" and "Lullaby of Broadway" in *Gold Diggers of 1935*) but also for some of his Broadway-to-Hollywood confreres, such as Bobby Connolly ("I'll Sing You a Thousand Love Songs" in *Cain and Mabel*, 1936; "Too Marvelous for Words" in *Ready, Willing and Able*, 1937), Seymour Felix ("Ice Cream Fantasy" in *Kid Millions*, 1934; "A Pretty Girl Is Like a Melody" in *The Great Ziegfeld*, 1936), and Dave Gould ("Rhythm of the Rain" and "Straw Hat" in *Folies Bergère*, 1935). At the same time, however, the musical genre was moving in a direction that was glossier, more homogeneous, more integrative, more plot-oriented, more personality-oriented, and less overtly spectacular than that of the early 1930s. This direction, anticipated by the Lubitsch and Mamoulian comedy-romances at Paramount, was consolidated by the Astaire/Sandrich collaborations at RKO, the Jeanette MacDonald/Nelson Eddy operettas at MGM, the Shirley Temple and Alice Faye vehicles at 20th Century-Fox, the Deanna Durbin films at Universal, and the Bing Crosby musicals at Paramount. The emphasis now was on consistency of tone and scale between musical numbers and narrative passages, and this moved the mainstream of the genre away from Berkeley, whose implementation of the Berkeleyesque became increasingly marginalized during the period.

At the same time, this was, for Berkeley, primarily a transitional period. He was employed more frequently as a director of entire films than as a specialist handling only the production numbers. Whether as overall director or contributor of individual numbers, the prevailing trends of the late thirties musical obliged Berkeley to think more in terms of incorporating the Berkeleyesque into an integrated whole. The result was a hybrid of the old-style Berkeleyesque spectacle forms and the new-style integrative/homogeneous forms.[1]

Gold Diggers of 1935 (1935)

Gold Diggers of 1935 (directed by Busby Berkeley) could have just as easily been placed at the end of the previous chapter as at the beginning of this one. The film encapsulates, in a particularly vivid way, the shifts in style that affected both Berkeley's work and the thirties musical in general. It represents precisely the dividing line, the fulcrum, between the two periods. *Gold Diggers of 1935* contains the last full explosion of the classic Warners/Berkeley spectacular style. At the same time, the film represents Berkeley's first strong gesture toward the changing trends of the late thirties musical.

Not counting *She Had To Say Yes*, a minor nonmusical comedy that Berkeley codirected in 1933, *Gold Diggers of 1935* was Berkeley's first assignment as a director of narrative cinema, and the first film, bar none, in which he directed both narrative scenes and musical numbers. For the first time, then, Berkeley had to evolve a conception of a whole musical film rather than of just individual musical numbers. Berkeley responded to this new situation by adopting a style of studied homogeneity in the ascendant Astaire/Sandrich vein. However, *Gold Diggers of 1935* sorely lacks the touch of deft, casual slickness that characterizes the best stretches of the Astaire/Sandrich collaborations. The film's attempts to impose a tone of sustained contrivance over the proceedings are generally strained and stilted, additionally hampered by the weak personalities of the principal actors and the unmodulated heaviness of Berkeley's style.

As in *Dames* (a film that in many ways points forward to *Gold Diggers of 1935*), the narrativized numbers in the early part of the film give way to performance spectacles in the latter part. Whereas *Dames* attempted to establish some sort of progression leading up to the big numbers at the end, *Gold Diggers of 1935* simply splits itself in two. One part consists of the final two numbers, "The Words Are in My Heart" and "Lullaby of Broadway"; the other part consists of everything else. The former represents perhaps the highest pinnacle ever achieved by Berkeleyesque cinema; the latter represents a first, tentative attempt by Berkeley to jump on the late thirties bandwagon.

The three major numbers in the first part of the film—the opening sequence, "I'm Going Shopping with You," and "The Words Are in My Heart" (first rendition)—are all in a narrativized, nonperformance, nonspectacular mode. In the Sandrichian vein, they work to break down the separation between the numbers and the narrative. This is primarily accomplished through the frequent mixing of recitative, song, and straight dialogue within the musical numbers and through the setting of everyday activities to choreographed rhythms. In the earlier Warners/Berkeley musicals, production numbers tended to be transcendent episodes in an otherwise relatively realistic context. In *Gold Diggers of 1935*, on the other hand, nonmusical passages are often as blatantly stylized and artificial as the musical numbers, with a consequent blurring of the distinction between the two.

The gritty urban/Depression atmosphere that formed the all-important background of the first three Warners/Berkeley musicals is referred to only once in *Gold Diggers of 1935*, and then rather obliquely and grotesquely. The film opens with a heavily caricatured park-bench bum, incongruously outfitted in an elegant suit and top hat. He is reading a swanky-looking magazine in which an ad touts the virtues of the Wentworth Plaza Hotel—"a name synonymous with luxurious living." A dissolve then transports the narrative to the confines of the hotel itself, where it remains for good. The Depression is never heard from again. (See photo 51.)

The plot concentrates on light romantic misunderstandings, without the slightest pretense of social consciousness (this withering away of the narrative's social framework is also evident in the previous Warners/Berkeley effort, *Dames*). True to the title of the film, several of the characters are obsessed with money, but this is no more than generalized greed, divorced from any explicit social context. Even the big show at the end seems inconsequential, merely a rich woman's idle whim rather than the life-and-death struggle of the classic Warner Bros. backstage musicals.

The opening sequence, after leaving the Depression behind, shows the staff members of the hotel polishing, dusting, mopping, gardening, painting, pruning, stacking, and wiping in time to the music on the soundtrack. The next number, "I'm Going Shopping with You," extends the same idea of life-as-choreography to a shopping trip taken by hotel clerk Dick

Powell and poor little rich girl Gloria Stuart. The third of the narrativized numbers, "The Words Are in My Heart" (first rendition), is in the I-feel-a-song-coming-on mode, delivered by Powell to Stuart and inspired by a motorboat cruise on a moonlit lake.

"The Words Are in My Heart"

In the last half hour, *Gold Diggers of 1935* abandons its narrativized musical format and reverts to a backstage structure (the occasion being a "Milk Fund Benefit" show) in order to present two mammoth numbers, "The Words Are in My Heart" and "Lullaby of Broadway," which represent the full maturity of Berkeley's spectacle style. The first of these, "The Words Are in My Heart," is the most accomplished of Berkeley's romantic/elegant numbers, a vein that also includes "Young and Healthy" (*42nd Street*), "The Shadow Waltz" (*Gold Diggers of 1933*), and "Don't Say Goodnight" (*Wonder Bar*).

The basic concept of "The Words Are in My Heart" is fraught with potential schmaltziness, kitschiness, and heaviness—an impression easily aroused by the number's treacly prologue, in which an overdressed Dick Powell and Gloria Stuart are seen simpering at each other in a blossomy moonlit garden. But these potential pitfalls are deftly sidestepped by the rigor, delicacy, and sheer audaciousness of the number's design. Although everyone remembers this number as the one with the fifty-six grand pianos, what is most remarkable is not the number and weight of this phalanx of pianos but the ways in which Berkeley plays against the grandiosity and weightiness inherent in the concept.

"The Words Are in My Heart" is based on a central paradox concerning heaviness and buoyancy. There are few objects that connote heaviness as much as a grand piano—the very name signals grandiosity. Yet the main conceit of the number is to treat these behemoths as the essence of gossamer, the airiest of bubbles, to spin them around like tops, send them gliding like figure skaters, waft them about like thistledown on an evening breeze. One's very sense of gravity is contradicted and confounded; nowhere is there a more explicit demonstration that the space of Berkeleyesque spectacle is a universe unto itself, with its own unique set of logical and physical laws, completely distinct from the world of the narrative.

The keynote of the style of "The Words Are in My Heart" is fluidity. Trick cuts juggle scales, locations, and objects in ever-shifting patterns. Combined, offsetting movements (e.g., the camera swivels in one direction while the pianos spin in another) create a floating effect that seems to levitate the pianos through space.

The prologue in the garden ends with a crane back to long shot. A matching dissolve converts Powell and Stuart into figurines in a toy-sized tabletop display, beside which are revealed a comparatively gigantic female trio singing at a white piano in an elegant setting. The shot tracks into the trio's pianist, then cuts to a close shot of what are apparently her fingers on the piano keys. The camera pulls back to reveal that the fingers actually belong to a blonde chorine seated at a white piano that is but one of many similar piano-and-chorine units, all arranged around a multitiered, curvilinear setting and all revolving in unison. A concealed cut shifts the action to a different location, revealing the pianos/girls now arranged in a back-to-back double row that recedes deep into the background. The two rows glide apart, come back together, and form a provocative series of undulating vulviform patterns. The pianos deploy into seven rows of eight each, completely filling the screen (see photo 50). Then they all glide offscreen, leaving the chorines behind to spread and swing their long, filmy white skirts.

The number's climactic shot is one of the most dazzling of Berkeley's career. A lone chorine is seen dancing atop four pianos that have been pushed together; her skirts swirl oddly about her, as if floating in midair. As the camera cranes up, the entire contingent of remaining pianos fly in from the sides of the frame, converging with magical smoothness into a perfect rectangle. The lights go down, and the chorine dances in a spotlit circle. The camera continues to crane back, passing through a latticework grille that materializes in the foreground and then dipping down to reveal a set of giant-sized piano keys. The entire shot has in fact been filmed in reverse-motion and presented to the viewer "backwards" (which accounts for the odd billowings of the dancer's skirt). This effect culminates the number's movement toward the defiance of gravity and the reversal of natural laws.

A cut and a pull back reveal the "giant" female singing trio at the piano. On its frontboard is seen the decorative latticework grille inside of which the body of the number has presumably taken place. In the coda, the trio stand up, blow out the candles, and glide up a shadowy staircase in the background. The camera tracks into a grandfather clock that is striking midnight, then sweeps over to the figurines in the toy garden. A matching dissolve returns the number to its original moonlit garden setting, where Powell and Stuart are now surrounded by softly falling blossoms. As they kiss, the camera pans down to a pool whose surface is choked with fallen blossoms; the blossoms float apart to reveal the final embrace in rippling reflection.

The coda of "The Words Are in My Heart" takes the feelings of fluidity and fleetingness established so strongly in the body of the number and attaches to them connotations of impermanence, temporality, and mortality (the blown-out candles, the shadows, the striking clock). These connotations are then transferred, with the utmost delicacy, to the framing tableau of the two young lovers (the falling blossoms, the rippling reflection).

Of great interest is the way that this note of impending ripeness established at the end of "The

Words Are in My Heart" is picked up and expanded in the film's next number, "Lullaby of Broadway," which is all about clocks, passing time, and sudden mortality. This strong thematic link between the two final numbers welds them together into a juggernaut that sweeps aside the inconsequential plot resolutions inserted between and after the two big numbers.

"Lullaby of Broadway"

"Lullaby of Broadway," the climax not only of *Gold Diggers of 1935* but of Berkeley's entire Warner Bros. period, has been widely and justly celebrated as one of the greatest achievements of the American musical film. It should be noted initially that no other Berkeley number has a more tenuous relationship to the surrounding narrative. While "The Words Are in My Heart," excessive and autonomous though it is, can ostensibly justify its presence in the narrative as a fitting climax to the Dick Powell–Gloria Stuart romance, "Lullaby of Broadway" can claim no such rationalization. The narrative is essentially resolved before the number begins. Although Dick Powell has a sizable supporting role in "Lullaby," the number is clearly, even ostentatiously, centered on Wini Shaw, a completely peripheral character in the surrounding narrative, where she is occasionally glimpsed as a cigarette-counter salesclerk at the hotel. The tone and style of "Lullaby of Broadway" have little in common with the surrounding narrative (or with the other musical numbers, except for the companion blockbuster, "The Words Are in My Heart"), which has virtually nothing to do with Broadway, New York City, nightclubs, or lullabies. To say that "Lullaby of Broadway" is grossly disproportionate to its narrative motivation would be an understatement. The number is completely anticlimactic and superfluous in terms of the film as a narrative, but completely climactic and essential in terms of the film as an occasion for spectacle.

"Lullaby of Broadway" plunges more bluntly into direct cinematic address than any previous Berkeley number. The curtains open to reveal Wini's face pinpointed in a field of black and slowly looming toward the camera. The opening movement effectively severs spectacle space from narrative space, quickly pulling the rug out from under the viewer's sense of context. In the black void of the prologue, it is difficult to tell whether the camera is moving toward Wini, or Wini is moving toward the camera. One's sense of direction is then confounded as the camera appears to dip Wini down, spin her around, and tilt her back. She puts a cigarette to her lips, and her face dissolves into a face-shaped aerial view of Manhattan. A series of dissolves and optical zooms moves the number into the heart of the city, ending on a clock tower whose circular face indicates that the time is 6:37 A.M.

The next section of the number is a series of vignettes depicting the awakening city in a manner reminiscent of the "city symphony" documentaries of the late 1920s.[2] A policeman is seen walking his beat;

milk is delivered; alarm clocks go off; awakening women pull on stockings and fasten brassieres; stacks of newspapers fall to the curb; commuters gulp down coffee, press through turnstiles, board subways; whistles sound; workers rush into offices; pencils are sharpened; an organ-grinder turns the crank of his instrument.

Although "Lullaby of Broadway" is one of Berkeley's most spectacularly stylized numbers, it does not highlight the extended camera movements or patterned overhead shots that are generally his trademarks. Instead, the main focus of cinematic spectacularization in "Lullaby of Broadway" is the *cut*. "Lullaby" spectacularizes editing, raising it out of its customary position of subordinate functionalism and turning it into an object of overt display. In contrast to the "invisible" (i.e., subordinate to the narrative) editing common to the classical narrative cinema, every cut in "Lullaby" is ostentatious, overloaded, designed to be "felt" by the spectator. This effect is accomplished in a number of ways, often used in excessive combination. The majority of the shots employ extreme off-angles (i.e., they are tilted out of true). Nearly every shot is composed around a sharply oblique angle that clashes with those of the shots immediately around it. Many shots are vignetted by means of a soft "vaseline" effect around the edges. High and low angles are often precipitously steep. Characters face and move in opposing directions in adjoining shots. Virtually no category of montage-oriented compositional conflict prescribed by Sergei Eisenstein—graphic, planes, volumes, spatial, light, tempo—is overlooked by Berkeley in "Lullaby of Broadway."[3] As a result, each shot tends to separate out into a flamboyantly self-enclosed unit, as if it were a microcosm of a Berkeleyesque production number—a little spectacle-within-the-spectacle or, to paraphrase an Eisensteinian term, a spectacle *cell*.

As well as the spaces between shots (i.e., cuts), "Lullaby of Broadway" also spectacularizes the spaces around shots (i.e., the framelines). The opening section of "Lullaby" (except for the face-in-the-dark prologue) is based on the principle of synecdoche (part for the whole) in such an ostentatious and excessive way as to make the viewer constantly aware of the arbitrary constraints of the frameline and of composition in general. Virtually no faces are seen in the "waking-up" section; if the prologue to the number is all face and no context, the "waking-up" section is all context and no faces. Instead, the section concentrates on *hands*—hands are seen collecting the milk bottles, pushing away the alarm clock, pulling on the stockings, opening the coffee-pot lid, inserting coins in the subway turnstile, turning the pencil sharpener, etc. The synecdochic structure of the opening, based on restriction and incompleteness, also serves to set up, by contrast, the number's climax, based on excess and satiety.

The opening's heavily marked concentration on the face (in the prologue) and the hand (in the "waking up" section) sets up a hybrid verbal/visual pun between the hands and faces of people and the hands and faces of *clocks*, which also figure very prominently in the number's design. The opening image of Wini's face as a white circle in the center of the frame is echoed by the image of the white, circular face of the clock at the beginning of the "waking up" section. A motif of circular movements, mostly clockwise, recurs throughout the prologue (the wheel of the dairy truck, the spinning turnstile, the pencil sharpener, the hand-organ), and beyond (the circular patterns of the climactic dance) as reminders of the hand of advancing time.

After the "waking up" section, "Lullaby of Broadway" launches into a passage of sustained intranumber narrative unprecedented (and subsequently unsurpassed) in any Berkeley number. Some previous Berkeley spectacles, such as "Shanghai Lil" and "I Only Have Eyes for You," established an initial narrative situation only to dissolve it eventually into pure spectacle. "Lullaby of Broadway" moves into large-scale spectacle while still sustaining a narrative line, somewhat in the manner of numbers like Astaire and Rogers's "Let's Face the Music and Dance" (*Follow the Fleet*, 1936) or Gene Kelly's "An American in Paris" (*An American in Paris*, 1951).

Maintaining the synecdochic and heavily angled style of the "waking up" section, the next section of the number shows Wini, accompanied by an inebriated Dick, returning home from a bout of all-night carousing. Stopping to give some milk to a stray kitten, Wini goes to bed, sleeping while the city works. The clock outside her window spins rapidly through the daylight hours and lights up with neon as night falls. The flashing neon falls on Wini's face as she wakes up. She gets dressed and sets out on another round of nightclubbing with Dick.

The nightclub they attend is unique. For one thing, Wini and Dick appear to be its only customers. Sitting in incongruous isolation at the club's only table, high above the dance floor, they watch a performance by the specialty dance team of Ramon and Rosita. An enormous crane shot back opens up the space of the number for the first time, signaling the shift to full-scale spectacle and revealing the full interior of the nightclub—extravagantly, even eerily vast, laid out in a complex pattern of tiers and steps. (See photo 52.)

Ramon and Rosita exit but quickly return, Rosita leading a brigade of tap-dancing women, Ramon leading a brigade of tap-dancing men. A series of wildly angled shots captures the mass tap dance, the frames surfeited with dancers, each break by one sex answered by a break from the other, the dancing feet booming ominously through the cavernous interior. (See photo 53.) The marking-off of the cuts is augmented by the dancing: each sequence of steps ends with an emphatic tap, followed by a pause, followed by a cut, as if the dancers were announcing the shot-divisions. The women fall back into the men's arms, then "unfall" by means of reverse motion. The cutting reaches a peak of intensity during an extended tap routine by three men, the shots jumping from one extreme angle to another, climaxed by a shot from underneath the floor, which has suddenly turned to glass.

It is difficult to describe in words the exhilarating frenzy of the climactic portion of "Lullaby of Broadway." Waving their extended arms, the chorus chants en masse to Wini, "Come on and da-a-a-a-nce!" She replies teasingly, "Why don't you come and get me?" They lure their willing victim down to the main floor and dizzyingly whirl her around (see photo 54). She runs out a glass double-door onto a high balcony, playfully shutting out the insistent chorus. Dick kisses her through the glass; the chorus presses forward; the doors fly open, pushing Wini over the ledge. The ground rushes up; the image spins and dissolves into the rapidly rotating face of the neon-illuminated clock. The clock comes to a rest, but its hands continue to spin, bringing on the advent of another morning.

The coda of the number is swift and haunting. The camera pulls back from the clock and through the window of Wini's apartment, tracking across the empty room to a crack of light under the front door. A cut to the other side of the door reveals the kitten waiting patiently for its bowl of milk. The city recedes again into a face-shaped vignette, which is then filled by the face of Wini. She removes the cigarette from her lips. This tantalizing detail confounds one's sense of time—is the entire body of the number supposed to have occurred within the duration of a single cigarette puff? Also, what exactly is the relationship of the ethereal Wini of the prologue to the playgirl Wini of the number's narrative—is she her spirit, her dreamer, her alter ego? These questions remain open; with an enigmatic, Cheshire Cat smile, Wini's face spins back around and recedes into the darkness from which it emerged.

It is intriguing to speculate on "Lullaby of Broadway" as a double-edged internal commentary on the crisis of the Berkeleyesque mode vis-à-vis the changing course of the Hollywood musical at this time. On one level, it culminates the excess and delirium that characterized Berkeleyesque spectacle in its early thirties heyday. But those very elements begin to turn in on themselves here. The vast set, vertiginous angles, expressionist lighting begin to seem empty, eerie, melancholy, nightmarish. The characteristically large chorus becomes oddly threatening, their stomping feet booming ominously through the cavernous nightclub, which takes on a haunted-house quality. On another level, it is possible to interpret "Lullaby of Broadway" as a reflection not on the Berkeleyesque past but on the future of the musical represented by RKO and MGM. In this reading, Wini and Dick become avatars of the debonair Astaire and Rogers; the vast nightclub set (unusually deco for Warner Bros.) is Van Nest Polglase with a hangover; and the big dance number is "The Continental" gone gothic. Like Berkeley's own career at Warner Bros., "Lullaby of Broadway" moves from populist cityscape (*42nd*

Street) to Sandrichian glitz (*Gold Diggers of 1935*)—that is, to the less social, more polished, more luxurious, and more constrictively narrativized world of the post-Astaire musical. Although these two readings contradict each other, that does not necessarily mean that they are incompatible. Instead, they can be seen as reflecting together the ambivalence and uncertainty facing the Berkeleyesque mode at this critical juncture in the history of the musical film.

Gold Diggers of 1937 (1936)

Despite his elevation to the dual role of director/choreographer, Berkeley continued to wear the single hat of choreographer in other directors' films. *In Caliente* (1935, directed by Lloyd Bacon), a Mexico-set musical, features two major Berkeley production numbers: "The Lady in Red," notable for its atmospheric candlelit opening and its attempts to mix spectacle space and narrative space, and "Muchacha," an onstage number that begins with a Mexican *bandito* plot and climaxes with a complex long take through a saloon packed to the rafters with an enormous ensemble of *vaqueros* and *señoritas*. *The Singing Marine* (1937, directed by Ray Enright) is notable for "Night over Shanghai," a mood piece whose morbid tone recalls "No More Love," "Lullaby of Broadway," and the middle section of "42nd Street" but whose constrained sense of spectacle is limited to intermittent touches (see photo 55). *Varsity Show* (1937, directed by William Keighley) is a modestly scaled campus musical until Berkeley's finale, a jubilant medley of college fight songs illustrated with appropriate choral formations.[4]

Gold Diggers of 1937 (directed by Lloyd Bacon) is a hodgepodge of Berkeleyesque and non-Berkeleyesque elements typical of Berkeley's late thirties work. The film opens with a brief pre-credits sequence of white-suited Dick Powell singing "With Plenty of Money and You" directly to the camera while standing against a black, featureless background. Three small-scale numbers are followed by the film's two big production numbers: "Let's Put Our Heads Together" and "All's Fair in Love and War."

"Let's Put Our Heads Together"

"Let's Put Our Heads Together" represents an attempt to adapt the Berkeleyesque production number to a narrativized context. The setting—a poolside party at a country estate—establishes the type of hermetic environment that encloses both narrative and musical elements. This contrasts with Berkeley's big backstage-musical numbers, which work more to segregate musical elements from narrative elements. Accordingly, "Let's Put Our Heads Together" is structured much differently from a characteristic Berkeley onstage number; it is much more amorphous. Its form is highly serial, syntagmatic, linear, with each element constantly spinning off laterally into another one.

The number begins with Dick Powell and Joan Blondell walking onto a dance floor and joining the couples there. As he and Blondell dance, Powell breaks into song, and a lengthy panning-cum-tracking shot follows the couple as they walk off the dance floor and continue the song beside a tree. A series of cutaways and panning shots leads to various groupings of two or three characters, one after another, each taking a couplet of the song. The chain eventually leads back to Powell and Blondell, now seated on a swing-seat. They kiss as an offscreen chorus takes up the last lines of the song, and the number appears to be finished.

But the camera continues to pan, picking up secondary leads Lee Dixon and Rosalind Marquis as they stroll by and launch into a reprise of an earlier tune, "Speaking of the Weather." They walk over to the swimming pool; Marquis dives in and joins four other bathing girls in a brief, toned-down water spectacle, with the girls forming a human chain of interlocked legs and torsos. Marquis emerges from the pool and joins Dixon in another apparent finale. But the camera pans with Dixon, following him to the tennis court, where he performs a lengthy tap dance as everyone stands around and watches. This climaxes with a double row of chorines linking arms to form a human bridge, across which Dixon walks on his hands. Another finale is reached, the audience applauds—but the music continues, and the next shot shows Glenda Farrell dancing with Victor Moore. However, this time the number really has ended, and Farrell and Moore's dance is merely a lead-in to the continuation of the narrative.

It is through a series of negatives that "Let's Put Our Heads Together" points up some of the central attributes of Berkeley's more characteristic production numbers. "Let's Put Our Heads Together" has no sense of a center, either spatially or structurally. Spatially, the center is continually shifting—from the dance floor to the garden to the swimming pool to the tennis court. The stars of the first part of the number, Powell and Blondell, disappear in the second half, when they are displaced by a second set of stars, Dixon and Marquis. The distinction between performers and audience is continually shifting. The number has little sense of symmetry, nor of the gradual, cumulative buildup to greater intensity and spectacle that is typical of other Berkeley numbers. Elements of potential spectacle—the water antics, the human bridge—remain brief and localized, without an opportunity to be expanded or elaborated. The beginning and end of the number are not clearly demarcated, leading easily from and to the narrative, which weakens the sense of separation and self-enclosure essential to full-scale Berkeleyesque spectacle.

"Let's Put Our Heads Together" is a curious number, full of small, isolated bits of invention, but it is ultimately too shapeless and lacking in cumulative impact to be considered a major Berkeley effort. Like "Let That Be a Lesson to You" in the upcoming

Hollywood Hotel (1937), it represents a tentative and not wholly successful attempt to build a bridge between the ambitions of Berkeleyesque spectacle and the constraints of the narrativized musical.

"All's Fair in Love and War"

On the other hand, the film's finale, "All's Fair in Love and War," represents a substantial return to the Berkeleyesque. It supplies all the elements missing in "Let's Put Our Heads Together": formal on-stage setting, symmetrical structure, strong cumulative sense of progression and "building," clearly demarcated separation from the surrounding narrative. Upon this structural base, "All's Fair in Love and War" adds the characteristic superstructural elements of Berkeleyesque spectacle: gigantic props, multiple props, outrageous metaphors, massed chorus formations, hand-and-arm drills (augmented with poles and pennants), trick transitions and camera effects. (Absent, however, are Berkeley's characteristic overhead geometric patterns, even though the parade of chorus girls in the latter part of the number would seem to provide a golden opportunity for them.)

"Let's Put Our Heads Together" is preceded by a careful and detailed establishment (via camera movements and foreground/background relationships) of the narrativized setting within which it takes place. In contrast, "All's Fair in Love and War" plunges directly into the type of abstract, decontextualized nonspace with which Berkeley frequently opened numbers in his post-1934 films ("Lullaby of Broadway," "Night Over Shanghai," "Brazil" in *The Gang's All Here*, "Love Is Back in Business" in *Call Me Mister*, "I've Gotta Hear That Beat" in *Small Town Girl*, etc.). Dick Powell, dressed in white, is spotlit alone in long shot on a black stage; a fast crane-down moves him into close shot. The number's early close shots of Powell are virtually identical to the pre-credits shot of him singing "With Plenty of Money and You" and thus work to associate the space here with the pre-credits space, located "outside" the film proper.

"All's Fair in Love and War" is one of Berkeley's most austerely designed numbers, maintaining a white-on-black motif throughout, with exclusively white props and costumes displayed against a featureless black field. Berkeley has said in interview that this austerity was forced on him by the parsimony of Warner Bros.:

> One time they wouldn't build a set for me because of the economy measures. Hal Wallis, then at Warners, said to me, "We don't want any more of these big expensive sets." So I said, "All right, don't give me any set. Just give me a black floor and a black cyclorama (backing)." I was so damned mad, I couldn't see straight because they wanted to get rid of all this cost.
>
> I said, "If you'll give me 50 boys and 50 girls, I'll

> do the number." And I did just that, using a plain black floor, a plain black background, and all the kids were dressed in white military uniforms. . . . This shows what can happen when you have to become completely resourceful and make use of a handful of essentials without a big set.[5]

Like many of Berkeley's published statements, this one is slightly misleading. Although it is true that no set is *seen* in "All's Fair in Love and War," this does not mean there is no set present. The set is concealed by the black-on-black decor. In the early stages of the number, various levels and steps are barely visible if one scrutinizes the frame, and a forest of concealed black pedestals enables Berkeley to produce one of his most inventive spatial effects at the end.

Although it is not as rich and complex as Berkeley numbers like "Shanghai Lil," "I Only Have Eyes for You," "Lullaby of Broadway," and "The Polka Dot Polka," "All's Fair in Love and War" contains an impressive roster of sleight-of-camera effects and visual tropes. A shot of Powell alone on the bare stage changes as the camera tracks into close shot, then pulls back to reveal that a formation of approximately forty oversized rocking chairs has materialized beside him, each one containing a romantic couple on its commodious seat (see photo 56). A concealed matching dissolve causes one of the chairs to change scale instantaneously, its seat becoming an even more enormous platform on which Lee Dixon performs a tap dance. The chair explodes into flying fragments, which reassemble into a cannon. The cannon fires white cannonballs, which fill the foreground to become close-up vignettes of various chorus girls and, finally, of star Joan Blondell.

It is the climax of the number that provides the most astounding effects. The women, victorious in the battle of the sexes, parade with banners on the ends of long poles, the entire ensemble reflected in the polished black floor (see photo 57). The ambiguous visual space created by the reflections sets up the subsequent series of transformations. The chorus girls line up in a double row and rotate the banners rapidly in vertical circles. However, each girl is now standing atop an invisible black pedestal, so that the banners, on their downward arc, extend below the apparent plane of the floor—an effect that is easily confused with the reflections of the banners "below" the plane of the floor in the preceding shots. To add to this confusion, at the end of the banner maneuvers, matching cuts are used to switch invisibly back and forth between the reflective-floor arrangement and the pedestals arrangement. The overall effect is as if the floor were continually melting away and reforming again—a subtly disorienting dissolution of spatial reality that confounds solidity and insubstantiality, object and reflection. This motif of dissolution/reformation is carried through at the end of the number. In reverse motion, a close-up of Joan Blondell is swallowed back up into the cannon, which flies apart to form into a giant rocking chair. The number ends as it began, with Powell standing alone on the bare black stage.

The obvious cross-reference in "All's Fair in Love and War" is to "Remember My Forgotten Man," which likewise is based on a mixture of sexual and military metaphors. However, in "All's Fair in Love and War" the associations are less specifically social-economic-historical than they are in "Remember My Forgotten Man." The opening of the number—Powell standing alone and erect in the frame—establishes an initial phallic association that is carried through in the cannons and rifles and in the dominance of Powell and fellow male Lee Dixon during the early part of the number. The hostilities proper, comprising the central section of the number, involve two motorized trenches ("No Man's Land" and "No Woman's Land") filled with uniformed women and men, respectively (see photo 58). The trenches converge and gunfire is exchanged, but the rifles are abandoned as the men wilt under a "gas attack" of perfume spray, followed up by a barrage of kisses. The men, blissfully defeated, disappear completely, and the screen is filled with women parading vigorously toward the camera (much like the men in the triumphal off-to-war section of "Remember My Forgotten Man"). This is followed by the banner-twirling section (described above), which climaxes with the women obscured behind a solid wall of fluttering banners. The progression of the number can be summed up as follows:

1. Women supplant men.
2. Abstraction supplants women.

This progression represents a major principle of Berkeleyesque cinema as a whole.

One might assume that the return to Powell at the end of the number signifies the reestablishment of male/phallic dominance. Although this interpretation is narrowly correct, it must be weighed against the experiential dimension of the number, which makes the final reassertion of the male principle seem paltry and attenuated in comparison to the rich panoply of femaleness that previously saturated the screen. In Berkeleyesque cinema, the interrelated pulls of the female and the abstract are powerful ones, and their regulation by structures of male dominance (often associated with narrative) is relatively weak.

Hollywood Hotel (1937)

After *Gold Diggers of 1935*, *Hollywood Hotel* (directed by Busby Berkeley) is Berkeley's most ambitious project as a director in the late 1930s. It evidences similar problems in integrating spectacle with narrative, and in sustaining a style over the course of an entire film rather than concentrating it all in the production numbers. As in *Gold Diggers of 1935* and *In Caliente*, the hotel setting (like the ocean liner and country estate in other musicals of the late 1930s and early 1940s) functions as a model for a self-enclosed, artificial world detached from social reality. The tone, like the setting itself, works to include the entire film—numbers and narrative alike—in a homogeneous unity. This contrasts with the Warners/Berkeley musicals of the early thirties, where this "island effect" was largely limited to the stage itself and the production numbers that took place upon it. One result of this structural consistency is that the spectacle side of the film is deflated and the narrative side correspondingly inflated. This strategy has much in common with the RKO/Astaire/Sandrich musicals, which synthesize the two sides of the film into a consistently lightweight tone. However, Berkeley, a creature of spectacle, lacks the light touch necessary to modulate the film's style in order to achieve this type of synthesis.

The decor of *Hollywood Hotel* is pompous and overornate, without the art deco slickness of the Astaire musicals. The eponymous Hollywood Hotel, central locale of the action, is a palatial establishment whose vast lobby features polished black floors, thick Greek columns, ornate railings, massive chandeliers, and banks of wide steps. The hotel's Orchid Room nightclub, where most of the musical numbers are performed, looks large enough to accommodate an army division comfortably. The room is festooned with huge (c. ten- to fifteen-foot high) "orchids." Even an "intimate" musical number ("Silhouetted in the Moonlight") between lovers Dick Powell and Rosemary Lane is staged in the vast, empty arena of the Hollywood Bowl, with deep-focus over-the-shoulder shots showing the two characters hundreds of feet apart. The frequently impressive fluidity of the camerawork in *Hollywood Hotel* (the movie is filled with vigorous crane shots, zip-pans, and fall-back tracking shots) becomes less snappy than ponderous in relation to its context. It ultimately serves to underline the heavy grandiosity of the settings and to overweight the trivial actions contained within them.

The dominant tone of the narrative is farcical screwball comedy, but given the ponderousness of the film's style and design, the result is strenuous, strident, unrelieved silliness. In an interview, director Howard Hawks criticized his classic 1938 comedy *Bringing Up Baby* because all its characters were too eccentric, without anyone to establish a framework of normality.[6] One wonders what Hawks might have thought of *Hollywood Hotel*, where it often seems as if the gate of a nearby "freak" show had been left open just before shooting began.

The film's parade of roaring grotesques includes screeching, egomaniacal movie-star Lola Lane; gratingly aggressive photographer Ted Healy; Johnnie Davis, the odd, somewhat epicene vocalist of the Benny Goodman orchestra; flamingly swishy tailor Curt Bois (flourishing a foot-long cigarette holder); apoplectic drive-in restaurateur Edgar Kennedy (see photo 59); caricature-specialist Fritz Feld as an eye-rolling, hysterical customer; cross-eyed, semi-idiotic man-chaser Mabel Todd; hideously "sweet," baby-talking gossip columnist Louella Parsons (playing herself); and walking non sequitur Hugh Herbert, who reacts with total, bug-eyed illogic to every situation he encounters.

Collectively, these characters exemplify the heavy comic touch afflicting most of Berkeley's directed films, which lack the flexibility and range of style conducive to an effective balance of comedy, narrative, and spectacle. Amidst this wall-to-wall pandemonium, low-key protagonist Dick Powell gets mostly lost in the shuffle, as does his romance with Rosemary Lane, as does the self-effacing charisma of guest star Benny Goodman, as does Warner Bros. veteran Glenda Farrell (in a small role as a wisecracking island of sanity).

In the almost uniformly hyperbolic atmosphere of *Hollywood Hotel*, the intrusion of Berkeleyesque spectacle seems nearly redundant. Indeed, elements of Berkeleyesque spectacle are confined mainly to the margins of the musical numbers and remain on a relatively limited scale. These include the series of exhilarating camera movements in the opening "Hooray for Hollywood" parade and the concealed trick cuts that invisibly bring the camera closer to and farther away from the stage in the Orchid Room numbers.

The film's most ambitious number, "Let That Be a Lesson to You," has a rambling, amorphous, de-centered structure similar to that of "Let's Put Our Heads Together" in *Gold Diggers of 1937*. Set at a hamburger drive-in, the number shifts awkwardly between narrativity (the irate owner keeps interrupting the song; the lyrics blend in and out of orders given for food), hyperbolic comedy (cross-eyed Mabel Todd sips down four glasses of soda through four straws at once; a poodle dances down the counter on its hind legs), and more characteristic Berkeley devices (song lyrics are passed fluidly from one passerby to the next; an oversized, forced-perspective eight-ball rolls in front of the camera at the end). The climactic number, a rendition of "Otchichornya," with Berkeley's camera lumbering over and around the large orchestra and vocal chorus, is the type of heavy, quasi-classical schmaltz more commonly encountered at studios such as MGM and Columbia.

Nowhere in *Hollywood Hotel* do the musical numbers cut loose into full-scale, sustained spectacle in the manner of the Warners/Berkeley musicals of the early 1930s; neither do they achieve the smooth balance of comedy, romance, and performance that characterizes the best passages of the Astaire-Rogers musicals. The result is a clumsy hybrid, too constricted to be satisfying as Berkeleyesque spectacle, but too inflated to be satisfying as lightweight musical comedy.

Gold Diggers in Paris (1938, directed by Ray Enright), a half-hearted finale to the Gold Diggers series, was Berkeley's last foray into musical spectacle at Warner Bros. His attempts in the late thirties to shift from a specialist to a full director and to branch out into other genres besides the musical were not successful or sustained enough to produce a major shift in his directorial identity. With the exception of the two big production numbers ("The Words Are in My Heart" and "Lullaby of Broadway") in the transitional *Gold Diggers of 1935*, Berkeley's most impressive work of this period occurs in those films on which he served solely as dance director, operating independently of the narrative and placing numbers within a show-within-the-show format. Included in this category are "Muchacha" (*In Caliente*), "Night Over Shanghai" (*The Singing Marine*), the *Varsity Show* finale, and "All's Fair in Love and War" (*Gold Diggers of 1937*).

Even these more successful numbers were increasingly hampered by budgetary restrictions, new developments in the genre, and the general decline of the Warner Bros. musical to a minor position in the studio's output. No longer in the forefront of the genre, Warner Bros. did not seem strongly committed to developing the musical in the new directions being pursued elsewhere, but at the same time the studio was not providing Berkeley with adequate resources to support the less fashionable (but far from dead) vein of Berkeleyesque spectacle. It was a good time for Berkeley to move on, and in 1939 he left Warner Bros. for MGM, where the musical was very much on the rise. MGM had both the commitment to developing new musical forms and the resources to sustain large-scale production numbers. However, Berkeley's tendency to capitalize on the latter far more than the former was to cause grave problems, even though the move to MGM initially brought renewed prestige and status to his apparently declining career.

MGM PERIOD (1939–1943)

9

From Warners to Metro

In 1939 Berkeley terminated his six-year association with Warner Bros. and moved to MGM—a decision that was bound to have an enormous effect on the course of the Berkeleyesque style in cinema. At that time the MGM musical, under the leadership of producer Arthur Freed, was developing more forcefully than any other studio's in the direction of big-star, strongly narrativized, integration-oriented productions. This movement would culminate in a series of acknowledged masterpieces of the "integrated" film musical: *Meet Me in St. Louis* (1944), *The Pirate* (1948), *On The Town* (1949), *An American in Paris* (1951), *Singin' in the Rain* (1952), *The Band Wagon* (1953), and *It's Always Fair Weather* (1955).

Berkeley directed four films for Freed in the early 1940s: *Babes in Arms* (1939), *Strike Up the Band* (1940), *Babes on Broadway* (1942), and *For Me and My Gal* (1942). He also contributed numbers to the Freed productions *Lady Be Good* (1941) and *Girl Crazy* (1943). These musicals are all highly narrativized in structure, pitched more toward song than toward dance or spectacular display, and strongly centered on the personalities of high-powered stars such as Mickey Rooney, Judy Garland, and Gene Kelly.

In this context, the exercise of Berkeleyesque spectacle was for the most part severely constrained. When asked in an interview to describe the difference between his Warner Bros. and MGM work, Berkeley explained:

> The crucial differences were determined by the story line. The Warner's musicals were generally built around a backstage plot, hence a certain type of musical number that was performed on stage as a formal spectacle. At Metro, on the other hand, the numbers were sort of slipped into the plot. If there was a love scene in a living room, one of the actors began to address the other with a song, and I remained in the living room for the ensuing dialogue in the sequence. And even if other characters came in, the scene remained very intimate. I didn't have the huge space that was at my disposal when I filmed such a sequence on what was supposed to be a theatre stage. . . . Generally I work with a large number of people, for spectacle means spectacular, and spectacular means that many people take part in very complex numbers. Instead of using a dozen girls as others do, I prefer to use forty-eight or sixty.[1]

In general, the late thirties–early forties was a period of regularization and maturation in the storytelling forms used by American cinema, leading to an overall increase in narrative consistency, complexity, and ambitiousness, as indicated by the more extensive use of flashback structures, subplots, and lengthy running times. There was a less freewheeling and casual approach to film storytelling than there had been in the early thirties, and this necessarily inhibited the use of extended Berkeleyesque flourishes. As a result, these flourishes were increasingly confined to localized and marginal instances.

On those occasions when the Berkeleyesque was given a little more room to cut loose, this tendency was generally directed away from the tone of erotic delirium that was nurtured by both the period (early 1930s) and studio (Warner Bros.) of his greatest earlier successes. The early 1940s in general and the MGM studio in particular were more inclined toward deeroticized sanctimoniousness, reinforced by the entrenchment of the regulatory Production Code. The Berkeleyesque impulse was accordingly diverted into the more acceptable channels of patriotism ("God's Country" in *Babes in Arms*, "The Ballad for Americans" in *Born to Sing*) and middlebrow culturalism (the finale of *Broadway Serenade*, "Fascinatin' Rhythm" in *Lady Be Good*). The latter mode provided the framework for Berkeley's first, promisingly (and, as it turned out, uncharacteristically) eccentric assignment at MGM.

Broadway Serenade (1939)

Released from his Warner Bros. contract, Berkeley was hired freelance by MGM to provide the final musical number for *Broadway Serenade* (directed by Robert Z. Leonard). This melodrama concerns the marital woes of a serious composer (Lew Ayres) who starves in a garret while his wife (Jeanette MacDonald) rises to fame as a singer in a Ziegfeldian revue. Berkeley's finale, which both climaxes and ends the film, is in the mode that nourished his biggest Warner Bros. backstage numbers: a realistically motivated stage number whose performance is expanded and embellished unrealistically. However, there are already creeping in here those elements of increased narrativity that were to constrain the development of Berkeleyesque spectacle during his MGM tenure.

The opening section of the number—a kitschy tableau of a shepherd piping away in a pastoral setting—takes its cue from sentiments voiced earlier by the Ayres character that he wants to capture in his compositions the panorama of music throughout the ages, starting from the first shepherd playing to his flock. The central section of the number, based on a conflict between classical and swing styles, encapsulates the musical/marital struggle between Ayres and MacDonald in the narrative. In addition, the final elevation/entrapment of MacDonald on a high pedestal epitomizes her elevation to stardom in the course of the story. Near the end of the number, Ayres himself appears briefly, pounding a grand piano while MacDonald smiles down at him from her lofty perch. This gaze cements their final reconciliation, which had been left slightly unresolved in the preceding narrative scene.

The number itself is in the venerable stage tradition of numbers in which music and musical instruments are made the explicit focus of the spectacle. The prologue (the primitive shepherd providing the first stirrings of musical composition) and conclusion (MacDonald atop a huge pedestal, reigning over an ornate neo-Grecian set filled with orchestra and choir) are in the middlebrow vein that MGM frequently reserved for its ventures into classical and semiclassical music. However, the long central section is one of Berkeley's most bizarre and striking creations: a dark, macabre fantasy that yokes the necrotic and the grotesque in the manner of a Mexican Day-of-the-Dead celebration.

After the opening establishment of the shepherd, the camera pulls back, squeezing through a window frame to reveal a gothically shadowed pianist banging away as he receives inspiration from the primitive source. The camera tracks into the piano keys and continues into a black space, out of which MacDonald appears in flowing black robes. A series of convoluted camera movements establishes the type of labyrinthine, disorienting space conducive to Berkeleyesque spectacle. The main set is a shadowy, sepulchral, multileveled structure, draped with black oilcloth and inset with crazily angled stairs. Rows of musicians, all wearing incredibly grotesque face-masks, and singers, dressed in dark winding-sheets, pop up on all sides. The pace of the number becomes frenetic as swing music begins to drown out the classical. Drummers pound out jungle rhythms, brass sections blare dissonantly, and jitterbuggers—also wearing grotesque, misshapen masks—jive convulsively. (See photo 60.) MacDonald is pulled down among the dancers and given a mask to wear as she dances with the most grotesque of the jitterbuggers.

The cacophony reaches its peak in a frenzied montage of various musical instruments, ending with a large gong that announces the number's passage out of the darkness and into the light. Transformed into a radiant majesty, MacDonald is revealed standing atop the pedestal with the orchestra below her. Despite the banality of these last images, the *Broadway Serenade* finale is for the most part a unique and fascinating number—a Berkeleyesque Dance of the Dead, a jitterbug with one foot in the grave, a morbid meeting of the *Ziegfeld Follies* and Forest Lawn.

The Mickey Rooney/Judy Garland "Trilogy"

The backbone of Berkeley's MGM tenure is his Mickey Rooney/Judy Garland "trilogy": *Babes in Arms*, *Strike Up the Band*, and *Babes on Broadway*. These are the only three of Berkeley's MGM musicals for which he directed both the numbers and the narrative. As such, they are important as examples of his attempt to fashion a more integrated style of musical in the MGM/Freed/1940s mode.

Besides their costars, the three films share similarities in tone, style, structure, and plot. Each film concerns the efforts of a group of youngsters, led by the Mickey Rooney character, to break into showbiz, culminating in their successful production of a stage show that wins the approval of the adult world. The general plot configuration—a series of rehearsals, setbacks, and financing problems leading up to the triumphant big show at the end—strongly evokes the pattern of the classic Warners/Berkeley backstage musicals of the early 1930s. But these surface similarities serve mainly to point up the more essential differences between the two series.

In the first place, there is Mickey Rooney. Despite Garland's costar billing, Rooney (who at this time was the number one box-office attraction in American movies) is decidedly the center of these films. In each film, the production of the big show is strongly tied to the Rooney character's struggles to overcome his immaturity and assert himself in the adult world. In *Babes in Arms* he must prove to his vaudevillian father that he is worthy of carrying on the family tradition on the stage. In *Strike Up the Band* he must convince his disapproving mother that he should follow a career in show business rather than, as his late father had wished, becoming a doctor. In *Babes on Broadway* he must learn that personal success is not as important as caring for others (which, in this case, means setting up a fresh-air fund for a group of underprivileged children). In contrast, the Garland character evidences no such conflicts or imperfections; she passes her time singing and waiting for the Rooney character to achieve grace. The success of the final show becomes a direct manifestation of the Rooney character's attainment of maturity and his entrée into the adult world. (See photo 61.)

Add to this the extremely aggressive acting style practiced by Rooney at this time, and the result is a performer who dominates these films in a way no performer (not even Cagney in *Footlight Parade*) ever dominated the classic Warner Bros. musicals of the 1930s, where the emphasis was more democratically apportioned among a cross-section of principals. This dominance of the Rooney character lends a greater degree of centralization to the narratives, which in turn imparts a greater degree of narrativization to the production numbers. Rather than being self-enclosed spectacles with at best a generalized relationship to the surrounding plot, these numbers become more the apotheoses of a single character. This character dominates both the dramatic elements of the narrative and the performance elements of the numbers, unifying them through his interdependent achievement of personal and theatrical goals.

Structurally and discursively, the Rooney/Garland musicals are more varied and integrated than were their Warner Bros. counterparts. One can classify the musical numbers in terms of two sets of paired oppositions: (1) performance/narrative and (2) realistic/unrealistic. "Performance" refers to numbers taking place in a formal performance situation (e.g., on a theatrical stage or a bandstand). "Narrative" refers to numbers intruding themselves directly into a fictional situation (e.g., two lovers, in the midst of a romantic scene, burst into a song affirming their love for one another). "Realistic" refers to numbers where the staging and the circumstances of the number appear to be realistically motivated, or "possible" (e.g., the number had been previously rehearsed in the narrative; the settings and effects are within the bounds of realistic possibility). "Unrealistic" refers to numbers whose circumstances and effects are blatantly "impossible" and signal a shift to another level of discourse for their comprehension (e.g., songs and elaborate dance routines are spontaneously generated by the characters; a stage number is filled with "impossible" effects such as trick cuts, instantaneous changes of setting, disembodied heads suspended in space, etc.).

One must note (inevitably) that these distinctions are not rigid. It is not uncommon to have overlappings of the opposed categories, passages from one to the other in the course of a single number, and ambiguous situations where the status is uncertain. With that proviso, the following chart is offered, categorizing the numbers of the classic Warners/Berkeley backstage musicals and those of the MGM Rooney/Garland "trilogy":

42nd Street:		
"You're Getting To Be a Habit"	Performance	Realistic
"Shuffle Off to Buffalo"	Performance	Realistic
"Young and Healthy"	Performance	Unrealistic
"42nd Street"	Performance	Unrealistic
Gold Diggers of 1933:		
"We're in the Money"	Performance	Realistic
"The Shadow Waltz" (1st)	Narrative	Realistic
"I've Got To Sing a Torch Song"	Narrative	Realistic
"Pettin' in the Park"	Performance	Unrealistic
"The Shadow Waltz" (2nd)	Performance	Unrealistic
"Remember My Forgotten Man"	Performance	Unrealistic
Footlight Parade:		
"Ah, The Moon Is Here"	Performance	Realistic
"Sitting on a Backyard Fence"	Performance	Unrealistic
"Honeymoon Hotel"	Performance	Unrealistic
"By a Waterfall"	Performance	Unrealistic
"Shanghai Lil"	Performance	Unrealistic
Dames:		
"When You Were a Smile"	Narrative	Unrealistic
"I Only Have Eyes for You" (1st)	Narrative	Unrealistic
"Try To See It My Way" (1st)	Performance	Realistic
"Dames" (1st)	Performance	Realistic
"The Girl at the Ironing Board"	Performance	Unrealistic
"I Only Have Eyes for You" (2nd)	Performance	Unrealistic
"Dames" (2nd)	Performance	Unrealistic
"Try To See It My Way" (2nd)	Performance	Realistic
Babes in Arms:		
"Good Morning"	Performance	Realistic
"You Are My Lucky Star"	Performance	Realistic
"Babes in Arms"	Narrative	Unrealistic
"Where or When"	Both	Both
"I Cried for You"	Narrative	Unrealistic
Minstrel Show	Performance	Realistic
"God's Country"	Performance	Realistic
Strike Up the Band:		
"Our Love Affair"	Narrative	Unrealistic
"La Conga"	Performance	Unrealistic
"Nobody"	Narrative	Unrealistic
"Little Nell from New Rochelle"	Performance	Realistic
"The Drummer Boy"	Performance	Realistic
"Strike Up the Band"	Performance	Realistic
Final Medley	Performance	Unrealistic
Babes on Broadway:		
"Anything Can Happen in New York"	Performance	Realistic
"How About You"	Narrative	Unrealistic
"Hoe Down"	Performance	Realistic
"Chin Up, Cheerio, Carry On"	Performance	Realistic
"Ghost Theatre"	Narrative	Unrealistic
"Bombshell from Brazil"	Performance	Realistic
"Franklin D. Roosevelt Jones"	Performance	Realistic

The majority of the numbers (and virtually all the

major numbers) in the classic Warner Bros. musicals fall into the performance/unrealistic mode—that is, they take place on the stage but then manipulate that context unrealistically. This is the mode in which Berkeleyesque spectacle thrived to the fullest extent.

The Rooney/Garland musicals (like MGM musicals in general) spread themselves more widely over the possible spectrum of musical-number modes. In addition, they make more extensive use of the narrative/unrealistic and performance/realistic modes, which have been by far the most commonly used modes in the history of the movie musical. These are also modes that are less amenable to Berkeleyesque spectacle than is the performance/unrealistic mode. The exercise of the Berkeleyesque is restricted in the first instance (narrative/unrealistic) by the demands of a narrative context, and in the second (performance/realistic) by the confined dimensions of a realistic performance space. In the Rooney/Garland films, the "unrealistic" mode is not used to open up the numbers to the extent that it does in the Warners/Berkeley musicals. Instead, the "unreality" (or "impossibility") of the numbers is largely restricted to their spontaneity, while the scale and effects of the numbers remain (except for some deviations around the edges) within the range of a conceivable stage production.

The distribution of the numbers in the two periods is also markedly different. In the classic Warners/Berkeley musicals (as described above), the major production numbers are typically "stacked" in a massive stage production that climaxes the film and that tends to eclipse the preceding narrative or, at least, to displace it strongly for the interim. This configuration works to segregate the numbers from the narrative, lumping them together into a monolithic bloc.

The Rooney/Garland musicals each contain seven major numbers (as opposed to typically between three and five in the Warner Bros. musicals), which are "spotted" throughout the film. There is no stacking of all or most of the big numbers at the end. Although a large-scale production number climaxes each of the Rooney/Garland films, some of their most spectacular and elaborate numbers ("Babes in Arms" in *Babes in Arms*, "La Conga" in *Strike Up the Band*, "Hoedown" in *Babes on Broadway*) are placed quite early in the proceedings.

The overall effect of these strategies is to integrate the numbers more strongly into the body of the film, to bring them more closely within the gravitational pull of the narrative. The potential segregation of the musical numbers is further broken down in these films by the frequent interruption of the numbers with dialogue and narrative passages (as in "Where or When" in *Babes in Arms*, "Our Love Affair" and "Nobody" in *Strike Up the Band*, "Anything Can Happen in New York" and "How About You" in *Babes on Broadway*). A similar effect is produced by the prominent inclusion of the audience in the same frame as the performance, constraining the performance space's potential to break away from the surrounding narrative space (as in "Lucky Star" and "God's Country" in *Babes in Arms*, "La Conga" and "The Drummer Boy" in *Strike Up the Band*, "Anything Can Happen in New York" and "Chin Up, Cheerio, Carry On" in *Babes on Broadway*).

A result of these integrative devices is the limitation of spectacle in the Rooney/Garland musicals. Although Berkeley managed to create some impressive production numbers during his MGM period, nowhere does he cut loose with the kind of unrestrained spectacle that characterizes "By a Waterfall," "I Only Have Eyes for You," "Dames," "Lullaby of Broadway," and "The Polka Dot Polka." In the classic Warner Bros. musicals (and in Berkeley's subsequent *The Gang's All Here*), spectacle frequently overwhelms narrative. In Berkeley's MGM musicals, spectacle is more frequently—and often uncomfortably—subordinated to narrative.

Babes in Arms (1939)

Babes in Arms (directed by Busby Berkeley), the first of the Rooney/Garland musicals that Berkeley directed, is the one with the closest surface relationship to the Warner Bros. musicals. At times it resembles a Baby Burlesk version of *42nd Street*, complete with Mickey Rooney as a high-pressure Julian Marsh-like director, bustling rehearsal scenes featuring a half-pint chorus line, and a pep talk in Judy Garland's dressing room before she goes on stage as a last-minute replacement for the original star. But the contrasts between *42nd Street* and *Babes in Arms* are more striking and essential than their similarities.

Following "Good Morning" and "You Are My Lucky Star," two small-scale numbers in intimate and informal performance situations, the film accelerates into spectacle for "Babes in Arms." The number has a strong narrative motivation. After having his theatrical ambitions denigrated by his father, Rooney stalks out angrily into the night, accompanied by his girlfriend Judy Garland and his baritone-voiced buddy Douglas McPhail. An exhilarating series of sweeping, synchronized camera movements falls back before the threesome as they stride through the back alleys of the neighborhood, singing their defiance ("They call us babes in arms,/But we are babes in armor!") while masses of torch-toting kids fall in behind them and take up the tune. The group convenes in a playground lot, where nursery rhymes counterpoint the main tune and a huge bonfire symbolizes the immolation of childish things.

It is very tempting to see in "Babes in Arms" a parallel between the Rooney character's declaration of independence and Busby Berkeley's recent break from Warners. Certainly, there is a striking contrast between the closely drilled regimental precision of Berkeley's Warner Bros. chorus lines and the explosive, disorderly, anarchic frenzy of his childish hordes here. "Babes in Arms" presents not a chorus but a mob, lurching about in a juvenile carambole. At the end, the camera cranes up to high-angle; however, the view from the top shows not a kaleidoscopic pattern of female bodies but a ring of children dancing madly around a raging bonfire.

Like *42nd Street*, *Babes in Arms* leads up to a big show, from which three production numbers are presented, but, unlike in *42nd Street*, the big show here is split up into three different segments, occurring at different points in the plot chronology and separated from each other by lengthy narrative passages. The first of these numbers, "Where or When," occurs at an early rehearsal session; the second, a Minstrel Show medley, takes place at the hometown premiere (see photo 62); the third and most ambitious, "God's Country," is set at the show's Broadway opening.

"God's Country" is a patriotic extravaganza of the type Berkeley would tackle again in *Born to Sing*'s "The Ballad for Americans." It begins on a small scale, with Rooney singing the introduction as he leads the orchestra. Then the ensemble (girls in frilly white dresses, boys in black suits) mingle with the audience before ascending the stage. This big-time Broadway stage (a backdrop depicting the Capitol Building, with an embankment of steps in front to hold the chorus) is, in fact, only a little bigger than its smalltown equivalent in the previous Minstrel Show number. The camerawork remains tight and close-in, and the dimensions of a realistic stage performance are strictly adhered to. Even a Berkeleyesque scale-shift remains within the limits of realism. The band marches down the steps, revealing behind them a row of jarringly tiny majorettes. However, plausibility prevails—the minuscule majorettes are revealed to be tots in costume when a row of grown-up girls file in behind them.

In the big Warner Bros. numbers, the stars might be emphasized at the beginning and at several points throughout, but, as a springboard to spectacle, the numbers would be taken over by the chorus, which then "absorbs" the stars. In "God's Country" (as in almost all of Berkeley's other big MGM numbers), the stars are never absorbed (this has important ideological as well as stylistic implications). The chorus remains an auxiliary, subordinate element, relegated to the background. The major emphasis is maintained firmly on the foreground—on the stars and, in "God's Country," on various Representative Americans (Indians, Ethnics, Polynesian, Miner, Hillbilly, Financiers), who are singled out to reflect MGM's reactionary vision of social consciousness.[2]

Strike Up the Band (1940)

Forty Little Mothers (1940, directed by Busby Berkeley) reunited Berkeley with his first movie star, Eddie Cantor. The film is not really a musical but a narrative containing two small-scale song numbers that have little or nothing to do with spectacle. Berkeley's next project, *Strike Up the Band* (directed by Busby Berkeley), is the most ambitious and interesting entry in the Rooney/Garland "trilogy," with two numbers ("La Conga" and "Strike Up the Band") that rank among Berkeley's most successful attempts to adapt the Berkeleyesque style to the MGM format. More than any of his other MGM films, *Strike Up the Band* strives toward the spectacular mode, although it ultimately remains within the standard narrativized format. It is a spectacle around the edges but a book musical at its heart.

"La Conga" is performed by bandleader Rooney and his orchestra at a school dance. Like several of the musical numbers in Berkeley's forthcoming *The Gang's All Here*, "La Conga" begins with an elaborate, extended camera movement up, over, and around the stars and the orchestra as they perform the first part of the number. However, the camera movements here remain tightly integrated with the movements of the performers, in contrast to the types of spectacularized, semiautonomous curlicues traced by the camera in *The Gang's All Here*.

The first part of "La Conga" is realistic in its presentation. It then moves into the unrealistic mode by drawing the audience of schoolchildren (nonprofessional, unrehearsed) into the performance. Rooney and Garland reappear, each leading a line of conga-dancing teenagers. This escalates into a mass dance routine involving elaborate large-scale formations. The climax comes when the camera tracks rapidly through the dancing kids, ending on a slightly high-angled close shot of two conga drums. This is followed by a cut to an apparently identical angle, with the two drums in the same position in the frame. But, as the camera pulls back, a Berkeleyesque trick is revealed. Masked by the cut, the drums have now been tilted forward to give the illusion of a high angle, and the pulling back of the camera reveals its position to have suddenly shifted into extreme low angle. The camera moves down an elongated double row of conga drummers with Rooney and Garland in the background. The couple run up into the foreground, crouch down, and shout into the camera, "Conga-a-a-a! Boom!"

Unlike most of Berkeley's MGM numbers, "La Conga" is in the performance/unrealistic mode, and this allows the spectacular elements freer rein than usual. However, these spectacle elements fall short of the classic Warner Bros. level, because performance space here is not segregated from narrative space. "La Conga" occurs not on a formal stage with a proscenium but on a dance floor. The audience is visible in the background throughout the number, packing the floor and the gallery above, with a good number of them participating in the dance itself. Accordingly, the "impossibility" of the number remains largely on the level of its spontaneity. Spatial and temporal reality are generally respected, with the exception of the trick cut and perspective change at the end. Similarly, despite the large-scale patterns of line and shade (girls in white, boys in black) formed by the dancers and frequently seen in high angle, these patterns do not attain the sheer abstraction of Berkeley's Warner Bros.

spectacles. The patterns remain too loose and informal for that, and the performers remain at least marginally individualized. Anatomy is not absorbed into geometry here, and the performers never quite become a fully formalized chorus, remaining suspended between that status and the status of extras in the narrative. (See photo 63.)

"La Conga" is an exciting and impressive number, but it stops well short of being a full-scale Berkeleyesque spectacle. Nevertheless, it was still a little too spectacular to suit the MGM studio style. Associate producer Roger Edens complained, "It started out simply as a song I had written for Judy to sing, based on the current dance craze, the conga. Then Berkeley got crazy and decided on blowing the whole number up into one of his 'typical finales,' using every possible camera angle he could think up."[3]

"Strike Up the Band" takes place on the stage of a Chicago theater as the finale of a student band contest in which Rooney and his group have triumphed. The main body of the number is a series of vigorous camera movements traveling over the orchestra and the chorus. Despite the enormous size of the ensemble, the "Strike Up the Band" number remains within the bounds of the commodious stage space established by a crane shot at the beginning of the number.

When the "Strike Up the Band" melody ends, the number segues into a reprise of all the earlier tunes.[4] At the same time, it moves more strongly into the performance/unrealistic mode, which is the prime matrix of Berkeleyesque spectacle. The pace quickens, and the space of the number becomes increasingly abstract and disorienting. With dizzying speed, large stage areas, props, settings, and groups of performers begin to materialize in forms that are difficult to account for in terms of the parameters previously established by the number. These apparitions include a long row of conga drummers, a large tree with couples lying on the grass around it, a flagpole, and an enormously long stage apron and flight of steps.

Space is manipulated by Berkeleyesque trick cuts in this final section. A dancer's skirt swirls by the camera, instantaneously shifting the location to reveal a female harpist with accompanying chorus in the background. A similar effect is used to move magically from Rooney's drums to a whole row of drummers. This is followed by a cut revealing a long, long double row of uniformed musicians. The camera moves forward rapidly down the center to Rooney and Garland perched atop a flight of steps in the background, where they raise an American flag (see photo 64). The number (and the film) ends with the happy couple's faces superimposed over the flag.

The most consistently successful of Berkeley's MGM musicals, *Strike Up the Band* represents not so much a modulation of the Berkeleyesque spectacle style to conform to the MGM narrativized format but an uneasy alliance between them. Rather than coalescing into sustained patterns, elements of Berkeleyesque spectacle are confined to brief, localized bursts that threaten the consistency of the narrative context without ever completely overwhelming it. Here (as in the best of his other MGM numbers) the Berkeleyesque seems to be straining against the limits imposed by its context. There is a resultant undertone of feverish tension that is quite different from the unfettered exuberance of Berkeley's best work at Warner Bros. and Fox.

Lady Be Good (1941)

Ziegfeld Girl (1941, directed by Robert Z. Leonard) is primarily a melodrama, although it contains two spectacle-oriented Berkeley numbers, "You Stepped Out of a Dream" and "Minnie from Trinidad." Both of them exhibit a stateliness of pacing and overelaborateness of decor that seem more Ziegfeldian than Berkeleyesque. (See photo 65.) These elements inhibit the development of the type of abstract, malleable space amenable to the rapid transmutations of Berkeley's major spectacles.

Lady Be Good (directed by Norman Z. McLeod) is a very book-oriented musical. Nearly all the numbers are performed in small-scale realistic contexts by the main actors, Robert Young and Ann Sothern, who portray a husband-and-wife songwriting team. Berkeley contributed three dance numbers, two of them very modest. The third, "Fascinatin' Rhythm," is a major accomplishment of Berkeley's MGM period and one of its closest approaches to the old-time Berkeleyesque style. However, much as "La Conga" had in *Strike Up the Band*, this increased exercise of the Berkeleyesque placed Berkeley at odds with the MGM establishment, as his out-of-control expansion of the final number sent the picture seriously over budget.[5]

It is notable that, although the number is supposed to be taking place as part of a Broadway show, there is absolutely no spatial context established to "contain" the performance—no shots of the audience, the orchestra, the stage curtain, last-minute backstage hubbub, etc. The number is set up by a bit of dialogue at the end of the preceding scene, when the Sothern character mentions that she expects her next show to be performed at the Melody Box Theatre. The scene dissolves to a theater ticket bearing the inscription of the Melody Box; then the camera cranes down through a black void toward a silhouetted pianist on the right side of a darkened screen.

The opening section features vocalist Connie Russell and the expanding, silhouetted, disembodied figures of each instrumentalist mentioned in the lyrics ("You can get it from the blare of a trumpet . . . ," etc.). An acrobatic tap dance by the three Berry Brothers precedes a solo tap by featured dancer Eleanor Powell atop a piano. While an unwinding curtain continuously moves leftward behind Powell, an unbroken tracking shot follows her to the right and forward as she taps her way past a series of five more grand pianos, each revealed in turn from behind a section of the curtain, which finally parts completely to reveal a large orchestra in the background. Powell dances in front of the orchestra, then is joined by a large male chorus for a final mass tap dance (see photo 66).

In order to enhance a Berkeleyesque sense of disorientation, the design of the number is keyed on a combination of offsetting movements. The leftward movement of the curtain is countered by the simultaneous rightward movement of Powell, the camera, and various moving platforms beneath Powell; the circular movement of the curtain offsets the forward movement of the camera in the latter part of the number. These, together with the lack of an external theatrical context, make it virtually impossible for the viewer to gauge the dimensions of the stage or the orientation of one part of the stage to another. Instead, Berkeley creates a dizzying impression of stages within stages, which open out into yet more stages—a labyrinthine, amorphous, slippery space that casts itself loose from narrative space and moves into the realms of abstraction and spectacle.

However, this movement toward spectacle and abstraction still stops short of the ecstatic, extreme level attained by the most grandiose of Berkeley's Warner Bros. numbers. The obvious cross-reference is to *Gold Diggers of 1935*'s "The Words Are in My Heart," which also features a panoply of grand pianos. However, where "Fascinatin' Rhythm" utilizes eight pianos, "The Words Are in My Heart" uses fifty-six, seemingly dancing on their own. Though extremely disorienting, the space of "Fascinatin' Rhythm" remains potentially "possible" (unlike the space of "The Words Are in My Heart," with its blatant spatial distortions and its paradoxical juggling of Brobdingnagian and Lilliputian modes).

"Fascinatin' Rhythm" never makes the final leap to abstraction and sheer spectacle. In the manner of Berkeley's other MGM work, the number always remains focused on individualized, foregrounded performers–Connie Russell, the Berry Brothers, Eleanor Powell—while the chorus and the spectacle elements (such as the giant silhouettes) remain subordinated, literally in the background. One could say that the grand pianos in "Fascinatin' Rhythm" remain themselves individualized, as they are brought onto the stage one by one, never coalescing into the abstract rows and vulviform patterns of "The Words Are in My Heart."

For Me and My Gal (1942)

Babes on Broadway (1942, directed by Busby Berkeley) is the last and least ambitious entry in Berkeley's Rooney/Garland "trilogy." It contains two relatively large-scale numbers: "Hoe Down," a lively but uneven rehearsal piece staged in a school auditorium, and "Franklin D. Roosevelt Jones," a static minstrel-show pastiche. A bombastic patriotic extravaganza, "The Ballad for Americans," was severed from *Babes on Broadway* and reattached to *Born to Sing* (1942, directed by Edward Ludwig), another kids-putting-on-a-show musical, featuring second-string MGM juveniles in place of Rooney and Garland.

For Me and My Gal (directed by Busby Berkeley) marks an inversion of Berkeley's usual priorities. For the first time, he served as director of the narrative passages of a musical while someone else handled the dance direction—in this case, Bobby Connolly, a contemporary of Berkeley on Broadway in the 1920s and at Warner Bros. in the 1930s. Moreover, *For Me and My Gal* is an unusually plot-heavy musical, strongly laced with MGM maudlinity. Wise guy Gene Kelly and nice kid Judy Garland are partners in romance and on the vaudeville stage. When World War I interferes with Kelly's career, he earns a 4-F by deliberately smashing his hand with a trunk lid. (See photo 67.) The patriotic Garland repudiates Kelly until he redeems himself by performing feats of incredible heroism on a French battlefield. The musical numbers are all in the performance mode, realistically motivated and staged. They create no major problems (such as characters breaking into spontaneous song-and-dance, or onstage numbers expanding impossibly) in relation to the realistic discourse of the narrative. For the most part, the numbers are straight onstage vaudeville performances, lacking scale, props, chorus girls, cinematic tricks, and virtually all other elements of Berkeleyesque spectacle.

For Me and My Gal would be of little interest to this study were it not for the fact that Berkeley in interviews spoke extremely highly of the film. When asked to select a favorite film to represent his work at a 1965 San Francisco Film Festival tribute, Berkeley chose *For Me and My Gal*.[6] It seems surprising that he would single out to epitomize his career a film that contains no recognizable elements of Berkeleyesque spectacle and that employed another person to handle the dance direction. This vaunting of *For Me and My Gal* indicates a possible desire on Berkeley's part to escape his identification with the Berkeleyesque and to prove himself as a versatile director capable of handling dramatic, nonmusical, and nonspectacle material. In interviews, Berkeley repeatedly asserted his competence at handling straight comedy and drama. He also claimed he had written into his studio contracts a guarantee that he be permitted to direct a certain number of nonmusical films.[7]

For Me and My Gal, with its restrained production numbers and its unusually serious, even mawkish dramatic passages, fits in neatly with this apparent desire on Berkeley's part to separate himself from the Berkeleyesque. He similarly expressed an otherwise inexplicable pride in his direction of *They Made Me a Criminal* (1939), a routine Warner Bros. crime melodrama, and *Take Me Out to the Ball Game* (1949), a later Freed musical for which he did not direct the dance numbers.[8] These films indeed demonstrate that Berkeley, had his film career not been so closely allied with the Berkeleyesque, might have developed into a competent studio contract-director—fully the equal of, say, a William Keighley or Ray Enright at Warner Bros., or a Robert Z. Leonard or George B. Seitz at MGM.

For Me and My Gal and *They Made Me a Criminal* have an analogous position in Berkeley's career to that of *Lady of the Pavements* (1929) in D. W. Griffith's, *The Man I Killed* (1932) in Ernst Lubitsch's, *Mr. and Mrs. Smith* (1941) in Alfred Hitchcock's, *The Spirit of St. Louis* (1957) in Billy Wilder's, and *The Last Tycoon* (1976) in Elia Kazan's. Each is an anomalous, anti-typecasting work that demonstrates its director's competence and versatility at the expense of those "signature" qualities on which his reputation is based.

Girl Crazy (1943)

The inherent conflicts between the Berkeley-esque/spectacle-oriented and the Freed/integration-oriented concepts of the musical film came to a head in a fourth Rooney/Garland vehicle, *Girl Crazy* (directed by Norman Taurog), based on George and Ira Gershwin's stage show. Berkeley was originally assigned to direct the entire film, as he had done in his previous three collaborations with Rooney and Garland. He began by shooting the film's finale, "I Got Rhythm," but soon found himself in serious disagreement with Freed and Freed's right-hand man, associate producer Roger Edens. As Edens later recounted: "We disagreed basically about the number's presentation. I wanted it rhythmic and simply staged; but Berkeley got his big ensembles and trick cameras into it again, plus a lot of girls in Western outfits, with fringe skirts and people cracking whips, firing guns . . . and cannons going off all over my arrangement and Judy's voice. Well, we shouted at each other, and I said, 'There wasn't room enough on the lot for both of us.'"[9] Berkeley was fired from the film. Norman Taurog replaced him as director. Charles Walters, later to become the most low-key of MGM's major musical directors, took over the dance numbers.

Unlike all the other numbers in the film, "I Got Rhythm," presented as an onstage performance at a rodeo festival, is kept fairly distinct from the narrative. The plot is completely resolved before "I Got Rhythm" begins. The number as a whole, staged at a previously unseen location, has the feeling of an appendage to the body of the film, a short subject after the feature. However, Berkeley uses this property of self-enclosure not as a launching pad for grandiose spectacle but as an opportunity for centripetal tightness. The number is set on a raised open-air platform in the middle of town (see photo 68), but the outer spatial context around the platform is only slightly indicated in the backgrounds and on the edges of the frame. It is also difficult to gauge the dimensions of the entire stage until there is a crane up to high-angle long shot about halfway through the number. For the most part, the camera remains close in, darting in and out, from side to side, and up and down to produce a fluidly shifting interplay of angle, depth, distance, motion, and rhythm.

The tightness of the camerawork also sets up a

sustained series of plays with the frameline and offscreen space, as various groupings of performers are whisked on and off the screen in a continual stream of surprising (but perfectly realistic) variations. For example, the opening section of the number begins on a close shot of Tommy Dorsey with his orchestra behind him. The camera pans left as Dorsey pulls Judy Garland onto the stage, tracks into a close shot of Garland, and accompanies her back and forth across the stage to reveal various groups of the cowboy/cowgirl chorus. The shot follows Garland down a line of sixteen chorus members sitting on a log that stretches deep into the background, then returns with her to the foreground, revealing Mickey Rooney now at the head of the line.

The basic ingredients of the number are simple, even if their manipulation is not. The chorus is large but not myriad; the stage is commodious but not enormous. The most elaborate props used are a series of sticks with streamers attached, which the chorus swing back and forth. An effect in which the chorus bow their heads so that their faces are hidden and only the cowboy hats on top can be seen is relatively simple compared to the more complex and abstract maneuvers performed by the cowboy-hatted chorus of Berkeley's "Cowboy Number" in *Whoopee!* Similarly, a double circle formed by the chorus around Rooney and Garland remains too simple and diffuse to become an abstract geometric pattern in the old Berkeleyesque manner. The only spectacularization of the camera occurs near the end when a reverse-motion effect makes the sticks jump up from the floor and into the chorus's hands.

The number ends with a literal bang. The chorus parts to reveal a cannon, which is pulled forward and fired into the camera at point-blank range. As the smoke clears, the camera tracks into a close two-shot of Rooney and Garland, who belt out the last line, "Who could ask for anything mo-o-o-o-o-re!"

Although not narrativized in the manner of the mainstream integrated musical, "I Got Rhythm" represents one of Berkeley's most successful attempts to modulate (rather than vitiate) the spectacle style in order to fit a smaller-scale narrativized context. However, this moderation of the Berkeleyesque was apparently still insufficient for the prevailing powers in the Freed unit, and he did not get a chance to develop it further. "I Got Rhythm" was the last musical number Berkeley directed at MGM until 1950, after his comeback.

Without the freedom to accelerate and to shift rapidly from one outrageous conceit to another, the high-powered Berkeleyesque spectacle style can easily incline toward heaviness and pompousness—a tendency already evident in such Warner Bros. numbers as "Goin' to Heaven on a Mule" (*Wonder Bar*) and "Otchichornya" (*Hollywood Hotel*). At MGM, Berkeley's numbers were for the most part either too bland and modest or too heavy and inflated. Nevertheless, he managed on a few occasions to adjust the Berkeleyesque style to its new context without fatally debilitating it. This resulted in a handful of numbers that, if not quite up to the level of his top Warner Bros. work, are still notable achievements: the finale of *Broadway Serenade*, "La Conga" and "Strike Up the Band" in *Strike Up the Band*, "Fascinatin' Rhythm" in *Lady Be Good*, and "I Got Rhythm" in *Girl Crazy*.

At no time during Berkeley's career were the tensions between the Berkeleyesque mode and its production context so pronounced as they were at MGM, and the friction that resulted was not always a productive one. At other studios, such as Paramount and Fox, a more retrograde approach to the genre, combined with a revival of the backstage format in its wartime-rally variant, created a congenial climate for freewheeling spectacle, although Berkeley was able to take full advantage of this more receptive framework only once, in *The Gang's All Here* (1943).

10 FOX PERIOD (1943)

The Gang's All Here (1943) and the Fox Musical

Busby Berkeley's period at 20th Century-Fox consists of exactly one film—*The Gang's All Here*, for which he directed both the narrative and the numbers. One of the most remarkable musicals ever made, *The Gang's All Here* contains more energy and imagination than all Berkeley's work for MGM put together.

Fox undoubtedly provided a more congenial environment for the full exercise of the Berkeleyesque than MGM had. Fox musicals of the early 1940s tended to be frothy, frivolous, and flashy, with a penchant for big-band swing music (Benny Goodman, Glenn Miller, Harry James, and Jimmy Dorsey made prominent guest appearances in several Fox musicals of the period) and exotic tropical settings (except for the Sonja Henie vehicles, which went to the opposite extreme, climate-wise).

Structurally, these musicals were generally quite loose, without a great deal of concern for integration, coherent narrativity, consistent characterization, or even simple logic. For instance,

Iceland, a 1942 Sonja Henie movie, set (as the title indicates) in Iceland, included an elaborate Polynesian hula-dance number—performed on ice-skates yet! (See photo 69.) In a similar vein, Fox's *Springtime in the Rockies* (1942) imported Carmen Miranda to Canada to perform a half-Portuguese, half-English rendition of "Chattanooga Choo Choo" in a multicolored Brazilian costume against a backdrop of the snowcapped Canadian Rockies. This tolerance for freewheeling absurdity and anomaly provided an appropriate context for *The Gang's All Here*, a Latinized musical set in New York and pitched at the opposite extreme from naturalism.

The Fox musical at this time was the haven of such stars as Alice Faye, Betty Grable, Sonja Henie, Carmen Miranda, Don Ameche, John Payne, and Cesar Romero. For the most part, these were pleasant, lightweight performers without high-powered star personalities—roughly the equivalents of Dick Powell, Ruby Keeler, and Joan Blondell from the Warner Bros. period, and a marked contrast to Mickey Rooney, Judy Garland, and Gene Kelly in the MGM musicals. As for the more obtrusive Carmen Miranda, she functions as a walking alienation-effect, much like Hugh Herbert in the Warners musicals; to conceive of an integrated or even remotely naturalistic musical starring Carmen Miranda seems a contradiction in terms.

Fox musicals of this period were lavish and opulent but largely without the accompanying weightiness that often characterized their MGM counterparts. Settings in the Fox musicals were splashy and spacious rather than heavy and overornate. In addition, Fox musicals were literally as well as figuratively more colorful than those made at MGM. During the 1940s, Fox used Technicolor more extensively than did any other studio.[1] Almost all big-budget Fox musicals, starting with *Down Argentine Way* (1940), were made in color, while MGM continued to stick mainly to black-and-white even in big-budget musicals. None of Berkeley's early MGM films was in color. *The Gang's All Here* was in fact his first color film (excepting the two-strip Technicolor of *Whoopee!*).

The major Berkeleyesque element lacking in the early forties Fox musicals was spectacle; though garish and excessive, they did not contain many large-scale production numbers. However, the format of the Fox musical was highly receptive to the incursion of Berkeleyesque spectacle—in contrast to the format of the MGM musical, which actively constrained it. *The Gang's All Here* followed in the footsteps of such Fox musicals as *Down Argentine Way* (1940), *That Night in Rio* (1941), *Moon Over Miami* (1941), *Week-end in Havana* (1941), and *Springtime in the Rockies* (1942), but it took a giant stride beyond them. For the first time since isolated numbers of the late 1930s such as "All's Fair in Love and War" and the *Varsity Show* finale, the Berkeleyesque was able to open up to its full extent, and this time (the only time, really, in Berkeley's career) it was able to operate across the length of an entire film.[2]

Garish Delirium

Perhaps the most striking limitation on Berkeley's abilities as a filmmaker is that, despite his unsurpassed brilliance in conceiving production numbers, he was unable to direct a *whole film* on any but a mediocre or routine level. As discussed earlier, this was largely a consequence of his attachment to a tradition based on self-enclosed, autonomous spectacle rather than on the attempted integration of music and narrative. What Berkeley lacked above all was any viable concept of a film as a whole.

Of the eleven musicals that Berkeley directed in toto, *The Gang's All Here* is the one that comes closest to achieving overall coherence without diminishing the excitement and excess associated with the Berkeleyesque. However, the solution achieved here is a highly eccentric one. When one calls *The Gang's All Here* a remarkable film, the adjective refers as much to its singularity as to its quality.

Essentially, Berkeley's solution in *The Gang's All Here* is to spectacularize the entire film, to convert it into a kind of macro-production-number from beginning to end. This is somewhat similar to what occurs in the RKO/Astaire/Sandrich films, where musical numbers and narrative passages flow into each other. But the strategy of the Astaire films is basically a moderate, classically balanced one: the naturalism of the narrative passages is decreased and that of the musical passages correspondingly increased so that they meet on a common middle ground, neither too restrictively naturalized nor too blatantly stylized.

The strategy adopted in *The Gang's All Here*, on the other hand, is radical and immoderate. The narrative passages are greatly denaturalized (to a certain extent, they are de-narrativized), while the musical numbers maintain their excessiveness, so that narrative and numbers alike exist on a precipitous level of garish delirium. There is little modulation in *The Gang's All Here*: it is like a control console on which every dial is turned up to Maximum—and the giddy, hallucinatory tone of the musical spectacles dominates the film rather than merely interrupting it. *The Gang's All Here* represents Berkeley's most sustained achievement in imposing the spectacle style across the entirety of a feature film.

There are several factors contributing to the peculiar balance struck by *The Gang's All Here*. In terms of the denaturalization and devaluation of the narrative, the screenplay and lyrics give the film a tremendous head start. Although popular song lyrics need not be Shakespearean in their eloquence, those of *The Gang's All Here* (written by Leo Robin) often reach extremes of nonsensicality. Prime examples include "Paducah," an arbitrary tribute to the sonorous possibilities of the name of a Kentucky town ("Paducah, Paducah,/If you want to,/You can rhyme it with bazooka./But you can't pooh-pooh Paducah,/That's another name for Paradise"), and "The Polka Dot Polka," a song based on the obscure correspondence between the words "polka" (as in the dance) and "polka dot" ("Oh, the polka dance, the polka dance, the polka dance is gone,/But the polka dot, the polka dot, the polka dot lives on"). The inanity of the lyrics is easily matched by that of the dialogue (Phil Baker: "Blossom, you old cabbage!"; Charlotte Greenwood: "It's more like cole slaw now"), which, moreover, is generally delivered fast and flat, without much inflection. The narrative itself is a typically trivial affair in which some blandly contrived romantic misunderstandings intrude occasionally upon the musical numbers and the lengthy comic shtick routines supplied by supporting players such as Carmen Miranda, Edward Everett Horton, Eugene Pallette, and Charlotte Greenwood.

The verbal level of the film—script, dialogue, and lyrics alike–is thus largely reduced to the level of meaningless babble. And it is upon this vapid base that Berkeley constructs a dazzling stylistic edifice of staggering crane shots, eye-popping colors, and unearthly decors. In effect, the style is so powerful and the script so weak in *The Gang's All Here* that the film works to obliterate the narrative and convert it into sheer spectacle.

Eccentric Editing

The devaluation of the "libretto" in *The Gang's All Here* extends to a formal as well as a verbal level. *The Gang's All Here* is a very strangely shot film. In a normal narrative film, or in the narrative passages of a normal musical, one would expect the dialogue scenes to be filmed according to the conventions of classical analytical editing style–that is, to be broken down into two-shots, single-shots, over-the-shoulder shots, reaction shots, point-of-view shots, shot/reverse-shot patterns, and so on. This conventional editing scheme is adhered to very weakly in *The Gang's All Here*. There is little cutting within the scenes and even less cutting that breaks the scenes down into analytical segments. By my count, all the narrative scenes in *The Gang's All Here* together contain only around ten apiece of these common analytical editing units: (1) reaction shots, (2) single-shots (only two of them close shots) other than reaction shots, (3) over-the-shoulder shots, and (4) cuts between master shot and medium two-shot.

It should be pointed out immediately that this stylistic configuration is not at all typical of the period, the studio, or the genre. Other Fox musicals of the early 1940s, such as *Week-end in Havana*, *That Night in Rio*, and *Moon Over Miami*, do not remotely resemble *The Gang's All Here* in their editing styles; instead, they rely much more heavily on conventional analytical editing patterns. For example, one single passage of dialogue between Betty Grable and Don Ameche in *Moon Over Miami* contains sixteen over-the-shoulder shots—that is, more than there are in the entirety of *The Gang's All Here*.[3]

From the paucity of analytical editing in *The Gang's*

All Here, it does not follow that Berkeley articulates narrative space in solidity and depth according to the principles of Bazinian deep-focus aesthetics.[4] On the contrary, the visual style of *The Gang's All Here* is oriented more toward a flattening of narrative space. There are few diagonals used in the film; compositions generally present the action frontally or in profile. Space and action tend to be organized horizontally, often through fast lateral camera movements that increase this flattening of space. Cuts are frequently used to follow the action laterally to an adjoining space, or to set up a camera movement for the same purpose. In effect, Berkeley cuts *across* space rather than cutting *into* space. Space in *The Gang's All Here* is not so much penetrated or analyzed as unscrolled, spun out.

A Musical Turned Inside Out

One effect of these stylistic tendencies—flatness, blatant artificiality, lack of cutting and close shots, devaluation of realistic narrative space—is to impart a distinctly stage-like quality to the narrative scenes of the film. The camera for the most part maintains a frontal "orchestra" view of the action; scenes are often "acted out" in a manner that makes the film at times seem almost like a documentary record of a stage performance. Hence, a central element of *The Gang's All Here*'s style is a lack of strong distinction between narrative space and stage/performance space, with a general gravitation of the film toward performance (i.e., spectacle) space. This effect is enhanced by one of the film's major motifs: a flowing together of audience/narrative space and stage/performance space, frequently underlined by camera movements (some of them quite spectacular) that link the two realms. These types of fluid transitions, coupled with the devaluation of the narrative and the theatricalization of narrative space, give an all-the-world's-a-stage aura to the film—or, to put it more precisely in Berkeley-esque terms, all the world's a spectacle space (rather than a narrative space).

Despite the presence of elaborate crane shots, garish colors, and gaudy decors, and despite the extreme theatricality of the acting and spatial presentation on the narrative side of the film, the narrative passages are nevertheless not identical with the spectacle numbers, whose scale, exaggeration, and spatial illogic still set them apart. However, the difference is more one of degree than of kind. The space of the numbers is continuous with that of the narrative, but it is much more heightened. Spectacle/stage space in *The Gang's All Here* is not distinct from narrative/offstage space (this contrasts strongly with the classic Warner Bros. musicals) but rather an extreme intensification of it.

While maintaining a strong link between the numbers and the narrative through camera movements and various spatial and editing strategies, *The Gang's*

All Here simultaneously maintains, on other levels, a distinctiveness of the musical numbers. In more typical Fox musicals of the period, such as *That Night in Rio* and *Week-end in Havana*, the narrative passages are characterized by an elaborate camera style (which includes editing, compositional complexity, elaboration of space in depth, etc.). The musical numbers, on the other hand, feature more restrained visuals. Their style is dominated by loose frontal medium shots. Cutting, angles, and sense of depth are limited. Camera movements are modest and serve mainly to follow the performers, much in the manner of a Fred Astaire dance number.

In *The Gang's All Here*, the effect is the opposite. As noted above, it is the narrative passages that feature less ambitious camerawork, more minimal editing, flatter spatial perspectives, and a more stage-like general appearance, while the musical numbers are characterized by more aggressive camerawork, more ambitious camera movements, more emphatic cutting, and a more complex sense of space. The overall effect is that the surrounding dramatic framework of the film becomes a stage-like framework in which are enclosed musical numbers that are highly cinematic. In some respects, the normal stylistic relationship of numbers and narrative is inverted in *The Gang's All Here*; it is like a musical turned inside out.

It is these strategies that enable *The Gang's All Here* to establish a de-narrativized context (similar to that of the revue or the backstage musical) for the enclosure of spectacle. However, this is accomplished without the separation of narrative and spectacle that characterizes the Warner Bros. musicals of the early 1930s. On the other hand, *The Gang's All Here* also avoids the awkward, unsatisfying hybridization of integration-oriented and spectacle-oriented styles that characterizes the Warner Bros. musicals of the late 1930s and the MGM musicals of the early 1940s.

Just as offstage space flows into onstage space in *The Gang's All Here*, narrative flows into spectacle and, ultimately, is absorbed into it. Other Fox musical comedies of the period, such as *That Night in Rio*, *Week-end in Havana*, and *Springtime in the Rockies*, are really more comedies than musicals. Their highly involved plots eventually prove a distraction from the musical aspects of the films, with the result that, in the later stages of the films, the musical numbers drop out and the plots take over.

In *The Gang's All Here*, the effect is just the opposite: the narrative feeds into the spectacle and eventually withers away. As an index of this, the fluid crossovers between offstage and onstage space eventually die out. The stage becomes more of an isolated, self-enclosed island, literally surrounded by water and screened from the audience by curtains of colored spray. Except for a hasty and perfunctory plot resolution sandwiched, barely, between the last two numbers, Berkeley reverts to the old "stacking" arrangement in *The Gang's*

All Here, with a climactic big show and a succession of production numbers at the end of the film.

"Brazil/You Discover You're in New York"

More than ever before, Berkeley's camera becomes a spectacularized element in *The Gang's All Here*—to a certain extent in the narrative passages and to an enormous extent in the musical numbers. Restless, active, swooping, swiveling, soaring, grand to the extent of obliterating its lightweight context, fast-paced and energetic where the narrative is often tedious and perfunctory, the camera largely detaches itself from the weak gravitational pulls of narrativity and naturalism and takes off into the upper regions of abstraction and spectacle. The camera in *The Gang's All Here* has the arbitrary power to fashion and refashion space, twisting and expanding and contracting and flattening it at will. In a sense, the camera explicitly "creates" the space in *The Gang's All Here*, rather than giving the illusion of representing or analyzing it.

The film opens in a void, with the half-lit face of a male singer (crooning "Brazil") that looms out of blackness as the camera cranes in. Without a visible cut, the camera pulls back to its original position, but the foreground is now occupied by bamboo poles that form a pattern of diagonal lines across the frame. This opening configuration moves the visual field from nothingness to abstraction. It also establishes the camera's power to conjure up spatial elements out of thin air: the diagonal lines are nonexistent when the space is first shown but appear magically and arbitrarily on the camera movement.

The camera continues moving laterally to the left, revealing the prow of a full-size cargo ship standing in real water. The shot cranes up, over, and around a roomy set representing a dock, passengers disembarking, cargo being unloaded, and the New York skyline in the background. A panning movement down an enormous load of fruit reveals Carmen Miranda standing underneath. As Miranda launches into "You Discover You're in New York," the camera pulls back to disclose a strolling Latin band behind her, then moves right to show costar Phil Baker pulling up in a car. The shot follows Baker as he joins Miranda, then cranes rapidly way back to disclose that this entire panorama has purportedly been taking place on the tiny stage of a nightclub (see photo 70). At this point the first visible cut in the film occurs.

The opening movement of *The Gang's All Here*—one of the most audacious flourishes of Berkeley's career—asserts, as the primary element in the film, the independent authority of the camera. The Berkeleyesque camera has the power to create space, to contextualize it, to redefine it, and to transform it, continuously and substantively. Like God at the Creation, the camera here begins in darkness, lets there be light, then adds, one by one, the sundry elements of its universe—sounds, patterns, objects, colors, settings, people, stars—and, at the end of the movement, supplies a fictional macrocosm to enclose the microcosm of the stage world.

The concept of the opening shot of *The Gang's All Here* is borrowed in part from an earlier Fox musical, *That Night in Rio*. That film similarly begins with a long take of a musical number (Carmen Miranda's immortal rendition of "Chica Chica Boom Chic") whose ontological status is ambiguous until a big crane shot back reveals the whole thing to be taking place on a nightclub stage. However, the effect in *That Night in Rio* is limited merely to surprise (the revelation that the number is taking place on the stage). It lacks the hyperbolic and transformative dimensions—the audacious "impossibilities"—that Berkeley adds in his variation. These include: the endlessly expanding space of the opening movement suddenly being contained within a stage about twenty feet wide; the three-dimensional ship becoming part of a two-dimensional backdrop; the water, the automobile, and the space with the bamboo poles seemingly vanishing into thin air. The opening of *The Gang's All Here* sets the pattern of paradox, hyperbole, and astonishment that will dominate the entire film.

"Paducah"

Most of the film's major numbers ("Brazil/You Discover You're in New York," "Minnie's in the Money," "The Lady in the Tutti-Frutti Hat," "No Love, No Nothin'," "Paducah," "A Journey to a Star" [second rendition]) begin with an especially extended, elaborate camera movement. Such a massive opening movement "loads" the number with an initial weight and inertia that increases its gravitational pull away from the surrounding narrative and into the realm of sheer, autonomous spectacle. The sense of separation is reinforced by the complex, often bewildering patterns traced by the camera movements. These create a kind of labyrinth effect, in which the viewer is disoriented from the original spatial context of the surrounding narrative and led into a new frame of reference with its own laws and relationships. The speed and immensity of these camera movements—sweeping rapidly over large and complex spaces—also creates a "blurring" effect that contributes to the film's pronounced tendency toward abstraction. The camera takes in too much information too quickly to be resolved into discrete, component parts. Instead, the film frequently gravitates toward generalized impressions of abstract shape and form.

The most important function of the opening camera movements is the connotations of spectacle that they immediately impart to the numbers, much of whose sense of scale and excess derives from the camerawork. Except for "The Lady in the Tutti-Frutti Hat" and the "Polka Dot Polka/A Journey to a Star" finale, the numbers rely little on gigantic sets, bizarre props, large-scale configurations of chorus girls, or special effects like trick cuts, dissolves, reverse-motion, etc. Indeed, the actual physical features of the numbers are often relatively modest. But the numbers can still convey a spectacular effect, largely by virtue of camera movements that imbue them with a sense of immensity, excess, complexity, and amazement.

A prime example of this type of effect is "Paducah," the opening number of the Garden Party Benefit show that climaxes the film. The number itself consists simply of Benny Goodman and his orchestra performing the song on a bandstand. But the opening camera movement alone is sufficient to qualify the number as spectacle, with the camera itself as the primary spectacular element.

The number begins on a close shot of a statue of a female nude, with mansion and guests seen in the background. The camera pulls back and swivels around the statue until a curtain of pink spray fills the frame. The spray descends slowly to reveal Goodman and his orchestra in the background, placed on a series of platforms against a gold-curtained backdrop with a large chandelier suspended over them on the left. After craning down rapidly into a close shot of Goodman in front of the orchestra, the camera swivels to the left, skims across the front row of reed-men, then moves right across the back row of horn-players. Upon reaching the piano, it cranes up sharply to the chandelier, from which it looks down in high-angle long shot on the whole band with Goodman now standing in the center. The shot holds as Goodman starts to sing, then descends slowly toward him, ending on an extreme low angle with the chandelier looming overhead. The first cut follows.

As for what a chandelier is doing in this open-air setting in the first place, and what exactly is holding it up against the clear night sky—these are questions that apply to the naturalistic universe and not to the realm of spectacle. The passage to that realm has been effected primarily through the agency of Berkeley's camera, with its visceral, roller-coaster-like excitement and the richly gratuitous variety of speeds, angles, distances, and directions it manages to compress into the course of a single movement.

"The Lady in the Tutti-Frutti Hat"

"The Lady in the Tutti-Frutti Hat," the most famous of the film's numbers, actually is less audacious cinematically than are either the opening or closing numbers. With the exception of the overhead kaleidoscopic patterns, everything in "The Lady in the Tutti-Frutti Hat" is more or less stage-possible. The number's impact is derived mainly from the fruity outrageousness of its imagery and the manic energy of its camera movements.

The number opens with another gargantuan movement, sweeping rapidly from the rear of the nightclub to the stage, picking out a single organ-grinder, following his monkey up a banana tree, and moving down a row of similarly be-monkeyed trees. By means of a concealed cut, it continues moving over a forest of cardboard palm trees, under which are sprawled a bevy of chorus girls in black halter-tops, yellow shorts, and yellow bandannas. The dimensions of the stage expand hyperbolically as the camera pulls back with the running chorus, sweeps rightward across the stage, and advances down a colonnade of banana trees to zero in on the inimitable Carmen Miranda as she arrives in an ox-drawn cart laden with bananas (see photo 71).

The number's first visible cut initiates another lengthy (but more static) take, which ends with the formation of a banana-xylophone. This leads into the revelation of the chorus wielding the now-legendary five-foot bananas (see photo 72). As they manipulate the bananas into a series of suggestive formations, the camera tilts precipitously from side to side, rocking the visual field back and forth like a storm-tossed boat. This is followed by a display of overhead geometrical patterns, forming a kind of king-sized fruit salad composed of giant bananas, giant strawberries, and spread-eagled chorus girls.

After a final workout with the bananas, the number concludes symmetrically with a crane away from Carmen Miranda in the banana cart, sweeps back over the grove of palm trees, and returns to the monkey and organ-grinder, now flanked by a row of organ grinders. "The Lady in the Tutti-Frutti Hat" ends on a tableau that confounds two-dimensional and three-dimensional space, with Miranda embedded in a perspective backdrop between a double row of oversized strawberries and underneath a plume of gigantic bananas (see photo 73).

"No Love, No Nothin'"

The next number, "No Love, No Nothin'," functions as a counterpoint to the other numbers in the film. Rather than working toward expansion and excess, it is based on limitations and constraint. Unlike the other numbers, which gradually reveal their space in a series of continuous and surprising expansions, "No Love, No Nothin'" begins with a high-angle long shot that immediately establishes the dimensions of the entire stage: a single-room set in which Alice Faye waits alone for her soldier husband to return from the war. These dimensions are rigorously adhered to throughout the number. Like most of the other numbers in the film, "No Love, No Nothin'"opens with an extended camera movement, but here the effect is to express confinement, not expansion. Imprisoned in her lonely apartment, Faye paces like a caged animal as the camera keeps following her back and forth from one end of the set to the other.

"The Polka Dot Polka/A Journey to a Star"

In contrast, the finale of the film—"The Polka Dot Polka" followed by a reprise of "A Journey to a Star"—is one of Berkeley's furthest excursions into unfettered abstract spectacle, ending with a total breakdown of spatial and realistic restraints. The number begins modestly with a couple of lengthy but relatively restrained camera movements following Alice Faye as she strolls through a group of polka-dancing children. Then, with stunning though somewhat awkward arbitrariness, a dissolve transforms the hand and wrist of one of the little girls into a giant mock-up of a hand and wrist, suspended in black space, with its lacy sleeve composed of neonized hoops. A spiraling camera movement leads into a complex curvilinear pattern of neonized hoops and singles out one of them, which floats downward into a vast sea of hoops. These hoops are manipulated by the blue-suited chorus in a series of synchronized hand-and-arm maneuvers against a glowing blue backdrop. An optical effect transforms the setting into a kind of inverted negative image of its former state. The hoops become solid disks (i.e., polka dots) and are waved and rolled about by the chorus; occasionally the disks come forward to fill the frame with pure color. (See photo 74.)

At this point, figures and forms begin to dissolve completely into a sea of spectacular abstraction. Alice Faye is seen in overhead shot, with a circular purple cape (i.e., polka dot) spread around her; a crane up reveals her to be in the center of a giant kaleidoscope.[5] While the kaleidoscope rotates, Faye's form disintegrates into constantly changing patterns of color, at a certain point merging with the fractured images of the chorus.

Then, soaring toward the camera one at a time, different colored disks loom up from the background, each one containing the disembodied head of one of the film's stars as he or she sings a line from "A Journey to a Star." As the last disk (a purple one containing Alice Faye) fills the frame, the shot pulls back to reveal a field of shimmering purple in which hover the disembodied heads of all the stars. A curtain of pink spray then washes away the image.

The looming disembodied heads of the finale recall the looming disembodied face that opened the film. Much as the film opens in a void, it closes with the dissolution of the image into pure color and shape. What Berkeley's spectacularized camera has done can also be undone. The end of the film is based on a series of purely formal, paradigmatic tropes and correspondences: the disembodied heads equal polka dots equal stars in the sky ("A Journey to a Star") equal the star actors of the film. The film is ultimately swallowed up by sheer spectacle, unbounded by the confines of the stage, the responsibilities of narrative, the dictates of logic, or even the laws of nature.

"What If?"

A tantalizing question raised by *The Gang's All Here* concerns the direction that Berkeley's career might have taken if he had gone to Fox instead of MGM in 1939, or if he had stayed on at Fox after *The Gang's All Here*. The prospect of a whole series of Berkeley wartime musicals in the manner of *The Gang's All Here* is very enticing. One imagines Berkeley would have been right at home at Fox, directing Sonja Henie ice fantasias, big-band swing frolics, leggy Betty Grable vehicles, and more Carmen Miranda musicals bursting with *carnivales*, parrots, and exotic tropical fruits.

Although these speculations are all moot ones, the high creative level of *The Gang's All Here* seems to indicate that Berkeley's decline at MGM was less the result of a degeneration of his talent than of unfavorable production conditions—including studio style, collaborators, and the particular form of the MGM musical in that period. Given a certain degree of elbow-room, Berkeley and the Berkeleyesque could still flourish, even in the context of a book-oriented musical (albeit one with a very high-handed treatment of the book). Unfortunately, Berkeley's wartime output after 1943 was curtailed by a series of personal and professional crises that sent his career into limbo until his comeback in 1948.

LATE PERIOD (1949–1954, 1962)

11

Simplification

After a five-year absence, Berkeley took his place again behind the camera, working as a dance director throughout the early 1950s. Although most of his work during this period was for MGM, his style was only slightly and intermittently affected by the concurrent developments in the movie musical that were being led by the Freed unit at the same studio. Relieved of the necessity of directing whole films, Berkeley could concentrate on his particular forte: the creation of spectacular production numbers. Hollywood style in the 1950s was generally more receptive to ostentatious spectacle than it had been at any time since the early 1930s, a development represented by such well-known technical enhancements as CinemaScope, 3-D, Cinerama, etc., and by the unprecedented popularity of such genres as the biblical epic and the science fiction film. In several respects, Berkeley's work in the early 1950s represents a revival of the spectacle-oriented mode that characterized his classic work of the 1930s.

The key factor in Berkeley's 1950s work, however, is *simplification*. Although several of his later numbers ("Going Home Train" in *Call Me Mister*, "Are You a Beautiful Dream?" in *Two Tickets to Broadway*, the "Smoke" number in *Million Dollar Mermaid*, "I've Gotta Hear That Beat" in *Small Town Girl*, the water-skiing finale of *Easy to Love*, "Totem Tom Tom" in *Rose Marie*) are based on concepts that are as impressive and spectacular as those of his great thirties numbers, their development is much briefer and more straightforward. The later numbers are conceptually more limited and unified, each one usually organized around a single, central effect (much in the manner of a novelty number on the musical stage), without the sense of a complexly orchestrated and interrelated *network* of different effects and levels that typifies Berkeley's previous spectacles. Berkeley's post-1950 work is not necessarily less grandiose than his most famous earlier numbers, but it is far less elaborate and complex.

Take Me Out to the Ball Game (1949)

For staging the musical numbers of *Romance on the High Seas* (1948, Warner Bros., directed by Michael Curtiz), Berkeley received his first screen credit since *Cinderella Jones* (directed by Busby Berkeley), an ill-fated Warner Bros. comedy/musical that was shot in 1944, put on the shelf for two years, reedited, and finally released in 1946. His comeback was then consolidated by his selection as director of *Take Me Out to the Ball Game*, a major MGM production. *Take Me Out to the Ball Game* is a pleasant, smoothly entertaining musical, and Berkeley expressed pride in both the film itself and the citations it received from trade publications.[1] His camerawork in the narrative passages is graceful and assured, keyed on medium two-shots, long takes, and smooth, uncomplicated camera movements. The comedy elements are, for the most part, brought off without that heaviness of touch that mars many of Berkeley's earlier efforts. The use of a baseball team in the plot enables Berkeley to develop the theme of the individual's relation to the group/ensemble/chorus, which is central to many of his classic production numbers and to the narratives of those films he directed. However, *Take Me Out to the Ball Game* also serves as an indication of changing trends in the musical film—trends that would have little to do with either Berkeley or the Berkeleyesque.

The direction of the musical numbers in *Take Me Out to the Ball Game* is credited not to Berkeley but to Gene Kelly and Stanley Donen, who were about to become prime contributors to the Freed-led, MGM-dominated "Golden Age" of the movie musical. Berkeley, in fact, exited the film before the musical numbers were shot.[2] With the exception of "Strictly U.S.A." (a large-scale number set at a dockside clambake), the numbers in *Take Me Out to the Ball Game* have little relation to Berkeleyesque spectacle. They are relatively small-scale affairs that place the major emphasis on comedy, transitions to the narrative, the cleverness of the lyrics, and the personalities and performance skills of the stars, rather than on spectacle and group dynamics.

Donen and Kelly (along with their colleagues in the Freed unit, Vincente Minnelli and Charles Walters) are frequently credited with having made the movie musical more "realistic" and "integrated." It would perhaps be more accurate to characterize their contribution not in terms of smoothing over the breach between the realistic (narrative) and antirealistic (spectacle) sides of the genre, but of articulating the tension between those sides in a particularly rich, vivid, and sophisticated manner. The classic Freed unit musicals of the 1950s are characterized by an enhanced complexity and heterogeneity of musical address on three different levels: (1) among the numbers (the numbers are spread collectively among a great variety of possible modes of discourse), (2) within the numbers (individual numbers shift freely among different modes of discourse), and (3) with regard to the numbers' relation to the narrative (numbers are freely and openly interwoven with the narrative in a variety of ways).

Although Berkeley's big numbers of the 1930s and early 1940s are certainly often complex, their complexity is of a different order. The complexity is more internalized and self-contained, rather than being located in the numbers' relation to the narrative and to the other numbers. Also, that internal complexity is primarily concentrated on formal elements (camera movements, editing patterns, chorus arrangements, etc.), rather than involving a variety of modes of performance discourse (i.e., addressing the number to the audience in a number of distinct ways).[3] As previously and frequently stated, the full exercise of Berkeley-esque spectacle depends on a clear separation of narrative space from performance space, within which the "impossible" can run rampant. The classic Freed musicals of the 1950s, on the other hand, are built on a more variegated and multipartite irruption of narrative space into performance space, and vice versa.

Moreover, the definition of the line between performance space and narrative space becomes more ambivalent and shifting in the Freed-style musicals. This can be seen in *Take Me Out to the Ball Game* numbers like "Yes, Indeedy," "O'Brien to Ryan to Goldberg," and "The Hat My Father Wore on St. Patrick's Day." These numbers play (often by means of fluid shifts in framing) on the presence of fictional spectators (e.g., the baseball team, the diners at the clambake) who have an ambiguous function halfway between that of fully narrativized characters and a formal performance audience. (See photo 75.) There is a similar ambivalence in the use of spaces (e.g., the baseball field, dining room, pier) that oscillate between narrativity and stagelike performance configurations. For example, in "O'Brien to Ryan to Goldberg," the space of the dining room periodically ceases to function as a realistic dining room and is momentarily transformed into a formal stagelike space. The foreground becomes like a stage apron, and the performances are directed outward, as if to an audience in the orchestra. Then a cut or camera movement restores the narrative context.

This type of flexible, open, narrativized space rules out the monolithic, self-enclosed framework so congenial to Berkeleyesque spectacle. On the other hand, those numbers that do take place on a formal proscenium stage (the opening Sinatra-Kelly tap dance to "Take Me Out to the Ball Game," the finale's reprise of "Strictly U.S.A.") adhere to the confines of a realistic stage performance, without any of the flights of fancy that mark Berkeley's most elaborate numbers. In either case, there is little opportunity for the old-style, full-scale Berkeleyesque mode to assert itself, even in the more simplified form characteristic of his later films.

The presence of producer Freed, budding codirectors Kelly and Donen, lyricists Betty Comden and Adolph Green, and stars Gene Kelly, Frank Sinatra, Jules Munshin, and Betty Garrett give *Take Me Out to the Ball Game* the appearance of a spring-training warm-up for *On the Town*, the ground-breaking landmark of the "new" musical (which was released later in 1949). Berkeley seems very much the odd man out in this collaboration. (See photo 76.)

Take Me Out to the Ball Game was Berkeley's last credit as a director. Although he continued to work for MGM in the 1950s, none of his subsequent work was with the Freed unit, which was then reaching the peak of its achievement. Berkeley's contributions were instead confined to more old-fashioned projects, such as the Esther Williams aquatic spectacles *Million Dollar Mermaid* and *Easy to Love*, the remake of *Rose Marie*, and the oddball, disorganized *Small Town Girl*.

Call Me Mister (1951)

Two Weeks with Love (1950, MGM, directed by Roy Rowland), an exercise in turn-of-the-century nostalgia modeled after the Freed classic *Meet Me in St. Louis*, represents the most minor work of Berkeley's late period. Its despectacularized musical passages are entirely consistent with the smooth, low-key, and rather bland charm of the rest of the film.

His next project, *Call Me Mister* (1951, 20th Century-Fox, directed by Lloyd Bacon) reunited Berkeley with Lloyd Bacon, the most simpatico of his old Warner Bros. directors. However, any resemblances between this film and *42nd Street* or *Footlight Parade* are purely superficial.

Call Me Mister does establish a backstage structure that recalls the classic Warners format. The story concerns a USO-like troupe entertaining Occupation troops in Japan immediately after the war. The numbers, with one exception, are all in the performance/realistic mode, mostly as rehearsals for the final show. Unlike in the classic Warner Bros. backstagers, there is no attempt here at "stacking" a few big numbers at the end. The film's nine numbers are sprinkled evenly throughout the narrative, and none is substantially bigger than the others. The fact that most of the numbers are seen only in rehearsal lends them a casual air that dilutes the formal rigor usually found in Berkeley's big numbers.[4] Most crucially, the numbers never take advantage of the backstage format to launch into full-scale spectacle. Instead, they remain mostly consistent—discursively and spatially—with a realistic stage context.

The first number, "Japanese Girl Like American Boy," sets a pattern followed throughout the film. The opening of the number (brightly clad Japanese chorines admiring a poster image of a virile G.I.) sets up a situation with potential to expand into Berkeley-esque spectacle. (See photo 77.) But the number does not build; instead, it lapses into a serial structure in which the elements established at the opening are dropped. The number moves on to (and ends with) a straight tap-dance routine involving star Betty Grable and three sailors. This happens time and again in the film. Elements (such as an atmosphere, a motif, a chorus, a setting) potentially receptive to spectacle are introduced at the outset of the numbers, but they do not lead to a cumulative buildup and spectacular payoff. Instead, each serves merely as a prologue to an extended performance sequence that concentrates exclusively on the singing and dancing skills of the main performers.

There is one major exception to the star-centered emphasis of the production numbers in *Call Me Mister*, and that is "Going Home Train," a rehearsal number occurring about midway through the film. A prologue shows stagehands responding to director Grable's orders as they display various bits of stage machinery that will be used in the ensuing number: steampipes, wires, props, a hand-cranked panoramic background. The number proper takes the form of a single, extended camera movement. It begins on a shot of the panoramic background scrolling outside the window of a moving train, then pans to a G.I. (Bobby Short) who launches into the song. The camera follows Short laterally right through three train cars full of homeward-bound soldiers (several of whom take up a bar or two of the song), passes momentarily outside the car, skims across a few windows, and moves back inside. The shot then reverses direction, following Short laterally left (passing briefly outside the train again) as he retraces his steps to the rear of the train. He climbs up on the roof, and the camera continues to follow him rightward across the roof and down to the engine cab. The shot reverses direction again, this time remaining outside the train as it moves across groups of singing G.I.'s leaning out the windows. After reaching the end of the last car, the camera holds while the train moves off into the background, with Short standing on the rear platform and singing the last lines. Steam billows up and obscures the departing train.

Unlike any of the other numbers in *Call Me Mister*, "Going Home Train" is primarily about a *group* rather than about a star performer or small group of star performers. Although Bobby Short is the main performer in the number, he is not really its star in the sense that Betty Grable, Dan Dailey, and Danny Thomas are the stars of the other numbers. Short brings no preestablished star identity into the number. He appears nowhere else in the film and is not even billed in its credits. Rather than gravitating toward Short and then remaining transfixed on him (as it does with the stars of the other numbers), the camera moves freely away from him, weaving in and out of the other G.I.'s. Short merges into them as a kind of unobtrusive collective spirit, rather than becoming a dominant center who swallows up the other elements of the number. Freed from the necessity of having to defer to central star personae, Berkeley is able to impose an overall formal shape on "Going Home Train" that sets it apart from the other numbers in the film and, considering the mediocrity of their heavily featured star performances, makes it far superior to them.

The prologue to the number, with its demystifying exposure of the elements of stage "magic," reserves the real magic for the camera itself. It is the camera, with the power to sweep effortlessly through a confined and crowded space, reversing directions and moving through walls at will, that transcends the stage limitations so carefully defined at the beginning of the number (and adhered to throughout it, without any Berkeleyesque expansions or "impossibilities"). After the number ends, a proscenium shot shows the stage setting in its entirety for the first time. It all seems rather mundane, a surprisingly ordinary space, without the camera's power to energize and transform it. Berkeley's camera is the true star of "Going Home Train."

However, although the extended camera movement of "Going Home Train" is extremely virtuosic, even magical, it is *not* spectacularized. The camerawork in "Going Home Train," no matter how elaborate, remains at all times integrated with the action. It basically follows the action, rather than describing excessive and semiautonomous patterns that overwhelm it in the manner of *The Gang's All Here* and several of Berkeley's big numbers of the 1930s.

Two Tickets to Broadway (1951)

Two Tickets to Broadway (RKO, directed by James V. Kern) is one of Berkeley's most obscure projects, but it is also one of his most successful in terms of tailoring his style to the demands of a narrativized musical. The many numbers in the film are, for the most part, small-scale and naturalistic. They take place in wholly narrativized locales or realistically treated stage spaces. With the exceptions of "Pelican Falls High" and "Manhattan," they involve a small number of performers, typically between two and four. The predominant camera style of the numbers is fluid and intimate. Although camera movements are often extended and complex, they remain (as in *Call Me Mister*'s "Going Home Train") generally keyed on the action and lack the ostentatious, semiautonomous force that characterizes much of Berkeley's 1930s and 1940s work.

This muting of the Berkeleyesque style is largely accomplished without the accompanying blandness and lack of ambition that afflicts other nonspectacularized Berkeley projects such as *Stage Struck* (1936), *Garden of the Moon* (1938), and *Two Weeks with Love* (1950). On the other hand, the numbers generally avoid the sense of strain and constriction that resulted from the conflict between ambitious Berkeleyesque concepts and their narrativized contexts in such films as *Wonder Bar* (1934), *Hollywood Hotel* (1937), and *Strike Up the Band* (1940). There *is* a sense of constriction in *Two Tickets to Broadway*, but it is inscribed in the numbers as a figure of style rather than merely being a symptom of the film's structural problems.

The opening number, "Pelican Falls High," is built around a series of extended camera movements following a parade of small-town well-wishers as they give local girl Janet Leigh a big send-off on her quest for showbiz success. After her bus departs, the camera, loosely representing a viewpoint from the rear of the moving bus, shows the waving townsfolk receding into the background. Then it continues to pull back through the previously unseen rear window of the bus and reveals Leigh slumped in the back seat, weary and teary.

This "threading-the-needle" effect—the camera emphatically pulling back through a door or window into an enclosed space—recurs in three subsequent numbers: "There's No Tomorrow," "Baby, You'll Never Be Sorry," and "The Closer You Are." Related to this motif is the numbers' prominent use of sheltered spaces (the awning and umbrella in "The Closer You Are"), obstructions (the parlor furniture in "Manhattan," the rooftop vents, antennae, skylights, and washlines in "Baby, You'll Never Be Sorry," the restaurant tables around which Janet Leigh and Tony Martin dance in "The Closer You Are"), and frame-within-the-frame devices (the spotlight that follows Martin throughout his "Pagliacci" rendition, the television monitor that displays the opening of "Big Chief Hole-in-the-Ground").

The spaces of the musical numbers, especially in the first two-thirds of the film, are usually carefully preestablished and delimited, without that sense of infinite expandability that marked the Berkeleyesque numbers of the 1930s and (to a lesser extent) the 1940s. "There's No Tomorrow" and "Baby, You'll Never Be Sorry" are both set within a small tenement rooftop area and adjoining apartment. "Manhattan" is confined to the cramped parlor, sitting room, and hallway of a boarding house. "Let the Worry Bird Worry for You" takes place within a small walled-in amphitheater-like area in the park.

The numbers' strongly defined sense of spatial constriction—doors and windows, obstructions and obstacles, cramped quarters and enclosed areas—mirrors the constriction of Berkeleyesque spectacle by the narrative context. Several of the numbers are broken up by interpolated dialogue and action. Transitions in and out of the numbers are continuous with the surrounding narrative (e.g., dialogue segues into the beginning of a song; the end of the song segues back into dialogue) without the powerful sense of self-enclosure found in Berkeley's major spectacles of the thirties. Spatial tricks are ultimately narrativized and naturalized, as when a slow pullback reveals "There's No Tomorrow" to be unexpectedly taking place on a rooftop.

On the whole, Berkeley's style is not so much diminished in *Two Tickets to Broadway* as it is modulated and miniaturized. "Manhattan" in particular is like a miniaturized Berkeleyesque spectacle—a vest-pocket edition of "Lullaby of Broadway"—with a chorus, a trip to the theater, a journey through New York "traffic," and a nightclub show all smoothly packed within the front parlor and hallway of a boarding house (see photo 78). "Let the Worry Bird Worry for You" ends with four mechanical chicks in their nest—an image taken directly from the end of "By a Waterfall." But the image here lacks the bathos and poignancy of its former appearance. Rather than contrasting resonantly with a dominant tone of grandiose spectacle (as in "By a Waterfall"), it blends seamlessly into the low-key silliness of the rest of the number.

The latter part of the narrative, centered around the production of a television variety show, returns Berkeley to the more familiar ground of the backstage format and enables him to pull off some genuinely spectacularized effects in the old Berkeleyesque manner. These include the *Olympia*-like cutting between slow motion and normal motion in the Charlivels' acrobatic number, the giant-sized records and turntable in the "Pagliacci" number, and the confounding interplay between foreground (Tony Martin singing) and back-projected background (Janet Leigh lounging sensuously in a surreal bedroom setting) in "Are You a Beautiful Dream?" (see photo 79).[5]

But even these returns to the Berkeleyesque are of a different order from the mode of "By a Waterfall," "Dames," and "Lullaby of Broadway." In the novelty-number manner of much of Berkeley's other late work, they concentrate on a single, monolithic gimmick (slow-motion, gigantism, back-projection) rather than leading the viewer through a complex series of evolutions and transformations that build up a spectacle world thoroughly distinct from that of the narrative.

Million Dollar Mermaid (1952)

Million Dollar Mermaid (MGM, directed by Mervyn LeRoy) is the first of two Esther Williams vehicles on which Berkeley collaborated. Strictly speaking, the film is not a musical but belongs to the genre that *Variety* dubs the "biopic." Here the biography depicted is that of the early twentieth-century swimming star and aquatic performer, Annette Kellerman. Into this format are inserted three water ballets, all set on the stage of the celebrated Hippodrome Theatre and together accounting for less than a tenth of the film's 115-minute running time. One of the numbers, a brief underwater ballet, was not staged by Berkeley. The other two, referred to in the credits simply as the "Fountain" and "Smoke" numbers, represent (especially the latter) some of the most impressive work of Berkeley's late period.

Water had always been one of Berkeley's favorite elements, providing a motif in several earlier numbers and a framework for one full-scale aquacade, "By a Waterfall." One major advantage of aquatic spectacles is that they offer Berkeley the opportunity to redouble the sequestration inherent in the backstage format. The swimming pool functions as a stage-within-the-stage that further differentiates spectacle space from narrative space. Water itself is a literally different element from the terra firma of the narrative, with tangibly distinct laws and properties, as well as built-in opportunities for such prime Berkeleyesque qualities as fluidity, mutability, surprise, and amorphousness.

The "Fountain" number is short and fairly simple; its monolithic structure, leading up fairly directly to one or two big effects, is typical of Berkeley's post-1949 work. The "Smoke" number is considerably more ambitious, although it still falls well short of the elaborateness of Berkeley's best work of the 1930s and 1940s. A wall of spray introduces the number; the lights go out, then come on again to disclose an eccentric spectacle. Against a background of billowing yellow smoke are seen two facing inclines, down which girls in yellow bathing suits slide on their bellies between the spread legs of muscular boys clad in bulging red swimtrunks. A cut to an undisclosed location shows a burst of red smoke, out of which emerges Esther Williams in a spangled red bathing suit. She slides on her feet down an enormous slide into the water, where she joins the swimming chorus.

Everyone submerges, and the number suddenly moves from the depths to the heights. High above the pool, out of a massive wall of red and yellow smoke, soar alternating swing-borne units of six males and six females, who swing and dive in unison. Williams, in isolated glory, concludes the procession, diving off a swing and emerging in the center of a double circle formed by the chorus. She grabs hold of a ring which hoists her high into the air (see photo 80), while far below the chorus forms overhead patterns that resolve into an explicit representation of an eyeball. Letting go of the ring, Williams plunges straight into the "pupil" (an inversion of the effect in "I Only Have Eyes for You," where Ruby Keeler ascends out of the pupil of a giant eyeball). Upon Williams's impact, the chorus spreads out into a rotating pinwheel pattern that is copied almost exactly from "By a Waterfall."

The number's final effect resolves the central water-and-fire motif in a strikingly paradoxical way. Out of the water emerges a trellis bearing an erect Williams, four recumbent nymphs, and 500 lighted sparklers, impossibly sparkling away (thanks to reverse-motion). (See photo 81.) The apparatus descends again, Williams blowing a kiss to the camera before she disappears into the depths for the last time.

By virtue of both its general aspect and specific borrowings, the "Smoke" number begs comparison with "By a Waterfall." The differences between them illustrate some essential differences between the two periods, even when one of the most ambitious and audacious of Berkeley's late numbers is being used as a standard of comparison. In the first place, the "Smoke" number is about half as long as "By a Waterfall" or the other major Berkeley numbers of the 1930s. Although perhaps the most complex of Berkeley's late numbers, it is far less complex than "By a Waterfall," which moves through a series of transitions to different levels (prologue/waterfall/pool/epilogue). The "Smoke" number, on the other hand, is all pitched on the same basic level; its shape is that of a single large bloc.

The structure of the "Smoke" number is less "democratic" and more star-oriented. Williams appears at the end of both the "Fountain" and "Smoke" numbers like a reigning queen, literally crowned and surrounded by her ladies-in-waiting. There is little of the interplay between the stars and the chorus that enriches "By a Waterfall," "Shanghai Lil," "I Only Have Eyes for You," etc. Although space is manipulated throughout the "Smoke" number (giant props, such as the slides, appear and disappear at will; the backgrounds are constantly changing), this manipulation is more subtle than ostentatious. There is nothing to compare with the audacity of, say, the sudden appearance of the stucco pool or the climactic removal of the chorus to the revolving platform in "By a Waterfall."

The relatively clear and simple organization of the "Smoke" number enables it to connect more easily with the surrounding narrative, rather than breaking off as an inwardly complex, self-enclosed microcosm in the manner of Berkeley's 1930s numbers. The soaring/submerging dynamic of the "Smoke" number encapsulates the central male/female conflict of the narrative. The film associates the female principle with water (the Williams character is described as "half woman, half fish"), while the male principle is associated with the sky (her frustrated suitor, played by Victor Mature, attempts to match her prowess by becoming an aviator). The females in the chorus wear yellow bathing suits and the males wear red. Williams's appearance in a red suit aligns her with the males, just as in the narrative her "masculinity" (i.e., she is independent and successful) produces an inferiority complex in the hero that blocks their romantic union. The "Smoke" number epitomizes the Williams character's status as superwoman, with the ability to fly through the air, plunge to the depths, and preside over miracles of fire and water. At the end of the film, this remarkable female has to be symbolically "castrated" (she lies crippled in a hospital bed) in order for the hero to be able, at last, to possess her.

Rose Marie (1954)

Small Town Girl (1953, MGM, directed by Leslie Kardos) offers a further demonstration of the simplification of Berkeleyesque spectacle in the 1950s. The numbers in the film are all defined by (and confined to) a single conceit or novelty effect: Bobby Van dancing around a dry goods store, Bobby Van kangaroo-hopping down Main Street, Ann Miller tap-dancing amid an orchestra comprised of disembodied arms and the instruments they are playing. The last, one of Berkeley's most memorably bizarre conceits, occurs in "I've Gotta Hear That Beat" (see photo 82), which climaxes with the magical materialization of approximately twenty giant tom-toms, suspended high above the stage and pounding out that eponymous beat.

Berkeley contributed numbers to a second, more minor Esther Williams vehicle, *Easy to Love* (1953, MGM, directed by Charles Walters). The most remarkable number is the final one, in which synchronized water-skiers take the place of the more traditional dancing chorus, and helicopter shots function as an augmented equivalent of the Berkeleyesque crane shot. As is typical in Berkeley's late period, the final number of *Easy to Love* sacrifices complexity for the sake of a sustained and monolithic effect.

Rose Marie (MGM, directed by Mervyn LeRoy) is the third film version of Friml and Harbach's famous operetta. In the operetta tradition, the film's lush production values are centered on scenic spectacle (in the form of both location shooting in the Canadian Rockies and elaborate backdrops contrived to match the locations) that is realistically tied to a strong narrative line.

"Totem Tom Tom" is the only number in the film with a significant relation to Berkeleyesque spectacle. Along with "Indian Love Call," "Totem Tom Tom" was the most celebrated number in the 1924 stage production. Dave Bennett's original staging featured novelty, with a chorus line dressed in totem-pole costumes. The 1936 film version of the number (staged by Chester Hale) stressed the exotic and the atmospheric, with an Indian brave and maiden dancing atop a giant tom-tom against a dusky horizon. Berkeley reconceived "Totem Tom Tom" into a mass pagan/erotic spectacle, much in the vein of his earlier work on the 1927 stage production *The White Eagle* and the 1932 film *Bird of Paradise*. (See photo 83.)

Although the number does not take place in a formal stage space, the setting—a kind of natural amphitheater enclosed by cliffs (Berkeley described it as "a mountain stronghold")—conveys, to a certain extent, the spatial sequestration typical of Berkeleyesque spectacle.[6] However, "Totem Tom Tom" is relatively restrained by Berkeleyesque standards. There are no extraordinary props employed, no exceptionally elaborate camera movements, no antirealistic manipulations or expansions of space, no trick cuts or other manifestations of Berkeleyesque sleight-of-camera. Instead, the major weight of the number's excess is concentrated on its tone of sustained erotic delirium, fraught with elements of gang-sex, sadomasochism, bondage, and rampant phallicism.

Except for some Indian girls forming immobile human totems in the upper background of the set, the only female in the number is the chieftain's daughter Wanda (Joan Taylor). She is surrounded by a large chorus of virile braves and a profusion of phallic imagery: a giant totem pole, stone pillars, spears, powder horns, and rigidly extended arms. The very setting, with its sheer, vaulting rock faces, exudes an air of priapic grandeur. Wanda performs a gyrating, open-legged dance and then languidly allows herself to be tossed from brave to brave in Apache-cum-*apache* fashion. At the climax, Wanda dashes up to the top of the cliff, and, in an exhilarating equivalent of orgasm, she is thrown down into the upraised, quivering arms of the braves below. They raise up her limp body, carry her over to the giant totem pole, and, holding her by the arms, pinion her against it (see photo 84). "Totem Tom Tom" is Berkeley's most explicitly erotic number since his pre-Code glory days with Warner Bros. and Goldwyn.

Jumbo (1962) and the Elephants' Graveyard

In the late fifties and early sixties, the movie musical was dominated by big-budget adaptations of Broadway hits in the integrative mode identified most strongly with Rodgers and Hart/Rodgers and Hammerstein. This provided the generic context for Berkeley's final screen credit. After an eight-year hiatus, he returned to the screen to work on *Jumbo* (aka *Billy Rose's Jumbo*, MGM, directed by Charles Walters), an elephantine film adaptation of the 1935 Rodgers and Hart show that had rung down the curtain on the old Hippodrome. Berkeley's credit on the film is as second unit director; the exact extent of his contributions is unclear.[7] Set in the turn-of-the-century circus world, *Jumbo* (the title itself referring to one of P. T. Barnum's most celebrated attractions) provided a fortuitous but fitting connection between Berkeley and the Barnumesque tradition that contributed so much to the evolution of the Berkeleyesque. (See photo 85.) It also marked the end of Berkeley's own three-ring circus; *Jumbo* was the last film credit he received.

During the 1950s, Berkeley had been able to regain a foothold that allowed for increased exercise of the Berkeleyesque mode. A trend toward the spectacular and the epic in some areas of the American cinema created certain limited opportunities for the exercise of the old-style Berkeleyesque. Working again primarily as a hired-gun specialist rather than a director of entire films, Berkeley was able to produce a series of impressive and nearly self-sufficient spectacles that approached the scale if not the complexity of his prime thirties work. In addition, he was able on occasion to modulate his spectacle style, in some instances inventively (*Two Tickets to Broadway*, the "Going Home Train" number in *Call Me Mister*), in other instances merely competently (*Take Me Out to the Ball Game*, *Two Weeks with Love*).

Although the Berkeleyesque declined in prominence and centrality over the course of the history of the movie musical, it never disappeared and was always available for periodic revivals, because the aggregate/spectacle side is an integral component of the genre itself. By the same token, the decline of the Berkeleyesque can be seen as merely the harbinger of the general decline of the entire movie musical genre. For all its pursuit of integration and sophistication, the musical is an inherently unrealistic and somewhat anomalous genre within the institution of mainstream cinema. A throwback to earlier forms of entertainment, the musical film's discursive complexity, contradictoriness, and even unwieldiness have always been more or less problematic. The cultural context necessary to sustain this living fossil apparently ceased to be available. The movie musical suffered a general collapse in the late 1960s, a collapse loudly trumpeted by several highly publicized, big-budget disasters (*Star!*, *Darling Lili*, *Lost Horizon*, etc.). Since then the "traditional musical"—meaning one that incorporates "impossibility" as a major element of its address (as discussed in chapter 2)—no longer has seemed a commercially viable proposition. Its place has been taken by "timid" musicals (basically films-with-music that repackage certain musical plot conventions but avoid or minimize sustained instances of impossibility—e.g., *Saturday Night Fever*, *Fame*, *Flashdance*, *Footloose*, *Dirty Dancing*) and by metamusicals (films that denaturalize the underlying assumptions of the genre and subject them to examination—e.g., *The Boy Friend*, *Cabaret*, *New York, New York*, *All That Jazz*, *Pennies from Heaven*). Occasionally, a brave attempt is made to revive the traditional musical, with predictably disastrous results, as represented recently by *Newsies*, perhaps the fastest-disappearing major studio release of 1992.

Within this limited generic horizon, the Berkeleyesque production number (and the "impossible" musical number in general) is only feasible in a heavily bracketed form—by being clearly marked as a subjective fantasy, as a Brechtian device, as something flagrantly nostalgic, archaic, campy, etc. It is in this context that a few large-scale Berkeleyesque film numbers have surfaced over the last twenty years—in such films as *The Boy Friend*, *Pennies from Heaven*, and (less purely) *Funny Lady*, *New York, New York*, *Grease*, and *All That Jazz*. When genres die, they often become adjectives—i.e., qualities or colorations (e.g., picaresque, gothic) that can be employed in the context of other forms. Such seems to be the destiny of the musical film and of that rambunctious mode of the musical that I have called the Berkeleyesque.

CONCLUSION: AUTHOR AND CONTEXT

This study has traced the course of the Berkeleyesque by focusing on the traditions that engendered it and that, when applied to a cinematic context, largely differentiated it from the mainstream of Hollywood filmmaking. The road from *Holka Polka*, Berkeley's first Broadway show, to *Jumbo*, his last motion picture, is a convoluted one, but its overall direction can be mapped around two complimentary poles. The first is the relationship of Berkeley's work to the Berkeleyesque—that is, to those elements of the "Tradition of Spectacle" that Berkeley assimilated and that became identified with his name. The second is the relationship of the Berkeleyesque to the various contexts in which Berkeley was working.

The extent to which Berkeley's work intersects with or deviates from the Berkeleyesque, and the extent to which his specific production situations provide a hospitable or inhospitable context for the Berkeleyesque, together constitute a model for conceptualizing his career. Berkeley's Broadway career can be conceived in these terms as a gradual movement toward those extant forms (spectacle, revue, precision dancing, etc.) that would eventually be identified with the Berkeleyesque. His film career, in turn, can be conceived as a series of production contexts (determined largely by the studio and the period involved) in which the Berkeleyesque could flourish to a greater or lesser degree. It was more likely to flourish at Warner Bros. than at MGM, more at Warner Bros. in the early 1930s than at Warner Bros. in the late 1930s, and so on.

Although by no means stagebound, the style of Berkeley's film numbers is crucially derived from stage traditions, and a recognition of this relationship is essential for understanding the shape and significance of his film career. Berkeley took a moribund, outmoded stage tradition and used it to revolutionize the nascent form of the movie musical. Rather than ousting retrograde stage influences from the temple of the musical film, Berkeley evolved cinematic equivalents ("spectacularization of the camera") for a particular, archaic stage tradition. At the same time, he retained, rather than replaced, a considerable repertoire of relevant stage techniques. Nearly all film musicals are built on a dialectic between theatrical and cinematic elements. However, the particular nature of Berkeley's mix (and of its sources) made the most effective mode of his style (the full-scale Berkeleyesque) less adaptable, less versatile, more quickly outdated, and more context-dependent than it probably would have been if he had specialized in other, less archaic, more integration-oriented modes.

The shape of Berkeley's film career as a whole reflects the problems involved in following a weakly narrativized tradition (the Tradition of Spectacle) within a strongly narrativized institution (American commercial cinema). The special natures of the musical genre (especially its discursive openness), of the early film musical's historical evolution (especially the popularity of the backstage format in the 1930s), and of the spectacle tradition that Berkeley applied to it enabled this atypical, narrow-ranged film artist to thrive, however tenuously and sporadically, within the context of commercial narrative cinema. As the musical film evolved in directions counter to the Berkeleyesque, Berkeley's incongruity and lack of range became more apparent, causing a general attenuation of his style through constriction, tension, blandness, and simplification.

Also involved here is a demonstration of the ways in which the concept of an "author" is constituted from an interplay of personal and extrapersonal factors. In the course of time, the label *busby berkeley* comes to be affixed to a number of elements that predate and surpass the individual Busby Berkeley, but at the same time the individual Busby Berkeley articulates those elements into forms that surpass their extrapersonal determinants. The artistry of numbers like "I Only Have Eyes for You" and "Lullaby of Broadway" cannot be accounted for entirely by preexisting traditions, genre conventions, ideological contexts, institutional priorities, etc. Even after these determinants have been factored out, there is a substantial excess remaining. However, Berkeley's artistry is still extremely dependent on those determinants. Outside the Tradition of Spectacle, outside the musical genre, outside the backstage format (or an equivalent thereof), outside the ideological context of the 1930s (the potential subject of another study), Busby Berkeley is a generally mediocre and insignificant artist.

There is always an outside to any model of intellectual inquiry, a falling short, a significant residue that escapes the system, and I would like to conclude this study with a recognition of its outside. In particular, the complex interrelationship between Berkeley's oeuvre and the ideological-historical-sociological context of the Depression era provides a rich field of inquiry that has only begun to be explored in such commendable studies of the Berkeley/New Deal relationship as Mark Roth's "Some Warners Musicals and the Spirit of the New Deal," John Belton's "The Backstage Musical," and Andrew Bergman's brief chapter on the classic Warner Bros. musicals in *We're in the Money*.

Also outside the scope of this study are qualities that are more difficult to analyze but nevertheless form an important dimension of Berkeley's work. With particular power, his best numbers evoke feelings of generosity, delight, joy, immensity, dazzlement, exhilaration, and erotic playfulness, achieved through a complexity and ingenuity of means far beyond the "naïveté" frequently attributed to them by naïve commentators. On both an emotional and formal level, Berkeley's cinema has an unusually direct impact. This directness can be ascribed in large part to that Tradition of Spectacle he apotheosized on the screen. It is a tradition that largely forgoes the mediating framework of narrative in favor of a series of concentrated, autonomous units in which spectacle can celebrate itself, infinite and omnigenous, dazzling and tremendous. Busby Berkeley was an artist with a very narrow range, but within that narrow range he could, at his best, contain multitudes.

NOTES

Introduction: Berkeley and the Berkeleyesque

1. Lester V. Berrey and Melvin van den Bark, *The American Thesaurus of Slang* (New York: Thomas T. Crowell, 1952), pp. 593–94.

2. Rowland Brown wrote and directed two remarkably offbeat crime dramas in the early 1930s: *Quick Millions* (1931) and *Blood Money* (1933); a combination of pugnacity and leftism reputedly shortened his directing career. Edgar G. Ulmer, a favorite of French auteurist criticism, worked almost exclusively in low-budget pictures; his work includes the film noir classic *Detour* (1945). Gerd Oswald brought an atmospheric style to such lurid thrillers as *A Kiss Before Dying* (1956) and *Screaming Mimi* (1958), as well as to several of the most highly regarded episodes of the *Outer Limits* television series. Monte Hellman's work includes the enigmatic western *The Shooting* (1967) and the existential road movie *Two-Lane Blacktop* (1971); still active, this talented stylist makes films infrequently and obscurely.

3. It is in the hyper-hyperbolic cartoons of Tex Avery or the formalist funny-business of Jerry Lewis that one possibly finds comparable examples of Hollywood filmmakers who were so aesthetically radical and yet able to work so successfully within popular idioms. Relevant comparisons to

Berkeley are also provided by specialists like the montage-sequence compiler Slavko Vorkapich and the credits-sequence creators Saul Bass and Maurice Binder. However, as this book will demonstrate, none of these cinematic analogues is as germane to Berkeley's film work as are theatrical figures such as P. T. Barnum, Florenz Ziegfeld, and R. H. Burnside.

4. A state popularly known today through the satirical sequences in the 1952 classic *Singin' in the Rain.*

5. David A. Cook, *A History of Narrative Film* (2d ed., 1990), p. 290; Arthur Knight, *The Liveliest Art*, p. 160; John Kobal, *Gotta Sing Gotta Dance: A Pictorial History of Film Musicals*, pp. 112, 121, 123, 127; Ethan Mordden, *The Hollywood Musical*, pp. 43–47; John Springer, *All Talking! All Singing! All Dancing! A Pictorial History of the Movie Musical*, p. 53.

6. Jane Feuer, *The Hollywood Musical*, pp. 23–26.

7. Tony Thomas and Jim Terry, *The Busby Berkeley Book*, pp. 24–25; Patrick Brion and René Gilson, "A Style of Spectacle: Interview with Busby Berkeley," *Cahiers du Cinéma in English*, no. 2 (1966): 32. The same story is related, with a few variations, in Bob Pike and Dave Martin, *The Genius of Busby Berkeley*, pp. 33–34; and in William Murray, "The Return of Busby Berkeley," *New York Times Magazine*, March 2, 1969, pp. 48–51.

8. Kobal, *Gotta Sing*, p. 121; Robert C. Roman, "Busby Berkeley," *Dance Magazine* (February 1967): 35; Springer, *All Talking!* p. 53; Brion and Gilson, "A Style of Spectacle," p. 28.

9. Bruce Babington and Peter William Evans, *Blue Skies and Silver Linings*, pp. 51, 54; Cook, *A History of Narrative Film*, p. 259; Jerome Delamater, "Busby Berkeley: An American Surrealist," *Wide Angle* 1 (Spring 1976): 30–37; Knight, *The Liveliest Art*, p. 160; William R. Meyer, *Warner Brothers Directors*, p. 29; Jean Mitry, *Histoire du Cinéma*, vol. 4, *Les Années 30*, p. 186.

In a later, more extensive discussion of Berkeley in *Dance in the Hollywood Musical*, Jerome Delamater gives ample recognition to the influence of the Ziegfeldian tradition on Berkeley's film work (pp. 27–48). More recently, there has been increased but still limited attention to the theatrical background of Berkeley's numbers in Rick Altman, *The American Film Musical*, pp. 201–204; and Gerald Mast, *Can't Help Singin': The American Musical on Stage and Screen*, pp. 116–17.

10. See Mordden, *The Hollywood Musical*, illustrations between pp. 73–74. Kobal (*Gotta Sing*, pp. 128–29) makes a very similar point, citing the *Ready, Willing and Able* number, a couple of other numbers from *The Great Ziegfeld*, and two numbers from *Dancing Lady* (1933). Non-Berkeley stage precedents can easily be found for all these "Berkeleyesque" numbers.

Chapter 1: Roots: From Barnum to Ziegfeld

1. Ethan Mordden, *Broadway Babies: The People Who Made the American Musical*, p. 3; Alan Williams, "The Musical Film and Popular Recorded Music," in Rick Altman, ed., *Genre: The Musical*, pp. 155–56.

2. Gerald Bordman, *American Musical Theatre: A Chronicle*; David Ewen, *The Story of America's Musical Theater*; Stanley Green, *The World of Musical Comedy*; Richard Kislan, *The Musical: A Look at the American Musical Theater*; Cecil Smith, *Musical Comedy in America.*

3. Kislan, *The Musical*, p. 113.

4. Patricia Mellancamp, "Spectacle and Spectator: Looking through the American Musical Comedy," *Cine-Tracts* 1 (Summer 1977): 28–35; Thomas H. Schatz, *Hollywood Genres: Formula, Film Making, and the Studio System*, pp. 194–212; Stanley J. Solomon, *Beyond Formula: American Film Genres*, pp. 71–75; Jacque Schultz, "Categories of Song," *Journal of Popular Film and Television* 8 (Spring 1980): 24–25; J. P. Telotte, "A Sober Celebration: Song and Dance in the 'New' Musical," *Journal of Popular Film and Television* 8 (Spring 1980): 2–5; Michael Wood, *America in the Movies*, p. 156; Rick Altman, *The*

American Film Musical, pp. 74–89; Timothy J. Scheurer, "The Aesthetics of Form and Convention in the Movie Musical," *Journal of Popular Film* 3 (Fall 1974): 308–17.

A notable exception to the integrationist consensus is Gerald Mast's *Can't Help Singin': The American Musical on Stage and Screen*. Although it is not a central element in his overall argument, Mast seems to accept quite cheerfully the inherent contradictions of the musical genre. For example, of George M. Cohan he writes: "He never quite left vaudeville behind—but neither have the very best American musical shows in some way or other. . . . But the problem of unity in this inherently disunified form is more paradoxical than later historians of the musical have been willing to admit" (p. 34). Most refreshingly, Mast sees such integrationist sacred-cows as Rodgers and Hammerstein's *Oklahoma!*, *Carousel*, and *South Pacific* as representing more loss than gain for the genre in the final balance (pp. 201–18).

Jerome Delamater, in his essay "Performing Arts: The Musical," in Stuart M. Kaminsky's *American Film Genres*, calls integration the "Platonic ideal" of the genre but acknowledges that this ideal can be too restrictive (p. 120).

5. "Discourse," a frequently used term in recent critical studies, refers to a distinct system of addressing the reader/spectator. Classical or conventionally realistic forms of art are commonly seen as those in which one mode of discourse is dominant. In musicals, the narrative/dialogue passages constitute one mode of discourse, while the singing/dancing passages constitute another, quite distinct way of addressing the spectator. The dominance of one discourse over the other in the musical is questionable or, at best, weakly resolved, and this is the beginning of the problem.

6. In ballad opera, spoken dialogue is combined with preexisting popular tunes to which new lyrics are added (e.g., *The Beggar's Opera*). Comic opera is similar to ballad opera but uses original music that is more central to the narrative (e.g., Gilbert and Sullivan's works). Operetta is related to the comic opera, but with greater emphasis on romance and melodrama.

7. Walt Whitman, *Leaves of Grass: The First (1855) Edition*, ed. Malcolm Cowley (New York: Viking Press, 1959), p. 85.

8. P. T. Barnum, *Struggles and Triumphs: Or, The Life of P. T. Barnum, Written by Himself*, ed. George S. Bryan, 1:183–97; Robert C. Toll, *On with the Show: The First Century of Show Business in America*, pp. 25–34.

9. Barnum, *Struggles and Triumphs* 1:195.

10. George L. Chindahl, *A History of the Circus in America*, pp. 92–95; John Culhane, *The American Circus: An Illustrated History*, pp. 95–107; Neil Harris, *Humbug: The Art of P. T. Barnum*, pp. 235–76; Toll, *On with the Show*, pp. 46–47, 61–62.

Historians offer differing interpretations of Barnum's contribution to the spectacularization of the American circus. Neil Harris and Robert C. Toll see Barnum as chiefly a publicist and figurehead for the various circuses he fronted, with Barnum's early partner W. C. Coup credited as the main innovative force. However, John Culhane's exhaustively researched history accords Barnum a more central creative role in his circuses.

11. Barnum, *Struggles and Triumphs* 1:193, 197–98.

12. Dailey Paskman, *"Gentlemen, Be Seated!": A Parade of American Minstrels*, pp. 21–31, 83–88; Toll, *On with the Show*, pp. 81–109, and Robert C. Toll, *Blacking Up: The Minstrel Show in Nineteenth-Century America*, pp. 52–57; Carl Wittke, *Tambo and Bones: A History of the American Minstrel Stage*, pp. 135–58.

13. Toll, *On with the Show*, p. 86.

14. Bordman, *American Musical Theatre*, p. 12. The final remark about the "not altogether healthy slapdash tradition" can be considered an example of pro-integration rhetoric.

15. Another key element (especially crucial to Berkeleyesque spectacle) that was minimized in minstrel shows was sex. The linking of sexuality with representations of African-Americans was a touchy area for white audiences of the time. The claims

by some authors (e.g., Erenberg and McLean) that a sexual dimension was absent in minstrel shows seem overstated; there was apparently a limited opportunity for such material in the form of female impersonations and double entendre jokes. See Lewis A. Erenberg, *Steppin' Out: New York Nightlife and the Transformation of American Culture, 1890–1930*, p. 19; Albert F. McLean, Jr., *American Vaudeville as Ritual*, p. 29; Paskman, *"Gentlemen, Be Seated!"*, pp. 85–88.

16. Some writers use the terms "vaudeville" and "variety" interchangeably. However, it is generally considered more accurate to use "variety" to denote an earlier, rowdier, less respectable phase of the form, before it was "cleaned up" (c. 1880) in order to broaden its appeal. See, for instance, Charles W. Stein, ed., *American Vaudeville as Seen by Its Contemporaries*, pp. 3–5, 6–9, 98–99.

17. Stuart Hall and Paddy Whannel, *The Popular Arts*, pp. 56–57; Peter Leslie, *A Hard Act to Follow: A Music Hall Review*, pp. 36–42, 49–50; McLean, *American Vaudeville as Ritual*, p. 34; Toll, *On with the Show*, pp. 189–92.

Several writers have linked the compartmentalized diversity of American vaudeville with the evolution of a heterogeneous mass urban audience in the late nineteenth-century United States. This connection would seem to be applicable to other aggregate entertainment forms as well. See John E. DiMeglio, *Vaudeville U.S.A.*, pp. 44, 197–99; McLean, *American Vaudeville as Ritual*, pp. 3–15, 33–37; Robert W. Snyder, *Voice of the City: Vaudeville and Popular Culture in New York*, pp. xiii–xvi.

18. DiMeglio, *Vaudeville U.S.A.*, pp. 35–37; George Gottlieb, "Psychology of the American Vaudeville Show from the Manager's Point of View," *Current Opinion* 60 (April 1926), reprinted in Stein, ed., *American Vaudeville*, pp. 179–81; McLean, *American Vaudeville as Ritual*, pp. 93–105; Snyder, *Voice of the City*, pp. 66–68; Marian Spitzer, "The Business of Vaudeville," *Saturday Evening Post*, May 24, 1924 (reprinted as "The Mechanics of Vaudeville" in Stein, ed., *American Vaudeville*, pp. 173–76); Toll, *On with the Show*, pp. 276–77.

19. Charles Higham, *Ziegfeld*, pp. 10–18; John F. Kasson, *Amusing the Million: Coney Island at the Turn of the Century*, pp. 57–72; Gary Kyriazi, *The Great American Amusement Parks: A Pictorial History*, pp. 42–65.

20. Foster Rhea Dulles, *A History of Recreation: America Learns to Play* (2d. ed.), p. 112; Harlowe R. Hoyt, *Town Hall Tonight*, p. 19; Julian Mates, *The American Musical Stage Before 1800*, pp. 136–37, 154–55, 180; Toll, *On with the Show*, p. 9.

21. Toll, *On with the Show*, p. 9.

22. Bordman, *American Musical Theatre*, p. 95.

23. Jean-Louis Baudry, "Ideological Effects of the Basic Cinematographic Apparatus," *Film Quarterly* 28 (Winter 1974–75): 41–42; Stephen Heath, "Film Performance," *Cine-Tracts* 1 (Summer 1977): 9–11; Stephen Heath, "Lessons from Brecht," *Screen* 15 (Summer 1974): 21–22; Stephen Heath, "Narrative Space," *Screen* 17 (Autumn 1976): 83, 90–100; Bill Nichols, *Ideology and the Image*, pp. 18–19, 49–57.

24. Opéra bouffe was a blend of satire, farce, song, and spoken dialogue that was especially popular in France during the Second Empire; its most famous practitioner was Jacques Offenbach. The Princess Theatre shows were an influential series of American musical comedies created by composer Jerome Kern, lyricist P. G. Wodehouse, and librettist Guy Bolton in 1915–18. Tailored to the confines of the diminutive Princess Theatre on West 39th Street, they downplayed spectacle in favor of intimacy and unity.

25. Bordman, *American Musical Theatre*, pp. 18–20; Mast, *Can't Help Singin'*, pp. 7–10; Julian Mates, "The Black Crook Myth," *Theatre Survey* 7 (May 1966): 31–43; Ethan Mordden, *Better Foot Forward: The History of American Musical Theatre*, pp. 10–13; Smith, *Musical Comedy in America*, pp. 13–22; Toll, *On with the Show*, pp. 173–77.

26. For example, the *New York Tribune* review of the opening performance commented, "The scenery is magnificent; the

ballet is beautiful; the drama is—rubbish." Quoted in Glenn Hughes, *A History of the American Theatre, 1700–1950*, p. 199.

27. Mates, "The Black Crook Myth," pp. 32–39.

28. These conclusions presuppose a conception of genre as being based on the maintenance of tensions and contradictions rather than on the resolution of them.

29. Mates, "The Black Crook Myth," p. 38.

30. John J. Jennings, *Theatrical and Circus Life; Or, Secrets of the Stage, Green-Room and Sawdust Arena*, pp. 162–65; A. Nicholas Vardac, *Stage to Screen: Theatrical Method from Garrick to Griffith*, pp. xvii–xxvi.

31. Vardac, *Stage to Screen*, pp. 1–19.

32. Barnard Hewitt, *Theatre U.S.A., 1668 to 1957*, pp. 265–68, 273–79.

33. Vardac, *Stage to Screen*, p. 65.

34. Brooks McNamara, "The Scenography of Popular Entertainment," *Drama Review* 18 (March 1974): 21.

35. Richard Moody, *America Takes the Stage: Romanticism in American Drama and Theatre, 1750–1900*, pp. 206–207, 218–19; Harold Scott, *The Early Doors: Origins of the Music Hall*, p. 14; Vardac, *Stage to Screen*, p. 68.

36. R. J. Broadbent, *A History of Pantomime*, pp. 172–75; Leslie, *A Hard Act to Follow*, pp. 43–45; Mates, *The American Musical Stage Before 1800*, pp. 156–64.

37. Broadbent, *A History of Pantomime*, pp. 182–83.

38. Ibid., p. 185; Leslie, *A Hard Act to Follow*, p. 45; Raymond Mander and Joe Mitchenson, *Pantomime: A Story in Pictures*, pp. 28–30; Mates, *The American Musical Stage Before 1800*, p. 159; Thelma Niklaus, *Harlequin*, p. 170; Scott, *The Early Doors*, pp. 34–35; Vardac, *Stage to Screen*, pp. 152–64; A. E. Wilson, *King Panto: The Story of Pantomime*, pp. 27–28, 34–35, 94, 158–59, 183.

39. Broadbent, *A History of Pantomime*, p. 185.

40. McNamara, "The Scenography of Popular Entertainment," p. 21.

41. Bordman, *American Musical Theatre*, p. 23; Mordden, *Better Foot Forward*, pp. 14–15; Laurence Senelick, *The Age and Stage of George L. Fox, 1825–1877*, pp. 138–43; Smith, *Musical Comedy in America*, pp. 23–27; Toll, *On with the Show*, pp. 176–77.

42. "Fun and Beauty at the Winter Garden," *New York Sun*, October 15, 1915; "New Winter Garden Spectacle Is Most Impressive Pictorially," *New York Mail*, October 15, 1915; "Winter Garden Gives Its Most Undressed Show," *New York World*, October 15, 1915.

Con., "Good Times," *Variety*, August 13, 1920.

"New Follies of Our Village," *New York Evening Telegram*, September 1, 1921.

M.M.B., "'Better Times' a Great Production," *New York Evening Post*, September 5, 1922; "'Better Times' Starts Run," *New York Sun*, September 4, 1922.

43. David Mayer III, *Harlequin in His Element: The English Pantomime, 1806–1836*, pp. 23–31.

44. Kislan, *The Musical*, pp. 74–76; Mates, *The American Musical Stage Before 1800*, pp. 178–79; Mordden, *Better Foot Forward*, pp. 9–10.

45. Clifford E. Hamar, "Scenery on the Early American Stage," *Theatre Annual* 7 (1948–49): 84.

46. Raymond Mander and Joe Mitchenson, *Revue: A Story in Pictures*, pp. 7–15; Mates, *The American Musical Stage Before 1800*, p. 179; Mordden, *Better Foot Forward*, pp. 9–10.

47. Charles Eidsvik, *Cineliteracy: Film Among the Arts*, pp. 113–22; John L. Fell, *Film and the Narrative Tradition*, pp. 12–36; Vardac, *Stage to Screen*, pp. 250–51.

48. Vardac, *Stage to Screen*, pp. 14, 43–45.

49. Ibid., pp. 9, 66, 198, 232–33.

50. For a fuller discussion of this aspect of realism, see Colin MacCabe's articles, "Realism and the Cinema: Notes on Some Brechtian Theses," *Screen* 15 (Summer 1974): 5–27, and "Theory and Film: Principles of Realism and Pleasure," *Screen*

17 (Autumn 1976): 7–27. MacCabe's concepts are dealt with at greater length in chapter 2.

51. Thomas H. Gressler, "A Review of the Term Revue," *Players* 48 (June–July 1973): 224.

Robert Baral (*Revue: The Great Broadway Period*) and Gerald Bordman (*American Musical Revue*) have written entire books on the subject without making any satisfactory attempt to define what they mean by the term "revue." The best attempt I have found is in Richard Kislan's *The Musical*.

52. Don B. Wilmeth, *Variety Entertainment and Outdoor Amusements: A Reference Guide*, p. 166.

53. McNamara, "The Scenography of Popular Entertainment," pp. 19–20.

54. Mander and Mitchenson, *Revue*, pp. 1–13.

55. A practice carried on in film titles like *Gold Diggers of 1933*, *Fashions of 1934*, *The Big Broadcast of 1936*, etc.

56. Mander and Mitchenson, *Revue*, p. 10.

57. Bordman, *American Musical Theatre*, p. 19; Bordman, *American Musical Revue*, pp. 14–21.

58. Bordman, *American Musical Revue*, p. 18.

59. Ibid., p. 31.

60. Baral, *Revue*, pp. 47–48; Bordman, *American Musical Theatre*, p. 250; Higham, *Ziegfeld*, pp. 75–77.

61. e. e. cummings, "Vive la Folie!" in George J. Firmage, ed., *E.E. Cummings: A Miscellany Revised* (New York: October House, 1965), p. 162.

62. As an index of this trend, newspaper reviews of the revues of the 1910s, when the form was still fresh, commonly lavished a great deal of space on praise and detailed description of the production numbers. By the late 1920s these elements were generally being passed over by reviewers, and more space was accorded to discussions of the comedy elements and of the anachronistic quality of the revue form as a whole.

63. Bordman, *American Musical Revue*, pp. 53–54.

64. Examples include the *Big Broadcast* series (1932, 1936, 1937, 1938), *International House* (1933), *Dancing Lady* (1933), *George White's Scandals* (1934, 1935), *Twenty Million Sweethearts* (1934), *Hollywood Party* (1934), *Transatlantic Merry-Go-Round* (1934), *Murder at the Vanities* (1934), *Go into Your Dance* (1935), *Every Night at Eight* (1935), *Broadway Melody of 1936* (1935), *Millions in the Air* (1935), *The Great Ziegfeld* (1936), *Born to Dance* (1936), *The Hit Parade* (1937), *Artists and Models* (1937), *Broadway Melody of 1938* (1937), *The Goldwyn Follies* (1938), *Artists and Models Abroad* (1938), etc.

65. Examples of the composer/performer biography mode are *Rhapsody in Blue* (1945), *Night and Day* (1946), *The Jolson Story* (1946), *Till the Clouds Roll By* (1946), *Words and Music* (1948), *Look for the Silver Lining* (1949).

Examples of the wartime-rally mode are *Star-Spangled Rhythm* (1942), *Stage Door Canteen* (1943), *Thousands Cheer* (1943), *This Is the Army* (1943), *Two Girls and a Sailor* (1944), *Four Jills in a Jeep* (1944), *Follow the Boys* (1944), *Hollywood Canteen* (1944).

Chapter 2: The Backstage Format

1. George Odell, *Annals of the New York Stage*, quoted in Bordman, *American Musical Theatre*, p. 7.

2. Bordman, *American Musical Theatre*, p. 114.

3. Rick Altman, in *The American Film Musical*, p. 205, notes that the backstage story flourished on Broadway in the 1920s, but primarily as a *non*-musical form.

4. Altman, *The American Film Musical*, p. 228; Mordden, *The Hollywood Musical*, pp. 48–49; Springer, *All Talking!* p. 53.

5. MacCabe, "Realism and the Cinema," pp. 7–12. See chapter 1, note 5, for a brief definition of "discourse."

6. Ibid., p. 12.

7. This definition is not airtight; it seems to work best at what might be called the musical genre's "center," both historically and qualitatively. It does not apply so well to some

films—such as *A Star Is Born* (1954), *Cabaret* (1972), *All That Jazz* (1979)—that are included by consensus in the genre's canon. However, these examples (at least) can be distinguished by the fact that they are all explicitly "metamusicals" (that is, films that reflect critically on the musicals/Hollywood/entertainment apparatus from positions that are—or at least purport to be—outside it to a certain extent).

8. William Murray, "The Return of Busby Berkeley," pp. 51–53. This conception of Berkeley's numbers is greatly at odds with the one presented by Rick Altman in *The American Film Musical* (pp. 227–34). In the first place, Altman (although he is certainly aware of the facts) discusses the Warners/Berkeley musicals in a manner that implies a common authorship for both the narrative portions and the production numbers. It seems highly questionable, even from the loosest or most generous auteurist reading, to regard *42nd Street*, *Gold Diggers of 1933*, *Footlight Parade*, and *Dames* as "Busby Berkeley films." They are Warner Bros. films in which Busby Berkeley numbers are included.

In addition, Altman attempts to read the classic Warners/Berkeley musicals in an integration-oriented way that overcentralizes the main romantic couple (usually designated—somewhat questionably—as Ruby Keeler and Dick Powell), with the plot thematics projected into the musical numbers and the final number resolving the entire film's various conflicts. This approach indicates the hazards of giving the Warners/Berkeley musicals a primarily narrative-oriented reading rather than a spectacle-oriented reading. Altman, whose important book is distinguished by its meticulous discrimination between different forms and phases of the musical, might have benefited from some additional category-drawing in this instance. One cannot interpret these Warners/Berkeley musicals in the same general way that one reads *Love Me Tonight*, *Shall We Dance*, or *Singin' in the Rain*. Gerald Mast, although his book on musicals is far less thorough and theoretically rigorous than Altman's, seems much more on target when he calls Berkeley's numbers "decorative epilogues to the narratives" (*Can't Help Singin'*, p. 149).

A more complex approach to the problem of the relationship between numbers and narrative in the Warners/Berkeley musicals is suggested in the discussion of *Gold Diggers of 1933* in Bruce Babington and Peter William Evans's genre study *Blue Skies and Silver Linings* (pp. 65–72). Although they concede that traditional notions of integration do not apply to Berkeley's numbers, the authors see integration operating in them on other levels. One is the relationship of the numbers to each other: Babington and Evans read the four major numbers of *Gold Diggers of 1933* as a self-enclosed network of comparisons and oppositions, similar to the interpretation below of the numbers in *Footlight Parade* (see the "Paradigm Parade" section in chapter 7). The numbers also intersect with the surrounding narrative in a generalized way, intensifying and hyperbolizing certain broad aspects of it (e.g., the central thematic relationship between sex and money). It should be noted that the authors have selected the one Warners/Berkeley musical (along with, possibly, *Dames*) that is the most receptive to this type of interpretation; I doubt whether such methods of analysis would be nearly as productive with, say, *42nd Street*, *Footlight Parade*, or the final numbers of *Gold Diggers of 1935*.

Most interestingly, Babington and Evans find significance in the very gap between numbers and narrative—through the ways these two sides of the film collide with and even contradict each other (e.g., the contrast between the demure Ruby Keeler character in the narrative scenes and the more sexually aware Ruby in the "Pettin' in the Park" number). The authors' subsequent analysis of the numbers does not strongly develop this aspect and instead primarily stresses links to the narrative. However, the basic concept introduced here suggests an approach to the Warners/Berkeley musicals as texts that are considerably more "open" than is normal in classical narrative cinema. This type of approach also seems much more apposite to aggregative entertainment forms than to integrative ones.

9. Arlene Croce, *The Fred Astaire and Ginger Rogers Book*, p. 36.

10. Roland Barthes, *S/Z*, trans. Richard Howard, pp. 88–90, 105, 173–74, 181–82.

11. Wilella Waldorf, "Earl Carroll's 'Vanities,'" *New York Post*, August 7, 1928.

12. "International Revue [Unsigned news item consisting mainly of a lengthy quotation from the *Philadelphia Public Ledger* review]," *New York Times*, February 10, 1930.

13. Jean-Louis Comolli, "Dancing Images: Busby Berkeley's Kaleidoscope," *Cahiers du Cinéma in English*, no. 2 (1966): 24.

14. Christian Metz, "The Imaginary Signifier," *Screen* 16 (Summer 1975): 44–45.

15. That the loss-of-focus may have been originally the result of technical sloppiness does not necessarily negate these claims. A decision would still have been made to leave it in the film, where it operates in the way described.

Chapter 3: Berkeley on Broadway

1. The obvious qualification to be appended to this statement is that there is a certain amount of overlap between these phases, as well as hybridizations of the different types of musical shows. The latter qualification applies particularly to mixtures of operetta and musical comedy in the early stages of Berkeley's Broadway career (*Castles in the Air*, *The Wild Rose*) and to mixtures of musical comedy and revue in the later stages (*Good Boy*, *Pleasure Bound*, *A Night in Venice*, *Broadway Nights*).

2. Gordon [only name given], "Holka Polka," *Wall Street News*, October 19, 1925; "'Holka-Polka' Lofty and Very Pleasing," *New York Times*, October 15, 1925; W.M., "Melody and the Harrolds Make 'Holka Polka' Good," *New York Tribune*, October 15, 1925.

3. Altman, *The American Film Musical*, pp. 133–35; Gerald Bordman, *American Operetta*, pp. 5–7; Kislan, *The Musical*, pp. 96–103.

4. See "Musical Comedy," in Hartnoll, ed., *The Oxford Companion to the Theater*, 4th ed.

5. Gilbert Gabriel, "Last Night's First Night," *New York Sun*, November 4, 1927; "Mark Twain's 'A Connecticut Yankee' Musicalized," *Stamford Advocate*, October 1, 1927.

6. The same burlesque-like mixture of the modern-day and the historical, with a dream as the link between them, is employed in the film *Roman Scandals* (1933), for which Berkeley directed the dance numbers.

7. The generally obsolete usage of the word "girls" to describe adult females is revived in this study in reference to those theatrical performers who were known as "chorus girls" and "showgirls." Such terms as "chorus women" and "show women," however politically commendable, seem idiomatically awkward and inaccurate. Lewis A. Erenberg's *Steppin' Out* contains an excellent discussion (pp. 215–22) of the function of immaturity and girlishness in constructing the popular image of chorus girls, as a means of ameliorating the challenge they posed to declining standards of Victorian sexuality.

8. Thomas and Terry, *The Busby Berkeley Book*, p. 22.

9. John Martin, "The Dance: New Musical Comedy Talent: Busby Berkeley's Direction Raises the Level of Our Stage Performances," *New York Times*, July 22, 1928.

10. Martin, "New Musical Comedy Talent."

11. Ibid.

12. Ibid.

13. "Broadway Portraits," *New York Amusements* 7 (July 16, 1928): 19.

14. Another example of a Berkeley stage technique that went against the grain of his later reputation occurred in the 1929 Shubert revue *Pleasure Bound*. The dance numbers, arranged by Berkeley in collaboration with John Boyle, featured

a figure identified as "The Girl on the End." Throughout the show, this chorus girl performed in a comically lackadaisical manner that set her apart from the synchronized peppiness of the rest of the chorus line.

In a letter to researcher Robert Darrell Moulton, Berkeley claimed credit for originating this device and gave the impression of having used it in more than one production, although I have found mention of it only in reviews of *Pleasure Bound*. In his study of Broadway choreography, Moulton cites "the little girl at the end of the line" as the main reason for including Berkeley among a select group of 1920s Broadway dance directors who "had tried to break up the 'mechanization' of the chorus line in musical comedy." Again, the contrast to Berkeley's later reputation is striking. Robert Darrell Moulton, "Choreography in Musical Comedy and Revue on the New York Stage from 1925 through 1950" (Ph.D. diss., University of Minnesota, 1957), pp. 48, 52.

15. Bordman, *American Musical Revue*, pp. 84–85; "Splash!" *New Republic*, August 22, 1928, p. 21.

16. Pierre de Rohan, "Creditable Revue Offers Beautiful Girls as Features," *New York American*, August 7, 1928.

17. Rowland Field, "The New Play—'Earl Carroll Vanities,'" *Brooklyn Daily Times*, August 7, 1928; E. W. Osborn, "Earl Carroll's Vanities," *New York Evening World*, August 7, 1928; Arthur Pollock, "Earl Carroll Reappears on the Scene with a New Edition of His 'Vanities' and Shows Improvement," *Brooklyn Daily Eagle*, August 7, 1928; "Premiere of Earl Carroll's 'Vanities' Tomorrow Night," *New York Evening Enquirer*, August 5, 1928; Wilella Waldorf, "Earl Carroll's 'Vanities,'" *New York Post*, August 7, 1928.

18. White Studio Key Book, n.c. 16,559, The Billy Rose Theatre Collection of the Lincoln Center Library for the Performing Arts, New York, N.Y., pp. 193–94.

19. J. H. Keen, "The Morning After," *Philadelphia Daily News*, August 8, 1927; "'Vanities' Found Lacking in Wit, but Very Magnificent," *New York Telegraph*, August 7, 1928.

20. Roxanne, "The Plays," *New York Telegraph*, August 12, 1928.

21. Roxanne, "The Plays"; "Splash!" *New Republic*.

22. E.F.M., "Professor Carroll's Course in Anatomy," *Boston Transcript*, October 15, 1928; Osborn, "Earl Carroll's Vanities."

23. De Rohan, "Creditable Revue"; "Earl Carroll's Vanities," *Philadelphia Evening Bulletin*, July 31, 1928; "Even Broadway at Last Begins To Understand," *Journal of Electrical Workers and Operators* (December 1928); Keen, "The Morning After"; "New 'Vanities' Stakes All on Its Comedians," *New York Times*, August 7, 1928; Osborn, "Earl Carroll's Vanities"; *Sid.*, "Plays on B'way—Vanities," *Variety*, August 8, 1928; Alison Smith, "Mr. Carroll Comes Back," *New York World*, August 8, 1928; "Splash!" *New Republic*; W.O'W., "Glorious Girls and Risible Sketches in New 'Vanities,'" *New York Journal*, August 7, 1928.

24. *Sid.*, "Plays on B'way."

25. "Earl Carroll's Vanities," *D.A.C. News* (September 1928), p. 70; *Sid.*, "Plays on B'way."

26. E.F.M., "Professor Carroll's Course."

27. Robert Coleman, "'Good Boy' Swift, Amusing, Tuneful Musical Comedy," *New York Mirror*, September 6, 1928; C.C.N., "'Good Boy' Deservedly Received with Novelty into Earning Merit," *New York Telegram*, September 6, 1928; Richard Watts, Jr., "'Good Boy' Opens with Novel Settings and Very Swift Pace," *New York Herald Tribune*, September 6, 1928.

28. H.T.P., "Off and On Go Panoramic Settings," *Boston Transcript*, April 17, 1929.

29. See the section on "Spectacle Forms" in chapter 1.

30. "Very Good, Mr. Hammerstein," *New York World*, September 7, 1928.

31. "Bizarre Effects Feature 'Good Boy' Hammerstein Hit," *New York American*, September 6, 1928.

32. Ibid.; "'Good Boy' Displays Scenic Novelties," *New York Times*, September 6, 1928; Burns Mantle, "'Good Boy'

Chockfull of This and That; Novel Attachments," *New York Daily News*, September 8, 1928; C.C.N., "'Good Boy' Deservedly Received"; H.T.P., "Off and On Go Panoramic Settings"; Stephen Rathbun, "'Good Boy' Opens," *New York Sun*, September 6, 1928; "Very Good," *New York World*; Wilella Waldorf, "A New Musical Comedy," *New York Evening Post*, September 6, 1928.

33. *The Passing Show* (newsletter of the Shubert Archive) 3 (Winter 1979): 12.

34. Sally Barnes, "Revues," *The Passing Show* 3 (Winter 1979): 2; Brooks McNamara, *The Shuberts of Broadway*, pp. 80–81, 96; Jerry Stagg, *The Brothers Shubert*, p. 214.

35. H. T. Craven, "Profusion of Stars in 'International Revue' Premiere," *Philadelphia Record*, February 4, 1930; "International Revue Has World Premiere at Shubert Theatre," *Camden Courier*, February 4, 1930; "International Revue Is Huge Production," *Philadelphia Inquirer*, February 4, 1930; "Luminaries from Two Continents Appear in Revue," *Philadelphia Ledger*, February 4, 1930; Arthur Ruhl, "Lew Leslie's 'International Revue' a Lavish Entertainment," *New York Herald Tribune*, February 26, 1930; Wilella Waldorf, "Lew Leslie's Extravaganza," *New York Post*, February 26, 1930.

36. "Flaming Feather Headdresses in 'International Revue,'" *Billboard*, March 20, 1930; Ruhl, "Lew Leslie's 'International Revue'"; "Variety of Colors and Costumes Follow Cosmopolitanism of 'International Revue,'" *Woman's Wear Daily*, February 26, 1930.

37. "International Revue," *Camden Courier*; "International Revue [unsigned news item consisting mainly of a lengthy quotation from the *Philadelphia Public Ledger* review]," *New York Times*, February 10, 1930; Jerome Kurtz, "International Revue," *Newark Ledger*, February 11, 1930; "Lew Leslie's 'International Revue' Heartily Applauded at the Shubert," *Newark News*, February 11, 1930; Elizabeth Perkins, "'International Revue' Gorgeous Dance Show," *Newark Star-Ledger*, February 11, 1930; Ruhl, "Lew Leslie's 'International Revue.'"

Chapter 4: Broadway Before Berkeley

1. "Ed Wynn Has a Hilarious Revue in 'The Perfect Fool,'" *New York Herald*, November 9, 1921; "Ed Wynn Now Shows Ability as Inventor," *New York Evening Journal*, November 18, 1921; "'Perfect Fool' Scores Before Wise Audience," *New York Evening Telegram*, November 8, 1921.

2. "Big Revue in Music Box," *New York Evening Telegram*, September 23, 1921.

3. "Winter Garden Has Excellent Revue," *New York Times*, June 25, 1925.

4. "'Better Times' Filled with Thrills," *New York Evening Journal*, September 4, 1922; "'Better Times' Starts Run," *New York Sun*, September 4, 1922; Alan Dale, "'Better Times' Is Sensation at Hippodrome," *New York American*, September 4, 1922; "Hippodrome Opens with 'Better Times,' A Sumptuous Spectacle," *New York Call*, September 4, 1922; Lawrence Reamer, "'Better Times,' Best of Hippodrome's Spectacles," *New York Herald*, September 4, 1922.

5. A nearly identical effect was used in the *Earl Carroll Vanities of 1925*, which opened on July 6, 1925. Stephen Rathbun, "'Earl Carroll Vanities' Opens," *New York Sun*, July 7, 1925; Helen Rockwell, "'Vanities' Girls in High Efficiency," *New York Telegram*, July 7, 1925.

6. In fact, some of the numbers discussed in the previous chapter as parts of shows on which Berkeley worked were probably (in some cases, certainly) not his creations, either in whole or in part. "The Machinery Ballet" in the *Earl Carroll Vanities of 1928* was staged by a team called the Marmeins. According to the programme for the *International Revue*, "The Rout" was staged and conceived by producer Lew Leslie and Anton Dolin, the up-and-coming ballet choreographer who was the featured dancer in the number. The scenic effects and

hyperfluid transitions of *Good Boy* were almost certainly less the work of Berkeley than of the show's various set designers and technicians, whose names were generally mentioned more prominently than Berkeley's in the reviews.

7. Bordman, *American Musical Theatre*, pp. 185, 200.

8. Charles Darnton, "Ziegfeld Follies," *New York Evening World*, June 22, 1915; "Ziegfeld Follies," *Louisville Herald*, July 3, 1915; Higham, *Ziegfeld*, p. 123; "New 'Follies' Is Prodigal," *New York Times*, June 6, 1922; C.P.S., "New 'Follies' Is a Dream of Beauty," *New York Post*, June 6, 1922 (source of quotation).

9. Bordman, *American Musical Theatre*, p. 35.

10. *Swing.*, "The Passing Show," *Variety*, January 31, 1919.

11. E.B.T., "Jape, Jabber and Jazz," *Boston Transcript*, February 2, 1926.

12. *Libbey.*, "Ziegfeld's Follies," *Variety*, August 10, 1927.

13. Higham, *Ziegfeld*, p. 178; Thomas and Terry, *The Busby Berkeley Book*, pp. 57, 89.

14. James Craig, "Vanities of 1923," *New York Mail*, July 6, 1923; White Studio Key Book, n.c. 16,553, The Billy Rose Theatre Collection of the Lincoln Center Library for the Performing Arts, New York, N.Y., p. 140, nos. 25, 26, and p. 148, no. 160; White Studio Key Book, n.c. 16,554, p. 358, no. 16.

15. Higham, *Ziegfeld*, p. 48.

16. Publicity postcard/photograph, located in Clippings File for *Better Times*, The Billy Rose Theatre Collection of the Lincoln Center Library for the Performing Arts, New York, N.Y.

17. White Studio Key Book, n.c. 16,556, p. 307.

18. Vardac, *Stage to Screen*, pp. 32–33, 72, 143, 150–61, 242.

19. "Greenwich Village Follies," *New York Herald*, September 1, 1921; "New Follies of Our Village," *New York Evening Telegram*, September 1, 1921; G.M.W., "Greenwich Village Follies," *Toledo Blade*, November 7, 1922; "'Lady Butterfly,' Lovely and Gay, at Globe Theater," *New York Tribune*, January 23, 1923; Norman Clarke, *The Mighty Hippodrome*, p. 116; M.M.B., "'Better Times' a Great Production," *New York Evening Post*, September 5, 1922; Heywood Broun, "The Music Box Revue," *New York World*, December 2, 1924; E.B.T., "'Models' Sans Gawking," *Boston Transcript*, November 17, 1925.

20. Clarke, *The Mighty Hippodrome*, p. 62; Higham, *Ziegfeld*, p. 82.

21. E.F.M., "Spectacle Galore, Served with Zest," *Boston Transcript*, September 17, 1929.

22. *Con.*, "A Night in Spain," *Variety*, May 11, 1927.

23. Weed Dickinson, "'Good Times' Had at Hippodrome," *New York Telegraph*, August 10, 1920; "Good Times," *New York Telegram*, August 10, 1920; Annalee Vernon, "'Good Times' at the Hip," *New York Garment News*, August 10, 1920.

24. Bordman, *American Musical Theatre*, p. 210; Clarke, *The Mighty Hippodrome*, pp. 13–37.

25. Clarke, *The Mighty Hippodrome*, pp. 100–26.

26. Kelcy Allen, "'Better Times' at Hippodrome," *Daily News Record*, September 5, 1922; "'Better Times,' at Hippodrome, Opens," *Brooklyn Citizen*, September 5, 1922; "'Better Times' Filled with Thrills," *New York Evening Journal*; "'Better Times' Starts Run," *New York Sun*; Dale, "'Better Times' Is Sensation at Hippodrome," *New York American*; "Hippodrome Opens with 'Better Times,' a Sumptuous Spectacle," *New York Call*; Reamer, "'Better Times,' Best of Hippodrome's Spectacles," *New York Herald*; *Sime.*, "Better Times," *Variety*, September 8, 1922.

27. Derek Forbes, "Water Drama," in David Bradby, Louis James, and Bernard Sharratt, eds., *Performance and Politics in Popular Drama*, p. 107.

28. Clarke, *The Mighty Hippodrome*, pp. 57–58, 108. The film *Million Dollar Mermaid* (1952; numbers by Berkeley) is based on the life of Annette Kellerman; several of its numbers are set in the (re-created) Hippodrome.

29. Dickinson, "'Good Times' Had at Hippodrome," *New York Telegraph*.

30. Baral, *Revue*, p. 51.

31. Ibid., p. 52. This number is related only by its title to the 1906 Hippodrome show.

32. Thomas and Terry, *The Busby Berkeley Book*, p. 70.

33. In *Footlight Parade* (1933), when an assistant suggests to idea-starved producer James Cagney that he do an American Beauty Rose number, Cagney replies derisively, "Stop, you're killing me! I almost fell out of my cradle when the Shuberts did it back in nineteen-hundred-and-twelve!"

34. M. Willson Disher, *Music Hall Parade*, p. 97.

35. "Summer Reaches the Winter Garden," *New York Times*, April 27, 1917.

36. "The Follies of 1909," *New York Dramatic Mirror*, June 26, 1909; "Follies of 1909," *Theatre Magazine* (August 1909).

37. "'Better Times' Filled with Thrills," *New York Evening Journal*.

38. White Studio Key Book, n.c. 16,553, p. 5, no. 42.

39. Baral, *Revue*, p. 125.

40. E.F.M., "An Americanized 'Paris,'" *Boston Transcript*, December 27, 1925; "Premiere of 'A Night in Paris' at the Majestic," *Brooklyn Standard*, December 29, 1925.

41. White Studio Key Book, n.c. 16,557, p. 172, no. 25.

42. *Waters.*, "I'll Say She Is," *Variety*, June 7, 1923; "'Up in the Clouds' Tuneful Comedy," *New York Evening Journal*, January 4, 1922.

43. Baral, *Revue*, p. 185.

44. Abe Laufe, *The Wicked Stage*, p. 50.

45. Joseph Mulvaney, "Beauty, Melody and Comedy Rule at Apollo," *New York American*, June 15, 1926.

46. E.B.T., "Gilded Banality," *Boston Transcript*, March 24, 1925.

47. Bordman, *American Musical Theatre*, p. 143.

48. White Studio Key Book, n.c. 16,562, p. 139.

49. Bordman, *American Musical Theatre*, p. 242.

50. H.T.P., "Bettered Humor, Routined Songs, Glint and Glow," *Boston Transcript*, June 15, 1924.

51. "'Better Times' Starts Run," *New York Sun*.

52. E.B.T., "Song of Solomon—1925," *Boston Transcript*, May 17, 1925; White Studio Key Book, n.c. 16,556, p. 338, nos. 11–13.

53. Mort Eiseman, "Scenes Swamped in 'Gay Paree,'" *New York Telegraph*, August 7, 1925.

54. E.B.T., "Song of Solomon," *Boston Transcript*.

55. E.F.M., "An Americanized 'Paris,'" *Boston Transcript*; "Premiere of 'A Night in Paris,'" *Brooklyn Standard*.

56. J. Brooks Atkinson, "Humor in a Stage Revue," *New York Times*, June 9, 1926; F. P. Dunne, Jr., "On a Large Scale," *New York World*, July 16, 1929.

57. J. Brooks Atkinson, "Show Business on Broadway," *New York Times*, July 16, 1929; Robert Garland, "Dancing Team of Three Kings Feature of 'Broadway Nights,'" *New York Telegram*, July 16, 1929.

58. Bordman, *American Musical Theatre*, p. 246.

59. E.F.M., "Spectacle Galore, Served with Zest," *Boston Transcript*.

60. "Carroll's 'Vanities,' with Peggy Joyce, Is Worth Seeing," *New York Herald*, July 6, 1923; E.B.T., "Unleavened, Unrehearsed," *Boston Transcript*, December 1, 1925.

61. Higham, *Ziegfeld*, p. 108.

62. Bordman, *American Musical Theatre*, p. 242; Photograph, *The Standard and Vanity Fair* (August 28, 1908), in Clippings File for *Ziegfeld Follies (1908)*, The Billy Rose Theatre Collection of the Lincoln Center Library for the Performing Arts, New York, N.Y.

63. "Audience Warm to 'Rose-Marie,'" *New York Sun*, September 3, 1924; Bordman, *American Musical Theatre*, p. 233; White Studio Key Book, n.c. 16,554, pp. 336, 426, 533.

64. White Studio Key Book, n.c. 16,554, p. 474, nos. 103–106.

65. Bordman, *American Musical Theatre*, p. 177.

66. Burns Mantle, "Strangers within the Gates," *New York*

Mail, January 5, 1922.

67. Higham, *Ziegfeld*, p. 108.

68. McCandlish Phillips, "Berkeley Seeks a Little Group—25 Gorgeous Girls," *New York Times*, March 17, 1970. (Presumably, Berkeley is referring here to "Dames.")

69. White Studio Key Book, n.c. 16,553, p. 5, no. 42; E.B.T., "Song of Solomon," *Boston Transcript*; White Studio Key Book, n.c. 16,559, p. 193, nos. 61, 63; White Studio Key Book, n.c. 16,558, p. 2, no. 41.

70. Bordman, *American Musical Theatre*, p. 166; Clarke, *The Mighty Hippodrome*, p. 47; *Con.*, "A Night in Spain," *Variety*; Atkinson, "Humor in a Stage Revue," *New York Times*. In *Footlight Parade*'s "By a Waterfall," the aquatic chorus at one point form into twin undulating snakes.

71. White Studio Key Book, n.c. 16,554, p. 381, no. 21; White Studio Key Book, n.c. 16,559, p. 54, no. 23.

72. Photograph, *Cleveland Review* (November 23, 1914), p. 2; Jerry Stagg, *The Brothers Shubert*, pp. 120–21; Mander and Mitchenson, *Revue*, illus. no. 33.

73. The "primitive" movie musicals of 1929–30, particularly those which are little more than transposed stage shows, constitute the most extensive filmed record of the Broadway stage techniques of the era. As such, they are referred to occasionally in this study.

74. F.D., "Night in Venice," (unidentified Chicago newspaper), November 26, 1929, in Clippings File for *A Night in Venice*, The Billy Rose Theatre Collection of the Lincoln Center Library for the Performing Arts, New York, N.Y.

75. E.B.T., "Fustian, Flesh and Foolery," *Boston Transcript*, November 9, 1926.

76. Brion and Gilson, "A Style of Spectacle," p. 32.

77. Allen Churchill, *The Theatrical Twenties*, p. 80.

78. E.B.T., "Song of Solomon," *Boston Transcript*.

79. "'Vanities' Found Lacking in Wit, but Very Magnificent," *New York Telegraph*, August 1, 1926.

80. See the "Black Crook" section in chapter 1.

81. Bordman, *American Musical Theatre*, pp. 40, 210.

82. Ibid., p. 8.

83. Ibid., p. 97; Derek Parker and Julia Parker, *The Natural History of the Chorus Girl*, pp. 23, 81–82; Smith, *Musical Comedy in America*, p. 53; Bernard Sobel, *A Pictorial History of Burlesque*, pp. 14–22; Toll, *On with the Show*, 216–221; Irving Zeidman, *The American Burlesque Show*, pp. 23–27.

84. Alan Hyman, *The Gaiety Years*, p. 67; Parker and Parker, *Natural History of the Chorus Girl*, pp. 53–59; Smith, *Musical Comedy in America*, pp. 113–17.

85. Smith, *Musical Comedy in America*, p. 155.

86. Moulton, "Choreography in Musical Comedy," pp. 2–4; Parker and Parker, *Natural History of the Chorus Girl*, pp. 102–12; "Professor Clark, of Columbia, Weds Mary Read [sic], Head of Tiller Dancers," *New York Herald Tribune*, October 23, 1937.

87. The idea of regimentation was often literalized in stage musicals by having chorus girls, usually in fetching "uniforms" of one sort or another, perform military-style marching drills. Berkeley, who had considerable experience in supervising parade drills during his World War I military service, employed the drill motif (with both male and female participants) in several of his film numbers, including "Remember My Forgotten Man" in *Gold Diggers of 1933*, "Shanghai Lil" in *Footlight Parade*, "All's Fair in Love and War" in *Gold Diggers of 1937*, and "The Song of the Marines" in *The Singing Marine*. Even when chorus members were not in uniform, the idea of regimentation was implicit in most Berkeleyesque production numbers. There is little room for individuality in the precision-dancing tradition; the emphasis is on repetition; and the chorus girls tend to become replicas of each other (an idea literalized in Berkeley's "I Only Have Eyes for You").

88. Gene Kelly, the next major figure in film choreography after Berkeley and Astaire, can be seen as a pioneer figure in the

trend to synthesize these two traditions of spectacle style and individual style. This perhaps accounts for the sense of effort and, at times, unwieldiness that underlies much of Kelly's work. The "purer" numbers of Berkeley and Astaire in their respective primes create more of an impression of organic unity and self-contained consistency.

Chapter 5: An Introductory Outline of Berkeley's Film Career

1. Douglas Gomery, *The Hollywood Studio System,* p. 25.
2. Ibid., pp. 63, 114.
3. Another issue that should at least be mentioned concerns the influence of events from Berkeley's personal life. Berkeley's career was punctuated by some major offscreen crises, including a protracted prosecution for second-degree murder (the result of a fatal traffic accident) in 1935–36, a scandalous alienation-of-affections suit involving nineteen-year-old actress Carole Landis in 1938, and a suicide attempt following the death of his mother in 1946. However, the concrete effect of these episodes upon Berkeley's numbers is inconclusive at best and raises questions of the relationship between biography and artistic production that are beyond the scope of this study.

Chapter 6: Early Period (1930–1933)

1. Steve Seidman, *Comedian Comedy: A Tradition in Hollywood Film,* pp. 1–57.
2. Ziegfeld also served, nominally, as coproducer of the movie version.
3. In addition to these three, there are nonspectacle numbers performed by Cantor and other cast members.
4. In this configuration, comic star Eddie Cantor holds a privileged, mediating position, with the prerogative to brush aside barriers and cross over from one side to the other: from narrative to spectacle (as in "My Honey Said Yes, Yes"), from male to female (he does a drag routine in the woman's shower room), and from white to black (he sings one number, "There's Nothing Too Good for My Baby," in blackface).
5. Brion and Gilson, "A Style of Spectacle," p. 34; David Martin, *The Films of Busby Berkeley,* pp. 8–9; Thomas and Terry, *The Busby Berkeley Book,* p. 72.
6. "This sadistic side fits in well with narrative. Sadism demands a story, depends on making something happen, forcing a change in another person, a battle of will and strength, victory/defeat, all occurring in a linear time with a beginning and an end. Fetishistic scopophilia, on the other hand, can exist outside linear time as the erotic instinct is focussed on the look alone." Laura Mulvey, "Visual Pleasure and Narrative Cinema," *Screen* 16 (Autumn 1975): 14.

Chapter 7: Classic Warner Bros. Period (1933–1934)

1. Gerald Mast, *Can't Help Singin',* p. 125, compares this end-heavy arrangement to the placement of the headliners on a vaudeville bill.
2. Croce, *The Fred Astaire and Ginger Rogers Book,* pp. 186–87.
3. See the "Placards" section of chapter 4.
4. Thomas and Terry, *The Busby Berkeley Book,* p. 50.
5. See chapter 4 for fuller descriptions of these theatrical motifs.
6. For another example of this theme, see Edmund Wilson, *The Thirties: From Notebooks and Diaries of the Period* (New York: Farrar, Straus and Giroux, 1980), p. 303: "Ideas of impotence were very much in people's minds at this period—on account of the Depression, I think, the difficulty of getting things going."
7. The use of extended lateral tracking shots to provide a gradual and controlled revelation of the spatial context in

"Honeymoon Hotel" and "Shanghai Lil" is somewhat similar to the use of treadmills in the 1928 stage production *Good Boy,* described in chapter 3.

8. An eyeline-match is a common editing technique used to create implicit spatial connections. A shot of a person looking is followed by a shot of what he/she is looking at. If consistent screen direction is maintained, we will assume that the looker and looked-at are present in the same space, even if we do not see them together in the same shot.

9. A match-on-action is a common editing technique in which an action carries over continuously from one shot to the next.

10. Andrew Bergman's *We're in the Money* contains a good overview of "Fallen Woman" melodramas (pp. 49–55).

11. Charles F. [Rick] Altman, "The American Film Musical: Paradigmatic Structure and Mediatory Function," *Wide Angle* 2 (January 1978): 11, 17. The term "paradigmatic" refers to "vertical" relationships of comparison and contrast. The term "syntagmatic" refers to "horizontal" relationships of proximity and sequence.

12. Thomas and Terry, *The Busby Berkeley Book,* p. 83.

13. As they can be in narrativized dream/imagination numbers such as Astaire and Rogers's "I Used To Be Color Blind" in *Carefree* (1938) and Kelly's climactic ballet in *An American in Paris* (1951).

14. It is instructive to note that "I Only Have Eyes for You," one of Berkeley's most spectacular numbers, involves no dancing to speak of: the chorus merely parades around and sways from side to side. In fact, there is very little dancing at all in *Dames,* the only such instances being a brief tap-dancing break by the chorus in the middle of "Dames," the even briefer tap demonstration by Keeler at the tryout, and the truncated chorus routine led by Joan Blondell in the final "Try To See It My Way" number. With a few notable exceptions (e.g., Cagney and Keeler's bartop dance in "Shanghai Lil," the mass tap dance at the nightclub in "Lullaby of Broadway"), dance is at best a minor or subsidiary element in Berkeley's full-scale spectacular film numbers, which are more concerned with pattern and movement than with fancy footwork.

Chapter 8: Later Warner Bros. Period (1935–1939)

1. It should be noted that the mid- and late 1930s is a transitional period for the musical in general. Just as Berkeley musicals of this period are marked by strained attempts to emulate the light-toned consistency of the Astaire-Rogers musicals, several of the Astaire-Rogers films are marked by awkward attempts to inject the Astaire style into a Berkeleyesque context, as represented by such sprawling numbers as "The Carioca" (*Flying Down to Rio,* 1933), "The Continental" (*The Gay Divorcee,* 1934), "Lovely to Look At" (*Roberta,* 1935), and "The Piccolino" (*Top Hat,* 1935).

2. Notable examples of this pioneer documentary film movement are Alberto Cavalcanti's *Rien Que les Heures* (1926), Walter Ruttman's *Berlin: Die Sinfonie der Grosstadt* (1927), and Dziga Vertov's *Chelovek S Kinoapparatom* (*The Man with the Movie Camera,* 1928). The "city symphony" documentaries typically present an impressionistic picture of a day in the life of a city.

3. Sergei Eisenstein, *Film Form: Essays in Film Theory,* ed. and trans. Jay Leyda (New York: Harcourt, Brace and World, 1949), p. 55.

4. Berkeley also served as the full director on three minor Warner Bros. musicals of the late 1930s: *Bright Lights* (1935), *Stage Struck* (1936), and *Garden of the Moon* (1938). They are all routine projects, lacking ambition in their musical numbers and bearing little relation to the Berkeleyesque.

5. Pike and Martin, *The Genius of Busby Berkeley,* p. 84.

6. Peter Bogdanovich, "Interview [with Howard Hawks]," *Movie,* no. 5 (December 1962): 11.

Chapter 9: MGM Period (1939–1943)

1. Brion and Gilson, "A Style of Spectacle," p. 27.
2. Some sample lyrics:
   Miner: "What about our wages when we dig?"
   Rooney: "Brother, teach 'em to jig! . . ."
   Hillbilly: "What about a pension for Ma and Pa?"
   Garland: "What about a pension for Artie Shaw!"
3. Hugh Fordin, *The Movies' Greatest Musicals,* p. 38.
4. The extension of a final number by means of reprises—a device often used in Berkeley's later films—works to give the finale a self-inclusive massiveness similar to that produced by the stacking of several numbers at the ends of the classic Warner Bros. musicals.
5. Fordin, *The Movies' Greatest Musicals,* p. 43.
6. Brion and Gilson, "A Style of Spectacle," p. 37; Pike and Martin, *The Genius of Busby Berkeley,* p. 117; Thomas and Terry, *The Busby Berkeley Book,* p. 33.
7. Brion and Gilson, "A Style of Spectacle," pp. 28–30; Pike and Martin, *The Genius of Busby Berkeley,* p. 99; Irene Thirer, "Hollywood Visitor: Busby Berkeley, Dance Master of the Movies" (unidentified New York newspaper, dated October 8, 1940; article located in Clippings File for Busby Berkeley in the Billy Rose Theatre Collection of the Lincoln Center Library for the Performing Arts, New York, N.Y.). In the Thirer article, Berkeley states flatly, "Drama . . . that's really my forte."
8. Meyer, *Warner Brothers Directors,* p. 37; Pike and Martin, *The Genius of Busby Berkeley,* p. 110; Eugenia Sheppard, "Oh, Fudge," *New York Post,* March 28, 1972; Thirer, "Hollywood Visitor."
9. Fordin, *The Movies' Greatest Musicals,* p. 83.

Chapter 10: Fox Period (1943)

1. Douglas Gomery, *The Hollywood Studio System,* p. 95.
2. As further amenities, Berkeley's move to Fox reunited him with Darryl F. Zanuck, the producer responsible for giving him free rein on *42nd Street,* and Harry Warren, the composer responsible for the most memorable melodies of Berkeley's Warner Bros. numbers.
3. The passage referred to in *Moon over Miami* is the first meeting between Grable and an inebriated Ameche at a patio table. Such density of analytical editing is not unusual in the film.
4. The writings of the French theoretician André Bazin have become a standard critical reference point for a film aesthetic based on the continuity of space and time achieved through depth-of-focus and unedited long-takes, rather than the segmentation of space and time achieved through editing.
5. As Berkeley described it, this kaleidoscope was formed by "two mirrors fifty feet high and fifteen feet wide which together formed a V design. In the center of this I had a revolving platform eighteen feet in diameter and as I took the camera up high between these two mirrors, the girls on the revolving platform below formed an endless design of symmetrical forms." Thomas and Terry, *The Busby Berkeley Book,* p. 153.

Chapter 11: Late Period (1949–1954, 1962)

1. Pike and Martin, *The Genius of Busby Berkeley,* p. 119.
2. Fordin, *The Movies' Greatest Musicals,* p. 242.
3. For a useful discussion of different modes of discourse in the musical, see Jacque Schultz, "Categories of Song," *Journal of Popular Film and Television* 8 (Spring 1980): 15–25.
4. It should be recalled that none of the big Berkeley numbers in the classic Warner Bros. musicals takes place in a rehearsal setting but only as part of a formal stage performance.
5. This last effect manipulates space in a richly paradoxical way that expresses the double pulls of longing and separation. For example, a camera movement toward Leigh in the background and apparently away from Martin in the foreground

also seems to move them closer together because of the way it magnifies Leigh's rear-projected image—so near yet so far away, so far away yet so near.

6. Thomas and Terry, *The Busby Berkeley Book,* p. 180.

7. In an interview with Dave Martin, Berkeley claimed to have directed all of the film's musical numbers except for "Little Girl Blue" and the "Sawdust, Spangles and Dreams" finale—easily the two most heavy-handed numbers in the film (Pike and Martin, *The Genius of Busby Berkeley,* p. 121). *The Busby Berkeley Book* credits him with the circus parade (misidentified as the opening sequence), "Over and Over Again," "This Can't Be Love," and "various other circus acts" (Thomas and Terry, p. 184). Based on a combination of external and internal evidence, I would equivocally assign to Berkeley at least the following five sequences: (1) the opening tent-raising sequence (but not Stephen Boyd's introductory song passage), (2) "Over and Over Again," (3) "The Circus on Parade," (4) "This Can't Be Love," and (5) the "Butterflies" trapeze act, including the segue into the storm sequence.

Berkeley wanted to end *Jumbo* with a climactic number "gradually building up into a spectacular three-ring circus." Instead, director Walters and associate producer Roger Edens opted to end the film with a leaden fantasy number directed by Walters himself (Pike and Martin, *The Genius of Busby Berkeley,* p. 121).

BIBLIOGRAPHY

Altman, Charles F. [Rick]. "The American Film Musical: Paradigmatic Structure and Mediatory Function." *Wide Angle* 2 (January 1978): 10–17.

Altman, Rick. *The American Film Musical*. Bloomington: Indiana University Press, 1987.

Altman, Rick, ed. *Genre: The Musical*. London: Routledge and Kegan Paul, 1981.

Ames, Jerry, and Jim Siegelman. *The Book of Tap*. New York: David McKay, 1977.

Astaire, Fred. *Steps in Time*. New York: Harper, 1959.

Babington, Bruce, and Peter William Evans. *Blue Skies and Silver Linings*. Manchester: Manchester University Press, 1985.

Baral, Robert. *Revue: The Great Broadway Period*. New York: Fleet Press, 1962.

Barnes, Sally. "Revues." *The Passing Show* 3 (Winter 1979): 1–3.

Barnum, P. T. *Struggles and Triumphs: Or, The Life of P. T. Barnum, Written by Himself*. Edited by George S. Bryan. 2 vols. New York: Alfred A. Knopf, 1927.

Barthes, Roland. *S/Z*. Translated by Richard Howard. New York: Hill and Wang, 1974.

Baudry, Jean-Louis. "Effects of the Basic Cinematographic Apparatus." *Film Quarterly* 28 (Winter 1974–75): 39–47.

Belton, John. "The Backstage Musical." *Movie*, no. 24 (Spring 1977): 36–44.

Bergman, Andrew. *We're in the Money*. New York: Harper and Row, Colophon Books, 1971.

Bordman, Gerald. *American Musical Comedy*. New York: Oxford University Press, 1982.

—. *American Musical Revue*. New York: Oxford University Press, 1985.

—. *American Musical Theatre: A Chronicle*. New York: Oxford University Press, 1978.

—. *American Operetta*. New York: Oxford University Press, 1981.

Braudy, Leo. *The World in a Frame*. Garden City, N.Y.: Anchor Books, 1976.

Brion, Patrick, and René Gilson. "A Style of Spectacle: Interview with Busby Berkeley." *Cahiers du Cinéma in English*, no. 2 (1966): 26–37.

Broadbent, R. J. *A History of Pantomime*. London: Simpkin, Marshall, Hamilton, and Kent, 1902; reprint, New York: Citadel Press, 1965.

Burton, Jack. *Blue Book of Broadway Musicals*. Watkins Glen, N.Y.: Century House, 1952.

Calhoun, Mary. *Medicine Show: Conning People and Making Them Like It*. New York: Harper and Row, 1976.

Cantor, Eddie, and David Freedman. *Ziegfeld: The Great Glorifier*. New York: Alfred H. King, 1934.

Carter, Randolph. *The World of Flo Ziegfeld*. New York: Praeger, 1974.

Chesire, D. F. *Music Hall in Britain*. Newton Abbot: David and Charles, 1974.

Chindahl, George L. *A History of the Circus in America*. Caldwell, Idaho: Caxton Printers, 1959.

Churchill, Allen. *The Theatrical Twenties*. New York: McGraw-Hill, 1975.

Clarke, Norman. *The Mighty Hippodrome*. South Brunswick, N.J.: A. S. Barnes, 1968.

Comolli, Jean-Louis. "Kaleidoscopie de Busby Berkeley." *Cahiers du Cinéma*, no. 174 (January 1965): 24–27. Translated as "Dancing Images: Busby Berkeley's Kaleidoscope." *Cahiers du Cinéma in English*, no. 2 (1966): 22–26.

Cook, David A. *A History of Narrative Film*. New York: W. W. Norton, 1981; 2d ed., 1990.

Croce, Arlene. *The Fred Astaire and Ginger Rogers Book*. New York: E. P. Dutton, 1972; reprint, New York: Vintage Books, 1977.

Culhane, John. *The American Circus: An Illustrated History*. New York: Henry Holt, 1990.

cummings, e. e. "Vive la Folie!" In George J. Firmage, ed., *E. E. Cummings: A Miscellany Revised*, pp. 159–63. New York: October House, 1965.

Damase, Jacques. *Les Folies du Music-Hall*. Paris: Editions "Spectacles," 1962; reprint (in English), London: Hamlyn, 1970.

Delamater, Jerome. "Busby Berkeley: An American Surrealist." *Wide Angle* 1 (Spring 1976): 30–37.

—. *Dance in the Hollywood Musical*. Ann Arbor, Mich.: UMI Research Press, 1981.

—. "Performing Arts: The Musical." In Stuart Kaminsky, ed., *American Film Genres*, pp. 120–40. Dayton, Ohio: Pflaum, 1974.

DiMeglio, John E. *Vaudeville U.S.A.* Bowling Green: Bowling Green University Popular Press, 1973.

Disher, M. Willson. *Music Hall Parade*. New York: Scribner's, 1938.

Dulles, Foster Rhea. *A History of Recreation: America Learns to Play*. 2d ed. New York: Appleton-Century-Crofts, 1965.

Dunn, Don. *The Making of "No, No, Nanette."* Secaucus, N.J.: Citadel Press, 1972.

Eidsvik, Charles. *Cineliteracy: Film Among the Arts*. New York: Horizon Press, 1978.

Elsaesser, Thomas. "The American Musical." *Brighton Film Revue*, no. 15 (December 1969): 15–16.

Engel, Lehman. *The American Musical Theater*. Rev. ed. New York: Collier Books, 1975.

Erenberg, Lewis A. *Steppin' Out: New York Nightlife and the Transformation of American Culture, 1890–1930*. Chicago: University of Chicago Press, 1984.

Ewen, David. *New Complete Book of the American Musical Theatre*. New York: Alfred A. Knopf, 1970.

—. *The Story of America's Musical Theater*. Rev. ed. Philadelphia: Chilton, 1968.

Farnsworth, Marjorie. *The Ziegfeld Follies*. New York: Bonanza Books, 1956.

Fell, John L. *Film and the Narrative Tradition*. Norman: University of Oklahoma Press, 1974.

"Feminine Beauty Is a Business." *Brooklyn Daily Eagle*, July 18, 1937.

Feuer, Jane. *The Hollywood Musical*. Bloomington: Indiana University Press, 1982.

Fischer, Lucy. "The Image of Woman as Image: The Optical Politics of *Dames*." *Film Quarterly* 30 (Fall 1976): 2–11.

Forbes, Derek. "Water Drama." In David Bradby, Louis James, and Bernard Sharratt, eds., *Performance and Politics in Popular Drama*, pp. 91–107. Cambridge: Cambridge University Press, 1980.

Fordin, Hugh. *The Movies' Greatest Musicals: Produced in Hollywood USA by the Freed Unit*. New York: Frederick Ungar, 1984; reprint of *The World of Entertainment: Hollywood's Greatest Musicals*, New York: Doubleday, 1975.

Freedley, George. "The Black Crook and the White Fawn." In Paul Magriel, ed., *Chronicles of the American Dance: From the Shakers to Martha Graham*, pp. 64–79. New York: Dance Index, 1948; reprint, New York: Da Capo Press, 1978.

Fumento, Rocco, ed. *42nd Street*. Wisconsin/Warner Bros. Screenplay Series. Madison: University of Wisconsin Press, 1980.

Gilbert, Douglas. *American Vaudeville: Its Life and Times*. New York: Whittlesey House, 1940.

Gomery, Douglas. *The Hollywood Studio System*. New York: St. Martin's, 1986.

Green, Abel, and Joe Laurie, Jr. *Show Biz: From Vaude to Video*. New York: Henry Holt, 1951.

Green, Stanley. *Encyclopaedia of the Musical Film*. New York: Oxford University Press, 1981.

—. *Encyclopaedia of the Musical Theatre*. New York: Dodd, Mead, 1976.

—. *The World of Musical Comedy*. 3d ed. New York: A. S. Barnes, 1974.

Green, William. "Broadway Book Musicals: 1900–1969." In *The American Theatre: A Sum of Its Parts*, pp. 246–71. (No editor listed.) New York: Samuel French, 1971.

Gressler, Thomas H. "A Review of the Term Revue." *Players* 48 (June–July 1973): 7–27.

Hall, Stuart, and Paddy Whannel. *The Popular Arts*. New York: Pantheon, 1965.

Hamar, Clifford E. "Scenery on the Early American Stage." *Theatre Annual* 7 (1948–49): 84–103.

Harris, Neil. *Humbug: The Art of P. T. Barnum*. Chicago: University of Chicago Press, 1973; Phoenix Books, 1981.

Hartnoll, Phyllis, ed. *The Oxford Companion to the Theatre*. 4th ed. London: Oxford University Press, 1983.

Hay, James. "Dancing and Deconstructing the American Dream." *Quarterly Review of Film Studies* 10 (Spring 1985): 97–117.

Heath, Stephen. "Film Performance." *Cine-Tracts* 1 (Summer 1977): 7—17.

—. "Lessons from Brecht." *Screen* 15 (Summer 1974): 103–28.

—. "Narrative Space." *Screen* 17 (Autumn 1976): 69–112.

Hewitt, Barnard H. *A History of the Theatre from 1800 to the Present*. New York: Random House, 1970.

—. *Theatre U.S.A., 1668 to 1957*. New York: McGraw-Hill, 1959.

Higham, Charles. *Ziegfeld*. Chicago: Henry Regnery, 1972.

Hirschhorn, Clive. *Gene Kelly: A Biography*. Chicago: Henry Regnery, 1974.

—. *The Hollywood Musical*. New York: Crown, 1981.

Hodgkinson, A. W. "*42nd Street* New Deal: Some Thoughts about Early Film Musicals." *Journal of Popular Film* 4 (1975): 33–47.

Howe, Arthur, ed. *Gold Diggers of 1933*. Wisconsin/Warner Bros. Screenplay Series. Madison: University of Wisconsin Press, 1980.

Hoyt, Harlowe R. *Town Hall Tonight*. Englewood Cliffs, N.J.: Prentice-Hall, 1955.

Hughes, Glenn. *A History of the American Theatre, 1700–1950*. New York: Samuel French, 1951.

Hyman, Alan. *The Gaiety Years*. London: Cassell, 1975.

Jennings, John J. *Theatrical and Circus Life; Or, Secrets of the Stage, Green-Room and Sawdust Arena*. St. Louis: Sun Publishing, 1882.

Jones, Carlisle. "Making Sixteen Damsels Dance Where But One Danced Before." *New York Herald Tribune*, March 18, 1934.

—. "Something New in Backgrounds Evolved by Hollywood Director." *New York Herald Tribune*, August 12, 1934.

Kasson, John F. *Amusing the Million: Coney Island at the Turn of the Century*. New York: Hill and Wang, 1978.

Kislan, Richard. *Hoofing on Broadway: A History of Show Dancing*. New York: Prentice-Hall, 1987.

—. *The Musical: A Look at the American Musical Theater*. Englewood Cliffs, N.J.: Prentice-Hall, 1980.

Knight, Arthur. "Busby Berkeley." *Action* 9 (May–June 1974): 11–16.

—. *The Liveliest Art*. New York: Mentor Books, 1959.

Kobal, John. *Gotta Sing Gotta Dance: A Pictorial History of Film Musicals*. London: Hamlyn, 1971.

Kreuger, Miles. *Show Boat: The Story of a Classic American Musical*. New York: Oxford University Press, 1977.

Kreuger, Miles, ed. *The Movie Musical from Vitaphone to 42nd Street: As Reported in a Great Fan Magazine*. New York: Dover, 1975.

Kyriazi, Gary. *The Great American Amusement Parks: A Pictorial History*. Secaucus, N.J.: Citadel Press, 1976.

Laufe, Abe. *The Wicked Stage*. New York: Frederick Ungar, 1978.

Leslie, Peter. *A Hard Act to Follow: A Music Hall Review*. New York: Paddington Press, 1978.

Loney, Glenn, ed. *Musical Theatre in America: Papers and Proceedings of the Conference on the Musical Theatre in America*. Westport, Conn.: Greenwood Press, 1984.

MacCabe, Colin. "Realism and the Cinema: Notes on Some Brechtian Theses." *Screen* 15 (Summer 1974): 5–27.

—. "Theory and Film: Principles of Realism and Pleasure." *Screen* 17 (Autumn 1976): 7–27.

MacQueen-Pope, W. *Nights of Gladness*. London: Hutchinson, 1956.

McLean, Albert F., Jr. *American Vaudeville as Ritual*. Lexington: University of Kentucky Press, 1965.

McNamara, Brooks. "The Scenography of Popular Entertainment." *Drama Review* 18 (March 1974): 16–24.

—. *The Shuberts of Broadway*. New York: Oxford University Press, 1990.

McVay, Douglas. *The Musical Film*. New York: A. S. Barnes, 1967.

Mander, Raymond, and Joe Mitchenson. *British Music Hall: A Story in Pictures*. London: Hart-Davis, 1968.

—. *Musical Comedy: A Story in Pictures*. New York: Taplinger, 1970.

—. *Pantomime: A Story in Pictures*. New York: Taplinger, 1973.

—. *Revue: A Story in Pictures*. New York: Taplinger, 1971.

Martin, David. *The Films of Busby Berkeley*. San Francisco: David Martin, 1964.

Martin, John. "The Dance: New Musical Comedy Talent: Busby Berkeley's Direction Raises the Level of Our Stage Performances." *New York Times*, July 22, 1928.

Mast, Gerald. *Can't Help Singin': The American Musical on Stage and Screen*. Woodstock, N.Y.: Overlook Press, 1987.

Mates, Julian. *The American Musical Stage Before 1800*. New Brunswick, N.J.: Rutgers University Press, 1962.

—. *America's Musical Stage: Two Hundred Years of Musical Theatre*. Westport, Conn.: Greenwood Press, 1985.

—. "The Black Crook Myth." *Theatre Survey* 7 (May 1966): 31–43.

Matlaw, Myron, ed. *American Popular Entertainment: Papers and Proceedings of the Conference on the History of American Popular Entertainment*. Westport, Conn.: Greenwood Press, 1979.

Mayer, David, III. *Harlequin in His Element: The English Pantomime, 1806–1836*. Cambridge: Harvard University Press, 1969.

Mellencamp, Patricia. "Spectacle and Spectator: Looking through the American Musical Comedy." *Cine-Tracts* 1 (Summer 1977): 28–35.

Metz, Christian. "History/Discourse: Note on Two Voyeurisms." *Edinburgh '76 Magazine*, no. 1 (1976): 21–25.

—. "The Imaginary Signifier." *Screen* 16 (Summer 1975): 14–76.

Meyer, William R. *Warner Brothers Directors*. New Rochelle, N.Y.: Arlington House, 1978.

Mitry, Jean. *Histoire du Cinéma*. Vol. 4, *Les Années 30*. Paris: Editions Universitaires, 1980.

Moody, Richard. *America Takes the Stage: Romanticism in American Drama and Theatre, 1750–1900*. Bloomington: Indiana University Press, 1955.

Mordden, Ethan. *Better Foot Forward: The History of American Musical Theatre*. New York: Grossman, 1976.

—. *Broadway Babies: The People Who Made the American Musical*. New York: Oxford University Press, 1983.

—. *The Hollywood Musical*. New York: St. Martin's, 1981.

Morley, Sheridan. *Spread a Little Happiness: The First Hundred Years of the British Musical*. New York: Thames and Hudson, 1987.

Moulton, Robert Darrell. "Choreography in Musical Comedy and Revue on the New York Stage from 1925 through 1950." Ph.D. diss., University of Minnesota, 1957.

Mueller, John. *Astaire Dancing: The Musical Films*. New York: Alfred A. Knopf, 1985.

—. "Fred Astaire and the Integrated Musical." *Cinema Journal* 24 (Fall 1984): 28–40.

Mulvey, Laura. "Visual Pleasure and Narrative Cinema." *Screen* 16 (Autumn 1975): 6–18.

Murray, Ken. *The Body Merchant: The Story of Earl Carroll*. Pasadena, Calif.: Ward Ritchie Press, 1976.

Murray, William. "The Return of Busby Berkeley." *New York Times Magazine*, March 2, 1969, pp. 26–27+.

Nichols, Bill. *Ideology and the Image*. Bloomington: Indiana University Press, 1981.

Niklaus, Thelma. *Harlequin*. New York: George Braziller, 1956.

Nye, Russell. *The Unembarrassed Muse: The Popular Arts in America*. New York: Dial, 1970.

Parker, Derek, and Julia Parker. *The Natural History of the Chorus Girl*. Indianapolis: Bobbs-Merrill, 1975.

Paskman, Dailey. *"Gentlemen, Be Seated!": A Parade of American Minstrels*. New York: Clarkson N. Potter, 1976.

The Passing Show. Newsletter of the Shubert Archive. Special Issue on the Revue. *See* Sally Barnes.

Pike, Bob, and Dave Martin. *The Genius of Busby Berkeley*. Reseda, Calif.: CFS Books, 1973.

Riis, Thomas L. *Just Before Jazz: Black Musical Theater in New York, 1890–1915.* Washington, D.C.: Smithsonian Institution Press, 1989.
Roman, Robert C. "Busby Berkeley." *Dance Magazine* (February 1967): 35–39.
Roth, Mark. "Some Warners Musicals and the Spirit of the New Deal." *Velvet Light Trap*, no. 17 (Winter 1977): 1–7.
Sadoul, Georges. *Dictionary of Film Makers.* Translated, edited, and updated by Peter Morris. Berkeley: University of California Press, 1972.
Schatz, Thomas H. *Hollywood Genres: Formula, Film Making, and the Studio System.* New York: Random House, 1981.
Scheurer, Timothy J. "The Aesthetics of Form and Convention in the Movie Musical." *Journal of Popular Film* 3 (Fall 1974): 307–25.
Schultz, Jacque. "Categories of Song." *Journal of Popular Film and Television* 8 (Spring 1980): 15–25.
Scott, Harold. *The Early Doors: Origins of the Music Hall.* London: Nicholson and Watson, 1946.
Seidman, Steve. *Comedian Comedy: A Tradition in Hollywood Film.* Ann Arbor, Mich.: UMI Research Press, 1981.
Senelick, Laurence. *The Age and Stage of George L. Fox, 1825–1877.* Hanover, N.H.: University Press of New England, 1988.
Sennett, Ted. *Hollywood Musicals.* New York: Henry N. Abrams, 1981.
Slout, William L. "The Black Crook: First of the Super Nudies." *Players* 50 (Fall–Winter 1975): 16–19.
Smith, Cecil. *Musical Comedy in America.* New York: Theatre Arts, 1950.
Snyder, Robert W. *Voice of the City: Vaudeville and Popular Culture in New York.* New York: Oxford University Press, 1989.
Sobel, Bernard. *A Pictorial History of Burlesque.* New York: Putnam, 1956.
Solomon, Stanley J. *Beyond Formula: American Film Genres.* New York: Harcourt, Brace, and Jovanovich, 1976.
Southern, Richard. *Changeable Scenery: Its Origin and Development in the British Theatre.* London: Faber and Faber, 1951.
Springer, John. *All Talking! All Singing! All Dancing! A Pictorial History of the Movie Musical.* New York: Citadel Press, 1969.
Stagg, Jerry. *The Brothers Shubert.* New York: Random House, 1968.
Stearns, Marshall, and Jean Stearns. *Jazz Dance: The Story of American Vernacular Dance.* New York: Macmillan, 1968; reprint, New York: Schirmer Books, 1979.
Steen, Mike. *Hollywood Speaks!: An Oral History.* New York: Putnam, 1974.
Stein, Charles W., ed. *American Vaudeville as Seen by Its Contemporaries.* New York: Alfred A. Knopf, 1984.
Steinke, Gary Lee. "An Analysis of the Dance Sequences in Busby Berkeley's Films: *Forty Second Street*; *Footlight Parade*; and *Gold Diggers of 1935.*" Ph.D. diss., University of Michigan, 1979.
Stern, Lee Edward. *The Movie Musical.* New York: Pyramid, 1974.
Taylor, John Russell, and Arthur Jackson. *The Hollywood Musical.* New York: McGraw-Hill, 1971.
Telotte, J. P. "A Sober Celebration: Song and Dance in the 'New' Musical." *Journal of Popular Film and Television* 8 (Spring 1980): 2–14.
Tessier, Max. "Busby Berkeley 1895–1976." *L'Avant Scene du Cinéma*, no. 206 (April 15, 1978).
Thomas, Tony. *Harry Warren and the Hollywood Musical.* Secaucus, N.J.: Citadel Press, 1975.
—. *That's Dancing!* New York: Harry N. Abrams, 1984.
Thomas, Tony, and Jim Terry. *The Busby Berkeley Book.* Greenwich, Conn.: New York Graphic Society, 1973.
Toll, Robert C. *Blacking Up: The Minstrel Show in Nineteenth-Century America.* London: Oxford University Press, 1974.

—. *The Entertainment Machine*. New York: Oxford University Press, 1982.

—. *On with the Show: The First Century of Show Business in America*. New York: Oxford University Press, 1976.

Tomlinson, David. "Berkeley, Busby." In Christopher Lyon, ed., *The International Dictionary of Films and Filmmaking*. Vol. 2, *Directors/Filmmakers*, pp. 43–45. Chicago: St. James Press, 1984.

Traubner, Richard. *Operetta: A Theatrical History*. Garden City, N.Y.: Doubleday, 1983.

Vallillo, Stephen M. "Broadway Revues in the Teens and Twenties: Smut and Slime?" *Drama Review* 25 (March 1981): 25–34.

Vardac, A. Nicholas. *Stage to Screen: Theatrical Method from Garrick to Griffith*. Cambridge: Harvard University Press, 1949; reprint, New York: Benjamin Blom, 1968.

Wayburn, Ned. *The Art of Stage Dancing*. New York: Ned Wayburn Studios, 1925.

Wilmeth, Don B. *American and English Popular Entertainment: A Guide to Information Sources*. Performing Arts Information Guide Series, vol. 7. Detroit: Gale Research, 1980.

—. *The American Stage to World War I: A Guide to Information Sources*. Performing Arts Information Guide Series, vol. 4. Detroit: Gale Research, 1978.

—. *Variety Entertainment and Outdoor Amusements: A Reference Guide*. Westport, Conn.: Greenwood Press, 1982.

Wilson, A. E. *King Panto: The Story of Pantomime*. New York: E. P. Dutton, 1935.

Wittke, Carl. *Tambo and Bones: A History of the American Minstrel Stage*. Durham, N.C.: Duke University Press, 1930.

Wolfe, Charles. "Busby Berkeley." In Jean-Pierre Coursodon, ed., *American Directors*, vol. 1, pp. 4–9. New York: McGraw-Hill, 1983.

Wood, Michael. *America in the Movies*. New York: Basic Books, 1975.

Zeidman, Irving. *The American Burlesque Show*. New York: Hawthorn, 1967.

STAGEOGRAPHY

The following chronological stageography is only for those Broadway (or Broadway-bound) productions in which Busby Berkeley contributed to the dance numbers.

1. HOLKA POLKA

Opened October 14, 1925. Lyric Theatre. 21 performances. Operetta.

Presented by Carl Reed. Music by Will Ortmann. Lyrics by Gus Kahn and Raymond B. Egan. Book by Bert Kalmar and Harry Ruby. Adapted from Derick Wulff's translation of the Czech operetta *Spring in Autumn* by W. Walzer. Staged by Oscar Eagle. Dances and ensembles by Busby Berkeley. Entire production and costumes designed by Livingston Platt. Musical program under the direction of Max Steiner.

Cast: Orville Harrold, Patti Harrold [Orville's daughter], Robert Halliday, Harry Holbrook, May Vokes, James C. Morton, Frances H. Cherry, Thomas Burke, Jr., Rosa de Cordoba and Edwin Strawbridge (specialty dancers), Marion and Martinez Randall (specialty dancers), Lisa Parnova (specialty dancer).

Ensemble: Ladies of the Ensemble (39), Gentlemen of the Ensemble (25).

Selected Numbers: "Home of My Heart," "Spring in Autumn," "In a Little While," "Chimes of the Chapel," "When Love Is Near," "Holka Polka," "I Want To Be a Bad Little Boy," "This Is My Dance."

Plot Summary: A Czech girl falls in love with a handsome American tourist, but her sophisticate mother tries to make her wed a baron. The girl's honest father, wrongfully accused of a past crime, saves the day and clears his name.

Comments: The up-and-coming team of Kalmar and Ruby were called in for a last-minute overhaul of the book, but their efforts were found lacking by the critics. Berkeley's handling of the large chorus received general acclaim. Attempting to appeal to Broadway's current vogue for dance crazes, the big "Holka Polka" number seems to have been a Charleston variation with a Czech accent.

2. CASTLES IN THE AIR

Opened November 22, 1925. Shubert Olympic Theatre (Chicago). Musical Play.

Presented by John Meehan and James W. Elliott. Music by Percy Wenrich. Lyrics and book by Raymond W. Peck. Staged by John Meehan. Ensembles by Busby Berkeley. Dances by John Boyle. Scenery by Rothe Studios. Production costumed by Booth, Willoughby & Jones, Inc., under supervision of Miss Viola. Orchestra under the direction of Max Steiner.

Cast: Vivienne Segal, Bernard Granville, Irving Beebe (replaced by J. Harold Murray during the Chicago run), Thais Lawton, Joyce White, Claire Madjette, Stanley Forde, Allen Waterous, Robert Williamson, Mary Hutchinson, Gregory Ratoff.

Ensemble: Singing Girls (19), Singing Boys (14), Specialty Dancers (17 women, 6 men—including coproducer John Meehan).

Selected Numbers: "Lantern of Love," "The Fox-Trot Lullaby" (aka "Baby"), "True Love and a Ring," "The Singer's Career, Ha! Ha!" "First Kiss of Love," "I Would Love To Fondle You," "Land of Romance," "Love Is King," "When the Only One Meets the Only One," "Girls and the Gimmes."

Plot Summary: An heiress's guardian hires a college boy to pose as a "Latavian" prince in order to cure the girl of her infatuation with royalty. It turns out that the "imposter" is a real prince.

Comments: An attempted synthesis of musical comedy and operetta formulas. Berkeley shared responsibility for the dance numbers with John Boyle, an accomplished technician whose fondness for jazz/tap rhythms, large-scale choral arrangements, and antiphonal rhythms indicates a possible influence on Berkeley's developing choreographic style. After nearly a year's successful run in Chicago, the company divided. One unit went to Broadway, where the show opened at the Selwyn Theatre on September 6, 1926. Berkeley was apparently associated only with the Chicago production. His name did not appear in the programme for the New York production; the ensembles were credited to Julian Mitchell, who had died shortly before the opening. The show was a minor hit in New York, where it ran for 160 performances.

3. THE WILD ROSE

Opened October 20, 1926. Martin Beck Theatre. 61 performances. Musical Play.

Presented by Arthur Hammerstein. Music by Rudolf Friml. Lyrics and book by Otto Harbach and Oscar Hammerstein II, based on the play *Hawthorne of U.S.A.* Book staged by William

J. Wilson. Dances by Busby Berkeley. Settings by Joseph Urban. Costumes designed by Mark Mooring. Orchestra under the direction of Herbert Stothart.

Cast: Lew Fields, Desiree Ellinger, Joseph Santley, Fuller Mellish, Inez Courtney, Joseph Macaulay, Gus Shy, Nana Bryant, Jerome Daley, The Randalls (dancers), The Pasquali Brothers (acrobats).

Ensemble: Ladies of the Ensemble (37), Gentemen of the Ensemble (31).

Selected Numbers: "Our Little Kingdom," "L'Heure D'Or (One Golden Hour)," "Her Eyes Are Brown," "The Wild Rose," "Lady of the Rose," "Lovely Lady," "It Was Fate," "Love Me, Don't You?" "Won't You Come Across?"

Plot Summary: In Monte Carlo, an American oil millionaire becomes involved in political intrigue when his young companion falls in love with a visiting Ruritanian princess. They follow her to her native land and foil a plot by bomb-throwing revolutionaries.

Comments: This plush operetta marked a disappointing reunion for the creators of *Rose-Marie*. Berkeley's dances, mainly in the folk/peasant vein, were absorbed into the show's general lavishness. William Collier replaced Lew Fields on opening night upon the latter's sudden illness.

4. SWEET LADY

December 1926–March 1927. Musical Comedy.

Presented by Thomas Ball. Music by Delos Owen and Thomas Ball. Lyrics by Bud Green. Book by Mann Page and Jack McGowan. Adapted from McGowan's farce, *Mama Loves Papa*. Book staged and directed by William Caryl (replaced by John Hayden). Musical numbers and dances staged and arranged by Busby Berkeley.

Cast: Gus Shy (replaced Roger Gray), Marie Nordstrom, Jane Taylor (replaced Vivian Marlowe), Harry Puck (replaced Lorin Raker, replaced by Alexander Gray), Inez Courtney, John Kane, Nina Penn (replaced by Mary Adams), Jeanette Fox-Lee, John Hundley (replaced Roy Gordon).

Ensemble: Girls (24), Boys (8).

Selected Numbers: "Sweet Lady," "Statues," "Mauve Decade," "On a Side Street," "Just Want You," "Will You Promise," "I Don't Want To Go Home," "I Adore You," "I'm Through with the Blues," "Sex Appeal."

Plot Summary: A young bride misunderstands her husband's involvement with a French actress. (He is an insurance man and was merely insuring the actress's legs for $200,000.) To retaliate, the bride goes on a cocktail spree and ends up at a playboy's apartment, where her husband discovers her. All is forgiven by the end of the Act Three.

Comments: Berkeley seems to have quickly adapted to the speed, novelty, and fancy footwork then fashionable in the musical comedy form, and his dance numbers monopolized what little favorable comment the show received. *Sweet Lady* closed out of town after a series of tryouts, including Syracuse (December), Detroit (December), Washington, D.C. (February), and Chicago (March). It was due to open in New York at the Imperial Theatre in September 1927. The above credits are based on the Washington run at the National Theatre. At the Syracuse premiere, Berkeley filled in at the last minute for conductor Ross Mobley upon Mobley's sudden illness.

5. LADY DO

Opened April 18, 1927. Liberty Theatre. 56 performances. Musical Comedy.

Presented by Frank L. Teller. Music by Abel Baer. Lyrics by Sam M. Lewis and Joe Young. Book by Jack McClellan and Albert Cowles. Production revised and staged by Edgar J. MacGregor (replaced John Hayden). Dances and ensembles staged by "Buzz" Berkeley. Scenery designed and executed by Kennel and Entwhistle. "Lady Do" dolls by Effanbee Dolls. Orchestra under the direction of Louis Gress.

Cast: Karyl Norman, Nancy Welford, Lew Hearn, Joseph Lertora, Sylvan Lee and Jane Moore (comedy dancers), Luis Alberini, Frances Upton, Maude Odell, Harriet Lorraine, Ralph Whitehead, Paul Darnelle and Ninon Natalie (specialty dancers—replaced Lisbeth Higgins and Cesar Romero).

Ensemble: Ladies of the Ensemble (24), Gentlemen of the Ensemble (8), The Four Buddies (4).

Selected Numbers: "Lady Do," "Dreamy Montmartre," "Too Blue," "O Sole Mi—Whose Soul Are You?" "Paris Taught Me Zis," "Double Fifth Avenue," "You Can't Eye a Shy Baby," "Little Miss Small Town," "In My Castle in Sorento," "Jiggle Your Feet."

Plot Summary: A handsome youth posing as a Parisian songstress is hired to seduce an evil duke and prevent him from marrying the daughter of a millionaire underwear manufacturer.

Comments: Lady Do was a star vehicle for Karyl Norman, well-known for his female impersonations in the Julian Eltinge/Bothwell Browne tradition. Although the reviews were lukewarm, nearly every one singled out the dance numbers for their intricacy and brisk, even violent, energy. During the first week of the run, Berkeley filled in for ailing actor Joseph Lertora as the Duke.

6. A CONNECTICUT YANKEE

Opened November 3, 1927. Vanderbilt Theatre. 418 performances. Musical Comedy.

Presented by Lew Fields and Lyle D. Andrews. Music by Richard Rodgers. Lyrics by Lorenz Hart. Book by Herbert Fields. Adapted from the novel by Mark Twain. Staged by Alexander Leftwich. Dances by Busby Berkeley. Scenery and costumes designed by John F. Hawkins, Jr. Art director, Herbert Ward. Musical director, Roy Webb. Entire production under the supervision of Lew Fields.

Cast: William Gaxton, Constance Carpenter, Nana Bryant, Jack Thompson, William Norris, June Cochrane, Paul Everton, William Roselle.

Ensemble: "Slaves, Knights, Ladies of the Court, Factory Hands, Etc." (12 women, 16 men).

Selected Numbers: "My Heart Stood Still," "Thou Swell," "On a Desert Island with You," "I Feel at Home with You," "A Ladies' Home Companion," "Nothing's Wrong," "Evelyn, What Did You Say?" "The Sandwich Men."

Plot Summary: In the course of a dream, a brash young man from Hartford, Conn., brings the industrial age and American slang to Olde Camelot. The dream enables him to find true romance in the waking present.

Comments: A major hit. According to *Variety* (October 12, 1927), Seymour Felix was called in to assist Berkeley during the tryouts. The show was revived on Broadway in 1943 in an altered and updated version. (See chapter 3 for a fuller description of this show.)

(THE GOLDEN DAWN)

Opened November 30, 1927.

Comments: Thomas and Terry credit the dance direction of this show to Berkeley (*The Busby Berkeley Book*, p. 21). The programme and the reviews all credit the dances to Dave Bennett. I have not found any evidence that Berkeley had anything to do with this show.

7. THE WHITE EAGLE

Opened December 26, 1927. The Casino. 48 performances. Musical play.

Presented by Russell Janney. Music by Rudolf Friml. Lyrics and book by Brian Hooker and W. H. Post. Adapted from Edwin Milton Royce's play, *The Squaw Man*. Staged by Richard Boleslavsky. Dances by Busby Berkeley. Scenes and costumes by James Reynolds. Technical director, Ben Webster. Music and orchestra under direction of Anton Heindl. Entire production under the personal direction of Olga Treskoff and Russell Janney.

Cast: Allan Prior, Marion Keeler, Lawrence D'Orsay, Kay Hawley, Hazel Glen, Oscar Shaw, Jr., John Mealey, Charles E. Gallagher, Forest Huff, Aysa Kaz (dancer), Paula Lind (dancer), Helen Grenelle (dancer).

Ensemble: The Twelve Chiefs (12), Indians (10), Squaws (17), Dancers (16 women), Officers of 16th Lancers (21), English Ladies (20), Butlers (3).

Selected Numbers: "Alone," "Thunder Dance," "Regimental Song," "Gather the Rose," "Smile, Darn You, Smile!" "Give Me One Hour," "Follow On," "Black Eagles."

Plot Summary: A British officer exiles himself to Colorado to save the family honor. He marries an Indian maiden who has saved his life. She commits suicide when he returns to England.

Comments: This expensive but unsuccessful production featured one of Friml's most ambitious scores, with leanings toward full-scale opera. Working with a huge chorus and lavish budget, Berkeley created some of his most spectacular stage numbers, including two Indian ceremonials that prefigure his later work in the films *Whoopee!* and *Rose Marie*.

(THE GREENWICH VILLAGE FOLLIES OF 1928)

Opened April 9, 1928.

Comments: Marshall and Jean Stearns's *Jazz Dance* (p. 164) mentions Berkeley as the dance director of this show (with considerable assistance from Buddy Bradley). The programmes and reviews credit the dances to Ralph Reader and Chester Hale.

8. PRESENT ARMS

Opened April 26, 1928. Lew Fields' Mansfield Theatre. 155 performances. Musical comedy.

Presented by Lew Fields. Music by Richard Rodgers. Lyrics by Lorenz Hart. Book by Herbert Fields. Staged by Alexander Leftwich. Musical numbers staged by Busby Berkeley. Art director, Herbert Ward. Scenery and effects by Ward and Harvey. Orchestra directed by Roy Webb. Entire production under the personal supervision of Lew Fields.

Cast: Charles King, Flora Le Breton, Joyce Barbour, Gaile Beverly, Florence Hunter, Busby Berkeley, Fuller Mellish, Jr., Franker Woods, Demaris Dore.

Ensemble: Ladies of the Ensemble (32), Gentlemen of the Ensemble (32).

Selected Numbers: "You Took Advantage of Me," "Tell It to the Marines," "Do I Hear You?" "A Kiss for Cinderella," "Is It the Uniform?" "Crazy Elbows," "I'm a Fool for You," "Down by the Sea," "Blue Ocean Blues," "Hawaii," "Kohala, Welcome."

Plot Summary: In Hawaii a marine poses as an officer in order to win the hand of his aristocratic sweetheart.

Comments: Berkeley's second collaboration with Rodgers and Hart. In addition to the frenetically fast-paced dances characteristic of current musical comedies, the show's military setting gave Berkeley the opportunity to stage two big military-drill numbers. He also played a marine sidekick of the hero and sang "You Took Advantage of Me" (the show's biggest hit) in a duet with Joyce Barbour.

9. EARL CARROLL VANITIES (Seventh Edition)

Opened August 6, 1928. Earl Carroll Theatre. 203 performances. Revue.

Entire production directed and produced by Earl Carroll. Music and lyrics by Grace Henry and Morris Hamilton. Additional music by George Bagby and G. Romilli. Dialogue by W. C. Fields and Paul Gerard Smith and staged by Edgar MacGregor. Musical numbers staged by Busby Berkeley. Settings designed by Hugh Willoughby. Costumes designed by Mabel E. Johnston and William H. Matthews. Art and technical direction by Bernard Lohmuller. Curtains by Dazian. Musical director, Ray Kavanaugh.

Cast: W. C. Fields, Ray Dooley, Joe Frisco, Gordon Dooley and Martha Morton, Dorothy Knapp ("The World's Most Beautiful Girl"), Lillian Roth, Richard Bold, Ernest Charles, Ray Leone, Cook Hanneford, Brian MacDonald, Beryl Halley ("The Form Divine"), Dorothy Britton ("Miss Universe"), Barto and Mann (specialty dancers), Maurice La Pue, Joey Ray, Naomi Johnson, Dorothy Lull (specialty dancer), The Vercell Sisters (dancers), Jean Tennyson, Adler and Bradford, Edward Graham, Vincent Lopez and His Band.

Ensemble: Complete information not available. The largest group noted in the programme is "The 32 Vaniteaser Dancers." Other numbers involve 16 Vanities Girls, 14 Yellow Roses, 7 Roman Goddesses and 16 Grecian Dancers, and the Double Dozen Tassellettes.

Selected Numbers: "Say It with Girls," "Pretty Girl," "Garden of Beautiful Girls," "The Dance Marathon," "The Pillar of Fame," "Vaniteaser," "Getting the Beautiful Girls," "Raquel Tango," "The Jewelled Curtain of Raquel," "Tourquois and Silver," "The Tassell Curtain," "Flutterby Baby," "The Butterfly and Spider," "The Portals of Mythology," "The Flaming Deity," "Blue Shadows," "Machinery Ballet," "Oh How That Man Can Love," "Watch My Baby Walk," "Once in a Lifetime," "The Curtain of Brilliants and Plumes," "Painting a Vanities Girl," "I'm Flying High," "The Collegiate Vaniteaser," "The Living Motion Picture Screen," "The Curtain of Plumes."

Summary: Revue in 2 acts and 47 scenes.

Comments: Among the W. C. Fields skits was his " 'Tain't a fit night out for man nor beast" routine (called "Stolen Bonds" here), which later became the basis of his classic short film, *The Fatal Glass of Beer* (1932). (See chapter 3 for a fuller description of this show.)

10. GOOD BOY

Opened September 5, 1928. Hammerstein's Theatre. 253 performances. Musical Play.

Presented by Arthur Hammerstein. Music and lyrics by Herbert Stothart, Bert Kalmar, and Harry Ruby. Book by Otto Harbach, Oscar Hammerstein 2nd, and Henry Myers. Book staged by Reginald Hammerstein. Dances staged by Busby Berkeley. Stage settings designed by John Wenger. Costumes designed by Mark Mooring. Mechanical and treadmill effects by Peter Clark, Inc., and Edward Dolan. Orchestra under the direction of Herbert Stothart.

Cast: Eddie Buzzell, Barbara Newberry, Helen Kane, Dan Healy, Sam Hearn, Effie Shannon, Evelyn Bennett, Charles Butterworth, Borrah Minevitch, Lester Bernard, Ariel Millars, Milton Douglass, Elsie Percival, Muriel Greel.

Ensemble: Members of the Chorus (41 women, 14 men).

Selected Numbers: "I Wanna Be Loved by You," "Good Boy," "The Voice of the City," "Some Sweet Someone," "I Have My Moments," "What Makes You So Wonderful?" "Manhattan Walk," "The Three Bears," "Oh, What a Man," "Nina."

Plot Summary: Arkansas boy, setting out to make a career on Broadway, meets girl, marries girl, fails to strike it rich, loses girl, gets rich, gets girl.

Comments: A musical comedy/revue/panorama dominated by its innovative staging. (See chapter 3 for a fuller description of this show.)

11. RAINBOW

Opened November 21, 1928. Gallo Theatre. 29 performances. Musical Play.

Presented by Philip Goodman. Music by Vincent Youmans. Lyrics by Oscar Hammerstein II. Book by Laurence Stallings and Oscar Hammerstein II. Book staged by Oscar Hammerstein II. Musical numbers staged by Busby Berkeley. Scenery designed and painted by Gates and Morange. Costumes designed by Charles LeMaire. Research and technical director, Leighton K. Brill. Orchestra under the direction of Max Steiner. Entire production under the personal direction of Mr. Goodman.

Cast: Louise Brown, Allan Prior, Charles Ruggles, Libby Holman, Harland Dixon, Helen Lynd, Brian Donlevy, Francetta Malloy.

Ensemble: Information not available.

Selected Numbers: "I Want a Man," "I Like You As You Are," "Let Me Give All My Love to Thee," "The One Girl," "I Look for Love," "Sunrise," "Hay! Straw!"

Plot Summary: In the days of '49, a cavalry scout kills an officer in self-defense, flees with the colonel's daughter on a wagon train to California, runs a gambling joint, and is eventually reinstated in the Army.

Comments: Touted as "another *Show Boat*," this ambitious attempt at Americanized operetta was a costly failure. The cavalry-post setting afforded Berkeley another opportunity for military-drill routines, and "Hay! Straw!" was a vigorous excursion into the hoedown field (later revisited by Berkeley in the film *Babes on Broadway*).

12. HELLO DADDY!

Opened December 26, 1928. Lew Fields' Mansfield Theatre. 198 performances. Musical Comedy.

Presented by Lew Fields. Music by Jimmy McHugh. Lyrics by Dorothy Fields. Book by Herbert Fields. Based on the farce *The High Cost of Loving*, adapted from the German by Frank Mandel. Book staged by Alexander Leftwich. Musical numbers staged by Busby Berkeley. Principal dance routines arranged by Buddy Bradley. The Fan Dance, Act 1, Scene 3, arranged by Madame Lenora. Settings designed by Herman Rosse. "Rosse Fabrics" of second act curtains from Dazian's. Costumes designed by Charles Le Maire. Musical numbers played by Ben Pollack and His Park Central Hotel Orchestra. Conductor, William Moore. Entire production under the supervision of John Murray Anderson.

Cast: Lew Fields, Mary Lawlor, Allen Kearns, Betty Starbuck, Billy Taylor, George Hassell, Wanda Goll, Allen Kearns, Theresa Maxwell-Conover, The Giersdorf Sisters.

Ensemble: Girls of the Chorus (16), Boys of the Chorus (8), Singers (8).

Selected Numbers: "In a Great Big Way," "I Want Plenty of You," "Futuristic Rhythm," "Let's Sit and Talk about You," "Out Where the Blue Begins," "Your Disposition Is Mine."

Plot Summary: Three middle-aged gentlemen are intimidated by a Purity League group into supporting a young woman of whom each believes himself to be the father.

Comments: A lightweight musical-comedy version of veteran comedy star Lew Fields's earlier production *The High Cost of Loving*. Berkeley shared credit for the dance numbers with Buddy Bradley, a brilliant African-American choreographer and behind-the-scenes dancing coach who was a leading force in introducing complex jazz-inspired rhythms on Broadway. The number that most impressed critics was "In a Great Big Way," a love song performed with comic apathy by secondary leads Billy Taylor and Betty Starbuck.

13. PLEASURE BOUND

Opened February 18, 1929. Majestic Theatre. 136 performances. Revue.

Presented by the Messrs. Shubert. Music by Muriel Pollock. Lyrics by Max and Nathaniel Lief and Howard Atteridge. Additional songs by Phil Baker and Maury Rubens. Book by Howard Atteridge. Book staged by Lew Morton. Dances arranged by Busby Berkeley. The Jack Donahue–John Boyle Girls' specialty dances arranged by John Boyle. Settings by Watson Barratt. Costumes designed by Ernest Schrapps. Harold Stern and His Orchestra.

Cast: Jack Pearl, Phil Baker, Aileen Stanley, Pepita (dancer), [Al] Shaw and [Sam] Lee, Marion Phillips, Grace Brinkley, Fred Hillebrand, John Humphrey Muldowney, Tito Coral, Veloz and Yolanda (dancers).

Ensemble: The Jack Donahue–John Boyle Girls (12—Lucille Osborn, Captain), Dancers (16 women), Show Girls (18), Boys (8).

Selected Numbers: "We Love To Go to Work," "Just Suppose," "We'll Get Along," "Band Box Dance," "Parisian Fashion Parade," "Mannikin Dolls," "Spanish Fado," "Sand Paper Number," "Doll Dance," "Glory of Spring."

Plot Summary: Revue in 2 acts and 12 scenes, strung around a slight plot involving a dress-making establishment.

Comments: The first of six Shubert productions on which Berkeley collaborated. *Pleasure Bound* was originally conceived as a straight musical comedy entitled *Well, Well, Well*; the book withered away as comedy and dance acts were added. The dance direction was predominantly in the venerable precision/novelty tradition and represented something of a step backward for Berkeley from the rhythmic innovations of the Rodgers and Hart shows. The most noteworthy dance element was the "Girl on the End" (described in chapter 3). The show was emceed by Phil Baker, who later costarred in Berkeley's film *The Gang's All Here*.

14. A NIGHT IN VENICE

Opened May 21, 1929. Sam S. Shubert Theatre. 175 performances. Revue.

Presented by the Messrs. Shubert. Music by Lee David and Maury Rubens. Lyrics by J. Keirn Brennan and M. Jaffe. [No book credit.] Book staged by Lew Morton and Thomas A. Hart. Staged by Busby Berkeley. Dances and ensembles by Busby Berkeley. Chester Hale Dances by Chester Hale. Settings by Watson Barratt. Costumes designed by Erté and Barbier. Other costumes designed by Ernest Schrapp. Max Meth Orchestra Ensemble. Under the personal supervision of Mr. J. J. Shubert.

Cast: Ted Healy, Ann Seymour, Mlles. Beth and Betty Dodge, Arthur and Morton Havel, Stanley Rogers, Moe Howard, Shemp Howard, Larry Fine, Laura Lee, John Byam, Jackie Paige, Halfred Young, Enjio Badii, Anita Case, Joe and Pete Michon, The Stevens Brothers and Their Bear, Betty Rees (dancer), Florence Powell (dancer).

Ensemble: The Chester Hale Girls (16), The Allan K. Foster Girls (13), Dancing Girls (8), Show Girls (14), Boys (10).

Selected Numbers: "Sliding Down a Silver Cloud," "One Night of Love," "Cellini's Plate," "Fans," "The One Girl" (composed by Vincent Youmans), "The Grand Staircase," "Lido Shores," "The Stork Don't Come Around Any More," "The Legend of Leda," "Tondelayo," "The Jungle," "St. Mark's Square."

Plot Summary: Revue in 2 acts and 25 scenes, tied to a plot about two bogus flyboys who, to impress their girls, pretend to fly to Venice but actually go over on an ocean liner.

Comments: Third and last in the Shuberts' *A Night in . . .* series, which previously included *A Night in Paris* (1926) and *A Night in Spain* (1927). The token plot quickly devolved into an aggregate of wildly assorted acts, including acrobats, Ted Healy and the Three Stooges, a wrestling bear, a burlesque of Elmer Rice's *Street Scene*, a jungle scene, a tableau of seminude sirens perched atop an iceberg, a "Legend of Leda" ballet, and even a few numbers that actually had some relevance to the show's Venetian setting. The Youmans song "The One Girl" was salvaged from the earlier flop, *Rainbow* (see No. 11 above).

15. BROADWAY NIGHTS

Opened July 15, 1929. The 44th Street Theatre. 40 performances. Revue.

Presented by the Messrs. Shubert. Music by Sam Timberg, Lee David, and Maurice Rubens. Lyrics by M. Jaffe. Book by Edgar Smith. Book staged by Stanley Logan. Staged by Busby Berkeley. Dances and ensembles by Busby Berkeley. Chester Hale Dance by Chester Hale. Settings by Watson Barratt. Costumes designed by Barbier. Other costumes designed by Ernest Schrapps. Orchestra under the direction of John McManus.

Cast: Dr. Rockwell, Odette Myrtil, Harry J. Conley, Joe Phillips, Frank Gaby, Harry Welsh; Dolores, Eddy and Douglas (adagio dancers); Laura Lee, Harry Stockwell, Sam Raynor, George Dobbs, Ruth Gormly; King, King and King (tap-dancers); Archie Foulke, Lillian Lane, Vivian Hunter, Miss Margaret Merle, Miss Joyce Coles (dancer), Madeline Meredith, Ethel Dunton, Betty Montgomery.

Ensemble: Chester Hale Girls (17), The Allan K. Foster London Palladium Girls (19), Show Girls (17), Boys (12).

Selected Numbers: "Why Don't We?" "Stranded in a One-Horse Town," "Hotsy Totsy Hats," "The Right Man," "White Lights Were Coming," "Train Effect," "Miles End Road," "Johann Strauss, Who Made the World Dance," "Heart of a Rose," "Arabian Nights," "I Kiss Your Hand, Madame," "Lobster Crawl," "Bracelet Number," "Baby's Doll," "The Orchid," "Come, Hit Your Baby."

Plot Summary: Vaudeville-style revue in 2 acts and 26 scenes, featuring the comic monologuist Dr. Rockwell. The flimsy connective plot involved a stranded theatrical troupe.

Comments: Yet another Shubert show in which a half-hearted plot was eclipsed by spectacle/revue elements. The production numbers combined fast-paced dancing in the latest fashion with derivative and old-fashioned concepts: the chorus took part in a floral number, posed as jewelry, formed a railroad train, and pelted the audience with rubber balls. *Broadway Nights* opened at the Majestic Theatre in Chicago on October 20, 1929, with Texas Guinan now starring and very much dominating the proceedings. Berkeley was still credited as the dance director.

16. THE STREET SINGER

Opened September 17, 1929. Sam S. Shubert Theatre. 191 performances. Musical Comedy.

Presented by Busby Berkeley. Music by Nicholas Kempner and S. Timberg and Richard Meyers. Lyrics by Graham John and Edward Eliscu. Book by Cyrus Wood and Edgar Smith. Entire production staged and directed by Busby Berkeley. Settings by Watson Barratt. "Street Scene" set and incidents shown through the courtesy of Wm. A. Brady, Ltd. Costumes designed by Barbier. Scanties and brassieres by the Model Brassiere Company. Orchestra under the direction of Pierre de Reeder.

Cast: Guy Robertson, Queenie Smith, Harry K. Morton, Nick Long, Jr., Nelly Kelly, Andrew Tombes, Jane Alden, Peggy Cornell, Ruth Shields.

Ensemble: Dancing Girls (17), Show Girls (12), Boys (8).

Selected Numbers: "You Never Can Tell," "I Am," "When Everything Is Hunky-Dory," "The Girl That I'll Adore," "You've Made Me Happy Today," "Somebody Quite Like You," "Statues," "Oh Theobald, Oh Elmer," "From Now On," "Knocking on Wood," "Ballet."

Plot Summary: "A Musical Comedy of Americans Abroad." Pygmalion story of a young American millionaire who wagers he can transform a street-singing gamin into a perfect lady in three months.

Comments: The only Broadway show that Berkeley entirely directed (as well as produced) in addition to staging the musical numbers. *The Street Singer*'s main attraction was the dancing, characterized by its breakneck pace (the show's publicity claimed the fastest-dancing chorus ever) and the strenuous, contorted postures struck by the chorus. The razzle-dazzle dancing clashed with the sentimental, operetta-ish book. The show was revived in 1931.

17. THE DUCHESS OF CHICAGO

Ca. November 1929. Musical Comedy.

Presented by the Messrs. Shubert. Music by Emmerich Kalman. Lyrics by Edward Eliscu. Additional numbers by Maurice Rubens and Sam Timberg. Book by Julius Brammer and Alfred Gruenwald. Dialogue directed by Stanley Logan. Staged by Busby Berkeley. John Tiller Girls with dances arranged by Mary Reade. Settings by Watson Barratt. Harold Stern's Ambassador Hotel String Ensemble.

Cast: Walter Woolf, Lillian Talz, Eric Blore, Jack Goode, Stephen Mills, Margaret Breen, Jose Mories, Arthur Treacher, Jules Epailly, Roy Byron, Richard Horne, Harold Clyde Wright, Peter Petraltis, Gene Scudder, William McLeod, Earl Plummer, Morton Griffith, Cortez and Helene (dancers).

Ensemble: Information not available. In Baltimore, the John Tiller Girls numbered 16. (An ad for the Philadelphia run promised "100–People on the Stage–100.")

Selected Numbers: "Look in My Eyes," "My Rosemarie," "In Chicago."

Plot Summary: Adaptation of the 1928 Viennese hit about a Chicago millionaire's jazz-mad daughter who meets a Graustarkian prince, setting the stage for a jazz-vs.-waltz battle in musical taste.

Comments: A hybrid of operetta and musical comedy, *The Duchess of Chicago* folded out-of-town after late-1929 tryouts in (in order) Springfield, Newark, Philadelphia, Baltimore, and Boston. The above credits are based on the Baltimore run at the Maryland Theatre (opened November 18). Berkeley's inventiveness seems to have been constrained by the show's lavish operetta elements and by the domination of the dance numbers by a troupe of John Tiller Girls (under the direction of Tiller's successor, Mary Reade).

18. RUTH SELWYN'S NINE FIFTEEN REVUE

Opened February 11, 1930. George M. Cohan Theatre. 7 performances. Revue.

Presented by Ruth Selwyn. Music and lyrics by Victor Herbert, George Gershwin, Rudolf Friml, Vincent Youmans, Roger Wolfe Kahn, Kay Swift, Philip Broughton, Will B. Johnstone, Ted Koehler and Harold Arlen, Ralph Rainger, Richard Myers, Ned Lehak, Manning Sherman, Edward Eliscu, Paul James, Ira Gershwin, Irving Caesar, and others. Sketches by Ring Lardner, Paul Gerard Smith, Eddie Cantor, Anita Loos and John Emerson, Geoffrey Kerr, H. W. Hanemann, Robert Riskin, Adorian Otvos. [Directed by Earl Carroll—not listed in the programme, but many reviews credit him.] Musical numbers staged by Busby Berkeley. Ballet numbers directed by Leon Leonidoff. Settings designed by Clarke Robinson. Electric Color Wheel Effects ("Get Happy" number) invented by J. W. Simmons. Costumes designed and executed by Kiviette. Produced under the personal supervision of Ruth Selwyn.

Cast: Ruth Etting, Harry McNaughton, Fred Keating, Joe and Pete Michon, Paul Kelly, Charles Lawrence, Helen Gray, Frances Shelly, Lynne Dore, Mary Murray, Gracella and Theodore, Lovey Girls, Diane Ellis, Michael Tripp, Wally Crisham, Oscar Ragland, Nan Blackstone, Earl Oxford, James Howkins, Peppi Lederer, Louise Barrett, Margarete Merle, Don Voorhees and His Orchestra.

Ensemble: 21, all female.

Selected Numbers: "Get Happy" (Arlen and Koehler), "Reve de Marquise," "Up Among the Chimney Pots," "The World of Dreams," "Toddling Along," "She's a Purty Little Thing."

Summary: Revue in 2 acts and 36 scenes, emceed by magician Fred Keating.

Comments: Produced at great expense (over $100,000) by Ruth Selwyn, twenty-four-year-old wife of Broadway producer Edgar Selwyn. Earl Carroll was called in at the last minute to revamp the show, replacing Alexander Leftwich as director. Despite the formidable roster of talent involved, this overstuffed production folded quickly. The musical numbers contained intimations of the peekaboo naughtiness found in several of Berkeley's film numbers: the show opened with showgirls making their way through an impressionistic Times Square setting to their dressing room, where they cavorted in lingerie; a later number provided a risqué bedroom variation on Goldilocks and the Three Bears. Star Ruth Etting was later directed by Berkeley in the film *Roman Scandals* (1933). Paul Kelly (later an outstanding character actor in such films as *The Roaring Twenties* and *Crossfire*) acted in the show while out on parole following twenty-five months in San Quentin for killing a man in a fight over Kelly's wife.

19. LEW LESLIE'S "INTERNATIONAL REVUE"

Opened February 25, 1930. Majestic Theatre. 95 performances. Revue.

Presented by Lew Leslie. Music by Jimmy McHugh. Lyrics by Dorothy Fields. Sketches by Nat N. Dorfman and Lew Leslie. Sketches directed by Edward Clarke Lilley. Special dance arrangements staged by Busby Berkeley. Incidental dances staged by Harry Crosley. Scenery designed and painted by Anthony W. Street. Costumes designed by Dolly Tree. Negligees by Saks, Fifth Avenue. Scanties and brassieres by the Model Brassiere Company. Orchestra directed by Harry Levant. Entire production staged and conceived by Lew Leslie.

Cast: Gertrude Lawrence, Jack Pearl, Harry Richman, Moss and Fontana, Jans and Whalen, Bernice and Emily (acrobatic dancers), Florence Moore, Anton Dolin, Viola Dobos, Argentinita (Latin dancer—dropped after the first week), Esther Muir, Livia Maracci, Richard Gordon, Rosemary Deering, McCann Sisters, Berinoff and Eulalie, Richard Ryan, Babs La Valle.

Ensemble: Chester Hale's International Girls (20), Show Girls (11).

Selected Numbers: "Exactly Like You," "On the Sunny Side of the Street," "Make Up Your Mind," "Boop-Boop-Poop-a-Doop," "The Margineers," "That's Why We're Dancing," "International Rhythm," "Keys to Your Heart," "Gypsy Love," "Cinderella Brown," "Here Comes the Bride," "Big Papoose on the Loose," "Floating Around."

Summary: Revue in 2 acts and 30 scenes.

Comments: A lavish revue in the declining Ziegfeldian tradition, with heavily Broadway-ized versions of foreign dance concepts (tango, *apache*, gypsy, Russian ballet, etc.). After a disastrously disorganized opening night, producer Lew Leslie (best known for the smash all-black revue, *Blackbirds of 1928*) radically reworked the show and managed to keep it alive for a couple of months. (See chapter 3 for a fuller description of this show.)

(NINA ROSA)

Opened September 30, 1930. Majestic Theatre. 137 performances. Musical Play.

Plot Summary: A hot-blooded Sigmund Romberg operetta, set in Peru, with a plot involving a hidden gold mine, an American engineer, a villainous gaucho, a romantic triangle, Inca sun-worship rituals, and sadomasochistic byplay.

Comments: In Thomas and Terry's *The Busby Berkeley Book* (p. 23), Berkeley seems to take credit for directing this show in its entirety. However, his name does not appear in the programme for the Broadway production or in any of the New York reviews that I have read. Berkeley did receive credit for staging the dances in several of the tryout productions (J. C. Huffman was regularly credited with staging the dialogue passages). When the show opened on Broadway, Berkeley's name was conspicuously absent from the programme; in fact, there was no dance director credited at all. A possible falling-out between Berkeley and the Shuberts is indicated here. In any event, the show contained a "Peruvian Sun Worship" number in the vein of pagan erotic spectacle explored by Berkeley previously in *The White Eagle* (1927) and subsequently in the films *Bird of Paradise* (1932) and *Rose Marie* (1954).

(FINE AND DANDY)

Opened September 23, 1930.

Comments: According to Bob Pike and Dave Martin's interview book, *The Genius of Busby Berkeley*, p. 134, it was while Berkeley was choreographing this show that Eddie Cantor discovered him and recommended him for the film *Whoopee!* The programmes and reviews credit the dances to Dave Gould, Tom Nip, Merriel Abbott, and Eugene Von Grone, with no mention of Berkeley. Because *Whoopee!* was shot well before *Fine and Dandy* opened, the chronology of Pike and Martin's story is open to question.

20. SWEET AND LOW

Opened November 17, 1930. Chanin's Forty-Sixth Street Theatre (moved to the 44th Street Theatre on January 19). 184 performances. Revue.

Presented by Billy Rose. Songs by Mr. Rose and His Friends [his "friends" included Harry Archer and Edward Eliscu, Charlotte Kent, William Irwin, Harry Warren and Ira Gershwin, Ned Lehak and Allen Boretz, Vivian Ellis, Spoliansky and Mort Dixon, Louis Alter, Phil Charig and Joseph Meyer]. Sketches by David Freedman. Staged by Alexander Leftwich. Dances by Danny Dare. Additional dances by Busby Berkeley. Settings designed by Jo Mielziner. Costumes by James Reynolds. Orchestra under the direction of Bill Daly.

Cast: James Barton (replaced Hal Skelly), Fannie Brice, George Jessel, Borrah Minevitch, Moss and Fontana (dancers), Hannah Williams, Jerry Norris, Roger Davis, Arthur Treacher, Paula Trueman, Roger Pryor Dodge and Company, Peggy Andre, Lucille Osborne, Hal Thompson.

Ensemble: Ladies of the Ensemble (25), Gentlemen of the Ensemble (8).

Selected Numbers: "Overnight," "Cheerful Little Earful," "Would You Like To Take a Walk?" "When a Pansy Was a Flower," "Ten Minutes in Bed."

Summary: Revue comprised of 26 numbers.

Comments: During tryouts the title was *Corned Beef and Roses*. The show started out as an intimate revue centered on producer Billy Rose's wife, Fannie Brice. Elaborate trappings and additional stars were added haphazardly until it became a high-budgeted hodgepodge with a heavy emphasis on raunchy humor. Danny Dare, Tamara Geva, Roger Pryor Dodge, and Sammy Lee all had a hand in the dance numbers, making Berkeley's contribution difficult to determine. *Sweet and Low* was Berkeley's final stint as a Broadway dance director before he pulled up stakes for Hollywood.

21. GLAD TO SEE YOU

November 1944. Musical Comedy.

Produced by David Wolper. Music by Jule Styne. Lyrics by Sammy Cahn. Book by Fred Thompson and Eddie Davis. Production staged and directed by Busby Berkeley (replaced by Daniel Laure). Dances and ensembles by Valerie Bettis. Settings by Howard Bay. Costumes by Travis Banton.

Cast: Jane Withers, Eddie Davis (replaced by Eddie Foy, Jr.), June Knight (replaced Lupe Velez), Kenny Bowers, Sammy White, Joseph Macauley, Gene Barry, Nancy Donovan, Jayne Manners, Alexis Rotov, Eric Roberts, Patsy O'Shea, Slam Stuart, Jimmy Gardiner, Whitney Sisters.

Ensemble: Information not available.

Selected Numbers: "B, Apostrophe, K, Apostrophe, Lyn," "I'll Hate Myself in the Morning," "I Lost My Beat," "Grownups Are the Stupidest People," "Ladies Don't Have Fun," "I Murdered Them in Chicago," "I'm Laying Away a Buck."

Plot Summary: A comedian and a boy-and-girl vaudeville team get into an overseas USO tour when they are mistaken for a magician and his two children.

Comments: Berkeley's attempt to return to Broadway after a fourteen-year absence was not a successful one. *Glad To See You* folded out of town after tryouts in Philadelphia (November) and Boston (December). By the time of the Boston engagement, Berkeley was no longer with the show.

22. NO, NO, NANETTE

Opened January 19, 1971. The 46th Street Theatre. 861 performances. Musical Comedy.

Presented by Pyxidium, Ltd. Music by Vincent Youmans. Lyrics by Irving Caesar and Otto Harbach. Book by Otto Harbach and Frank Mandel. Adapted and directed by Burt Shevelove. Dances and musical numbers staged by Donald Saddler. Tap supervisors, Mary Ann Niles and Ted Cappy. Production designed by Raoul Pène du Bois. Musical direction and vocal arrangements by Buster Davis. Production supervised by Busby Berkeley.

Cast: Ruby Keeler, Jack Gilford, Bobby Van, Helen Gallagher, Susan Watson, Patsy Kelly, Roger Rathburn, Loni Zoe Ackerman, K. C. Townsend, Pat Lysinge, and The Busby Berkeley Girls.

Ensemble: Nanette's Friends (36, of which approximately 22 are women).

Selected Numbers: "Tea for Two," "I Want To Be Happy," "Telephone Girlie," "Take a Little One-Step," "You Can Dance with Any Girl at All," "I've Confessed to the Breeze," "Call of the Sea," "Too Many Rings Around You," "Where-Has-My-Hubby-Gone Blues."

Plot Summary: A free-thinking flapper and her flirtatious father come to their senses after a series of misunderstandings and misadventures in Atlantic City.

Comments: Berkeley was originally signed as sole director and choreographer for this smash revival of the 1925 musical, which had been only a moderate hit in its initial run. Before rehearsals began, coproducer Cyma Rubin, exasperated by Berkeley's apparent senility, replaced him as director with Burt Shevelove. Donald Saddler, originally hired as Berkeley's assistant, took over the choreography. Berkeley's new duties were as "consultant and advisor to the producers." His function seems mainly to have been to chat with reporters and appear on talk shows. According to Don Dunn's revealing but depressing account, *The Making of "No, No, Nanette"*, Berkeley's primary chore during rehearsals was to staple together the pages of the constantly rewritten script as they were delivered.

FILMOGRAPHY

The following filmography is an attempt to list all of Berkeley's known film credits, but it is selective in terms of the information included in each entry, concentrating on those individual contributions most relevant to the musical numbers. For more exhaustive credits on each film, the reader is referred to Tony Thomas and Jim Terry's *The Busby Berkeley Book* and the filmography by Ralph Crandall that is appended to the Patrick Brion and René Gilson interview in *Cahiers du Cinéma in English*, no. 2.

1. **WHOOPEE!** 1930. Goldwyn/United Artists. Produced by Samuel Goldwyn and Florenz Ziegfeld. Directed by Thornton Freeland. Dances staged by Busby Berkeley. Based on the 1928 musical play by William Anthony McGuire, Gus Kahn, and Walter Donaldson. Songs by Walter Donaldson and Gus Kahn; Nacio Herb Brown and Edward Eliscu. With Eddie Cantor, Eleanor Hunt, Paul Gregory, John Rutherford, Ethel Shutta. Two-strip Technicolor.

2. **PALMY DAYS.** 1931. Goldwyn/United Artists. Produced by Samuel Goldwyn. Directed by Edward Sutherland. Dances directed by Busby Berkeley. Songs by Con Conrad and Ballard MacDonald; Harry Akst and

Eddie Cantor, Bennie Davis; Cliff Friend. With Eddie Cantor, Charlotte Greenwood, Barbara Weeks, George Raft, The Goldwyn Girls.

3. **FLYING HIGH.** 1931. MGM. Directed by Charles F. Riesner. Dances directed by Busby Berkeley. Based on the 1930 musical play by Buddy DeSylva, Ray Henderson, and Lew Brown. Songs by Jimmy McHugh and Dorothy Fields; Ray Henderson and Buddy DeSylva, Lew Brown. With Bert Lahr, Charlotte Greenwood, Pat O'Brien, Kathryn Crawford.

4. **SKY DEVILS.** 1932. United Artists. Produced by Howard Hughes. Directed by Edward Sutherland. Dances directed by Busby Berkeley. Musical score by Alfred Newman. With Spencer Tracy, William Boyd, Ann Dvorak, Yola D'Avril.

5. **NIGHT WORLD.** 1932. Universal. Directed by Hobart Henley. Dances staged by Busby Berkeley. Musical score by Alfred Newman. With Mae Clarke, Lew Ayres, George Raft.

6. **BIRD OF PARADISE.** 1932. RKO. Produced by David O. Selznick. Directed by King Vidor. Dances directed by Busby Berkeley. Musical score by Max Steiner. With Dolores Del Rio, Joel McCrea, John Halliday.

7. **THE KID FROM SPAIN.** 1932. Goldwyn/United Artists. Produced by Samuel Goldwyn. Dances directed by Busby Berkeley. Songs by Harry Ruby and Bert Kalmar. With Eddie Cantor, Lyda Roberti, Robert Young, Ruth Hall, The Goldwyn Girls.

8. **42ND STREET.** 1933. Warner Bros. Produced by Darryl F. Zanuck. Directed by Lloyd Bacon. Dances staged and directed by Busby Berkeley. Songs by Harry Warren and Al Dubin. With Warner Baxter, Bebe Daniels, George Brent, Una Merkel, Ruby Keeler, Dick Powell, Clarence Nordstrom, Ginger Rogers, Guy Kibbee, Ned Sparks, Allen Jenkins.

9. **GOLD DIGGERS OF 1933.** 1933. Warner Bros. Directed by Mervyn LeRoy. Numbers staged and directed by Busby Berkeley. Songs by Harry Warren and Al Dubin. With Warren William, Dick Powell, Ruby Keeler, Joan Blondell, Aline MacMahon, Ginger Rogers, Guy Kibbee, Ned Sparks, Clarence Nordstrom.

10. **SHE HAD TO SAY YES.** 1933. First National/Warner Bros. Directed by Busby Berkeley and George Amy. With Loretta Young, Winnie Lightner, Lyle Talbot, Hugh Herbert.

11. **FOOTLIGHT PARADE.** 1933. Warner Bros. Directed by Lloyd Bacon. Dances created and staged by Busby Berkeley. Songs by Harry Warren and Al Dubin; Sammy Fain and Irving Kahal. With James Cagney, Joan Blondell, Ruby Keeler, Dick Powell, Guy Kibbee, Ruth Donnelly, Claire Dodd, Hugh Herbert, Frank McHugh.

12. **ROMAN SCANDALS.** 1933. Goldwyn/United Artists. Produced by Samuel Goldwyn. Directed by Frank Tuttle. Numbers staged and directed by Busby Berkeley. Songs by Harry Warren and Al Dubin; Harry Warren and L. Wolfe Gilbert. With Eddie Cantor, Ruth Etting, Gloria Stuart, David Manners, Verree Teasdale, Grace Poggi, The Goldwyn Girls.

13. **FASHIONS OF 1934.** 1934. First National/Warner Bros. Produced by Henry Blanke. Directed by William Dieterle. Numbers created and directed by Busby Berkeley. Songs by Sammy Fain and Irving Kahal. With William Powell, Bette Davis, Verree Teasdale, Reginald Owen, Dorothy Burgess.

14. **WONDER BAR.** 1934. First National/Warner Bros. Produced by Robert Lord. Directed by Lloyd Bacon. Numbers created and directed by Busby Berkeley. Songs by Harry Warren and Al Dubin. With Al Jolson, Kay Francis, Dolores Del Rio, Ricardo Cortez, Dick Powell, Hal LeRoy, Hugh Herbert.

15. **DAMES.** 1934. Warner Bros. Directed by Ray Enright. Numbers created and directed by Busby Berkeley. Songs by Harry Warren and Al Dubin; Sammy Fain and Irving Kahal; Allie Wrubel and Mort Dixon. With Ruby Keeler, Dick Powell,

Joan Blondell, ZaSu Pitts, Guy Kibbee, Hugh Herbert.

16. GOLD DIGGERS OF 1935. 1935. First National/Warner Bros. Directed by Busby Berkeley. Dances created and staged by Busby Berkeley. Songs by Harry Warren and Al Dubin. With Dick Powell, Gloria Stuart, Adolphe Menjou, Glenda Farrell, Hugh Herbert, Alice Brady, Frank McHugh, Wini Shaw.

17. IN CALIENTE. 1935. First National/Warner Bros. Directed by Lloyd Bacon. Musical numbers directed by Busby Berkeley. Songs by Allie Wrubel and Mort Dixon; Harry Warren and Al Dubin. With Dolores Del Rio, Pat O'Brien, Leo Carrillo, Edward Everett Horton, Glenda Farrell, Wini Shaw, The DeMarcos, Phil Regan.

18. BRIGHT LIGHTS. 1935. First National/Warner Bros. Directed by Busby Berkeley. Songs by Harry Ruby and Bert Kalmar; Allie Wrubel and Mort Dixon; Harry Akst and Grant Clark. With Joe E. Brown, Ann Dvorak, Patricia Ellis, William Gargan.

19. I LIVE FOR LOVE. 1935. Warner Bros. Produced by Bryan Foy. Directed by Busby Berkeley. Songs by Allie Wrubel and Mort Dixon. With Dolores Del Rio, Everett Marshall, Guy Kibbee, Allen Jenkins.

20. STARS OVER BROADWAY. 1935. Warner Bros. Produced by Sam Bischoff. Directed by William Keighley. Dances directed by Busby Berkeley and Bobby Connolly. Songs by Harry Warren and Al Dubin; Carson J. Robison. With Pat O'Brien, James Melton, Jane Froman, Jean Muir, Frank McHugh, Phil Regan.

21. STAGE STRUCK. 1936. Warner Bros. Produced by Robert Lord. Directed by Busby Berkeley. Songs by Harold Arlen and E. Y. Harburg. With Dick Powell, Joan Blondell, Warren William, Frank McHugh, Jeanne Madden, The Yacht Club Boys.

22. GOLD DIGGERS OF 1937. 1936. First National/Warner Bros. Produced by Hal B. Wallis. Directed by Lloyd Bacon. Numbers created and directed by Busby Berkeley. Songs by Harry Warren and Al Dubin; Harold Arlen and E. Y. Harburg. With Dick Powell, Joan Blondell, Victor Moore, Glenda Farrell, Lee Dixon.

23. THE GO-GETTER. 1937. Cosmopolitan/Warner Bros. Produced by Hal B. Wallis. Directed by Busby Berkeley. With George Brent, Anita Louise, Charles Winninger.

24. THE SINGING MARINE. 1937. Warner Bros. Directed by Ray Enright. Numbers directed by Busby Berkeley. Songs by Harry Warren and Al Dubin; Harry Warren and Johnny Mercer. With Dick Powell, Doris Weston, Lee Dixon, Hugh Herbert, George "Doc" Rockwell, Larry Adler.

25. VARSITY SHOW. 1937. Warner Bros. Directed by William Keighley. Finale created and directed by Busby Berkeley. Songs by Richard Whiting and Johnny Mercer. With Dick Powell, Priscilla Lane, Fred Waring and His Pennsylvanians, Rosemary Lane, Johnnie Davis, Lee Dixon, Buck and Bubbles.

26. HOLLYWOOD HOTEL. 1937. First National/Warner Bros. Produced by Hal B. Wallis. Directed by Busby Berkeley. Songs by Richard Whiting and Johnny Mercer. With Dick Powell, Rosemary Lane, Lola Lane, Benny Goodman, Ted Healy, Johnnie Davis, Alan Mowbray, Frances Langford, Louella Parsons, Hugh Herbert, Glenda Farrell.

27. GOLD DIGGERS IN PARIS. 1938. Warner Bros. Produced by Sam Bischoff. Directed by Ray Enright. Numbers staged and directed by Busby Berkeley. Songs by Harry Warren and Al Dubin; Harry Warren and Johnny Mercer. With Rudy Vallee, Rosemary Lane, Hugh Herbert, Allen Jenkins, Gloria Dickson, The Schnickelfritz Band.

28. MEN ARE SUCH FOOLS. 1938. Warner Bros. Directed

by Busby Berkeley. With Wayne Morris, Priscilla Lane, Humphrey Bogart, Hugh Herbert.

29. GARDEN OF THE MOON. 1938. Warner Bros. Directed by Busby Berkeley. Songs by Harry Warren and Al Dubin; Harry Warren and Johnny Mercer. With Pat O'Brien, John Payne, Margaret Lindsay, Johnnie Davis, Joe Venuti and His Swing Cats.

30. COMET OVER BROADWAY. 1938. First National/Warner Bros. Directed by Busby Berkeley. With Kay Francis, Ian Hunter, John Litel, Donald Crisp, Minna Gombell.

31. THEY MADE ME A CRIMINAL. 1939. Warner Bros. Directed by Busby Berkeley. With John Garfield, Claude Rains, Ann Sheridan, The Dead End Kids.

32. BROADWAY SERENADE. 1939. MGM. Produced and directed by Robert Z. Leonard. Finale created and directed by Busby Berkeley. Music by Tchaikovsky (arranged by Herbert Stothart and Edward Ward), lyrics by Gus Kahn. With Jeanette MacDonald, Lew Ayres, Frank Morgan, Ian Hunter.

33. BABES IN ARMS. 1939. MGM. Produced by Arthur Freed. Directed by Busby Berkeley. Based on the 1937 musical play by Richard Rodgers and Lorenz Hart. Songs by Richard Rodgers and Lorenz Hart; Harold Arlen and E. Y. Harburg; Nacio Herb Brown and Arthur Freed; Bob Carleton; Roger Edens; Eubie Blake and Noble Sissle; John Philip Sousa. With Mickey Rooney, Judy Garland, Charles Winninger, Guy Kibbee, June Preisser, Grace Hayes, Douglas McPhail.

34. FAST AND FURIOUS. 1939. MGM. Produced by Frederick Stephani. Directed by Busby Berkeley. With Franchot Tone, Ann Sothern, Ruth Hussey, Lee Bowman.

35. FORTY LITTLE MOTHERS. 1940. MGM. Produced by Harry Rapf. Directed by Busby Berkeley. Songs by Nat Simon and Harry Tobias. With Eddie Cantor, Rita Johnson, Bonita Granville, Ralph Morgan.

36. STRIKE UP THE BAND. 1940. MGM. Produced by Arthur Freed. Directed by Busby Berkeley. Songs by Roger Edens; Roger Edens and Arthur Freed; George Gershwin and Ira Gershwin. With Mickey Rooney, Judy Garland, Paul Whiteman, June Preisser, William Tracy.

37. BLONDE INSPIRATION. 1941. MGM. Produced by B. P. Fineman. Directed by Busby Berkeley. With John Shelton, Virginia Grey, Albert Dekker, Charles Butterworth.

38. ZIEGFELD GIRL. 1941. MGM. Produced by Pandro S. Berman. Directed by Robert Z. Leonard. Musical numbers directed by Busby Berkeley. Songs by Roger Edens; Roger Edens and Ralph Freed; Nacio Herb Brown and Gus Kahn; Walter Donaldson and Harold Adamson. With Judy Garland, James Stewart, Hedy Lamarr, Lana Turner, Tony Martin, Charles Winninger, Edward Everett Horton, Al Shean.

39. LADY BE GOOD. 1941. MGM. Produced by Arthur Freed. Directed by Norman Z. McLeod. Musical numbers staged by Busby Berkeley. Songs by George Gershwin and Ira Gershwin; Roger Edens; Roger Edens and Arthur Freed; Jerome Kern and Oscar Hammerstein II. With Eleanor Powell, Ann Sothern, Robert Young, John Carroll, Lionel Barrymore, Red Skelton, Connie Russell, Virginia O'Brien.

40. BABES ON BROADWAY. 1942. MGM. Produced by Arthur Freed. Directed by Busby Berkeley. Songs by Roger Edens; Roger Edens and Ralph Freed; Burton Lane and Ralph Freed; Burton Lane and E. Y. Harburg; Harold Rome. With Mickey Rooney, Judy Garland, Virginia Weidler, Ray McDonald, Richard Quine.

41. BORN TO SING. 1942. MGM. Produced by Frederick Stephani. Directed by Edward Ludwig. Finale created and directed by Busby Berkeley. Songs by Earl Robinson and John

Latouche (finale); Earl Brent; Earl Brent and Lennie Hayton; Nacio Herb Brown and Arthur Freed. With Virginia Weidler, Ray McDonald, Rags Ragland, Douglas McPhail.

42. FOR ME AND MY GAL. 1942. MGM. Produced by Arthur Freed. Directed by Busby Berkeley. Dance direction by Bobby Connolly. Songs by George W. Meyer and Edgar Leslie, E. Ray Goetz; Roger Edens; Richard A. Whiting and Ray Egan; Nat D. Ayer and A. Seymour Brown; Henri Christine and E. Ray Goetz; Turner Layton and Henry Creamer; Chris Smith and Jim Burris; Walter Donaldson and Joe Young, Sam M. Lewis; Harry Williams and Jack Judge; Lee M. Roberts and J. Will Callahan; Felix Powell and George Asaf. With Judy Garland, Gene Kelly, George Murphy, Marta Eggert, Ben Blue.

43. GIRL CRAZY. 1943. MGM. Produced by Arthur Freed. Directed by Norman Taurog. Dance direction by Charles Walters. "I Got Rhythm" number directed by Busby Berkeley. Songs by George Gershwin and Ira Gershwin; Roger Edens. With Mickey Rooney, Judy Garland, Gil Stratton, Rags Ragland, June Allyson, Tommy Dorsey and His Orchestra.

44. THE GANG'S ALL HERE. 1943. 20th Century-Fox. Produced by William LeBaron. Directed by Busby Berkeley. Songs by Harry Warren and Leo Robin; S. K. Russell and Ary Barroso. With Alice Faye, Carmen Miranda, Phil Baker, Benny Goodman, Eugene Pallette, Charlotte Greenwood, Edward Everett Horton, Tony DeMarco, James Ellison, Sheila Ryan. Technicolor.

45. CINDERELLA JONES. 1946 (shot in 1944). Warner Bros. Produced by Alex Gottlieb. Directed by Busby Berkeley. Songs by Jule Styne and Sammy Cahn. With Joan Leslie, Robert Alda, Julie Bishop, Edward Everett Horton.

46. ROMANCE ON THE HIGH SEAS. 1948. Warner Bros. Produced by Alex Gottlieb. Directed by Michael Curtiz. Musical numbers created and directed by Busby Berkeley. Songs by Jule Styne and Sammy Cahn. With Jack Carson, Janis Paige, Don DeFore, Doris Day, Oscar Levant, S. Z. Sakall, Eric Blore, Franklin Pangborn, The Samba Kings. Technicolor.

47. TAKE ME OUT TO THE BALL GAME. 1949. MGM. Produced by Arthur Freed. Directed by Busby Berkeley. Dances directed by Gene Kelly and Stanley Donen. Songs by Adolph Green and Betty Comden, Roger Edens; Albert Von Tilzer and Jack Norworth; Jean Schwartz and William Jerome. With Frank Sinatra, Esther Williams, Gene Kelly, Betty Garrett, Jules Munshin. Technicolor.

48. TWO WEEKS WITH LOVE. 1950. MGM. Produced by Jack Cummings. Directed by Roy Rowland. Musical numbers staged by Busby Berkeley. Songs by Walter Donovan and Arthur Fields; Edward Madden and Gus Kahn; Lucien Denni and Roger Lewis; James V. Monaco and William Jerome; Oscar Straus and Stanislaus Stange; Joe Goodwin and Joe McCarthy; Arthur G. Robyn and Thomas T. Railey; Ivan Caryll and C. H. S. McClellan. With Jane Powell, Ricardo Montalban, Louis Calhern, Ann Harding, Carleton Carpenter, Phyllis Kirk, Debbie Reynolds. Technicolor.

49. CALL ME MISTER. 1951. 20th Century-Fox. Produced by Fred Kohlmar. Directed by Lloyd Bacon. Dances directed by Busby Berkeley. Based on the 1946 musical play by Arnold M. Auerbach and Harold J. Rome. Songs by Harold J. Rome; Sammy Fain and Mack Gordon; Earl K. Brent and Jerry Seelen; Frances Ash. With Betty Grable, Dan Dailey, Danny Thomas, Dale Robertson, Benay Venuta, Bobby Short. Technicolor.

50. TWO TICKETS TO BROADWAY. 1951. RKO. Produced by Howard Hughes. Directed by James V. Kern. Musical numbers created and directed by Busby Berkeley. Songs by Jule Styne and Leo Robin; Jule Styne and Bob Crosby;

Richard Rodgers and Lorenz Hart. With Tony Martin, Janet Leigh, Gloria DeHaven, Eddie Bracken, Ann Miller, Bob Crosby, Joe Smith, Charles Dale, The Charlivels. Technicolor.

51. MILLION DOLLAR MERMAID. 1952. MGM. Produced by Arthur Hornblow, Jr. Directed by Mervyn LeRoy. "Fountain" and "Smoke" numbers directed by Busby Berkeley. Musical direction by Adolph Deutsch. With Esther Williams, Victor Mature, Walter Pidgeon, Maria Tallchief. Technicolor.

52. SMALL TOWN GIRL. 1953. MGM. Produced by Joe Pasternak. Directed by Leslie Kardos. Musical numbers staged by Busby Berkeley. Songs by Nicholas Brodszky and Leo Robin. With Jane Powell, Farley Granger, Ann Miller, S. Z. Sakall, Robert Keith, Bobby Van. Technicolor.

53. EASY TO LOVE. 1953. MGM. Produced by Joe Pasternak. Directed by Charles Walters. Musical numbers created and directed by Busby Berkeley. Songs by Mann Curtis and Vic Mizzy; Johnny Green, Carmen Lombardo and Gus Kahn; Paul Lincke. With Esther Williams, Tony Martin, Van Johnson. Technicolor.

54. ROSE MARIE. 1954. MGM. Produced and directed by Mervyn LeRoy. Musical numbers staged by Busby Berkeley. Based on the 1924 musical play by Otto Harbach, Oscar Hammerstein II, and Rudolf Friml. Songs by Rudolf Friml and Otto Harbach, Oscar Hammerstein II; Rudolf Friml and Paul Francis Webster; George Stoll and Herbert Baker. With Ann Blyth, Howard Keel, Fernando Lamas, Bert Lahr, Joan Taylor. Eastmancolor. CinemaScope.

55. BILLY ROSE'S JUMBO. 1962. MGM. Produced by Joe Pasternak and Martin Melcher. Directed by Charles Walters. Second unit direction by Busby Berkeley. Based on the 1935 musical play by Ben Hecht, Charles MacArthur, Lorenz Hart, and Richard Rodgers. Songs by Richard Rodgers and Lorenz Hart. With Doris Day, Stephen Boyd, Jimmy Durante, Martha Raye. Metrocolor. Panavision.

Further Comments

In the absence of further corroboration or specification, the following possible uncredited contributions by Berkeley have been omitted from this filmography:

In Robert Darrell Moulton's 1957 dissertation "Choreography in Musical Comedy and Revue on the New York Stage from 1925 through 1950" (p. 45), it is claimed that Berkeley staged dances for several unspecified silent films and also for the pioneer talkie *The Jazz Singer* (Warner Bros., 1927).

According to Thomas and Terry (*The Busby Berkeley Book*, p. 25), Berkeley arranged the dances for *Kiki* (United Artists, 1931), a Mary Pickford comedy with a show-business setting.

Several filmographies (e.g., those accompanying Brion and Gilson's interview in *Cahiers du Cinéma in English*, no. 2; Charles Wolfe's entry on Berkeley in *American Directors*; and the entries on Berkeley in Stanley Green's *Encyclopaedia of the Musical Film* and Georges Sadoul's *Dictionary of Film Makers*) credit Berkeley with staging the numbers for *Twenty Million Sweethearts* (Warner Bros., 1934) and/or *Go Into Your Dance* (Warner Bros., 1935).

According to Thomas and Terry (*The Busby Berkeley Book*, p. 28), Berkeley supervised some sequences of *The Wizard of Oz* (MGM, 1939) and *Bitter Sweet* (MGM, 1940).

In an interview with Charles Higham in *Hollywood Cameramen* (Bloomington: Indiana University Press, 1970), p. 88, cinematographer James Wong Howe attributes the dances in *Yankee Doodle Dandy* (Warner Bros., 1942) to Berkeley.

In the filmography of *The Movies' Greatest Musicals* (p. 535), Hugh Fordin credits Berkeley with the staging of one musical number (unspecified) in *Cabin in the Sky* (MGM, 1943).

INDEX

FILM AND CULTURE
A SERIES OF COLUMBIA UNIVERSITY PRESS

EDITED BY JOHN BELTON

What Made Pistachio Nuts? Early Sound Comedy and the Vaudeville Aesthetic
Henry Jenkins

Projections of War: Hollywood, American Culture, and World War II
Thomas Doherty

Laughing Screaming: Modern Hollywood Horror and Comedy
William Paul

Laughing Hysterically: American Screen Comedy of the 1950s
Ed Sikov

Primitive Passions: Visuality, Sexuality, Ethnography, and Contemporary Chinese Cinema
Rey Chow

The Cinema of Max Ophuls: Magisterial Vision and the Figure of Woman
Susan M. White

Black Women as Cultural Reader
Jacqueline Bobo

Picturing Japaneseness: Monumental Style, National Identity, Japanese Film
Darrell William Davis

Attack of the Leading Ladies: Gender, Sexuality, and Spectatorship in Classic Horror Cinema
Rhona J. Berenstein

This Mad Masquerade: Stardom and Masculinity in the Jazz Age
Gaylyn Studlar

Sexual Politics and Narrative Film: Hollywood and Beyond
Robin Wood

The Sounds of Commerce: Marketing Popular Film Music
Jeff Smith

Orson Welles, Shakespeare, and Popular Culture
Michael Anderegg

Pre-Code Hollywood: Sex, Immorality, and Insurrection in American Cinema, 1930–1934
Thomas Doherty

Sound Technology and the American Cinema: Perception, Representation, Modernity
James Lastra

Melodrama and Modernity: Early Sensational Cinema and Its Contexts
Ben Singer

Wondrous Difference: Cinema, Anthropology, and Turn-of-the-Century Visual Culture
Alison Griffiths

Hearst Over Hollywood: Power, Passion, and Propaganda in the Movies
Louis Pizzitola

Masculine Interests: Homoerotics in Hollywood Film
Robert Lang

Special Effects: Still in Search of Wonder
Michele Pierson

Designing Women: Cinema, Art Deco, and the Female Form
Lucy Fischer

Cold War, Cool Medium: Television, McCarthyism, and American Culture
Thomas Doherty

Katharine Hepburn: Star as Feminist
Andrew Britton

Silent Film Sound
Rick Altman

Home in Hollywood: The Imaginary Geography of Hollywood
Elisabeth Bronfen